Byron: A Survey

BYRON: A SURVEY

Bernard Blackstone Litt.D.

Longman

LONGMAN GROUP LIMITED
London
Associated companies, branches and representatives throughout the world

© Bernard Blackstone 1975

First published 1975

ISBN 0 582 48354 9   cased
     0 582 48355 7   paper

Library of Congress Catalog Card Number: 74–84345

Set in 10 on 12 pt Monotype Baskerville
Printed in Great Britain by
Western Printing Services Ltd, Bristol

for Shirley and Tony Irving

O saepe mecum tempus in ultimum

CONTENTS

Preface   ix

Part One: The Rock and the Flower

1 Tough and Tender   3
2 The Literary Satires   43
3 Poems of Transit   62
4 The First Pilgrimage   79

Part Two: The Gulf and the Fountain

5 The Turkish Tales   111
6 *Hebrew Melodies*   129
7 Poems of the Separation   146
8 Poems of Exile   164

Part Three: The Maze and the Morass

9   The Second Pilgrimage   181
10 The Dramas and *The Island*   231
11 Social and Political Satire   270
12 *Don Juan*   287

Select Bibliography   351

Index   359

Abbreviations used in the notes

CH   *Childe Harold's Pilgrimage*
DLM   *The Late Lord Byron*, by Doris Langley Moore, Murray, 1961
LJ   *The Works of Lord Byron: Letters and Journals*, ed. R. E. Prothers, 6 vols, Murray 1898–1901 (reference by volume and page, e.g. *LJ* v, 193)
MLJ   *Byron's Letters and Journals*, ed. Leslie A. Marchand, 3 vols, Murray 1973–4 (reference by volume and page, e.g. *MLJ* ii, 84)
PW   *The Works of Lord Byron: Poetry*, ed. E. H. Coleridge, 7 vols, Murray 1898–1904 (reference by volume and page, e.g. *PW* ii, 6)

PREFACE

Among the reactions of shock, incredulity and grief which swept the Western world when the news came out of Missolonghi that Byron was dead, there are three which have always interested me by virtue, first, of their representative character, and second, of their relevance to my approach in the present study. The response of the Greeks themselves was immediate. Easter celebrations were suspended. Klephtic ballads were composed:

> The klephts gave to Byron the name of father
> Because he loved the klephts of ....
>
> The woodlands weep, and the ....
> The castle of Missolonghi groans,
> .... Byron lies dead at Missolonghi.

And it was proposed that the body of ..... the ..... in the ..... running out from ..... at Somerset to ..... grief-stricken ..... world until he finally brought himself to say the words 'Byron is dead'. Into an outcrop of rock. The third reaction, three months later, was recorded by the peasant poet John Clare:

> I was wandering up Oxford Street . . . when my eye was suddenly arrested by straggling groups of the common people collected together & talking about a funeral. I did as the rest did though I could not get hold of what funeral it could be but I knew it was not a common one by the curiosity that kept watch on every countenance. By & by the group collected into about a hundred or more when the train of a funeral suddenly appeared on which a young girl that stood beside me gave a deep sigh & uttered 'Poor Lord Byron'.

All three responses are essentially gestures, movements of empathy. The wish is to embrace, to receive into a fold, as it were, whether that fold is a compassionate heart, a body of ethnic tradition, or a much-loved landscape. All three would have pleased Byron, the first for its acceptance into the clan, the family, and the third for its unconscious negation of the values which had led Dean Ireland to exclude him from the Abbey. As for Tennyson's boyish dramatics, they constitute the kind of symbolic gesture which is itself poetry. The poetry lies in the gesture, the symbolism in its recognition of Byron's exilic status—the acceptance explicit in his own words, 'I should prefer a grey Greek stone over me to Westminster Abbey'— and in kinship of solitude between poet and poet.

All three gestures are also acts of criticism, judgments on Byron as man and poet. It is interesting that the least verbal comes from a boy who was to be one of England's most profuse writers, and the most voluble from a gang of bandits-cum-freedom fighters. The servant girl's sigh adds a feminine component, her words express perhaps some kind of lower class moral comment as well as compassion. But she is pitying Byron within her *topos* of London, as the hero restored in death to his native land. While Tennyson, it seems to me, is consciously or unconsciously integrating Byron into a 'ground' of uncluttered landscape which, different as it is in so many respects from the sun-scorched barrenness of the Attic and the Anatolian scene, nevertheless shares with them the attributes of solitude and silence. And through the austerity of the outer landscapes the two poets meet in an inner dimension of alienation amidst success, of triumph through defeat, of schizophrenia: the poetic mask hiding, in both cases, such formidable concatenations of personalities ribald and romantic, mocking and moralistic.

What all these three 'gestures' have in common is a relation to place and time which makes them, I like to think, the ancestors of my present study. For what I have tried to do in these pages is to approach Byron, to understand him and ultimately to interpret him within his basic 'ground', which was, by his own repeated confession, that of the Eastern Mediterranean. I am essaying a species of 'topocriticism', as far removed from reading *about* Byron in libraries or from conversations *about* Byron in the memoirs of Lady This and Captain That, as can be imagined. This is not to say that I am writing a 'With Byron through Greece', or 'In the Steps of the Poet', or anything at all like that. The reader will look in vain for the type of topographic detail ('Joannina, when Byron descended upon

it on that bright October day of 1809, was a glittering city of
minarets and cypress groves . . .') which has a rightful place in books
of travel but none whatever in works of criticism.

A good many books on Byron which set out with the best intentions
to discuss his poetry in depth have found themselves deflected all
too often into the by-ways of biography and amateur psychology.
This deflection I think I have avoided by my approach along
the lines of what I have called, half-seriously, topocriticism.
Half-seriously, that is, as far as the pompous word is concerned;
but very seriously indeed in pressing the claims of a gestalt approach.
For Byron is, with Wordsworth, one of our two great topical poets—
in the sense of 'regional', sinking roots into a *topos*. Wordsworth's
topos is a narrow one, the Lake District, and this limits his appeal
to the European reader. Byron's is a very broad one, the whole of
Europe and the Mediterranean world, and this makes him strange to
the English reader. Mosques, temples, bazaars, dervishes, pashas,
deserts, wadis, don't go down very easily to a palate accustomed to
clergymen, farmers, public-houses, markets, churches and cottages.
So that Byron has never seemed quite real to an English audience,
though his work was very real to himself and to his Mediterranean
readers. As we come closer to Europe in what remains of this century
we shall probably come closer to Byron.

To explain in what sense my own approach is 'topocritical' I
shall have to indulge in some reminiscence: this is strictly confined
to the Preface, and bears upon the conditions, the history so to
speak, within which my study has been composed. I trace the
writing history back to 1952, and the inaugural lecture, on the text
'I should prefer a grey Greek stone above me to Westminster Abbey',
which I delivered at the inception of my tenure of the Byron Chair
in the University of Athens. The writing continued through the
decade of classes, public lectures and seminars on Byron which I
gave in that University, and ended with the notes I drew up for a
recent seminar on 'Byron and Eliot' in the American University of
Beirut. The feeling and thinking and acting history originated much
further back, in a pilgrimage to Little Gidding with T. S. Eliot in
1936, and culminated in another pilgrimage, this time to Missolonghi to receive the Freedom of that City a quarter century later. I
say culminated, not ended, for the fifteen years of immersion in the
Islamic world which lay ahead for me were to prove just as significant for my understanding of Byron as my familiarity with the
world of Hellenism.

These reminiscences will not be unacceptable, I hope, in the sesquicentennial year of Byron's death, when an element of com- memoration and piety enters inevitably into our thinking about him—and if it does not, then so much the poorer is our thinking! But I introduce them here for practical and not for anecdotal purposes. They suggest themselves to me as the simplest, the most direct and the most concrete means I can find of explaining how I came to write this book and what the reader may expect from it. It isn't gossip, it isn't psycho-analysis, it is a consideration of Byron the poet in terms—mostly implicit rather than explicit—of his grounding in certain places and times, and the ways in which his understanding of life branched and flowered from that grounding. Most works of criticism, and even a large number of novels and biographies, have little connection with the times and places within which they were written—the cluttered desk, the clustering book-shelves, the window looking out on college court or green fields or city street—and when the last page is brought to its dramatic or meditative close, and we say, 'It is finished', there is a sudden hiatus: here the object hangs, poised in its own stillness, but detached from the long months or years of toil and frustration and momentary illuminations that lie behind it.

More memorable scenes, and events more closely intertwined with my theme, encircle this study of Byron. The four beginnings and endings I have just mentioned constitute a sort of parallelogram of forces within which, over the years, it has been pulled into shape— often, as it has seemed to me, without my active contrivance. The parameters are clearly those of pilgrimage and home-coming, of tomb and triumph. Gestalt is a word which has rather gone out of fashion, but it is now familiar enough for me to anglicise it as gestalt in lower case and without italics: it is, then, as a gestalt poet, one whose most 'metaphysical' insights are rooted in 'significant soil', that I present Byron in the following pages: a poet who, like the 'mon- archical insect' which was his favourite emblem of freedom and fruition, circles round and voyages away from and returns treasure- laden to his honey-combed hive.

On the road to Little Gidding Eliot talked of Byron's feeling for places and for history, for the local pieties and for the rise and fall of empires. Our point of departure had been Byron's college in Cambridge, and our point of arrival was a place intimately linked with the University through its founder, Nicholas Ferrar, and the many 'people, not wholly commendable, / Of no immediate kin or kindness, / But some of peculiar genius, / All touched by a common genius', of whom George Herbert and the 'broken king' spring most vividly to mind. I wondered, as we stood on that windy Huntingdonshire upland, if Sir John Byron had accompanied his royal master to Little Gidding as he later followed Prince Charles into exile; and it was not difficult to imagine Byron himself, if some Regency time machine could have whisked him back into the seventeenth century, as one of those 'not wholly commendable' intruders at the 'Arminian nunnery', trotting over from Trinity to consult Nicholas Ferrar in much the same way that he rowed over to the Armenian monastery on S. Lazzaro in Venice to talk with Father Pasqual, in 1816, about the Pauline epistles.

A foolish fancy, perhaps. As Eliot wandered with his Kodak 'behind the pig-sty to the dull façade / And the tombstone' an even more incongruous, almost a psychedelic college of poets and places, of times and traditions flashed across my mind. Superimposed on the twentieth-century poet threading his seventeenth-century scene was the early nineteenth-century poet 'stumbling o'er recollections' as he picked his way among crumbling columns and over mouldering vaults in the Forum Romanum six score years before. The collage was to seem less incongruous in 1943, when we had the complete *Four Quartets* before us, and could appreciate how 'this grace dissolved in place' was the master motif of Eliot's poem as it had been of *Childe Harold's Pilgrimage*.

For me, at all events, the moment was a seminal one, and I believe it was on this first pilgrimage that the lines of my subsequent thinking about Byron were laid down. It may even be that some sort of unconscious resolve was made to study Byron, as I later came to do, 'in the field'. It is a long time ago now, but I still seem to hear the prompting voice which suggested that I might get nearer to Byron in the Levant than in libraries, that an immersion in 'those magical and memorable abodes' which had 'made him a poet', as he repeatedly declared, might help to make me a better critic than I could otherwise hope to be.

Here, at any rate, was my 'field'. For the belief that a writer is best appreciated on his own ground I had the authority of Byron himself. Again and again, in the letters and journals, he speaks of the joy and the illumination which comes from reading the classics amid the scenes which gave them birth. He declaims *Medea* on the Symplegades, Homer on the plain of Troy, crows over Wordsworth for getting his facts wrong about the Greek climate and landscape, and regrets he has left the Anthology at home. Was it not possible, I asked myself, that something of the memorableness if not the magic of Byron's abodes might rub off onto me if I stayed in them long enough? I had no illusions that any 'influence of the clime' would 'shed its Ionian elegance' over my mind as it had over that of Haidée's piratical papa; and Dr Johnson's satirical 'Who drives fat oxen must himself be fat' had long ago punctured the identification bubble. But memorableness, yes—for memorable spells meaningful, and meaning is best apprehended in its springs and fountains, in the Little Gidding spirit of 'You are here to kneel / Where prayer has been valid'. 'With those countries, and events connected with them', he told Moore in 1816, 'all my really poetical feelings begin and end.' A remarkable statement, which Byron repeated in a variety of terms; to interpret it properly, we must look again at those 'magical and memorable abodes' celebrated in his 1818 dedication of the second *Pilgrimage* to Hobhouse. 'Memorable', I have suggested, implies 'meaningful', for we do in fact remember those things which had meaning for us. 'Magical' includes the notion of transmutation, of 'the enchanter's wand': the Byron of Athens, Constantinople, Ephesus and Rome is and yet is not the Byron of the Highlands, Newstead, Harrow and Trinity. 'Abodes' are dwelling-places, 'notre vieille Europe aux anciens parapets' experienced as temenos rather than tourist trap, or as a gigantic hive, in Byron's favourite metaphor, to which the golden bees return again and again. 'Magical' and 'memorable' intertwine: the magical is memorable because it transmutes, the memorable is magical because of the thousand scattered moments, each a point of time but 'out of Time's covenant', within which the miracle of understanding has occurred, and which we remember with awe and gratitude.

The painful mix-up of experience which spells 'life' for those of us who are not saints or sages, the gap between the potential and the actual, or however we like to put it, is the matter of Byron's work and no talk of magical or memorable, any more than of Wordsworthian 'spots of time' or Shelleyan glimpses of an 'Intellectual Beauty', is allowed to mask the impact of that 'naked vision'. I use the term which Eliot applies to Blake's devastating intellectual honesty. Blake would, I think, have applied it to Byron; no keener eye than his followed Byron's Orc-like progress through Europe, no more discerning insight recognised Byron's role as prophet and as scapegoat in the world of his time. *Don Juan* is the final paradigm of this, though we should not in making *Don Juan* our trend poem ignore the masterpieces which led up to it and without a study of which its real meaning is hardly discernible. Above all, we must study *Childe Harold* in its polyphonic relationship with the later poem. In *Don Juan* Byron takes up again, and restructures and inverts and counterpoints anew all those themes which are explicit and implicit in his preceding stabs at a synthesis, as Blake in *Jerusalem* reshapes the mythology and the lyricism and the irony which run through *Innocence and Experience* and *The Marriage of Heaven and Hell* and the earlier Symbolic Books.

It is above all in *For the Sexes: The Gates of Paradise* (begun 1793 as an emblem book, when it was called 'For Children: The Gates of Paradise', and completed with a verse commentary in around 1818, thus spanning the major Blakean and Byronic avatars) that we find a projection of the sexual component of existence so closely patterned on Byron's *curriculum vitae* external and internal that I find it difficult to believe Blake had not Byron in mind as he wrote it. If this conjecture is correct, it lends weight to my use of the poem as a kind of 'control' in my final chapter, which discusses *Don Juan*; if I am wrong, the thematic links between the two poems are still remarkable enough to make the one a valuable commentary upon the other, and as such I have treated it in this last chapter, employing lines from *For the Sexes* as section headings.

The Blake section headings may be thought of as an 'external' control, framing the development of the several themes in *Don Juan*, and doing this from the sexual-psychological angle. I have been more ambitious than ever this bizarre procedure suggests, and have tried to set up an 'internal' control throughout the chapter by interpolating, at strategic points, lines from Eliot's 'Burnt Norton' which seemed to me to connect with the metaphysical level of the poem. Here, also, I have a strong suspicion that Eliot was thinking of Byron as he wrote section II of his poem. If, once again, I am wrong, then once again it hardly matters. The exegetic force remains intact. But those 'Garlic and sapphires in the mud' seem to my mind much more intimately connected with the slime of Venice's canals and the bejewelled countesses who 'smelled so of garlic', according to Shelley, 'that an ordinary Englishman cannot approach them', than with the bucolics of an English village. The line takes me further back, to Little Gidding itself with its pig-sty and the muddy road leading to it, in which at one point our car was almost immobilised. The garlic lay, perhaps, on the breaths of those Cromwellian soldiers who tore down the original west end of the chapel with its organ (hence the present 'dull façade'); the sapphires may have been puddle-reflected splinters of the Huntingdonshire sky, or on another level, that 'dolce color d'oriental zaffiro' which Eliot like Dante habitually sees as the hue of sanctity, 'blue of Mary's colour', and which here would surround the tombstone and the Renaissance ascetic who lies beneath.

'Garlic and sapphires in the mud / Clot the bedded axle-tree.' The participle is a pun if we connect Eliot's line with Byron's *serventismo*. 'In royalty's vast arms he sighed for beauty'—Juan at the court of Catherine the Great: in Teresa's slim arms Byron must often have longed for freedom. Escape to freedom in Missolonghi is escape to mud again, this time the mire and muddle of a provincial marsh town where the burning axle-tree of his Apollonian progress is 'clotted' for ever, the garlic of his less savoury sexual exploits and the sapphires of his genius bogged down in mess and machination, the maze finally subsiding into the morass.

Byron's last scene presents us with a triumph of irony, almost of farce, as though he were living a pathetic-risible episode from his own *Don Juan*. The irony struck me, if I may revert for a moment to my own second pilgrimage, as I stood on the spot where Byron had died to receive the honour he himself had received in 1824. Irony, incongruity, and yet connectiveness. Little Gidding was here with its dull façade and its tombstone: English fenland shook hands with Aetolian marsh, and Tennyson's 'glooming flats' were not far away. At Little Gidding I had been granted an odd vision of a modern poet and his 'field' palimpsested on a nineteenth-century poet and his European 'abodes'. In the intervening quarter of a century, most of it lived in those abodes, the two poets had grown closer together in my imagination: I felt they had been after the same thing, the recovery of a culture, a *Europa liberata*, and that both had failed. Nicholas Ferrar had failed too, with his vision of a City of God built in the England of George Herbert, Lancelot Andrewes and Sir Thomas Browne. 'Wandering alone by Delphi's sacred side', Byron's vision had been of a Greece set free, and in her freedom a beacon to Europe. Eliot's dream in *The Rock* and *Four Quartets* had been nearer to Ferrar's in its Anglicanism: the dream of a national homecoming, a family reunion, as it were, in the bosom of Ecclesia Anglicana and of sanctity. But he was a great European too.

From Little Gidding to Missolonghi, between tomb and tomb, the way had lain through the Waste Land foreseen by Byron (was it not to that Wanderer 'in the Wilderness' that Blake had inscribed his

Ghost of Abel?) and mapped by Eliot in the most representative poem
of its age. Where was sanctity now? Mud yes, garlic yes, but where
were the sapphires? Orts and fragments from the masters swirled
through my brain—'Delphi's sacred side' . . . 'The Sacred Wood' . . .
'Where prayer has been valid'—it all seemed very far away, in the
fifties, as I stood there among the ambassadors and the archimand-
rites, the eagles and the trumpets. *Was* there anything sacred any
more? After Hitler, after D. D. T., after the technocratic revolution?
The brass bands blared, compliments were exchanged between the
representatives of Hellas and Great Britain, funeral odes followed
doxologies, speeches were punctuated by national anthems. It was
all very good and very proper. But was it sacred? A shadow passed
across the sun. I glanced down at the scroll in my hand. *Hieras
poleos Mesolonghiou*—it was 'of the sacred City of Missolonghi' that
I was now a freeman. The thought was comforting. Yes, yes, and
again yes! It was ironic, certainly, that after the sublimities of
Athens, the monitory desolation of Ephesus, the seductions of
Venice, the instructive majesty of Rome, the most famous poet of his
age should come here to die. 'Here ends Childe Harold his last
Pilgrimage.' Ironic, but in the Byronic idiom. The minor poet who
wrote that line had understood. Here Byron, the Byron of *Childe
Harold*, had found himself again. If 'Where life is lost, or freedom
won' is the best place to be, if the courage of simple folk confers
sanctity, then he had 'chosen his ground' well, and could take his
rest. Over Byron's statue the dark cypresses waved slowly, there was
still an echo from those filial klephts, those ululating Suliotes, still a
tear from the woodlands and a groan from the castle of Missolonghi.
In the distances of the Ionian sea Ithaca's twin peaks brooded where
'sad Penelope o'erlooked the wave' for sight of her returning Ulysses;
across the Gulf lay Patras, where Byron first set foot on the sacred
soil; to the north, some fifty miles away, was Prevesa, the scene of
his final landfall. Yes, a homecoming of a sort for Byron, in 1824.
In my end is my beginning.

Little Gidding 1936—Istanbul 1949—Athens 1952—Beirut 1974.

Acknowledgements

I have to thank the British Council and Longman Group for permission to reproduce parts of essays 215, 219 and 223 in the 'Writers and Their Work' series.

We are grateful to the following for permission to reproduce copyright material:

Faber and Faber Ltd and Harcourt Brace Jovanovich Inc., for 15 lines from 'Burnt Norton' and other short extracts from 'Burnt Norton' and 'East Coker' from *Four Quartets* by T. S. Eliot. Reproduced by permission of the Publishers.

Part One

THE ROCK
AND THE FLOWER

1

TOUGH
AND TENDER

'I have hazarded my reputation and feelings . . .'

Most juvenile verse is either decadent or delinquent, and sometimes
it is both. Decadence means writing in an outworn tradition, or in
exaggerated revolt against it: stasis or spasm. Delinquency is a slap in
the face to established religious, social or political values. Keats's
early verse is silly-decadent, with touches of unconvincing delinquency
caught from Leigh Hunt. Coleridge is silly-decadent too, with large
infusions of delinquency Socinian, necessitarian and pantisocratic.
Shelley is delinquent in the main, with Godwin, Rousseau and the
physiocrats behind him; his decadence stems from the Tale of
Terror. Wordsworth's early verse (wisely unpublished by its author,
but collected in an appendix to volume I of the standard edition) is
quite undelinquent: it ranges through a quaint spectrum of decadence sentimental, Chattertonian, Gothic and charnel-house.

Byron is both decadent and delinquent, in a rather low key.
Institutions are criticised in *Hours of Idleness*, but on the basis of
accepted values. Where Shelley is outspoken, Byron is cagey. Sexual
freedom is welcomed, but as a departure from the recognised norm.
Religious divergence is along respectable deist lines. His decadence
too is conventional, functioning within late eighteenth-century
modes: the Della Cruscans, the bluestockings, the horror comics,
Ossian. This makes for dullness, and much of *Hours of Idleness* is very
dull indeed; but there is an undertone of irony which alerts us to
possible ambiguities. We cannot always be certain how to take him—
we suspect that a sleight of hand is being practised on us: an attitude
adopted in one poem is abandoned in the next, and not infrequently

Byron seems to be parodying himself. This unwillingness to be
pinned down is a trick he may have caught from Thomas Moore, his
chief model for the amatory and horrific poems. *The Poetical Works
of the late Thomas Little, Esq.*, that erotic bible of Byron's boyhood,[1]
presents some coy 'editorial' disclaimers, ranging from rejections
of 'spurious copies of this song' (footnote to 'Oh! nothing in life
can sadden us') to such solemn disavowals of the Tale of Terror as

I should be sorry to think that my friend ['Thomas Little'] had any serious
intentions of frightening the nursery by this story; I rather hope, though the
manner of it leads me to doubt, that his design was to ridicule that distem-
pered taste, which prefers those monsters of the fancy, to the 'speciosa
miracula' of true poetic imagination . . .

(footnote to 'The Ring', a 'Gothic' poem). This is a device by which
the author eats his cake and has it. Byron was never to renounce it
entirely, and a great deal of spurious criticism of his best work
derives from his own disparaging comments. In *Hours of Idleness* the
device functions, mainly in the amatory poems, as tongue-in-cheek
hyperbole:

> 'Tis said that Berenice's hair,
>   In stars adorns the vault of heaven;
> But they would ne'er permit *thee* there,
>   *Thou* wouldst so far outshine the seven.
>
> For did those eyes as planets roll,
>   Thy sister-lights would scarce appear:
> E'en suns, which systems now controul,
>   Would twinkle dimly through their sphere.[2]

'Little' had gone back to Sedley and Rochester for his brand of
gallantry, Byron goes back to them for his conceits, but, alas, the
element of wit is lacking. Or is it, as I have suggested, supposed to
reside in the hyperbole itself? We cannot tell, and this pervasive
uncertainty may go some way to accounting for our sense of unease
as we read *Hours of Idleness*.

The juvenilia came out in a series of privately printed volumes:
Fugitive Pieces, 1806; *Poems on Various Occasions*, early 1807; *Hours of
Idleness*, later in 1807; *Poems Original and Translated*, 1808. The first
two issues were anonymous, though two poems in *Fugitive Pieces* are
signed BYRON; the last two volumes have Byron's name on the
title-page. *Hours of Idleness* is rightly regarded as the definitive issue:
its predecessors lead up to it, and its successor is described on the
title-page as a 'Second Edition'. Byron's title-pages are often significant, and not least for their epigraphs. In these early examples we

may trace the gradual emergence of a triple theme which is to permeate the whole of his succeeding work. *Fugitive Pieces* has no epigraph, but it has a title vignette of Venus Anadyomene in her shell with attendant cupids. The predominantly amatory character of the 'Pieces' is plainly avowed. The Rev. J. T. Becher, Byron's Southwell friend and mentor, thought some of them too 'warm', and the issue was suppressed. *Poems on Various Occasions* has no frontis-piece, but it has the motto 'Virginibus Puerisque Canto': a re-inforcement of the friendship motif is suggested, and this is borne out by the inclusion of Byron's most important schooldays poem, 'Childish Recollections'. A sterner note now begins to sound with the translation of Horace's 'Justum et tenacem propositi virum' and the 'Answer to a Beautiful Poem', which announces that

> The Patriot's and the Poet's frame
>   Must share the common tomb of all:
> Their glory will not sleep the same;
>   *That* will arise, though Empires fall.

Byron the poet-warrior is adumbrated.

Hours of Idleness likewise lacks a frontispiece, but its title-page bears a triple epigraph from Homer, Horace and Dryden. *Poems Original and Translated* omits the line from Horace; we guess at a pruning-out of the amatory poems: and this has in fact been done. The five new pieces are celebrations of friendships and laments for lost childhood. The frontispiece, a lithograph of Harrow-on-the Hill, stands above a couplet from 'Childish Recollections' which clinches the volume's nostalgic impact:

> 'Ida! blest spot, where Science holds her reign!
> How joyous once I join'd thy youthful train!'

Taking *Hours of Idleness* and *Poems Original and Translated* together as an expression of Byron's final choice among his juvenilia, we can, I think, arrive at certain conclusions about the kind of poet Byron is, and, more important, about the kind of poet he is going to be. One impression which emerges forcibly is his uncertainty of stance and of aim. All these 'decisions and revisions which a minute will reverse' —hesitations which affect the balance in succeeding issues of his major themes as well as his sureness of touch, his sincerity, if you like, in treating the themes themselves—suggest a talent basically unsure of itself. Together with the decadence and the delinquency we note a *tertium quid*, doubt. It is not just philosophical doubt or adolescent despondency; it is an 'existential *angst*' which will shortly ripen into the famous Byronic 'guilt', the *weltschmerz* which fascinated a century.

Let us glance back at that threefold epigraph to *Hours of Idleness*, and the whole title-page on which it figures. The subtitle, 'A Series of Poems, Original and Translated, by George Gordon, Lord Byron, a minor', is followed by

Μητ' αρ με μαλ' αινεε μητε τι νεικει   Homer, *Iliad*, 10

Virginibus puerisque Canto.   Horace

He whistled as he went for want of thought.   Dryden

A curious mixture of aggression and deprecation, of tough and tender! The title *Hours of Idleness* itself is a species of challenge: lords have a prescriptive right to be idle, and these light verses are all *you* have a right to expect from their scribbling! But this is immediately followed by the self-defensive 'A Minor'. Then, with the Homeric line, we swing back to a posture of proud defiance: 'I care neither for your praise nor your blame.' Horace reverts to the tender; and Dryden, finally, introduces the note of insouciance with reference not to the reader but to the poems themselves, establishing a tone, an attitude of thoughtlessness which includes the elements of spontaneity and freedom.

The Preface to *Hours of Idleness* (omitted from the E. H. Coleridge edition) reinforces our sense of Byron's lack of poise. Here is the mixture as before of truculence, deprecation and pleading. The author 'might be . . . more usefully employed'. The poems 'are the fruits of the lighter hours of a young man who has lately completed his nineteenth year'. Byron has 'hazarded [his] reputation and feelings in publishing this volume'. If it is condemned, he will 'submit without a murmur'. He has 'not aimed at exclusive originality', still less has he 'studied any particular model for imitation'. The tone teeters between the Johnsonian pompous and the schoolboyish cheeky: there are some painful attempts at wit:

I . . . content myself with the not very magnificent prospect of ranking amongst 'the mob of gentlemen who write';—my readers must determine whether I dare say 'with ease', or the honour of a posthumous page in 'The Catalogue of Royal and Noble Authors',—a work to which the Peerage is under infinite obligations, inasmuch as many names of considerable length, sound, and antiquity, are thereby rescued from the obscurity which un-luckily overshadows several voluminous productions of their illustrious bearers.

Painfully inept, even at the age of twenty, for the barbed intelligence which was so soon to sparkle in *English Bards and Scotch Reviewers* and the Grand Tour letters, and to dazzle, not very much later, in *Waltz* and *The Curse of Minerva*. We remember the Preface to *Endymion*, written it is true when Keats was three years older than Byron, and with no attempt at wit, written without Byron's Harrow and Cambridge background and under the stress of urgent financial and emotional problems, but breathing an air of 'sincerity and strength', even one might say of wisdom, which was quite outside the range of the young Byron:

Knowing within myself the manner in which this Poem has been produced, it is not without a feeling of regret that I make it public.

What manner I mean, will be quite clear to the reader, who must soon perceive great inexperience, immaturity, and every error denoting a feverish attempt, rather than a deed accomplished. . . .

The imagination of a boy is healthy, and the mature imagination of a man is healthy; but there is a space of life between, in which the soul is in a ferment, the character undecided, the way of life uncertain, the ambition thick-sighted: thence proceeds mawkishness, and all the thousand bitters which those men I speak of must necessarily taste in going over the following pages.

I am being unfair in setting the worst paragraph of Byron's Preface side by side with the best of Keats's. And of course *Endymion* is not juvenilia;[3] *Poems 1817* was that, the collection which includes 'To Some Ladies', and the three unbelievably bad, bad quite outside Byron's range, sonnets to Woman. But to compare the two Prefaces as wholes is not unfair, and it is illuminating. Keats's clearsightedness at twenty-three, his very real humility in face of great art, contrasts strongly with Byron's disingenuous assumption of diffidence, and his manifest incapacity for self-criticism.

'My springs of life were poisoned'

I have referred to Keats's personal problems in the hinge years 1816–17. Byron had his problems too, not less crucifying than Keats's. The 'doubt' which I added as a *tertium quid* to the two 'notes' of juvenile verse, decadence and delinquency, was not an after-thought: doubt moves in the depths of *Hours of Idleness*, surfacing in particular poems such as 'The Prayer of Nature'[4] (religious doubt) and 'Damaetas' (social doubt), but pervasive through the whole collection as an undertone of despair. This, I think, is what Keats felt when he addressed Byron, in a very bad sonnet dated 1814, as the poet of 'O'ershadowing sorrow'. And Byron in *his* hinge years, 1804–05, had very good personal reasons for sorrow, for doubt and despondency—at least as good as Keats's.

I am not writing yet another gossiping 'study' of Byron, in which the *oeuvre* is remorselessly (or sometimes remorsefully, the critic succumbing with gasps of protest to the biographer) sacrificed to the *vie*: my aim is now, in considering the early poems, as it will continue to be in assessing the mature works, to focus attention on the individual poem, the stanza, the line, the word. But to go to the other extreme is self-stultifying. Byron is a very human poet, grappling with human problems in their immediacy: and the immediate data from which he starts off are found, where Montaigne and Shakespeare found them, in his own mind and heart. Even Shakespeare and Homer would be more intelligible to us if we knew more about their lives. I say 'even', for these are writers working, like Dante and the Attic dramatists, on planes transcending the personal: planes which Byron rarely achieves. His epic, *Don Juan*, is a 'human comedy', not a divine. But we are thankful for what we know of Dante's life as we read the *Vita Nuova*, we should be thankful for any new light on Shakespeare as we read the Sonnets, and we are thankful again for the very complete documentation available to us, as we study Byron's early poems, in his schoolboy letters to Augusta and others.

Keats wrote, in his sonnet, of Byron's 'o'ershadowing sorrow'. The phrase links up, in my mind, with a phrase of Byron's. As we read those desperate letters of his to his half-sister and the Pigots,[5] written between March 1804 and January 1807, we see the rejection of his mother building up from 'this female *Tisiphone*' (to Augusta, 10 August 1805), through 'my amiable Alecto' (to J. M. B. Pigot, 9 August 1806), 'my Hydra' (to Elizabeth Pigot, 10 August 1806), to a final 'that upas tree, that antidote to the arts' (to J. M. B. Pigot, 26 August 1806). Earlier letters to Augusta had complained of Mrs Byron's '*diabolical* disposition' (18 August 1804) and suggested that 'she is certainly mad' (5 June 1805). The upas tree is Byron's 'o'ershadowing sorrow'. Byron's mother is nowhere mentioned in *Hours of Idleness*, that ingenuous record of Byron's early loves and detestations, but, as the *shadow*, she is ubiquitously present.

Poor Catherine Gordon of Gight! Scottish heiress, descendant of James I of Scotland, dumpy, semi-illiterate and finally alcoholic, she fell to the blandishments of that almost incredibly 'romantic' villain, Captain ('Mad Jack') Byron, who had already seduced,

married and exhausted the fortune of the Marchioness of
Carmarthen.[6] It is easy to see that Catherine had what is called 'a
good heart'. A good heart was needed to continue to love Mad Jack,
who ran through her fortune of more than £23,000 in less than a
year, escaped to France to avoid his creditors, returned to England
in time for the birth of his son in 1788, but was back in France by
September 1790; whence he wrote to his sister on 16 February 1791:

> With regard to Mrs Byron, I am glad she writes to you. She is very amiable
> at a distance; but I defy you and all the Apostles to live with her two months,
> for, if any body could live with her, it was me. . . . For my son, I am happy
> to hear he is well; but for his walking, 'tis impossible, as he is club-footed.

No need to enquire where Byron got his wonderful prose style
from—it's all there in Mad Jack's letter. A remarkable vindication
of the Abbé Mendel! We pause in admiration over the prose, but
shake our heads over the sentiment. Mad Jack showed no further
interest in his club-footed son. 'Sinking lower and lower in degradation and debt,'[7] he died in Valenciennes on 2 August 1791. In an
odd way his fascination persisted. After the first wild outburst of
grief, audible in the street outside,[8] Mrs Byron gradually turned in
upon herself, nursing her grievances: the wound festered, and
Mad Jack's son became a sort of whipping boy, adored like his
father for his attractions, execrated for his misdeeds. *Odi et amo.*
Oedipean shades press upon us here, and are not to be ignored; in
the Byronic sexual panorama, as in any discussion of the famous
Byronic 'guilt', we have to take the mother figure into account. The
father figure is more easily discernible: George Gordon and Augusta
got together in a pathetic 'our father right or wrong' league against
the Hydra, and Mad Jack's independence of convention, his complete scorn of conformity, became a guiding light for his son through
the shoals and shallows of Southwell small-town society as well as,
later, in the whirlpools of London and Venice. We can, perhaps,
trace his lifelong hatred of 'cant' back to this source.

But that Byron's childhood was traumatic, to a degree surpassing
anything experienced by Coleridge, Shelley or Keats, is certain; and
the fact has to be taken into account in any assessment of his
emotional development. Mrs Byron alternately lavished caresses on
her son and pursued him with blows and shouts of 'You lame brat!'
The grim opening of his final play, *The Deformed Transformed*—

Bertha. Out, Hunchback!
Arnold.   I was born so, Mother!

testifies to the persistence of his resentment.[9] Almost as unbearable as these violent outbursts on Catherine Byron's part must have been the day to day intercourse, if we can call it that, of a mind as brilliant as Byron's with such an *esprit borné*. If Byron is so very much the poet of fugue, of almost hysterical escape from every life situation in which he finds himself trapped, the initial impulse was the overmastering need to get away from his foolish mother. And this is abundantly borne out by the letters.

The upas tree is a favourite emblem in Romantic iconography. It is exploited, indeed overexploited, by both Coleridge and Shelley—but with Byron it has its roots in these very real childhood torments and deserves a more serious consideration. The theme of death is pervasive in the early poems. In *Childe Harold* it deepens into a recognition of the 'death wish'. Byron's existential vision here anticipates Freud: such passages as

> There is a very life in our despair,
>   Vitality of poison—a quick root
>   Which feeds these deadly branches. . . .   (*CH* III, xxxiv)

and

> Our life is a false nature—'tis not in
>   The harmony of things,—this hard decree,
>   This uneradicable taint of Sin,
>   This boundless Upas, this all-blasting tree. . . .   (*CH* IV, cxxvi)

go far to explain Byron's appeal for his generation, a generation which suffered from the Enlightenment's loss of faith without the compensation of the Enlightenment's social complacency. But I anticipate. Our concern for the moment is with *Hours of Idleness*, where the death wish is pervasive rather than overt. Perhaps I can put it in its right relationship to the other themes of that volume by way of an imaginary object, a fabricated 'visual aid'.

'This boundless Upas, this all-blasting tree'

I invite my reader to contemplate a non-existent frontispiece. Byron liked frontispieces,[10] but they were expensive luxuries for a boy printing his own verses, and *Hours of Idleness* lacks even a title-vignette. We can, however, easily supply one for him: and it will, I suggest, serve not only as a graphic panorama of Byron's emotional state in 1807 but also as a thematic index to the volume. *Hours of Idleness* is very much of a jumble, at first sight, and any device which helps to get some order into the chaos should be welcome. Let us begin, then, with the architectural, which constitutes a big part of Byron's imagery in the juvenilia and later, and set a Gothic abbey in the centre of our design. In its cloisters we note a bevy of feasting monks, quaffing wine from skull-cups incessantly replenished by 'Paphian girls'. To the right of the abbey, in the middle distance, a classical temple: boys are at play in its *temenos*. From the architectural we pass to the natural, or elemental. Towering above the abbey and the temple, in the far distance, we see a mountain diversified with caves. Its summit is obscured by clouds, which open from moment to moment to emit lightning flashes and disclose the forms of armed warriors, warlocks, bards. Hermits sit at the entrances to the caves (we are moving down the slope of the mountain now) deep in their devotions. From the snow-capped peaks (one cannot avoid clichés in such a reconstruction) streams flow down with all the turbulence of Coleridge's Alph, to sink in tumult, not to a lifeless ocean but to the placid waters of a lake in the foreground of the abbey, a lake on whose banks a young man and a girl are walking hand in hand. A mermaid, complete with comb and mirror, rises from its centre. But on the left of the abbey, balancing the temple to the right, an enormous upas tree spreads its shade over abbey, school, lake and wandering lovers.

My design is a messy one, and a purist might relate it rather to the baroque exuberance of 1607 than to the chaste Regency taste of two centuries later. This objection I would not quarrel with—indeed, I would welcome it, as signalising that curious 'metaphysical' note in Byron which makes him the most 'emblematic' of the Romantic poets, a writer delighting in hints, allusions and cryptograms, working within ambiguities and multiple levels of meaning. The relation is perhaps more with Quarles and Wither than with Donne. 'Know ye the land where the cypress and myrtle/Are *emblems* of deeds that are done in their clime'—so he begins *The Bride of Abydos* half a decade later: but the emblematising (my italics) is already there in *Hours of Idleness*. This makes him the closest to Blake of all the Romantics. 'Where man is not, nature is barren': nature constitutes the human cryptogram.

I have assembled my imaginary frontispiece out of a variety of bits and pieces. The classical temple is Harrow, straight from the *Poems Original and Translated* lithograph and line 150 of 'Childish Recollections'. The mermaid is the Aphrodite Anadyomene of the *Fugitive Pieces* title-vignette, transmogrified into a supporter from the Byron coat of arms.[11] The upas tree comes from the 1804–07 letters. The mountain is Lachin Y Gair, focusing the maternal dynastic strain in *Hours of Idleness* while the abbey is of course Newstead, embodying the paternal. 'Paphian girls' figure in stanza vii of *Childe Harold* I. The lake is Newstead lake, but as we read on in Byron (for my frontispiece will prove to be a key to his total *oeuvre*) it is also Lake Leman, and even, in some of its sinister aspects, the lake at Joannina. The boy and girl wandering by the lake are Byron and Mary Chaworth, but also, in a later scenario, Byron and Augusta. The incidental human figures, schoolboys, monks, and hermits (one might have added fishermen and hunters, objects of Byron's detestation) are self-explanatory.

Turning back from our imaginary frontispiece to the existent title-page to which we have already directed a good deal of attention (but with Byron there is no limit to the degrees of attention to which he may be profitably subjected) we note in the triple epigraph a division of subject matter—epic, amatory, reflective—which is itself a very valid index to his themes in *Hours of Idleness* and also in his work as a whole. Consider this stanza from one of the latest of his writings, the eighth Canto of *Don Juan*:

> Reader! I have kept my word,—at least so far
>   As the first Canto promised. You have now
> Had sketches of Love—Tempest—Travel—War,—
>   All very accurate, you must allow.
> And *Epic*, if plain truth should prove no bar;
>   For I have drawn much less with a long bow
> Than my forerunners. Carelessly I sing,
>   But Phoebus lends me now and then a string. . . .   (st. cxxxviii)

The wisdom of spontaneity: 'Carelessly I sing' . . . 'He whistled as he went for want of thought.' Love: 'Virginibus Puerisque Canto.' Power: the Homer motto. In this adherence to a kind of thematic programme, as in many other respects which will surface later in this discussion, Byron shows himself as an extraordinarily *continuous* poet: and at the same time as a poet with a very clear idea of his 'field'. The field is a wide one: love, power, the wisdom of 'want of thought', and we have already seen that Byron is unsure about how to exploit it. His poetic development will prove to be an unceasing quest for proportion: for the exact blending of the themes of love, wisdom and power in a synthesis which will adequately express that view of life that we still, even when we are not thinking of Byron's work, call 'Byronic'.

There are a few adjectives, derived from proper names, which stand out as something special in the annals of literature. Homeric, Virgilian, Dantesque, Chaucerian, Shakespearian—and to these we must certainly add Byronic—are epithets which connote as well as denote: their meaning spreads out from the purely literary context to wider 'existential' fields. Such epithets as Miltonic, Swiftian, Wordsworthian, Keatsian, Tennysonian have a limited impact: we think of a particular kind of subject matter, an individual style. But those of our first group refer to 'worlds' of experience and of ways of embodying that experience: these worlds are created and projected by their creators on to the European consciousness, so that it is still possible in 1931, for instance, to have one of the characters in Virginia Woolf's *The Waves* say to another 'You are not Byron, you are yourself', and leave the reader in no doubt of what is being implied.[12] Can we imagine anyone saying 'You are not Wordsworth, you are yourself?' No doubt there exists the possibility of an illicit identification with Byron, as one might identify with a film star, but the prolongation of such an influence over such a stretch of time shows that deeper influences than hero-worship are at work. The Byronic 'world' has continents which could be discovered and explored by Kierkegaard, Nietzsche, Arnold, Eliot, Freud, and Jung. Not all these later discoverers acknowledged their debt (Nietzsche was an honourable exception), but it is not difficult to trace Byron's tracks in their snow.

'The rocks where the snow-flake reposes'

My last paragraph may seem a digression, and perhaps it is: but the bane of Byron criticism has always been the inability or unwillingness of his commentators to see him in a total perspective, to recognise his role as doctrinal to a continent as Milton declared himself to be to a nation. Or, if they recognise it, they shrug it off as an aberration of the European *zeitgeist*. In particular, they have been unwilling to dig for the roots of Byron's role in the soil where, if anywhere, it is to be found; his early experiences and his early formulations of those experiences in verse. The verse itself may be undistinguished; we need not anthologise it, but we cannot ignore it.

I have used the catchphrase 'tough and tender' liberally enough: its essence is there in the *Hours of Idleness* title-page; but perhaps the time has come to pin it down a bit more precisely. Byron is tough in his dynastic descent from the Buruns and the Gordons, he is tough too in his literary pedigree from Chaucer and Henryson through Skelton and Dryden, Johnson and Churchill, down to Gifford in his own day. His tenderness is all his own: we can trace no ancestral links. He is tender about small unprotected things, wild flowers and insects and fishes, children in distress, old charwomen sweeping up and lighting fires, and about what we now call the environment, unpolluted stretches of sea and land, pure air, the monuments of the past permitted to exist undespoiled in their gestalt. Tenderness doesn't mean sloppiness. He discerns in Dante 'a tenderness beyond all tenderness'; and in Byron, tough as he is, we may detect a compassion beyond that of the Coleridge who weeps over a tethered donkey but declares that he would,

supposing it his duty . . . order the military execution of a city . . . and then in awe listen to the uproar, even as to a Thunderstorm . . . the awe as tranquil, the submission to the inevitable, to the Unconnected with my own Self, as profound.[13]

It is Wordsworth, another quietist, who writes sonnets in support of capital punishment, and reminds the Deity that 'Carnage is thy daughter'.[14] Coleridge, voyaging to Malta, witnessed the slow torture of a migrant hawk as it flew from mast to mast of the five ships in his convoy in search of footing while the crews shot at it, and retired to the seclusion of his cabin to write a 'man of feeling' note in his diary.[15] Byron would have done something about that hawk.

Byron never uprooted plants from their native rocks and painfully lugged them home to live a caged existence (when they survived), in Dove Cottage garden,[16] but his solicitude for the 'young oak . . . in the garden of Newstead Abbey, planted by the author in the 9th year of [his] age' which he found many years later 'choked up with weeds and almost destroyed',[17] and his determination that it shall survive, opens up a dimension of Byronic 'Nature poetry' which is persistently ignored by those commentators, such as Professor Ernest J. Lovell, Jr, PhD, of Texas, who are determined to see Byron as the bastard son of William Wordsworth.[18] Byron *cared* for trees he had planted himself, for geese he had bought for slaughter and brought up by hand and found he had grown too fond of to kill, for fishes in his ponds and dogs in his hall; and extending from this domestic enclave to the European menagerie of apes and cranes and bears and tortoises remarked on by Shelley,[19] his solicitude also included the undefended columns and architraves, amphitheatres and temples threatened alike by ignorant Turks and educated Britons.

'To an Oak at Newstead', dated 1807, is the 'paternal' equivalent of the 'maternal' dynastic expression of tenderness-cum-toughness which is posited in 'Lachin Y Gair'—to which I shall turn in a moment. Here the young oak (strength) dies because it is planted under the aegis of a tenderness which is powerless to protect it. A long shadow stretches from here to *The Corsair*.[20]

> I left thee, my Oak, and, since that fatal hour,
>   A stranger has dwelt in the hall of my Sire;
> Till Manhood shall crown me, not mine is the power,
>   But his, whose neglect may have bade thee expire.

Strength needs tenderness: this constant theme of Byron's verse (the plays, above all, are based on it) opens up in the juvenilia. And tenderness needs strength: this is the moral of 'Lachin Y Gair'. Wisdom lies in the recognition of this nexus. Non-recognition brings the calamities of *Manfred, Sardanapalus, Cain, Werner*. *Don Juan* moves between the tough and tender poles. In *The Vision of Judgment* Byron is tough with Southey and tender with George III. Bligh's toughness in *The Island* is offset by the tenderness of Neuha, the slaveship is counterpointed by the island of erotic permissiveness. Wisdom, which Byron was always hoping to achieve, and never did, consists in the ability to move from the love–power level to a new dimension which reconciles the poles without negating them. Cant is a recognition of the one pole (power) while paying lip-service to the other (love as tenderness, philanthropy, devotion, patriotism, or whatever other form 'love' may take).

Along the wisdom–power–love spectrum the poems of *Hours of Idleness* and other juvenilia resolve themselves into correspondent groups. In one we have the Newstead poems, projecting the paternal hubris on the one hand, and the Highland poems (including 'Lachin Y Gair', 'I would I were a careless Child', 'When I roved a young Highlander', as well as the Ossianic and ballad imitations) on the other. Byron's family traumas—the parental conflict, and the Newstead guilt-complex—are powerful forces here. 'The shade of power' (*CH* II, ii) flits between the battlements of Newstead and the peaks of Loch na Garr. The shade of love moves between the tea-parties and amateur theatricals of Southwell, the 'hills of Annesley, bleak and barren' where he worshipped Mary Chaworth, and the schoolrooms and dormitories and playing-fields of Harrow. 'Virgines puerosque amo.' Wisdom is a more fleeting guest, as dubious as love and power but, we feel, more ardently welcomed. It emerges in the deist piety of 'The Prayer of Nature', in the self-analysis of 'To Edward Noel Long, Esq.', and in 'Childish Recollections'. The satiric component of *Hours of Idleness* is also a factor in 'wisdom': for simplicity's sake, I defer its consideration to my later chapter on *English Bards and Scotch Reviewers, Hints from Horace*, and *The Curse of Minerva*.

Let us begin then with power, and with the Highland poems. Here Byron is probing his earliest contacts with landscape and with dynastic and ethnic forces working within landscape, themes to be taken up later (with dazzling effect) in *Childe Harold* and *The Island*. And at once I enter this caveat: neither 'wisdom' nor 'love' can be left out of account as we explore the power systems of the dynastic poems. The earliest and most complex of them, 'Lachin Y Gair', interweaves love with freedom and the fight for freedom in anticipation of the Maid of Saragoza stanzas of Canto I of *Childe Harold*; wisdom is implicit, but we feel it in the delicate balance throughout the poem of Byron's pride-in-ancestry and his sense of what in *Manfred* he is to call 'the o'er-ruling infinite', the sombre 'genius' of the Highlands which gives meaning to 'the forms of my Fathers'.

Swinburne was right in singling out 'Lachin Y Gair' in his 1866 essay, for here we have the Ur-Byron, the Byron uncorrupted by 'Saxon pride' or Oriental luxury. What moves us is not the form, the technical accomplishment—to our ears the anapaests are too jaunty for comfort—but the evident sincerity. The poem is the product of loneliness and deracination: a small boy's attempt to cope. But from the outset his search for a 'correlative', a father figure such as the mountain was for Wordsworth, is bedevilled by the awkward fact that mountains are associated not with Mad Jack but with his appallingly unimpressive mother. If only the pedigrees could have been reversed, and his father come from the stern, romantic Highlands, his insufferable mother from the soft, decadent English midlands! In a mind which worked so consistently in images and mythologies as Byron's did, I cannot help feeling that this baffling anomaly added a warp which complicated an already tortuous inner landscape.

To return to the poem. Written at Newstead, it repudiates 'gay landscapes, . . . gardens of roses', in favour of

> the rocks, where the snow-flake reposes,
> Though still they are sacred to freedom and love.

We ask, 'why *though*?' The answer leads us to the crux of Byron's paradoxical vision.[21] Love and the passion for freedom are warm, violent emotions; the summits of mountains are cold and bleak. Yet freedom has always found its refuge among mountains, and as for love, as Johnson remarked in his *Letter to Lord Chesterfield*, 'The shepherd in Virgil grew at last acquainted with Love, and found him a native of the rocks'. This is the kind of violent antithesis which delighted Byron.

It is better to have the whole first stanza before us.

> Away, ye gay landscapes, ye gardens of roses!
>   In you let the minions of luxury rove;
> Restore me the rocks, where the snow-flake reposes,
>   Though still they are sacred to freedom and love:
> Yet, Caledonia, belov'd are thy mountains,
>   Round their white summits though elements war;
> Though cataracts foam 'stead of smooth-flowing fountains,
>   I sigh for the valley of dark Loch na Garr.

There is a violent revulsion away from the English midlands to the austere north. Roses are counterpointed with snowflakes; fountains with cataracts, gardens with rocks.

The young Byron turns to the austerities of the rock and the snowflake. I should like to linger for a moment here, because the antithesis of tough and tender in its physical mode—expressed, that is, in juxtapositions of flower and crag, of butterfly and desert, and so on—is a permanent Byronic oxymoron serving a variety of purposes. Byron likes to bring tough and tender violently together, as for instance in his comment that there is in Dante a 'tenderness beyond all tenderness'[22] even in Hell, where its gates are constructed by the triple power of force, wisdom and *love*.[23] The point of the 'though' is that the very existence of the snowflake depends on the hardness and iciness of the rocks on which it falls. Softness, warmth, cosiness would at once destroy it. The oxymoron guarantees the phenomenon. The 'love' of the mountain peak for the snowflake is precisely its coldness, its hardness, its immitigable austerity. This is the 'midwinter Spring' of Eliot's 'Little Gidding'. The stern is the natural protector of the ethereal, a point Byron will make constantly in his later writing:

> But from their nature will the Tannen grow
>   Loftiest on loftiest and least sheltered rocks,
>   Rooted in barrenness . . .   (*CH* IV, xx)

Barrenness: rock weathered by sun and wind, or friated by roots, lapses into sand, chemically neutral, but magically fruitful. That the 'tannen', the pinetree, is itself tough, is a point that links it to the snowflake via the rock in a nexus which is peculiarly Byronic. The growth of the tannen depends on the snowflake to this degree, that the snowflake preserves its identity throughout the winter but sacrifices it in the spring for the sake of plant growth. Already the Byronic interchange between the elements, which is also Heraclitean, is making itself heard. 'Earth lives the death of water.' Or of air, the snowflake being a magical stasis of water in air, subdued (by its material form) to earth, and shortly to be resolved through fire (the sun's rays) into that vapour which, like Shelley's cloud, will repeat the cycle *ad infinitum*.

I do not pretend that these affinities were consciously present in Byron's mind when he wrote *Hours of Idleness*. That they were implicit can be shown in any sensitive account of Byron's imagery. And, in particular, of his imagery of love, as we shall see when we come to a consideration of the Turkish Tales. Love is essentially self-giving, an intercourse of high and low, of Blake's 'mutual creations and destroyings' throughout the four elements. The heat streaming from the sun in late spring inevitably destroys the snowflake. This is the annihilation of individuality in the cosmic love, the 'love which moves the sun and the other stars' (already Byron's affinities with Dante begin to manifest themselves). The snowflake melts, trickles down into the 'dark valley' of the second half of the stanza, or percolates into the crevices of the upper rocks to subdue them into a suitable humus for the 'tannen'. As water it breaks down the rocks into life-giving soil, or rises again as mist into the atmosphere to fulfil another stage of its eternal cycle. As source of the mountain torrents it supplies the water without which the mountain freedom fighters (whether of the Scottish or the Greek Highlands) would be unable to carry on their struggle.

I am reading 'Lachin Y Gair', I admit, in the light of Byron's later career as man and poet, but this is not illegitimate in the case of a writer so *continuous* as Byron shows himself to be from beginning to end of his work. And already the peculiar coordinates of Byron's Man–Nature construct are beginning to reveal themselves. We shall never understand Byron's 'Nature poetry' if we attempt to approach it through the fixities and definites of the Wordsworthian schema, or via Coleridge's symbolic universe of God speaking to man through a physical cryptogram. Byron's Nature is endlessly fluid, Heracleitus' πάντα ῥεῖ, a theatre of exchange among a variety of planes. The snowflake is an etherial visitant, a heavenly star or flower descending on the barren but heroic surface of the rock. It

would appear to have little contact with 'the fury and the mire of
human veins'. But it is the point of Byron's inclusive vision, here in a
nuclear and later in a wealth of expanded forms, to link up the
human and the natural-divine not in a metaphysical synthesis, like
Wordsworth's, but in a working family relationship. 'Where rose the
mountains, there to him were *friends*/Where rolled the ocean, there
he found his *home*.' In Blake's phrase, 'For the human family we
live', and the human includes the natural and the divine. This is
Byron's major theme of reciprocity, of self-giving, of sacrificial
death and resurrection. It suffuses *Childe Harold*: with its opposite,
assertion of the selfhood against the communal good, it forms the
dramatic agon of the Turkish Tales. Nor, even in these projections
of human passion, is the snowflake, now in the form of the wild
flower springing from the barren rock, forgotten:

> Strange—that where Nature loved to trace,
> As if for Gods, a dwelling place,
> And every charm and grace hath mixed
> Within the Paradise she fixed,
> There man, enamoured of distress,
> Should mar it into wilderness,
> And trample, brute-like, o'er each flower
> That tasks not one laborious hour;
> Nor claims the culture of his hand
> To bloom along the fairy land,
> But springs as to preclude his care,
> And sweetly woos him—but to spare! (*The Giaour* 46–57)

It seems a mere aside in the human turmoil of *The Giaour*, but it is
central to Byron's vision. And it is brilliantly prophetic of twentieth-
century man's attitude to the 'sweet especial rural scene'. As Gerard
Manley Hopkins remarks, 'when we mend her we end her'; but so
potent now is the prestige of technology, even in remote rural areas
of the Mediterranean, that any unspoiled 'rural scene' is regarded
as unbearably crude unless the culture of man's hand through
many a laborious hour can be brought to bear to smooth the living
rocks with concrete and replace the wild flowers with roses and
double dahlias.

These desecrations of the lowlands, the seashore, are escaped in
the solitudes of the mountain fortresses. The tender is protected by
the tough. To return to 'Lachin Y Gair': the rocks which support
freedom, in their capacity as fortress, and love, in their capacity as
Eden, also support the snowflake, the sky-flower, the etherial visitant,
in their capacity as sterile medium. The verse is antiphonally

structured, working between England's 'tame and domestic' beauties and the Highland peaks, and, at the microscopic level, between the delicacy of the snowflake, its etherial, complex pattern, and the brute solidity of the rock which protects it from annihilation. These are the paradoxes which, transposed into terms of 'the sexual strife', await us in the Turkish Tales, a decade or more later.

The point of 'Lachin Y Gair' is made in its first stanza; the rest elaborate, with autobiographical touches. Byron wears the Highland dress, listens to 'traditional story', calls, with Ossianic fervour, on the shades of dead heroes. The forms of his Fathers 'dwell in the tempests of dark Loch na Garr'. The chthonic, racial forces arise from the rocks to meet the descending benediction of the snowflake. How prophetic this is of Byron's later psychodrama—of the proffered grace, as in Manfred's 'There is a calm upon me',[24] and the dark, turbid resistances in the hero's soul which reject the uncovenanted mercy! This situation of ascents and descents is one we must return to in our consideration of the love–hate patterns of the Turkish Tales.

The remaining Highland poems simply reinforce (or perhaps weaken) the impact of 'Lachin Y Gair'. 'When I roved a young Highlander' softens the flower–rock antithesis to an amatory stereotype. Climbing the 'steep summit' of 'Morven of snow', fearless and unlettered, he has no feeling but for his Mary:

> Yet it could not be Love, for I knew not the name,—
> What passion can dwell in the heart of a child?
> But, still, I perceive an emotion the same
> As I felt, when a boy, on the crag-cover'd wild.

Here the interest of the poem lies in the self-analysis. While still a boy, Byron is probing boyish reactions. Not emotion recollected in tranquillity, but recollection assessed in emotion. Past and present flow one into the other, exercising judicial reappraisals. We are conscious of an antithesis, hardly clear to Byron himself, between the 'steep summits' and the sexual lowlands. The Byron of 1807 prefers to posit his dilemma in terms of an appeal to Fortune to

> take back these cultur'd lands,
> Take back this name of splendid sound!
> I hate the touch of servile hands,
> I hate the slaves that cringe around:
> Place me among the rocks I love,
> Which sound to Ocean's wildest roar:
> I ask but this—again to rove
> Through scenes my youth hath known before.
>
> ('I would I were a careless child' St. 2)

His wish was not to be granted: instead, he was to assuage more complex—and less innocent—urges for 'freedom and love' in scenes which partly reproduced, partly contradicted these childhood austerities; combining, indeed, an apotheosis of the rose garden of Newstead with a magnification of the peaks of dark Loch na Garr.

'Where, now, the bats their wavering wings extend'

Power, in the Highland poems, was mysterious, vague, Ossianic. The 'forms of my Fathers' sank back into, or momentarily emerged from, mists and precipices. Newstead is more definite. The forms of his maternal forefathers find it hard to compete with these insistent barons and cavaliers. A strong instinct for reality, for what is here and now, always competes in Byron with a thirst for the remote, the primitive, the exotic. On the spot at Newstead he integrates with Newstead. And the personal pull towards his father, as he allies himself with his half-sister Augusta against the impossible Mrs Byron, shifts him into a peculiar stance vis-à-vis the Abbey and its history. 'Mad Jack', in his (to Byron) admirable role—gallant, *insouciant*, gay, independent, suicidal—sums up the whole history of the Byrons, and of the Abbey which is their conquest and their home and their monument. And now guilt enters the picture: the guilt of sacrilege, of the *temero templa*, desecration of the holy places. Byronic guilt stems from identification with his father's ill-treatment of Mrs Byron, personal guilt in his own repudiation of her, dynastic guilt in his occupation of the desecrated Abbey of Newstead.

All this makes for intense confusion in Byron's mind—essentially a frank, open and honest one—and this is reflected in the conflicting stances of *Hours of Idleness*. 'On Leaving Newstead Abbey' is a perfect paradigm of disequilibrium. Even the initial regret for decay cannot be wholehearted in the poet who in 'Lachin Y Gair' preferred thistles to roses.

> Through thy battlements, Newstead, the hollow winds whistle:
> Thou, the hall of my Fathers, art gone to decay;
> In thy once smiling garden, the hemlock and thistle
> Have choak'd up the rose, which late bloom'd in the way.

English roses are ousted by Scots thistles: the Byrons by the Gordons in the poisonous shape (hemlock) of the poet's mother. Yet, while roses are beautiful, hemlock and thistle have a morbid, 'romantic' charm. And they recall Socrates' sacrifice, Bruce's determination.

Perhaps to bloom 'in the way' is to bloom as an impediment to the self-knowledge, self-mastery, which was coming to seem a 'way' to the young Byron.[25] Byron teeters here, I feel, among a wealth of options. Yet Newstead is stable as a matrix, a womb of forces, hollow as the winds yet fruitful (in Shelley's 'West Wind' sense) as they are.[26] He addresses the 'hall' directly, as later he was to invoke the great pregnant monuments of Greece and Italy, as a focus of tensions, or 'parallelogram of forces', rich in seminal possibilities. Already Byron's unique dialectics, personal-dynastic-architectural-physical, is taking shape. Personal and hereditary, secular and religious pull one against another here. We are directed forward, if we have the whole Byronic opus in mind, to the Greek-Turkish, classical-Christian ethos of Athens. Newstead is, for the moment, Byron's Parthenon, focusing dynastic, religious, social-political dilemmas later to be evaluated in the tales, dramas and narratives, and above all in *Childe Harold*.

This inclusiveness of the Abbey as symbol is formulated in the later 'Elegy on Newstead Abbey' where the building is addressed as 'fast-falling, once-resplendent dome!' Dome is a catchword in Augustan and Regency verse for any extensive and well-proportioned edifice (the twin word 'pile' rather expressing weight and mass). Byron may be using it in its accepted sense; yet remembering his serious concern with words, we may suggest (especially as this is the first line of the poem, with no exigencies of rhyme involved) that 'dome' does present a structure which includes and, as far as it can, mediates. Most old prints of Newstead show it rising from its lake as a kind of efflorescence of the watery powers which are conveyed in the Byron emblem of mermaid and looking-glass and which he later celebrated in the first of his Venice stanzas in *Childe Harold* IV. A print in Allan Cunningham's *Anniversary* for 1829 shows the lake as almost a Lake Leman, with a sailing boat and the lights of Newstead reflected in the water; the accompanying poem reminds us that

> Proud baron's hall, and poet's tower,
> And artist's toil, all have their hour;
> For this will sink and that will pass,
> Like autumn's fruit and summer's grass:
> Man's art to them their being gives,
> But Byron is of God, and lives.

This 'living' character, deeply intertwined with the spirit of place, gives dramatic intensity to the Newstead poems.

The drama lies, as I have already suggested, in the contradictions. Inclusivity here is not harmony. An intricate warp-and-woof underlies the Newstead poems and the *Hours of Idleness* lyrics generally. The Ossianic epigraph of 'On Leaving Newstead Abbey' sounds the first dissonance:

Why dost thou build the hall, Son of the winged days. Thou lookest from thy tower today: yet a few years, and the blast of the desart comes: it howls in thy empty court.

Tempus edax rerum: human pride versus the destructive forces of time. This note rings not only through *Hours of Idleness* and *Hebrew Melodies*: it is the keynote of *Childe Harold* and the Tales. A blast blows from 'the desart', from the inhuman void. If 'Loch na Garr with Ida looks on Troy' in *The Island*, here Newstead with Ephesus looks on the Empty Quarter. Ossian had not intended this with his 'desart'; but Byron, deep in Jones and Waring, Weston and the Koran, conflates Ossian and the topographically alien and remote but psychologically akin diagrams of Jami and Ferdausi.[27] Blowing from the desert, the blast comes with the aridity and the blessing of sand, disinfecting the damp Nottinghamshire valleys and uplands. This spatial nexus, cunningly established through the Ossianic motto, is even more boldly (and unjustifiably) reinforced by a projection of the medieval Byrons as Crusaders.

> Of the mail-cover'd Barons, who, proudly, to battle,
>   Led their vassals from Europe to Palestine's plain.
> The escutcheon and shield, which with ev'ry blast rattle,
>   Are the only sad vestiges now that remain.

That these imaginary Crusaders were conjured up in Byron's mind by 'some groups of heads on the old panelwork at Newstead' is an index of how much his mythopoeic faculty could be aroused by architectural detail: a point valuable as we plot his later development.

'Only connect!' Forster's slogan is vital in any intelligent assessment of Byron, most complex of Romantic poets. We have to connect past with present, East with West, classical (Virgil, Horace, Pope, Gray, Collins) with romantic (Ossian, Blake, Wordsworth, Shelley), and architecture with landscape and the flesh-and-blood which animates it. Byron's imagination is synoptic: it takes in, as the Metaphysicals' did, enormous ranges of 'disparate' material. The tendency of the other Romantics (with Blake always the great exception) was to contract and delimit: Wordsworth with his corner in the Lakes, Shelley with his vegetarian ethical paradise, Keats commuting between Wardour Street middle ages and bosky snoozings in the Vale of Health, Coleridge dreaming dreams in 'a lonely farmhouse between Porlock and Linton'. Byron, on the contrary, continuously expands, moving outwards in ever-widening circles.

And within the circles, eddies of irony. Those 'mail-cover'd barons'—the irony here, implicit in the smug 'proudly, to battle' and 'the only sad vestiges' of the quatrain's final line, would escape Byron's contemporary readers. As so often, he is playing tricks with us. The carapace, the 'mail', the outer shell of force, of religion, covers . . . what?[28] It is 'vassals', not so well armoured, who are led to their deaths 'on Palestine's plain'. What remains of all this slaughter? 'The escutcheon and shield' rattle 'with ev'ry blast' that blows along the wall: this is the spider's carapace, long abandoned. A social criticism is implied, as well as the dynastic *angst* more cogently expressed in the great Haram passage (lines 288–351) of *The Giaour*. Even the choice of metre, the jaunty anapaestic tetrameter, finds its ironic raison d'être. Constantly, in reading Byron, even the young Byron, we have to be alive to these tongue-in-cheek possibilities. *Crede Byron*—yes, but with a pinch of salt. He may be laughing at you.

Ossian, at first sight a rooted inmate of the Highland stretches of *Hours of Idleness*, weaves about among the Newstead and even the Harrow poems, proffering a key which unlocks a great variety of doors. It is significant that both Byron and Blake, the freest of the Romantics, admired and 'imitated' Ossian. Both denied the Wordsworthian permanence, the 'stonifying', as Blake expressed it, of a reality which to them only existed in its flow. For Blake it is the 'joy as it flies' that matters; and Byron is a lifelong enemy of 'system' and 'permanence'.[29] This gives a vital quality even to the minor lyrics of *Hours of Idleness*: one feels that something is happening in them, though below the surface. Falling between Wordsworth's stasis and Shelley's evanescence, they revolve around elemental axes which lend them a curious assurance. This is Ossian's world, a world of apparently undirected flow, a stream of consciousness which moves between psychic poles, and perhaps it was this sense of release from the rational modes of thought and expression which fascinated the eighteenth and early nineteenth centuries. Macpherson provided some of the facilities of the psychiatrist's couch. Even today, reading 'Fingal' or 'Temora' in a relaxed mood, one feels oneself carried into 'strange seas of thought' or day-dreaming. 'Why dost thou build the hall, Son of the winged days . . .?' Macpherson's rhythms are irresistible and his interweaving of the human with the cosmic, his creation or revivifying of an antique world where man merged with his environment, penetrates Byron's early poems and provides a direction for his later. 'Through thy battlements, Newstead, the hollow winds whistle': the inter-penetration of human, elemental and architectural which is Byron's basic pattern is already here. Though the wind is uncontrollable, blowing where it listeth, yet it is modified in its effects by the material on which it operates. The pathos of human destiny, enshrined in crumbling artefacts, makes itself heard in this wind music: the Abbey becomes a species of Aeolian harp playing variations on the Ossianic epigraph.

Free association is the underlying principle of both Blake's and Byron's poetics: in the later Symbolic Books and *Don Juan* a technique already apparent in the early lyrics is carried to its furthest point. To grasp its origins it is worth while making a close study of Blake's 'Prologue to King John', 'The Couch of Death', 'Contemplation', and 'Samson', side by side with Byron's 'The Death of Calmar and Orla' and 'Oscar of Alva'. The cry 'O man, how great, how little thou! O man, slave of each moment, lord of eternity!' from 'Contemplation', or 'Brother in brother's blood must bathe, rivers of death!' from 'Prologue to King John'; the picture of mother and sister gathered to the sick bed of a youth in 'The Couch of Death', and 'the aged woman's cry', 'O my child, my child! is thy breath infected? So is mine. As the deer wounded, by the brooks of water, so the arrows of sin stick in my flesh; the poison has entered into my marrow' in the same piece; the theme in 'Samson' of the strong yet vulnerable man who tells his wife 'this secret of my birth' and is destroyed—all these elements of the Byronic destiny move powerfully through Blake's Ossianic imitations and are recreated in 'My springs of life were poisoned' (*CH* III, vii), in *Hebrew Melodies*, and in the Annabella context within which the *Melodies* were written.

Moreover, we can detect in Byron's 'The Death of Calmar and Orla' the beginnings of what I have called the Byronic 'vortex', that constant ideogram of himself which he presents now in terms of 'a whirling gulf of phantasy and flame' (*ibid.*), now in terms of 'a wandering hell in the eternal space', a ruined star, or of a whirlpool in the ocean depths. The opening paragraph of 'Calmar and Orla' brings together this and a number of related themes.

Dear are the days of youth! Age dwells on their remembrance through the mist of time. In the twilight he recalls the sunny hours of morn. He lifts his spear with trembling hand. 'Not thus feebly did I raise the steel before my fathers!' Past is the race of heroes! But their fame rises on the harp; their souls ride on the wings of the wind; they hear the sound through the sighs of the storm, and rejoice in their hall of clouds. Such is Calmar. The grey stone marks his narrow house. He looks down from eddying tempests: he rolls his form in the whirlwind, and hovers on the blast of the mountain.

That grey stone appears again and again in Byron, as an eikon of the austere dignity of the grave: in *The Giaour*, for instance, and so personal a remark as 'I should prefer a grey Greek stone over me to Westminster Abbey' (*LJ* vi 196). 'Their fame rises on the harp' introduces the theme of the bard, of traditional song and oral legend, which fascinated Byron throughout his life,[30] and which induces him to bring a fictitious bard, 'old Robert', into 'On Leaving Newstead Abbey', as the inspirer of the equally fictitious Crusaders to battle 'on Palestine's plain'. The bard thus links Ossian and the Byronic destiny past (in his ancestry) and future (in his own death in fighting the infidel): the prophetic resonances which impressed Blake in Byron begin to sound.[31]

As though conscious that the Crusader claim is very dubious, Byron brings forward other instances of his ancestors' fighting in a noble cause. Four brothers died for their king on the field of Marston Moor; others fell in the Hundred Years War:

> Paul and Hubert too sleep in the valley of Cressy;
>   For the safety of Edward and England they fell:
> My Fathers! the tears of your country redress ye:
>   How you fought! how you died! still her annals can tell.

The awkward syntax of the third line betrays Byron's embarrassment. It is not the Byrons who are 'redressed' by the tears of their country; what he really means is that the noble deeds which evoke their country's tears redress the original guilt of their usurpation of Newstead. In advance, of course, since Henry VIII's gift of the Abbey to 'Sir John Byron the Little, with the great beard', was not until 1540. Their blood shed at Marston Moor confirms their expiation; a cancelled reading in stanza v stresses the religious context: 'For Charles the Martyr their country defending.'

The place of sacrilege in the whole complex of Byronic guilt is worth investigating. It recurs, and more openly, in 'Elegy on Newstead Abbey'. The Ossianic epigraph here is: 'It is the voice of years, that are gone! they roll before me, with all their deeds.' Once more the building functions as a voice, as revealing more than words

can say, a theme to which Byron is to return again and again in
Childe Harold and the Tales, and with special poignancy in the Forum
stanzas, since for him Rome is the 'mother of the soul' as Newstead
is the father:

> Tully was not so eloquent as thou,
> Thou nameless column with the buried base!   (*CH* IV, cx)

The 'deeds' are now identified as acts of piety and impiety:

> NEWSTEAD! fast-falling, once-resplendent dome!
>   Religion's shrine! repentant HENRY's pride!
> Of Warriors, Monks, and Dames the cloister'd tomb,
>   Whose pensive shades around thy ruins glide.

'Henry II', Byron's note informs us, 'founded Newstead soon after
the murder of Thomas à Becket.' The trilogy of warriors, monks and
dames neatly presents the power–wisdom–love complex under the
one dome, and not necessarily in the succession wisdom–power–love.
The confusions imposed on Byron by his heredity and his 'en-
lightened' society led him into ambivalent reactions to religion and
especially to the monastic and eremitical life. We feel that he is
strongly drawn to the aspect of wisdom projected in the complete
self-giving of the monk, yet that, like the young man in the Gospel
story who 'had great possessions', he cannot abandon himself to it
and feels the need to protect and justify himself (and his usurping
ancestors) by raking up the old charges of monastic lechery,
gluttony and winebibbing. This is a point to which I must return
later, for Byron's dealings with monasticism were by no means
confined to the historical; even the poem under discussion moves
through an extraordinary complex of ambiguities. The 'dark pile'
rises from 'the wild', from the abode of 'outlaws'; the monk who
seeks shelter in its 'gloomy cells and shades profound' (an echo from
Eloisa to Abelard) is abjuring 'a world he ne'er could view', or
repenting of 'blood-stain'd Guilt', or finding refuge from 'stern
Oppression'. The analysis, however callow, shows that the schoolboy
has done some thinking on the subject. But he has come to no
conclusions. A stanza complaining that

> . . . Superstition's crimes, of various dyes,
>   Sought shelter in the Priest's protecting cowl

is followed immediately by

> Where, now, the grass exhales a murky dew,
>   The humid pall of life-extinguish'd clay,
> In sainted fame, the sacred Fathers grew,
>   Nor raised their pious voices, but to pray.

> Where, now, the bats their wavering wings extend,
>   Soon as the gloaming spreads her waning shade;
> The choir did, oft, their mingling vespers blend,
>   Or matin orisons to Mary paid.

Intellectually confused, perhaps, but the confusion is dynamic, not supine, and issues as writing in a series of powerful contrasts which, though not yet combined into 'ideograms', achieve by simple visual impact an effect which is wellnigh as telling. 'Where, now, the bats their wavering wings extend' is both visual and auditory—the 'wavering' is felt in the rhythms—and is a line of which no poet need be ashamed. Many others in *Hours of Idleness*, such as 'Gilds with faint beams the crystal dews of rain', in 'Childish Recollections', and 'The yellow harvest's countless seed', in 'Imitated from Catullus', have a Pre-Raphaelite delicacy which suggests what Byron *might* have done as a lyrist if his destiny had not led him to the massive and dramatic triumphs of *Childe Harold* and *Cain*. Yet the early possibilities are absorbed, not abandoned; these *aureae felicitates* of the juvenilia are the materials which Byron's 'lion paw' was to pat with such effortless ease into the great stanzas of *Don Juan* or the rippling tetrameters of *The Giaour*.

The theme of wisdom is largely muted in *Hours of Idleness*, which is what we should expect of juvenilia. Gestures towards piety such as 'The Prayer of Nature' are unconvincingly Popean. It is in the longer 'confessional' poems, 'Childish Recollections' and 'To Edward Noel Long, Esq.', which are poems of childhood and childhood friendships, that we find Byron working his way towards some kind of 'philosophy'. He never reached it, because like Virginia Woolf he is not a 'one-maker': reality resides, for him, in the flux of events and the unformulable void beyond it; events as the voice of the void, the void as the matrix of events. Childhood is Byron's Eden because events strike with keener impact on spirits not yet subdued by what Traherne called 'the dirty devices of the world'. The satirical Theophrastan sketch 'Damaetas' is a picture of perverted boyhood such as Byron was again to essay, less virulently but more cogently, in *Hints from Horace*, lines 221–4:

> Observe his simple childhood's dawning days,
> His pranks, his prate, his playmates, and his plays:
> Till time at length the mannish tyro weans,
> And prurient vice outstrips his tardy teens!

This dread of the perversion of love moves beneath the nostalgia of 'Childish Recollections'.

'Dissolving in the Fond Caress'

Byron's early 'love' poetry has some interest for the prosodist and the
historian of poetic forms and fashions. It is not as bad as Keats's,
because Byron has a firmer grasp of form, is less sentimental, and
writes under the guidance of better models. Chief among these are
Prior and Moore. Moore himself wrote in the line of Sedley and
Rochester, as the Preface to *The Poetical Works of the late Thomas
Little, Esq.* (1801) makes clear. 'Little' goes to the limit of permissiveness for his time, and Byron lapped him up eagerly; as late as
1820 we find him writing to Moore, now a firm friend: 'I have just
been turning over *Little*, which I knew by heart in 1803, being then
in my fifteenth summer. Heigho! I believe all the mischief I have
ever done, or sung, has been owing to that confounded book of
yours!'

Byron's models in 'Little' are considerably more accomplished,
more pointed, and more spicy than his own schoolboy imitations,
but it is only fair to note that the best of his amatory (and satirical)
verses were progressively pruned out, under the eye of his clerical
friend the Rev. John Thomas Becher, as the editions marched from
Fugitive Pieces to *Poems Original and Translated*. Some stanzas from a
suppressed poem, 'To Mary', give a better idea of what he could
do in the 'Little' vein than anything surviving in the collected
Works:

> No more that bosom heaves for me,
> > On it another seeks repose,
> > Another riot's on its snows,
> Our bonds are broken, both are free.
>
> No more with mutual love we burn,
> > No more the genial couch we bless,
> > Dissolving in the fond caress;
> Our love o'erthrown will ne'er return.
>
> Though love than ours could ne'er be truer,
> > Yet flames too fierce themselves destroy,
> > Embraces oft repeated cloy,
> *Ours* came too *frequent*, to endure.   (sts 4–6)

> Even now I cannot well forget thee,
> > And though no more in folds of pleasure,
> > Kiss follows kiss in countless measure,
> I hope *you* sometimes will regret me.

> And smile to think how oft were done,
>   What prudes declare a sin to act is,
>   And never but in darkness practice,
> Fearing to trust the tell-tale sun.
>
> And wisely therefore night prefer,
>   Whose dusky mantle veils their fears,
>   Of *this* and *that*, of eyes and ears,
> Affording shades to those that err.
>
> Now, by my soul, 'tis most delight
>   To view each other panting, dying,
>   In love's *extatick posture* lying,
> Grateful to *feeling*, as to *sight*.   (sts 9–12)

Apart from the liveliness of the verse, and the closeness of the sentiment to Blake's recommendation of 'naked in the sunny beams
delight' in 'lovely copulation, bliss on bliss, with Theotormon',
Byron's use of the '*In Memoriam* stanza', hardly found between
Tennyson's time and that of its originators, Ben Jonson and Lord
Herbert of Cherbury, is noteworthy. So too is the reference forward
of 'flames too fierce themselves destroy' to 'the sword outwears its
sheath' in the best of all his lyrics, 'So we'll go no more a'roving',
some ten years later.

The amatory poems which survived Mr Becher's red pencil are
frigid and deadly dull, without even the 'stuffed owl' quality which
makes Keats's

> Ah! who can e'er forget so fair a being?
>   Who can forget her half retiring sweets?
>   God! she is like a milk-white lamb that bleats
> For man's protection

worth at least a hoot of delighted laughter. Byron the schoolboy puts
on the mask of the sated, the Cavalier lover, strives to be clever
and knowing. There are a few compensatory touches. Some satirical-
amatory verses, such as 'To a Vain Lady', show an early interest, of
a clinical kind, in feminine psychology. Tough and tender meet here,
as again in the anapaestic 'To Caroline': one wonders how many
lovers of seventeen have reminded their mistresses

> That the time must arrive, when, no longer retaining
>   Their auburn, those locks must wave thin to the breeze,
> When a few silver hairs of those tresses remaining,
>   Prove nature a prey to decay and disease.

Hardly inspiriting; and another poem 'To Caroline' envisages consummation of their love in the tomb, a Marvellian touch. Tough is at odds with tender in another set of verses which deplore the poet's passive acceptance of his fate:

> Was my eye, 'stead of tears, with red fury flakes bright'ning,
>   Would my lips breathe a flame which no stream could assuage,
> On our foes should my glance lanch in vengeance its lightning,
>   With transport my tongue give a loose to its rage.

This is Ercles' vein, hardly preferable to the maudlinly abject tone of most of these poems, in which they are so often reminiscent of Wyatt. If, as some critics have suggested, Wyatt may be using the love situation as cover for other grievances and frustrations, which could not be ventilated with safety, the same explanation may fit Byron. There are many varieties of love, and Byron at this date was starved of most of them, not least of the maternal. Poems like 'To a Fair Quaker' initiate that nostalgic, Egeria-worshipping vein which later produced some of the best of the *Hebrew Melodies*:

> Sweet girl! though only once we met,
> That meeting I shall ne'er forget;
> And though we ne'er may meet again,
> Remembrance will thy form retain.

This is the undemanding note of 'She walks in beauty, like the night' of 1814. It differs in kind, though not perhaps in intensity, from that of 'Hills of Annesley, bleak and barren', the only early love poem of Byron which, it seems to me, sounds the note of genuine anguish:

> Hills of Annesley, Bleak and Barren,
>   Where my thoughtless Childhood stray'd,
> How the northern Tempests, warring,
>   Howl above thy tufted Shade!
>
> Now no more, the Hours beguiling,
>   Former favourite Haunts I see;
> Now no more my Mary smiling,
>   Makes ye seem a Heaven to Me.

Written in 1805, 'shortly after the marriage of Miss Chaworth', as Byron's subtitle states, these verses were not published in his lifetime. Byron probably thought them too revealing, or realised that their stark immediacy would have shattered the frigid mould of *Hours of Idleness*.

'Friendship, the dear peculiar bond of youth'

With these very few exceptions, the amatory poems are tedious in the extreme, as Byron acknowledges in the original (*Poems on Various Occasions*) paragraph of 'Childish Recollections', where he renounces the 'unvarying song of varied loves' in favour of the remembrance of boyhood friendships at Harrow. Again 'The Death of Calmar and Orla' provides the nucleus:

No maid was the sigh of his soul; his thoughts were given to friendship—to dark-haired Orla, destroyer of heroes! Equal were their swords in battle; but fierce was the pride of Orla:—gentle alone to Calmar. Together they dwelt in the cave of Oithona.

The elements of a Byronic cosmology emerge here: love; friendship; war; death; the sheltering cave. All will be 'expansed' in the Turkish Tales, in *Don Juan* and *The Island*. War, death, love and friendship are projected in their classical heroic mould in Byron's very free translation of the Nisus and Euryalus episode from the *Aeneid*, which he himself links with 'Calmar and Orla' in a note to the Ossianic imitation. But for the moment the cave is 'Ida', the fostering womb of Harrow school which supplies for Byron so many of the assurances his miserable childhood had lacked.

'Childish Recollections' is Byron's longest and most important poem before *English Bards and Scotch Reviewers*. In its original version it begins with a paragraph of renunciation of girls and poems about them, together with the world and its snares of ambition:

> Censure no more shall brand my humble name,
> The child of passion and the fool of fame.
> Weary of love, of life, devour'd with spleen,
> I rest a perfect Timon, not nineteen;
> World, I renounce thee! all my hope's o'ercast!
> One sigh I give thee, but that sigh's the last.
> Friends, foes, and females, now alike, adieu!
> Would I could add remembrance of you, too!

A blanket condemnation: Byron is to distinguish in his second version. Memory itself is deprecated here: 'the curse of memory', he calls it, 'hovering in [his] dreams', ruling his senses 'with tyrannic sway'.[32] But in the *Hours of Idleness* version he recants:

> The Sun of Memory, glowing through my dreams,
> Though sunk the radiance of his former blaze,
> To scenes far distant points his paler rays,
> Still rules my senses with unbounded sway,
> The past confounding with the present day. (22–6)

Misanthropy and renunciation of his early erotic verse come
together here. What remain are the memories of Harrow school.
'Childish Recollections' has been called Byron's 'Tintern Abbey';
but Byron's early paradise (the word occurs at line 218) is social, not
solitary, and active, not contemplative. Or where contemplative, a
shared contemplation (see the lines from the original version given as
footnote, *PW* I, 99). The poem is an ardent eulogy of boyhood
friendships. Childhood is the period of frankness, spontaneity and
participation, as against the caution and the cant of adult years.

> Hours of my youth! when, nurtur'd in my breast,
> To Love a stranger, Friendship made me blest,—
> Friendship, the dear peculiar bond of youth,
> When every artless bosom throbs with truth;
> Untaught by worldly wisdom how to feign,
> And check each impulse with prudential rein;
> When, all we feel, our honest souls disclose,
> In love to friends, in open hate to foes;[33]
> No varnish'd tales the lips of youth repeat,
> No dear-bought knowledge purchased by deceit;
> Hypocrisy, the gift of lengthen'd years,
> Matured by age, the garb of Prudence wears:
> When, now, the Boy is ripen'd into Man,
> His careful Sire chalks forth some wary plan;
> Instructs his Son from Candour's path to shrink,
> Smoothly to speak, and cautiously to think;
> Still to assent, and never to deny—
> A patron's praise can well reward the lie:
> And who, when Fortune's warning voice is heard,
> Would lose his opening prospects for a word?
> Although, against that word, his heart rebel,
> And Truth, indignant, all his bosom swell.   (55–76)

This is mature writing, already focusing Byron the cant hater, the
opponent of inner as well as outer servitude, whose lifelong struggle
against the Philistines filled Goethe and Matthew Arnold with
'reverential awe' and may still have something to say to us today.

But Byron, as he confesses in the next paragraph, is not by nature a
satirist. *Facit indignatio versus.* The most attractive portions of
'Childish Recollections' are those which celebrate and commend.
Yet the tone is never mawkish. A shrewdly assessive mind probes the
varied strata of Harrow life. His own leadership among the boys:

> Here first remember'd be the joyous band,
> Who hail'd me chief, obedient to command;
> Who join'd with me in every boyish sport,
> Their first adviser, and their last resort;   (99–102)

anticipates Conrad's in *The Corsair*:

> No matter where—their chief's allotment this;
> Theirs to believe no prey or plan amiss.
> But who that CHIEF? his name on every shore
> Is famed and feared—they ask and know no more.[34]

There is, it appears, no competition. But on the dubious upper-echelon levels of adult authority the case is different. A Greek-Turkish conflict begins to develop between boys and masters; and among the Turks, which is Ali Pasha, which the Sultan? The debate is a lively one, carried on outside 'Childish Recollections' in the satirical character sketch of 'Pomposus' in 'On a Change of Masters in a Great Public School' and in the MS lines reproduced as a footnote to p. 91 of vol. i of the standard edition (*PW*). Byron was persistently in search of a father figure, and he reacted strongly where this was proffered but not supplied; there was even stronger reaction when the emotional centre of Harrow was in any way threatened.

Under the benevolent tuition of 'Probus', Byron and his schoolmates 'search'd the classic page,/Culling the treasures of the letter'd sage'. This is the earlier version; in *Hours of Idleness* the second line reads 'And fear'd the Master, though we lov'd the Sage'. Both readings are valuable; the earlier should not be ignored. We are only too eager to think of Byron at Harrow as the rebellious schoolboy delighting in games, rags, escapades, and only too unwilling to recognise the thirst for knowledge and for wisdom which led him to 'search the classic page' and put his findings to such good use in *Childe Harold*. Throughout his life Byron showed a profound respect for true learning and piety, as witness his correspondence with Professor Clarke of Cambridge and his Armenian studies with Father Pasqual in the Mekhitarist monastery in Venice.[35]

A brilliant picture of day-to-day pursuits at Harrow occupies the long section of 'Childish Recollections' stretching from line 121 to line 184. Gray presides over these lines, but the detail has an immediacy beyond Gray. The opening is general enough:

> High, through those elms with hoary branches crown'd,
> Fair IDA's bower adorns the landscape round;
> There Science, from her favour'd seat, surveys
> The vale where rural Nature claims her praise;
> To her awhile resigns her youthful train,
> Who move in joy, and dance along the plain.   (121–6)

On closer scrutiny, we note an antithesis absent from 'On a Distant

Prospect of Eton College'. 'Fair Ida's bower *adorns the landscape round*'—the citadel of 'Science' throws its benison of wisdom over the 'vale of rural Nature', and the vale returns the blessing with the gifts of health and spontaneity and energy. Blake's 'joy in the springing day' is not cramped here; it flourishes, and reverberates back from 'vale' into 'Hill', from 'green retreat' (135) into classroom:

> Th'allotted hour of daily sport is o'er,
> And Learning beckons from her temple's door.   (149–50)

The daily pursuits themselves mingle, or alternate, the active with the contemplative, the social with the solitary (139–46); the school meets the rural world outside in verbal or physical battle (137–42, 273–82), and the agon passes into legend handed down from generation to generation of schoolboys (140–84). Here we have not only Byron's abiding reverence for tradition, but also his sense of interrelationship, of community transcending class divisions yet acknowledging them, and above all of the vital intercourse of City and Temenos, of the divine centre penetrating into, as it draws its nutriment from, the natural world of fruition and generation and decay. This, to my mind, is the dominant theme of *Childe Harold*, the theme of the central realm.

This preoccupation, in 'Childish Recollections', is the main representative of the strand of *wisdom* within the threefold woof of wisdom, power and love. It is wisdom mediated by words, in 'the classic page', by personality, in 'the letter'd sage' Dr Drury, by atmosphere, in the Ossianic mournfulness of 'The sighing weeds, that hide their nameless grave' (162), by tradition, and by that whistling for want of thought which penetrates schoolday activities with a gay spontaneity integrating the boy with his natural environment.

After wisdom, *power*. Tradition, and particularly schoolboy tradition, celebrates power rather than wisdom, or wisdom embedded in power. The 'dusky wall' of the schoolroom shows name after name of those who once possessed 'the reins of power' (169). And here the hereditary Ossianic and Newstead threnos resounds:

> Here mingling view the names of Sire and Son,
> The one long grav'd, the other just begun:
> These shall survive alike when Son and Sire,
> Beneath one common stroke of fate expire;
> Perhaps, their last memorial these alone,
> Denied, in death, a monumental stone,
> Whilst to the gale in mournful cadence wave
> The sighing weeds, that hide their nameless grave.   (155–62)

The fascination of 'Childish Recollections' lies in its function as a crucible. The energies boiling up here, power struggling with wisdom, wisdom tangled with love, re-emerge in *Childe Harold*, under another sun, as straightforward strands of power politics, Christian-Islamic morality, hetero-homosexual love, to recomplicate themselves, the moment Byron returns to the grey skies of England, in the crypto-grams of the Turkish Tales and *Hebrew Melodies*. Plainly what is at issue in 'Childish Recollections' is not the simple 'crabbed age and youth' antithesis on which the poem seems to be built, but a conflict of values which includes but transcends the generation gap. Byron is already posing the complex of searching dilemmas which is shortly to constitute him, in *Childe Harold* and the Turkish Tales, Europe's analyst in chief.[36]

The 'fairy realm' (184) of 'Ida' links on to the 'fairy land' (*Giaour*, 55) of Greece through this same nexus of tradition. Byron hears the Giaour's saga built up by tavern-haunters in Greece as he does that of the schoolboys in his own dormitory at Harrow. Both are equally fragile.

> Yet a few years, one general wreck will whelm
> The faint remembrance of our fairy realm.   (183–4)

Boyhood joys will be forgotten in the plunge into dissipation (189–191). But the sudden appearance of an old schoolfellow disperses the nonsense of fashionable intrigue.

> The smiles of beauty, though those smiles were dear,
> Could hardly charm me, when that friend was near.   (201–2)

'Reality' is identified with the fragility of boyhood society or the Greek landscape. Conversely, we can see fragility built into any valid pattern of reality. Lines 209–42 present a potent image of Byron's perennial Paradise theme, and echo in a curiously pro-phetic way the Islamic threnodies he was reading around this time in Stephen Weston's *Arabic Aphorisms*.[37] I call the echo prophetic, since Byron always needed another 'home' to replace 'Ida', and the East was to become that home for him. Byron confesses himself

> one, who thus for kindred hearts must roam,
> And seek abroad, the love denied at home.
> Those hearts, dear IDA, have I found in thee,
> A home, a world, a paradise to me   (215–18)

and directly quotes Jami's lines (from Weston):

> Since thee I've lost, I've no affection known,
>   And though 'midst crowds, I seem to stray alone

in his sustained lament for a family life denied him:

> I hear—I wake—and in the sound rejoice!
> I hear again,—but ah! no Brother's voice.
> A Hermit, 'midst of crowds, I fain must stray
> Alone . . . (233-6)

A penultimate section of 'Childish Recollections' singles out five
of Byron's special friends at Harrow for affectionate reminiscence.
'Alonzo' (John Wingfield)[38] is the 'best and dearest' of his friends.
Emphasis is laid, as in *Lycidas*, on shared studies:

> Oft have we drain'd the font of ancient lore,
> Though drinking deeply, thirsting still for more (253-4)

(a couplet which should give pause to those critics who persistently
underplay Byron's knowledge of and love for the classics), as well as
shared sports:

> Together join'd in cricket's manly toil,
> Or shar'd the produce of the river's spoil;
> Or plunging from the green declining shore,
> Our pliant limbs the buoyant billows bore:
> In every element, unchang'd, the same,
> All, all that brothers should be, but the name. (259-64)

'Davus' (John Cecil Tattersal) is remembered for his candour and
'liberality', his love of punning, his curious diffidence:

> Yet, with a breast of such materials made,
> Anxious to please, of pleasing half afraid. (269-70)

Already Byron's analytical powers are at work. The third friend
'Lycus' (Lord Clare), of whom Byron later wrote, 'I have always
loved him better than any *male* thing in the world', evokes a eulogy
considerably toned down in the *Hours of Idleness* version (286-300)
from its *Poems on Various Occasions* original:

> For ever to possess a friend in thee,
> Was bliss unhop'd, though not unsought by me;
> Thy softer soul was form'd for love alone,
> To ruder passions and to hate unknown;
> Thy mind, in union with thy beauteous form,
> Was gentle, but unfit to stem the storm;
> That face, an index of celestial worth,
> Proclaim'd a heart abstracted from the earth.
> Oft, when depress'd with sad, foreboding gloom,
> I sat reclin'd upon our favourite tomb,
> I've seen those sympathetic eyes o'erflow,
> With kind compassion for thy comrade's woe. . . .

We can ill spare these fervent lines, with their glimpses of school-boy sensibility, for the comparatively frigid tribute in the later volume.

'Fair Euryalus', the Earl of Delawarr, stands out as 'a heart untainted', one constitutionally alien to 'the flow of compliment, the slippery wile'—possessing, then, all those virtues of sincerity, spontaneity, and indignant rejection of intrigue which were for Byron the schoolboy, and continued to be for Byron the man, the chief of human qualities. And the last friend 'Cleon', Edward Noel Long, is also hailed as 'honest, open, generous', but with, it seems, an added dimension of 'purity': 'No vice degrades that purest soul serene' (328). It is worth observing that this is the note which rings through the later poem 'To Edward Noel Long, Esq.', which includes recollections of the two friends' Cambridge days together (Long was the only one of the five who went up with him to Cambridge). This is a night poem, as distinguished from the daylight brilliance of 'Childish Recollections', and memories of Harrow now return with that added note of purity and mystery which moonlight bestows. This is a poem rich in permanent Byronic ideograms, set in dramatic contrast. 'The gathering storm' is counterpointed with 'the sky's celestial bow'; 'this sequestered scene' of slumber is contrasted with 'the joyous days' of childhood. The sequestered, moonlit scene casts its pure radiance back over the past, defecating memory of its more violent aspects. This is a 'Childish Recollections' in reverse in two senses: it is not only a night poem where the original was a day poem, but it interprets the past in the mournful light of the present, instead of bringing the present into vivifying relationship with the past. The moral note, already struck in the 'purest soul' line quoted above, suffuses 'To Edward Noel Long, Esq.':

> Yes, I will hope that Time's broad wing
> Will shed around some dews of spring:
> But, if his scythe must sweep the flowers
> Which bloom among the fairy bowers,[39]
> Where smiling Youth delights to dwell,
> And hearts with early rapture swell;
> If frowning Age, with cold controul,
> Confines the current of the soul,
> Congeals the tear of Pity's eye,
> Or checks the sympathetic sigh,
> Or hears, unmov'd, Misfortune's groan
> And bids me feel for self alone;
> Oh! may my bosom never learn

> To soothe its wonted heedless flow;
> Still, still, despise the censor stern,
>   But ne'er forget another's woe.
> Yes, as you knew me in the days,
> O'er which Remembrance yet delays,
> Still may I rove untutor'd, wild,
> And even in age, at heart a child.   (27–46)

The determination is firm, but acknowledges the potency of 'the world's slow stain'. Byron the agonist for the framebreakers, for the Irish Catholics, for the oppressed Italians and the enslaved Greeks, is projected in these lines. That is the public Byron; but the Byron who continues to be a child, the Byron who laments the wounded eaglet and the crushed flower, the tired old charwoman and S.T.C. the unappreciated poet, is also present.

'To Edward Noel Long, Esq.' ends with a projected visit by them both from Cambridge to Harrow. The moon still reigns, but before she makes her third circuit

> I trust, that we, my gentle Friend,
> Shall see her rolling orbit wend,
> Above the dear-lov'd peaceful seat,
> Which once contain'd our youth's retreat;
> And, then, with those our childhood knew,
> We'll mingle in the festive crew;
> While many a tale of former day
> Shall wing the laughing hours away;
> And all the flow of souls shall pour
> The sacred intellectual shower,
> Nor cease, till Luna's waning horn,
> Scarce glimmers through the mist of Morn.   (97–108)

The moon, which opens and closes the poem, sheds her softening influence over its ethos—which is indeed the ethos of Edward Noel Long himself. The close of 'Childish Recollections' is very different, above all in its original form.[40] The opening stanzas of *Childe Harold* are clearly adumbrated in these lines:

> No social solace from a friend, is near,
> And heartless strangers drop no feeling tear.
> I seek not joy in Woman's sparkling eye,
> The smiles of Beauty cannot check the sigh.
> Adieu, thou world! thy pleasure's still a dream,
> Thy virtue, but a visionary theme;
> Thy years of vice, on years of folly roll,
> Till grinning death assigns the destin'd goal,
> Where all are hastening to the dread abode,
> To meet the judgment of a righteous God.

Thirty even bitterer lines follow. The *Hours of Idleness* conclusion is
milder, but sad enough. Byron *tries* 'to think with pleasure on the
past alone' (376) but melancholy keeps breaking in. In a remarkable
image, Harrow is seen not as something static but as a ship which
'proudly steers through Time's eventful tide'. It is a permanency,
whether as the school actually attended in childhood or as the
receptacle of sustaining childhood memories. Byron's problem is
consistently with time: he tries to solve it here by an apotheosis of
'Ida', by positing a childhood matrix to which return can from time
to time be made. But no one as intelligent as Byron could continue
to function along the old school network. Europe provided him with
another matrix, infinitely more ancient, more complex and more
extended in time and space.

Notes and references

1   See below, pp. 29ff.
2   'To M—', *PW* i, 68–9.
3   See my study of Keats, *The Consecrated Urn*, pp. 190–202, for an
     account of Keats's fluctuating reactions to Byron, and an assessment
     of *Endymion*'s debt to *Manfred*.
4   A poem (*PW* i, 224) which falls outside the canon but is listed by
     E. H. Coleridge under the *Hours of Idleness* heading.
5   The Pigots were a Southwell family. Elizabeth Bridget Pigot and her
     brother John were among the closest of Byron's boyhood friends.
6   She died, after five years of marriage to Captain Byron, in 1784.
     Augusta, the poet's half-sister, was the only surviving child of the
     marriage.
7   L. A. Marchand, *Byron: a biography*, 3 vols, Murray, 1958, i, 31.
8   *Ibid.*, i, 32.
9   Mary Shelley declared that Byron's lameness was never out of his
     mind for a moment. References to it crop up continually in his
     letters and journals and in contemporary accounts of his life and
     conversation. E. H. Coleridge's note (*PW* v, 477) should be
     consulted.
10   Cf. *MLJ* ii, 15: 'No let some charming cuts and frontispiece/Adorn
     my volume, and the sale increase'.
11   One of those symbolic 'accidents' that stud Byron's 'life of allegory'.
     Byron noted the resemblance of his own mermaid to Scott's in a
     letter of 12 January 1822.
12   In a good deal of reading of ephemeral literature—thrillers, science
     fiction—over the past decades, I have been struck with the frequency
     of references to Byron, often in the most unexpected contexts. A

valuable piece of research might be done on the persistence of Byron as a 'folk figure' in the twentieth century.

13   *Notebooks of S. T. Coleridge*, ed. Kathleen Coburn, vol. ii, entry 2551.
14   See below, pp. 173ff.
15   *Notebooks of S. T. Coleridge*, ii, 2090.
16   Dorothy Wordsworth's Journal for June 1800 reveals this as a kind of obsession. See particularly the entries for June 4–7.
17   *PW*, i, 257.
18   This is a point I discuss at some length in 'Byron and the levels of landscape', in *ARIEL*, vol. v, no. 4, (1974), 3–20.
19   *Collected Letters of P. B. Shelley*, ed. Frederick L. Jones, O.U.P. 1964 ii, 324, 330.
20   *The Corsair* III, xxiii. 'His heart was formed for softness—warped to wrong/Betrayed too early, and beguiled too long.'
21   In Moral *Aphorisms in Arabic* (tr. by Stephen Weston, London, 1805), which Byron was reading at this time, we have 'Go now and seek for the rose and the lilly in the hard stone, and the dry clod'—a sentence which might stand as motto to the present chapter.
22   See below, p. 116.
23   *Inferno* III, lines 4–6.
24   *Manfred* III, i, 6–18.
25   See my 'Byron and Islam: the triple Eros', *Journal of European Studies*, December 1974, for documentation.
26   Norman Abbey, in *Don Juan* XIIIff, presents the final degradation of the Abbey—the worms as devourer. See below, pp. 337–9.
27   Cf. 'Byron and Islam', *loc. cit.*
28   The critique of power implicit here suffuses the Venetian plays and is expressed in similar metaphors of masks and carapaces (see below, p. 238).
29   Cf. The 'Letter on . . . Bowles Strictures', quoted on p. 51 below.
30   See below, pp. 99, 129.
31   Byron's own high opinion of this poem is conveyed in a letter to Edward Noel Long (23 February 1807, first published by Leslie A. Marchand, Byron's *Letters and Journals*, 2 vols, Murray 1973, vol. i): 'I consider my last "Newstead" as my "chef d'oeuvre".'
32   Here too appears the 'poison'd cup' of his early life, reverted to in *Childe Harold* III, vii.
33   Byron is remembering Johnson's love for 'an honest hater' which he commends again in *Don Juan* XIII, 7.
34   'Theirs but to do and die'—Byronic echoes in the Victorians, especially Tennyson and Arnold, is a theme worth investigating. The passage is from *The Corsair*, lines 59–62. In 'Byron and Islam' *loc. cit.* I have given reasons for supposing that Conrad is a hero with peculiarly Byronic traits.
35   *LJ* iv, 9–11.
36   *Pace* Matthew Arnold, who preferred Goethe for this role, no doubt because Goethe was more highly serious and presented his case book with a Germanic thoroughness which Byron not only never attempted but positively eschewed.

37   See my paper, 'Byron and Islam', *loc. cit.*, for a study of this early
        Islamic strain in Byron.

38   A poignant passage in *Childe Harold* (I, xci–xcii) laments Wingfield's
        death at Coimbra (and see below, p. 88).

39   This repeated collocation of 'fairy' with 'flowers' (see above, pp.
        18–21) links Byron's Harrow with his Islamic years and opens a
        window into the fragrant prism of his Turkish Tales. 'Be assured I
        have not changed, in all my ramblings, Harrow & of course *yourself*
        never left me, and the

    —"dulces reminiscitur Argos"

    attended me to the very spot to which that semi-line alludes
    in the mind of the fallen Argive', he writes in December 1811 to his
    old schoolmate William Harness. Some seven weeks earlier he had
    complained to Dallas (October 11th): 'Instruct Mr. Murray not to
    allow his Shopman to call the work—"Childe *of Harrow's* Pilgrimage"
    !!!!!!—as he has done to some of my astonished friends who wrote to
    inquire after my *Sanity* on the occasion as well they might.' A Freudian
    slip, not the less revealing for being made by proxy.

40   In *Poems on Various Occasions*; see *PW* i, 103n.

2
THE
LITERARY SATIRES

English Bards and Scotch Reviewers (1809) was Byron's answer to the *Edinburgh Review's* contemptuous dismissal of his first volume of verse, the *Hours of Idleness* (1807). The critique had wounded him deeply. 'He was very near destroying himself', his friend Hobhouse reports, perhaps with some exaggeration. In his journal five years later Byron reminisces:

I . . . read it the day of its denunciation—dined and drank three bottles of claret (with S. B. Davies, I think), neither ate nor slept the less, but, nevertheless, was not easy till I had vented my wrath and my rhyme, in the same pages, against every thing and every body.

One may comment that this was by no means the 'submitting without a murmur' promised by his *Hours of Idleness* Preface in case of adverse criticism. This suggests that Byron had not really anticipated such criticism, or had failed to steel himself against it.

'Lords too are Bards'

Byron's first full-length satire is in Pope's couplet and to some extent in Pope's manner, though it lacks the polished urbanity of 'the little Queen Anne's man'. Its rasp and occasional buffoonery betray the influence of the mock epic satirists closer to Byron's own day, notably of Gifford in his *Baviad* and *Maeviad* (1794–5). Churchill's *The Apology* (1761), which challenges the secretive tyranny of the mid-century reviewers, is an even closer parallel. In tone and layout *English Bards* is astonishingly original, shot through and through with the Byronic attributes of gusto, humour, sheer farce and wry magnanimity so alien to the great Popean virtues of moderation, decorum, virulent understatement, and symmetry. In what follows I shall be discussing Byron's first satire not simply as a detached poem, but in the context of his total outlook in the years 1807–09, pressing into service moreover material in his later journals.

Byron's Preface is characteristically aggressive. All his friends, he says, have urged him to publish the satire anonymously. But 'I am not to be terrified by abuse, or bullied by reviewers'. He has attacked no one personally 'who did not commence on the offensive'. And his object in writing the satire is defined: 'not to prove that I can write well, but, *if possible*, to make others write better' (Preface to the second, third, and fourth editions). This statement of aims is important: it shows that Byron was adopting the traditional Jonsonian (and Johnsonian) stance, derived from Juvenal, of *castigat ridendo mores*: his purpose is didactic and therapeutic. In the later social satires he largely abandons this aim.

The Preface to the first edition began with the statement:

With regard to the real talents of many of the poetical persons whose performances are mentioned or alluded to in the following pages, it is presumed by the Author that there can be little difference of opinion in the Public at large; though, like other sectaries, each has his separate tabernacle of proselytes, by whom his abilities are over-rated, his faults overlooked, and his metrical canons received without continued scruple and without consideration. But the unquestionable possession of considerable genius by several of the writers here censured renders their mental prostitution more to be regretted.

Among the writers was, of course, Wordsworth, whose 1807 volume Byron had reviewed in that year. It is to be noted that Byron does not deny the genius, but objects to its prostitution. His aim is to restore the catholicity, as it were, of English poetry, which has been disrupted by a host of sectaries. This is Byron's common stress on unity and a continuing tradition. It is to this end that the destructive and instructive wit of his poem is directed.

Wit, humour, farce, spleen—the poem moves through a gamut of tones. Byron's wit is a facet of his eighteenth-century heritage, his descent from Dryden and Pope and Johnson, and beyond them from Sedley and Rochester. It is closer to Rochester and Dryden in its energy and large carelessness, to Pope in its mordancy and scope. It is more genial than Pope's, however. Byron does not spare his victims, but he is seldom bitter. Laughing at others, he takes the occasion to laugh at himself:

> No Muse will cheer, with renovating smile,
> The paralytic puling of Carlisle . . . (725-6)

(where the mild absurdity of 'renovating smile' clashes with the ferocity of 'paralytic puling' to produce an 'aesthetic shock')—yes, but:

> Lords too are Bards: such things at times befall,
> And 'tis some praise in Peers to write at all. (719-20)

Through it all there runs a stream of fun-making, of farce, a revelling
in the incongruous. The effect is of impromptu—the art of the
improvisatore, the 'note' of Byron's conversational wit as described by
Scott: 'Byron occasionally said what are called good things, but
never studied for them. They came naturally and easily, and mixed
with the comic or serious, as it happened' (*LJ* ii, 355n). Assailing one
of the most egregious, if harmless, of the age's poetasters, Coleridge's
bookseller friend Amos Cottle (1768?-1800), Byron distils the
maximum of amusement out of his victim's name.

> Oh, AMOS COTTLE!—Phoebus! what a name
> To fill the speaking-trump of future fame!—
> Oh, AMOS COTTLE! for a moment think
> What meagre profits spring from pen and ink!
> When thus devoted to poetic dreams,
> Who will peruse thy prostituted reams?
> Oh! pen perverted! paper misapplied!
> Had COTTLE still adorned the counter's side,
> Bent o'er the desk, or, born to useful toils,
> Been taught to make the paper which he soils,
> Ploughed, delved, or plied the oar with lusty limb,
> He had not sung of Wales, nor I of him. (399-410)

Now this may strike us as cruel and snobbish, the noble lord
assailing a tradesman. But that is not the point. Byron had no
contempt for tradesmen or ploughmen if they wrote good poetry,
as he recognised Burns did, and Bloomfield. Hogg he describes in a
letter to John Murray of 3 August 1814 as 'a man of great powers and
deserving of encouragement'; similar praise is accorded to Hogg in a
letter to Tom Moore of the same date. Praise of Bloomfield (who
'made [Charles Lamb] sick') is retracted in *Hints from Horace*, 731.
But he objected to bad poetry from Cottle as much as from the
Earl of Carlisle; and what amused him about Cottle was the name.
This would not have amused Dryden or Pope: it belongs to Byron's
Shakespearean side, his love for puns, for word play, for ludicrous
rhymes.[1] His mock-Miltonic catalogue of odd-sounding proper
names in *Don Juan* VII, xvi-xvii, is a later example.

Schoolboy humour, perhaps. There's a lot of it in Byron, and particularly in the letters, for which his first editor and biographer, Tom Moore, makes solemn apology. Hobhouse too thought Byron's letters 'sad trash', unfit for publication (*DLM*, 218). But what to Moore and Hobhouse seemed unworthy the dignity of a major poet strikes us today as the kind of informality, ease and naturalness we look for from someone of the stature of Shakespeare or Byron, someone not concerned with making an effect. And with it goes a kind of humility. The Letters and Journals show Byron laughing at himself, at his ambiguous fame:

> Murray [Byron's publisher] has had a letter from his brother bibliopole of Edinburgh, who says, 'he is lucky in having such a poet'—something as if one was a packhorse, or 'ass or anything that is his'; or, like Mrs Packwood, who replied to some enquiry after the Ode on Razors—'Lawks, sir, we *keeps* a poet'. The same illustrious Edinburgh bookseller once sent an order for books, poesy, and cookery, with this agreeable postscript—'The *Harold* and *Cookery* are much wanted'. Such is fame . . .[2]
>
> (Journal, 13 Dec. 1813)

This is that 'wisdom of sheer roguish pranks' which, as Nietzsche says about Socrates, 'constitutes the best state of soul in a man'. It is the voice of our non-Romantic Byron, with the keenest of noses for the ridiculous, the slyest eye for his own status in an hierarchy which includes Homer and Horace, Shakespeare and Dante. 'How I do delight in observing life as it really is!—and myself, after all, the worst of any', he exclaims a little later in this 1813–14 journal. 'But no matter—I must avoid egotism, which, just now, would be no vanity.' It is precisely this observation of life as it is, with all its curious quirks and quibbles, that gives Byron's humour its strength and resilience.

'What an antithetical mind!'

Byron detested stereotypes, took delight in odd personalities, in the little lunacies that break the mould. We understand him best on this side if we see him as one of the last of the great English eccentrics, keeping a pet bear at Trinity ('Sir, I mean him to sit for a fellow-ship' was his reply to his tutor's plaintive demurrer), peopling his Venetian palace with a collection (according to Shelley) of three monkeys, eight mastiffs, five peacocks, five cats, one eagle, one

crow, one falcon, two guinea hens, one wolf and an Egyptian crane;
boxing with Cribb or Jackson in the intervals of writing his Eastern
romances, enjoying bacon and eggs and beer at one moment and
haute cuisine at another, he qualifies for the judgement he himself
passed on Burns: 'What an antithetical mind! tenderness, roughness
—sentiment, sensuality—soaring and grovelling, dirt and deity—all
mixed up in that one compound of inspired clay!' This was the
Byron from whom his fellow Romantics, and later Victorians,
averted their eyes.

Bigotry, cant, the universal assumption of masks in society, and
above all in English society, these are the targets he has constantly
under fire in *English Bards* and almost every succeeding major poem.
Cant is a special subject for Byron, though deeply involved with
bigotry and masquerade: I shall return to it later in this chapter.
If I pause for a moment over the compassionate understanding of
Burns evident in that analysis of his character and genius, and over
the theme of the masquerade as the antithesis of the Byronic love of
'life as it really is', it is less to trace these topics in *English Bards*
(though they are patently there) than to lay foundations, at this
early point, for much I shall later have to say, and still more I shall
have to leave implicit, in my comments on *Childe Harold*, the
dramas, and *Don Juan*.[3]

I wonder how the deuce anybody could make such a world—for what
purpose dandies, for instance, were ordained—and kings—and fellows of
colleges—and women of 'a certain age'—and men of any age—and myself,
most of all! . . . is there anything beyond?—*who* knows? *He* that can't tell.
Who tells that there *is*? He who don't know. And when shall he know?
Perhaps, when he don't expect, and generally when he don't wish it. In this
last respect, however, all are not alike: it depends a good deal upon
education—something upon nerves and habits—but most upon digestion.

Thus Byron in his journal for 18 February 1814. It's not complex or
profound, it's just an intelligent and thoughtful man mulling things
over without any preconceptions about a 'Wisdom and Spirit of the
Universe' or an 'Intellectual Beauty'; trying to worry things out on
the small basis of fact we are given. Reading his private journal we
feel ourselves to be in the presence of an agile and in many ways a
subtle mind. Byron the man comes to life for us as he sat night after
night at his desk in his rooms in Albany or his palace at Ravenna,
his journal open before him and a glass of hock or madeira at his
elbow. Let us eavesdrop a little further. Solitude—is it good for one,
he ponders?

Redde a little—wrote notes and letters, and am alone, which Locke says is
bad company. 'Be not solitary, be not idle.'—Um!—the idleness is trouble-
some; but I can't see so much to regret in the solitude. The more I see of
men, the less I like them. If I could but say so of women too, all would be
well. Why can't I ? I am now six-and-twenty; my passions have had enough
to cool them; my affections more than enough to wither them—and yet—
always *yet* and *but*—'Excellent well, you are a fishmonger—get thee to a
nunnery'.—'They fool me to the top of my bent'.

There we have Byron the cynic and misanthropist. We think we
have pinned down our butterfly. But then suddenly there emerges
another Byron—equally voluble, equally 'humorous': the man of
energy who is also the divided mind, the split soul:

No letters today—so much the better—there are no answers. I must not
dream again—it spoils even reality. I will go out of doors, and see what the
fog will do for me. Jackson has been here: the boxing world much as usual.
I shall dine at Crib's tomorrow.[4] I like energy—even animal energy—of all
kinds; and I have need of both mental and corporeal. I have not dined out,
nor, indeed, *at all*, lately; have heard no music—have seen nobody. Now
for a *plunge*—high life and low life. Amant *alterna* Camoenae.[5]

(Journal, 23 Nov. 1813)

Other humorists may work more deeply in a more restricted
field: Jonson among the gulls and tricksters of Jacobean London,
Butler with the solemn lunacies of Caroline sectarians, Sheridan in
the glittering world of the salons. Byron casts his net wider, if his
fishing is more desultory than theirs. I shall continue, in the present
chapter, to weave threads from his journals and critical writings in
prose around the satiric centre in *English Bards*, returning to this
centre to digest, as it were, what I have trapped. Byron touched life
at many points. Admire as we may the more admirable of his
contemporaries, the fact remains that Byron simply knew more
about life—experienced more, and reflected on a wider range—than
Wordsworth or Coleridge, than Shelley or Keats; and what he
knew made him, not infrequently, smile where Wordsworth or
Keats would have wept. In particular he had a deep conviction of
the *limitations* of human knowledge and human powers, as against
the 'human perfectibility' convictions of Shelley or Wordsworth's
'egotistical sublime'. His London life touched all strata of society,
from peers to prostitutes, and on his travels abroad, as he notes in
his journal, he is 'Today in a palace, tomorrow in a cow-house—
this day with the Pacha, the next with a shepherd'.

Byron's love of simplicity, genuineness, true emotion, which we
have noted in the *Hours of Idleness*, is a constant current in the later

work, and especially in *Childe Harold*. He comes close here to his
antetype Wordsworth, but within a wider spectrum. It might be
argued that Byron's Haroun al Raschid mingling with the crowd
is nearer to actuality than Wordsworth's immersion (which was
hardly more than spectatorial) in Cumberland peasant life. Byron's
contacts followed a time-hallowed Sufi tradition, though I do not
suggest they were motivated by anything more than his love of
social variety. 'It is too late for Matlock', he writes to Tom Moore
on 5 September 1813, 'but we might hit upon some scheme, high
life or low,—the last would be much the best for amusement. I am
so sick of the other, that I quite sigh for a cidar-cellar, or a cruise
in a smuggler's sloop' (*LJ*. ii, 261). He was amused too by oddities.
'I love phenomena', he writes in his Diary on 26 January 1821.
Again it is a question of anything that breaks the mould. He prides
himself in a letter to Murray of 23 September 1830 on knowing the
Italians 'from the Conte to the Contadino' (he later declines an
invitation to write a book about Italian society because this would
be a betrayal of his hosts). At the same time he takes his accumula-
tion of worldly knowledge very lightly: writing to John Hamilton
Reynolds in 1814 he notes:

it was my lot to be thrown very early upon the world, to mix a good deal in
it in more climates than one, and to purchase experience which would
probably have been of greater service to anyone than myself.

In *Don Juan* IV, cvii, he sees his own life as 'at once adventurous
and contemplative'. This wealth of experience, coupled with a
curious modesty in evaluating it, are factors in Byron's spectrum of
life and society that mark him off from his contemporaries, including
even Shelley, who brought his anti-modern-Italian prejudices with
him from England.

It is precisely this sense of the complexity and limitations of
human experience that establishes the tone for *English Bards and
Scotch Reviewers*. The title itself is a kind of oxymoron. We expect a
defence of the poets against their critics, but this is far from Byron's
intent. He occupies a middle ground. The tone of maturity, of
experience, is so firm that we find it hard to remember that this is
juvenile work, written before the Eastern tour and the first years of
fame. The poem opens with a Popean prologue on the prevalence
of vice and its exposure by 'wit', followed by a disclaimer on Byron's
part of any such high pretensions: his aim is simply to 'chase'
literary 'follies':

>Laugh when I laugh, I seek no other fame,
>The cry is up, and scribblers are my game.   (43-4)

He himself has published 'A schoolboy freak, unworthy praise or blame'; it met with critical condemnation—but with what title, Byron asks, do hacks like Jeffrey set themselves up as judges? The age itself is degenerate. 'Bards and censors are so much alike' that there is little to choose between them.

From this tentative opening Byron swings into a sustained panegyric of the great Augustan age. A lifelong admirer of Pope, Byron did not share his fellow Romantics' contempt for eighteenth-century poetry.

>Time was, ere yet in these degenerate days
>Ignoble themes obtain'd mistaken praise,
>When Sense and Wit with Poesy allied,
>No fabled Graces, flourish'd side by side;
>From the same fount their inspiration drew,
>And, rear'd by taste, bloom'd fairer as they grew.
>Then, in this happy isle, a POPE's pure strain
>Sought the rapt soul to charm, nor sought in vain;
>A polish'd nation's praise aspired to claim,
>And raised the people's, as the poet's fame.
>Like him great DRYDEN pour'd the tide of song,
>In stream less smooth, indeed, yet doubly strong.
>Then CONGREVE's scenes could cheer, or OTWAY's melt;
>For Nature then an English audience felt—
>But why these names, or greater still, retrace,
>When all to feebler Bards resign their place?
>Yet to such times our lingering looks are cast,
>When taste and reason with those times are past.   (103-20)

The standpoint is firmly neoclassical, though we note the parenthesis 'or greater still' (Shakespeare? Milton?) in line 117. Sense, Wit, Taste, Reason, all the old counters devalued by Wordsworth and Coleridge, are brought provocatively back into currency. 'Nature' is Pope's Nature, not Wordsworth's: the human norm, the accepted world picture, the congruence of what is described with what is.[6]

'Cant, multiplied through all the varieties of life'

In what follows, Byron's scorn is directed against cant and disproportion; in particular, against the inflation of human potentialities. His standpoint is already that expressed in his *Letter on . . . Bowles' Strictures on Pope*, written some ten years later:

The truth is, that in these days the grand 'primum mobile' of England is *cant*; cant political, cant poetical, cant religious, cant moral; but always cant, multiplied through all the varieties of life. It is the fashion, and while it lasts will be too powerful for those who can only exist by taking the tone of the time. I say *cant*, because it is a thing of words, without the smallest influence upon human actions; the English being no wiser, no better, and much poorer, and divided among themselves, as well as far less moral, than they were before the prevalence of this verbal decorum.

The insight is prophetic as well as topical; cant, developed beyond Regency limits, was to be Britain's *primum mobile* for a century to come. This fact alone would account for Byron's down-grading by the Victorians. There were other considerations, of course, including Byron's scepticism about the inevitability of progress and the attainment of security. One of mankind's greatest 'idols' (in Bacon's sense of the word) is the thirst for permanence, and the compulsion to read permanence into a universe which is the theatre of incessant change.

I do hate that word 'invariable'. What is there of *human*, be it poetry, philosophy, wit, wisdom, science, power, glory, mind, matter, life, or death, which is 'invariable'?

It is not simply Bowles that Byron is undermining here, but a whole human tendency: the bias towards disproportion, towards exaggeration and complacency.

Returning now to *English Bards*, we note that exaggeration, in its literary manifestations, works both ways—towards Grand Guignol on the one hand and silly sooth on the other. 'Tales of Terror jostle on the road' with 'strange, mysterious Dullness': Wordsworth's 'Idiot Boy' is a freak, a departure from 'Nature', as culpable in one direction as Mrs Radcliffe's Gothic horrors are in the other. In Scott's lays, 'mountain spirits prate to river sprites'; Southey's Thalaba, 'Arabia's monstrous, wild and wondrous son' overthrows 'More mad magicians than the world e'er knew' (143–56, 202–16). From inflated themes we pass to inflated (or its opposite, sub-poetic) diction. Wordsworth is concerned to show 'That prose is verse, and verse is merely prose'; Coleridge, 'To turgid ode and tumid stanza dear', substitutes obscurity for sublimity (235–64). It is penetrating, entertaining, and just: Coleridge's early verses *are* tumid and turgid, Wordsworth's rustic vignettes *are* obsessively *simpliste*. But Byron knows where to stop. We find no attacks on 'Tintern Abbey', no echoes of Southey's sneer at *The Ancient Mariner*.

From lyrical and narrative poetry Byron turns to the drama of his day, applying the same standards of proportion and lucidity. Here we are even further removed from good sense, from 'Nature':

> Now to the Drama turn—Oh! motley sight!
> What precious scenes the wondering eyes invite:
> Puns, and a Prince within a barrel pent,
> And Dibdin's nonsense yield complete content.   (560–3)

In the rage for sensation, the boy actor Master Betty—the 'infant Roscius'—has been hailed as a new Garrick. Nothing survives of the stage once adorned by Shakespeare, Massinger, Otway and Sheridan. The emphasis is on scenic display, oblivious of the virtues of plot and characterisation. Opera has ousted tragedy and comedy alike.

> Then let Ausonia, skilled in every art
> To soften manners, but corrupt the heart,
> Pour her exotic follies o'er the town,
> To sanction Vice, and hunt Decorum down: . . .
> Let high-born lechers eye the lively Presle
> Twirl her light limbs, that spurn the needless veil;
> Let Angiolini bare her breast of snow,
> Wave the white arm, and point the pliant toe; . . .
> Whet not your scythe, Suppressors of our Vice!
> Reforming Saints! too delicately nice!
> By whose decrees, our sinful souls to save,
> No Sunday tankards foam, no barbers shave;
> And beer undrawn, and beards unmown, display
> Your holy reverence for the Sabbath-day.   (618–37)

The fun is irresistible; the vertiginous descent from the opera house to the yokels deprived by the Society for the Suppression of Vice of their beer and Sunday shave establishes a new order of paradox, which Byron was to exploit further in *Don Juan* (in which poem may also be found a very similar and more devastating exposure of two-standard morality in his appeal to Mrs Fry, X, lxxxv–lxxxvii).

A concern for the sad condition of British drama persisted throughout Byron's career. 'It is impossible not to allude to the degraded state of the stage,' he writes in 1812, referring to his own Drury Lane prologue in a letter of 30 September to Lord Holland, and as late as 1821 we find him writing, à propos of *Marino Faliero*, 'I have had no view to the stage; in its present state it is, perhaps, not a very exalted object of ambition; besides, I have been too much behind the scenes to have thought it so at any time'. In the Drury Lane address he pleads for 'Nature for our guide', and in 1814 he welcomes the advent of Kean: 'There is a new actor named Kean come out . . . his Style is quite new, or rather *renewed*, being that of Nature' (letter to J. W. Webster, 20 February 1814). Johnson's Prologue 'At the Opening of the Theatre in Drury Lane 1747' was very probably in his mind as he wrote his own exordium.

So much for the 'bards', working in their main fields of lyric, romance and drama. But what of the 'reviewers'? Though we might expect Byron's main animus to be directed here, we find him rapidly checked by the barrenness of his subject matter. The poem actually begins with an attack on the 'Scotch Reviewers'—but Byron knew very little about them. And what he believed he knew was mistaken. It was not Jeffrey, but Brougham, who had written the *Hours of Idleness* review. And of Jeffrey and his character he has no personal knowledge. He can only play, rather feebly, on the resemblance of his name to that of the infamous 'hanging judge' of James II's day:

> Health to immortal JEFFREY! once, in name,
> England could boast a judge almost the same;
> In soul so like, so merciful, yet just,
> Some think that Satan has resigned his trust,
> And given the Spirit to the world again,
> To sentence Letters, as he sentenced men.   (438–43)

The tone is modulating here from sarcasm to irony, a much keener weapon, and one which Byron is to use with some skill in the middle and concluding sections of his poem. It is the *Dunciad* which is now the Popean model, rather than the *Moral Essays* or *An Essay in Criticism*; the details become scurrilous and, as Byron admitted six years later, too personal. One entry in his Journal for 1816 reads: 'Too ferocious—this is mere insanity'; and many more express regret at having written the satire at all. But Byron did not reach his full command of irony until thirteen years later, in *The Vision of Judgment*. In that poem he was to have the target, Southey, well between his sights. The contemptuous geniality with which he disposes of the Laureate is much more devastating than the Dunciadic scurrility of his onslaught on Jeffrey.

'Where Attic flowers Aonian odours breathe'

Even in writing his first and most spleenful satire Byron could not be less than himself, a poet of Shakespearean diversity of tone. All is not invective and denigration. There are tributes to 'neglected genius', to Burns, Campbell, Crabbe, Cowper. Beside the humour and even farce of his comments on minor poets (their names forgotten today) we have the elegiac tenderness of the lines on his Cambridge contemporary, Henry Kirke White (831–48), which may have contributed a resonance to *Adonais*, the elevation of the paragraph on Wright's *Horae Ionicae* (867—80), where Canto II of *Childe Harold* is anticipated, and the moral indignation of those sections of the poem which deal with the opera, the dance and the gaming-house.

The closing paragraphs of *English Bards* are already modulating from the English scene to the Mediterranean:

> Yet once again, adieu! ere this the sail
> That wafts me hence is shivering in the gale;
> And Afric's coast and Calpe's adverse height,
> And Stamboul's minarets must greet my sight.   (1017–20)

Byron's next satires, *Hints from Horace* and *The Curse of Minerva*, were composed 'Where Attic flowers Aonian odours breathe'. He is now in his right setting and there is a sense of relaxation, of poise, of urbanity. We have left the glooms and glumpiness of Newstead, Cambridge, London. In bright air, Byron can write airily and dismissively of

> The groves of Granta, and her Gothic halls,
> King's Coll, Cam's stream, stain'd windows, and old walls
>   (*HH* 27–8)

and patronisingly of Jeffrey:

> Again, my Jeffrey—as that sound inspires,
> How wakes my bosom to its wonted fires!
> Fires, such as gentle Caledonians feel
> When Southrons writhe upon their critic wheel, . . .   (*HH* 589–92)

And though he recurs to his old *Hours of Idleness* grievance, and even threatens the 'Dear damned contemner of [his] schoolboy songs' with his 'hate', he wryly confesses himself baffled by Jeffrey's bland omission to reply to *English Bards and Scotch Reviewers* (599–626).

Hints from Horace is then, in some sense, a continuation of the earlier satire. The old themes are taken up—fury at the reception of *Hours of Idleness*, dislike of the Lake School of poets (and we note that Southey is becoming the main target of attack, in lines 653–62), support for neoclassical standards. But the bulk of the poem is occupied with technical points—with judgements on what kind of form is suitable for what kind of subject, on the relative merits of blank verse and couplets, and so on. It is, in fact, a 'Poetics', or Criticism', based on Horace's Epistle *Ad Pisones*, or *De Arte Poetica*, and the original Latin text is run along at the bottom of each page so that the reader may judge how well Byron is doing his job of adapting his classical model to Regency conditions. 'Imitations of Horace', or of Juvenal, had been a favourite form in the preceding age: Pope gives us one example, Dr Johnson another. For Byron, plainly, the challenge to his virtuosity was attractive, and he does give us a satire *sui generis* which yet sticks pretty closely to its original. Written in 1811, during his Athenian sojourn, *Hints from Horace* is a kind of aesthetic stocktaking, a summing-up of his criteria and allegiances. Decorum is firmly stressed, as was 'Nature' in *English Bards*.

> The greater portion of the rhyming tribe
> (Give ear, my friend, for thou hast been a scribe)
> Are led astray by some peculiar lure.
> I labour to be brief—become obscure;
> One falls while following Elegance too fast;
> Another soars, inflated with Bombast: . . .
> New words find credit in these latter days
> If neatly grafted on a Gallic phrase;
> What Chaucer, Spenser did, we scarce refuse
> To Dryden's or to Pope's maturer Muse.
> If you can add a little, say why not,
> As well as William Pitt, and Walter Scott?
> Since they, by force of rhyme and force of lungs,
> Enrich'd our Island's ill-united tongues.   (*HH* 39–86)

It is judicious, neatly turned, relaxed, without the coiled spring tension of *English Bards*. There is nothing original in the praise of decorum. Yet Byron does not leave the matter there. He goes a step beyond the standpoint of the earlier satire. Even 'correctness' must give way to the 'glowing thoughts' of genius:

> And must the Bard his glowing thoughts confine,
> Lest Censure hover o'er some faulty line?
> Remove whate'er a critic may suspect,
> To gain the paltry suffrage of '*Correct*'?
> Or prune the spirit of each daring phrase,
> To fly from Error, not to merit Praise?   (*HH* 417–22)

It would be futile to maintain that *Hints from Horace* is a work which has much attraction for the modern reader; that is perhaps less its fault than a consequence of our lack of interest in its themes. But to read it is to gain an expansion of one's knowledge of Byron's

mind, and a correction of what seems to be the ingrained prejudice
that he was not a very serious literary practitioner. His next satire,
The Curse of Minerva, may be more congenial because more dramatic
and more rooted in the Greek scene. Its stage is the Parthenon, its
actors Athena, Byron, Elgin, its time scheme in one sense a single
evening and in another sense the whole of history. Technically, the
unities are preserved; psychologically, we are in a world of multiple
dimensions. To count it a literary satire we have to give 'literary'
a rather wide sense; perhaps 'cultural' would be better, or even
'ethnic'. 'Satire' too might well be replaced by 'polemic' or 'diatribe'.

To understand what sort of a poem *The Curse of Minerva* is we
should remember Byron's curious faculty for falling in love with a
place as easily as with a person, and perhaps more easily; and I am
not using 'fall in love' figuratively. We have to remember the
tenderness of 'How Venice once was dear' in *Childe Harold* IV, iii,
the old attachment to Harrow, the indignation at the suggestion
that Troy was a myth. Athens too has now (1811) been taken under
Byron's wing. He feels keenly the depredations practised on her yet
remaining glories by such antiquaries as Lord Elgin. *Quod non
fecerunt Goti, hoc fecerunt Scoti,*[7] were the words 'very deeply cut', as
Hobhouse reports, in the plaster wall which filled the gap left by
Elgin. In his confrontation with Athena on the floor of the ruined
Parthenon Byron stresses the point (125–56) that her 'plunderer' is
a Scot, not an Englishman. Britannia's honour is thus, to some
extent, saved.

Perhaps I might at this juncture try to correct a misconception
about Byron's attitude to 'antiquities'—a misconception current
since Lady Blessington reported that 'antiquities had no interest for
him', and repeated *ad nauseam* up to the present day. It is true that
Byron had no love for antiquities as such, as relics of the past torn
from their context and mummified in museums and galleries. But he
did care enormously, passionately, for 'antiquities' as 'eternities', if
I may so put it, as manifestations of the living past which itself is an
aspect of the eternal moment through which man lives and is lived.
In the extant evidences of the ancient world, through which that
world still, in a way, breathes and comforts and reproaches modern
man, in this he *was* interested (if one can apply so feeble a word to
Byron's total commitment). The commitment was more than a
speculative one: as I have suggested in an earlier essay, it was
Byron's unique task to make himself a vehicle of reintegration of
past and present, of revitalisation of a space–time continuum

covering the Mediterranean world. And this task he undertook in a series of atoning *gestures* leading up to the final sacrificial act. One minor gesture among many which has been totally misunderstood is his swim from Sestos to Abydos. To his biographers and commentators this was a feat of physical skill of which Byron was childishly proud and to which he referred too often; but for Byron himself it was a work of historical salvage, a reinsertion through living action of a portion of the past into the present, an act of piety, a triumph over time.

It is an index of the extraordinary *continuity* of Byron's mind (through all its surface fluctuations and inconsistencies) that *The Curse of Minerva* develops a theme already adumbrated in *English Bards and Scotch Reviewers*, 1027–32:

> Let ABERDEEN and ELGIN still pursue
> The shade of fame through regions of Virtù; . . .
> And make their grand saloons a general mart
> For all the mutilated blocks of art.

But now, in 1811, he is on the spot, standing within the temple these 'Scoti' have desecrated:

> As thus, within the walls of Pallas' fane,
> I mark'd the beauties of the land and main,
> Alone, and friendless, on the magic shore,
> Whose arts and arms but live in poets' lore;
> Oft as the matchless dome I turn'd to scan,
> Sacred to Gods, but not secure from Man,
> The Past return'd, the Present seem'd to cease,
> And Glory knew no clime beyond her Greece!   (CM 55–62)

It is from such a rooting in a here-and-now that stretches out to historical and mythological vistas that Byron's imagination always draws its best sustenance. Conditions are ideal for the creation of a great poem. And a great poem *The Curse of Minerva* undoubtedly is. One wonders why its importance has been so assiduously soft-pedalled.

The work opens with Byron's most magnificent couplets.

> Slow sinks, more lovely ere his race be run,
> Along Morea's hills the setting Sun;
> Not, as in northern climes, obscurely bright,
> But one unclouded blaze of living light . . .

This whole passage, down to line 54, is a brilliant land-and-seascape diptych exhibited first in the light of the setting sun and then under the full moon. It was transferred bodily to the opening of the third

canto of *The Corsair* when Byron, for various reasons, abandoned any
idea of publishing *The Curse*. In an earlier essay I have suggested
that it 'fits much better there'; this is a judgement I should now
like to recant. It does fit beautifully into the Tale, but the Tale
could do without it. Not so the satire; it is an essential note in its
counterpoint. For it is only in the context of light and space, island
and promontory, sea and mountain, that Byron's impassioned plea
receives its full meaning. Note—and this is crucial to Byron's
stance—that there is no antiquarianism, no Hellenic purism. The
Parthenon presides over the total history of Greece, which includes
the Turkish occupation as well as the classical past. Byron reminds
us, subtly, that under the moon which is Islam's symbol as well as
Diana's, the mosque as well as the temple is 'sacred', and that the
olive is a holy tree for the Koran[8] as for the cult of Pallas.

> But lo! from high Hymettus to the plain
> The Queen of Night asserts her silent reign;
> No murky vapour, herald of the storm,
> Hides her fair face, or girds her glowing form.
> With cornice glimmering as the moonbeams play,
> There the white column greets her grateful ray,
> And bright around, with quivering gleams beset,
> Her emblem sparkles o'er the Minaret:
> The groves of olive scatter'd dark and wide,
> Where meek Cephisus sheds his scanty tide,
> The cypress saddening by the sacred mosque,
> The gleaming turret of the gay kiosk,
> And sad and sombre mid the holy calm,
> Near Theseus' fane, yon solitary palm.　　　　　　　(33–46)

Here we have Byron's inclusive vision, couched in a medium
brilliantly adapted to its complexities. This is the Popean regular
couplet: no enjambements, no metrical looseness. Yet Byron makes
it *dance*—and of course it dances *because* it keeps to the pattern, with
subtle variations of rhythm insufficient to disturb the basic design.[9]
The dance here is an intellectual, one might almost say a metaphysical thing: a dance of contrasts, of cultures and emblems of
cultures, the interweaving of domes and minarets with columns and
cornices, a marriage of atoning gestures. Sad cypress (already noted
by Byron for its presence in Muslim graveyards) raises its sword
above the thalassic flow of fruitful olive groves. And it is into this
ethnic symbiosis, this delicate balance of cultures, that Elgin so
crassly intrudes.

Among all the other things we can identify *The Curse of Minerva*

as being—satire, description, polemic, apology, prophecy—it is
worth noting that it is also an example of that ancient form the
'vision': a 'kind' dear to the Middle Ages and popular right up to
our own day. As Byron muses within the desecrated temple, Pallas
herself appears to him—majestic, but no longer the awesome power
of old time:

> . . . though still the brightest of the sky,
> Celestial tears bedimmed her large blue eye;
> Round the rent casque her owlet circled slow,
> And mourned his mistress with a shriek of woe! (*CM* 85–8)

(How Byronic that owlet! for the ancients a stereotype of wisdom,
but here rescued from the abstract and made into something living
and feeling, sharing its mistress's sorrows as might a faithful dog or
horse.) The situation closely resembles that at the opening of *Childe
Harold* II,[10] but now it is 'august Athena' herself who speaks,
delivering a sustained invective on Lord Elgin which occupies the
rest of the poem.[11] First tracing the fortunes of the 'relics torn that
yet remain' on the Acropolis—

> *These* Cecrops placed, *this* Pericles adorned,
> *That* Adrian rearl'd when drooping Science mourned—

relics which have ' 'scaped from the ravage of the Turk and Goth',
she pours savage scorn on their latest plunderer:

> So when the Lion quits his fell repast,
> Next prowls the Wolf, the filthy Jackal last. (99–114)

Then comes the curse itself: a retraction of 'her counsels' (i.e. of
wisdom) from the land that gave Elgin birth, and the subsequent
train of evils moral, political and cultural. The presence of the
marbles in London will prove the degradation of art, not its
salvation. Here Byron's satire is at its naughtiest (note how the
'languid maid's' sly interest is suggested in line 187):

> Round the throng'd gate shall sauntering coxcombs creep,
> To lounge and lucubrate, to prate and peep;
> While many a languid maid, with longing sigh,
> On giant statues casts the curious eye;
> The room with transient glance appears to skim,
> Yet marks the mighty back and length of limb;
> Mourns o'er the difference of *now* and *then*;
> Exclaims, "These Greeks indeed were proper men!" (183–90)

Next the canker of corruption, of perfidy, implicit in Elgin's criminal deed, will spread to every aspect of English life. Her allies will fall away from her; her empire will decay:

> Look to the East, where Ganges' swarthy race
> Shall shake your tyrant empire to its base.   (221–2)

The final defeat will come with the moral and economic collapse of Britain herself:

> Look last at home—ye love not to look there
> On the grim smile of comfortless despair:
> Your city saddens: loud though Revel howls,
> Here Famine faints, and yonder Rapine prowls. . . .
>
> Now fare ye well! enjoy your little hour;
> Go, grasp the shadow of your vanish'd power;
> Gloss o'er the failure of each fondest scheme;
> Your strength a name, your bloated wealth a dream. . . .
>
>   (239–62)

We are again in the presence of the prophetic Byron, with a statesman's eye for cause and effect, the Byron who in the House of Lords opposed the death penalty for the Nottingham frame-breakers, and described the Act of Union between England and Ireland as a union 'between the shark and its prey'. And again we may guess how such predictions would appear to his own age of colonial and commercial expansion. We have less excuse, today, for disregarding *The Curse of Minerva*.

Notes and references

1   Wilkes's jibe at Elkanah Settle in Boswell's *Life of Johnson* is the direct ancestor of this, and Arnold found similar ammunition in 'Wragg': ' . . . has anyone reflected what a touch of grossness in our race . . . is shown by the natural growth among us of such hideous names—Higginbottom, Stiggins, Bugg?' (*Essays in Criticism*, I, 'The Function of Criticism').

2   The joke still amused Byron five years later:

> Along thy sprucest book-shelves shine
> The works thou deemest most divine—
> The *Art of Cookery*, and mine,
>   My Murray.
> *To Murray*, 11 April 1818.

3   M. K. Joseph's discerning *Byron the Poet* (Gollancz, 1964) has some

excellent remarks on Byron's attitude to cant, system, and 'entusymusy'.

4 'Gentleman' Jackson was Byron's boxing instructor. Tom Cribb (1781–1848) was one of the most famous professional pugilists of his day.

5 'This journal is a relief. When I am tired—as I generally am—out comes this, and down goes everything. But I can't read it over; and God knows what contradictions it may contain. If I am sincere with myself (but I fear one lies more to one's self than to any one else), *every page should confute, refute, and utterly abjure its predecessor.*' My italics. With such an anticipation of Keyserling's 'no truth can be expressed except by profound contrapuntal opposition', and with Byron's ever alert sense of the possibility of deceiving oneself, we can safely confront the Byron gossips, with their eternal 'Byron told Medwin . . .' and 'Byron confided to Lady Blessington that . . .', with the 'very self and voice' which is breathing in his own poems and journals. The letters, where he may be spoofing, are more suspect.

6 Cf. Byron's comment on Kean's acting in *Richard III*: 'Life—nature—truth without exaggeration or diminution. Kemble's Hamlet is perfect;—but Hamlet is not Nature. Richard is a man; and Kean is Richard. Now to my own concerns' (1814 Journal: *LJ* ii, 385–6).

7 What the Goths had spared, the Scots destroyed.

8 See Koran, sura 24, 'The Chapter of Light': 'His light is as a niche in which is a lamp . . . it is lit from a blessed tree, an olive neither of the east nor of the west, the oil of which would well-nigh give light though no fire touched it—light upon light!' (*The Koran*, trans. by E. H. Palmer, Oxford University Press, 1928.)

9 For the kind of couplet which cannot dance because it is too dissolute, too far emancipated from its frame, the reader may compare Keats's *Endymion*. For a couplet like Byron's, but used for quite other purposes, he might look at lines 47 to 90 of *The Rape of the Lock*.

10 See below, pp. 92ff.

11 Apart from the poet's intervention to protest that Elgin was not an Englishman, already noted.

3

POEMS
OF TRANSIT

'Redeemed from worms and wasting clay'

Byron's lyric impulse cut across the divisions of time and place: we
can distinguish 'the Newstead–Harrow–Cambridge period' from
'the years of Pilgrimage' in terms of major works, satiric and
romantic, but the springs of love and death were perennial wherever
he might roam. *Hours of Idleness* did not exhaust all he had to say on
these themes. Malta, Athens, Pindus, Constantinople gave new
colourings to a somewhat faded spectrum. Few of these Pilgrimage
lyrics are memorable as poetry, but as documents, as pointers to
Byron's developing interests, they merit our attention.

But first let us look at what *is* a major lyric, one written before his
departure for the East. 'Lines Inscribed Upon a Cup Formed from
a Skull' is dated 1808. It is a Newstead poem, relating to the convivial period of Byron's pre-Tour residence at the Abbey. The fact
that the 'Lines' were published together with the seventh edition of
Childe Harold (I and II) in 1814 may encourage us to assimilate them
to that other 'skull poem' constituted by stanzas i to viii of Canto II.
There, the skull is all that remains of some long-dead saint, sage or
sophist. Byron contemplates it under brilliant Athenian skies, now
narrowing his gaze to 'its broken arch, its ruined wall', now expanding it to the skull's architectural analogues in the ruins which
surround him. The 'Lines' are written under grey English skies,
amid Gothic ruins, and the skull is a monkish skull. In an earlier
essay[1] I have discussed the poem as a Hamletish exercise in paradox,
moving between the grave and the upper air. But it is more than
that, and invites a closer analysis.

Let us think of it first as a Gothic poem, in its setting, which is also Gothic. The Gothic identity was thrust on Byron, and while with one side of his being he embraced it—'the old English baron' of his schoolmates' jeers, the descendant of the Crusaders of his own dreams—with others (the Highland boy of his childhood, the cosmopolitan of his exile) he rejected it. Nevertheless it plays an important part in his total make-up. He was born, after all, into a Gothic period, the age of Gray, Walpole, Percy, Ann Radcliffe, Chatterton, Blake; and the lord of Newstead could hardly escape his context. But the classics, and later the classical world, pulled in an opposite direction. Harrow balances Newstead; Trinity, with its mixture of Gothic, Tudor and neoclassical, fuses a variety of worlds. His rooms on the north side of Nevile's Court looked to the left on the medieval hall, to the right on Wren's baroque masterpiece, the Library. It is not irrelevant to mention these factors in the total 'field' of a poet whose significance is so peculiarly bound up with time and place.

The return to Newstead, in the summer of 1808, is a reversion, culturally, to the Gothic, and personally to the convivial, with Cambridge friends. The upturning of the skull (for the *fact* we may, for once, accept Medwin's account) effects a communication from past to present. The skull of the old monk speaks to Byron. We expect a minatory tone—Byron's ancestors had after all profited from the dissolution of the monastery—but no, nothing could be sweeter than the skull's address.

> Start not—nor deem my spirit fled:
> In me behold the only skull,
> From which, unlike a living head,
> Whatever flows is never dull.

'Nor deem my spirit fled': Byron is already asserting that kind of immortality—one might call it animistic—which belongs to the clinging of 'spirit' around 'spot', and which is to permeate *Childe Harold*. The skull addresses the drinker in measured tones.

> I lived, I loved, I quaff'd, like thee;
> I died: let earth my bones resign;
> Fill up—thou canst not injure me;
> The worm hath fouler lips than thine.

There is a touch of satire: the drinker's lips are not too clean, the conversation round the table at Newstead in 1808 is far from prudish—but better anything than the worm!

> Better to hold the sparkling grape,
>   Than nurse the earth-worm's slimy brood;
> And circle in the goblet's shape
>   The drink of Gods, than reptile's food.

The poem progresses by a series of small shocks: first, that the skull should have been made into a goblet (a species of sacrilege); second, that the skull should speak (a kind of miracle); third, that what it says is so unexpected (paradox); fourth, that it talks better sense dead than alive (irony).

> Where once my wit, perchance, hath shone,
>   In aid of others' let me shine;
> And when, alas! our brains are gone,
>   What nobler substitute than wine?

Hamlet and Falstaff meet here: 'I am not only witty myself, but the cause that wit is in other men.' 'Where once . . .' refers to the great hall of Newstead, in the old monastic days; but also to the smaller hall of the skull, from which the brains have been removed in favour of wine (as happens all too often to living skulls—'O that a man should put an enemy into his mouth, to steal away his brains!'). In this, Byron's most 'metaphysical' poem, we move on a variety of levels, between past and present, grave and dining-table, living and dead, wine and worms. Yet the thing is done with such skill, such a concealment of art by art, that we miss the means while remaining alive to the effect.

> Quaff while thou canst: another race,
>   When thou and thine, like me, are sped,
> May rescue thee from earth's embrace,
>   And rhyme and revel with the dead.

The monitory note at last appears: 'Quaff while thou canst . . .' The poem, which has hitherto been moving vertically, from the yawning grave to the yawning mouth, and in a circle from drinker to drinker, now expands to an unknown, incalculable future: a horizontal progression in time. 'Another race' may displace Byron's as his displaced the monks, but there is still the ironic hope that sacrilege will restore communication. What returns from the dead is not the soul, that dubious entity, but 'the silent and enduring bone'.

> Why not? since through life's little day
>   Our heads such sad effects produce;
> Redeem'd from worms and wasting clay,
>   This chance is theirs, to be of use.

Note the 'ambiguities'. 'Through life's little day' our heads produce nothing but nonsense or worse. *This* skull is 'redeemed' by the Christlike wine from 'worms' (earthworms or maggots of the brain?) and 'wasting clay' (clay which wastes, degenerates, i.e. the body; or clay which destroys, i.e. the earth of the grave?). 'This chance is theirs, to be of use.' The dry comment is perfectly 'metaphysical'; it might have come from a sceptical Herbert.

A *jeu d'esprit*? Yes, but viewed in a wider perspective not uninformed with Byron's perennial concern for unity and continuity. Body and soul are indivisible. Individuals are fleeting formations of atoms, which may take any shape in the course of time. My skull becomes your goblet, my enduring bone teaches you a better lesson than my flexible tongue could ever compass. In contrast to the later, parallel situation in the Olympeion, the 'field' is not mentioned unless in the 'Where once' of stanza 4: we have living man and skull, not man, skull, tout and temples. This is not yet gestalt writing. Unless we see the wine as a kind of inner gestalt, contained by, rather than containing, the resurgent skull. This deflates human pretensions. The skull does not matter: any skull may serve as a container for the drink of the gods. The continuity of the wine, the product of vintage after vintage through the ages, is thus more important than the skull, alive or dead, which holds it. Any old skull will serve: what is important is that the wine should be good! Mr Weston, one imagines, would have approved.

'Now at length we're off for Turkey'

The Gothic macabre of 'Lines Inscribed Upon a . . . Skull' is rapidly effaced by the new experiences, in lucid Mediterranean vistas, of Byron's voyage from Falmouth to Constantinople. A jocose poem of parting sweeps the old shadows away:

> Huzza! Hodgson, we are going,
>   Our embargo's off at last;
> Favourable breezes blowing
>   Bend the canvass o'er the mast.
> From aloft the signal's streaming,
>   Hark! the farewell gun is fired;
> Women screeching, tars blaspheming,
>   Tell us that our time's expired.
>   Here's a rascal
>   Come to task all,

> Prying from the Custom-house;
>> Trunks unpacking,
>> Cases cracking,
> Not a corner for a mouse
> 'Scapes unsearch'd amid the racket
> Ere we sail on board the Packet.

Four equally vigorous stanzas follow. Even the *expectation* of travel—for Byron writes this to Hodgson from Falmouth broads, 'on board the Lisbon Packet'—opens a new comic vein. The rhythms, the abandonment to the here and now, the alternate long and short lines, conjure up the tars' song and hornpipe in *Dido and Aeneas*— 'Take a boozy short leave of your nymphs on the shore . . .':

> Now at length we're off for Turkey,
>> Lord knows when we shall come back!
> Breezes foul and tempests murky
>> May unship us in a crack.
> But, since Life at most a jest is,
>> As philosophers allow,
> Still to laugh by far the best is,
>> Then laugh on—as I do now.
>>> Laugh at all things,
>>> Great and small things,
>> Sick or well, at sea or shore;
>>> While we're quaffing,
>>> Let's have laughing—
> Who the devil cares for more?—
> Some good wine! and who would lack it,
> Ev'n on board the Lisbon Packet?

Like Aeneas, Byron is cutting himself adrift from emotional ties. Gaiety may obscure a certain element of guilt. But the breach is essential for Byron as man and poet. In its 'light' way, 'Lines to Mr Hodgson' projects many of the values of the new, the mature Byron of the Levantine tour. It even anticipates the 'Pyrrhonism' of *Don Juan*. Its command of rhythm is superb; the completely original stanza or paragraph form is tailored for this occasion and no other, like one of Donne's 'Songs and Sonnets'. Its immediacy is equally impressive: we are right there, on the Lisbon Packet with Byron, enjoying the bustle and the confusion and the clash of little human schemes, distresses, recoveries which delighted him as he watched, participated and reflected. 'The Lisbon Packet' is a microcosm of Byron's universe-to-be, and a magnificent comic poem in its own right. Arnold excluded it from his anthology; later seekers-out of 'Beauties' have followed suit.

None of the subsequent lyrics of transit is quite so good as this. Perhaps Byron's major energies were channelled into the veins of observation, reflection, dramatisation which fed his masterpiece. And from that poem the comic note is absent. It emerges in his letters home, to some extent; but *Childe Harold* is almost unremittingly serious. I find this odd, and cast around for an explanation. Perhaps the minor poems of the Tour will suggest one.

If we are to take in the whole of Byron's lyric output in the early period which includes *Hours of Idleness* and covers the period of the Tour, we must regress a little to 1808. A number of poems listed in E. H. Coleridge's edition as 'Miscellaneous' hardly deserve comment: they are detritus from *Hours of Idleness*, and wisely unpublished by Byron. Some lyrics are interesting as documents. We see Byron watching and recording his own emotional states with what is, as far as he can manage it, a detached interest. There are 'love' poems, that is to say poems about moves in a love game, or game of the sexes, almost inconceivable in its artificiality to us today. There are some poems of deeper impact, 'To an Oak at Newstead', 'On Revisiting Harrow', both of 1807, which require no further comment than what I have given the *Hours of Idleness* lyrics on these themes. A poem of 2 December 1808, 'To a Lady, on being asked My Reason for Quitting England in the Spring', interests us for its introduction of the exilic note.

> When Man, expell'd from Eden's bowers,
>   A moment linger'd near the gate,
> Each scene recall'd the vanish'd hours,
>   And bade him curse his future fate.
>
> But, wandering on through distant climes,
>   He learnt to bear his load of grief;
> Just gave a sigh to other times,
>   And found in busier scenes relief.

The gloomy wanderer is here already, poised to jettison the jolly traveller of 'The Lisbon Packet'. The stanzas which follow pose Byron's basic oxymorons: the outsider's mingled gloom and neurotic exhilaration, the lingering over the past clashing with anticipation of a future which is 'cursed'. And in flight, in the poem's concluding stanza, he escapes too from temptation:

> In flight I shall be surely wise,
>   Escaping from temptation's snare;
> I cannot view my Paradise
>   Without the wish of dwelling there.

Alas, the escape is to be brief enough. Byron moves from 'Paradise' to 'Paradise'—all equally delusory, equally painful in the outcome. 'With dreadful faces thronged, and fiery arms.' The 'rosy urchin' of H.M.S. *Spider* clearly attracted him, and when he got to Spain there were 'the ladies of Cadiz'. Malta came up with something more serious in 'fair Florence', the adventurous Mrs Spencer Smith, 'A very extraordinary woman . . . of whose escape the Marquis de Salvo published a narrative', he writes to his mother from Malta: 'She has since been shipwrecked, and her life has been from its commencement so fertile in remarkable incidents, that in a romance they would appear improbable' (15 September 1809). I think it is important to note that Byron wrote about this liaison at Malta, and also about his relations with Spanish women, and his ambiguous invitation from Ali Pasha 'to visit him often, and at night, when he was at leisure' (letter of 12 November 1809), *to his mother*, the last person, one would have thought, to have been informed of such matters. But if Byron was crowing over his release from maternal apron-strings, and needling his mother on the points of Mary Chaworth and Lord Grey de Ruthyn,[2] the ploy is explicable. So too is the subsequent exacerbation of the feeling of guilt which failure to arrive at Newstead before his mother's death excited in him, and which split over into the complex guilt patterns of the *Tales* and *Manfred*.

'Delirium is our best deceiver'

The Malta lyrics, 'To Florence', and 'Lines Written in an Album', are frigid and conventional enough. 'Stanzas Composed During a Thunderstorm' (11 October 1809) spring from a deeper nerve, and merit our attention as Byron's first response to his new creative centre, 'the Archipelago', and in a situation of confrontation with the elements such as always stimulated him. These stanzas have an exultation of rhythm we have not met with in his lyrical writing since 'Lachin Y Gair'.

> Our guides are gone, our hope is lost,
>   And lightnings, as they play,
> But show where rocks our path have crost,
>   Or gild the torrent's spray.
>
> Is it a cot I saw, though low?
>   When lightning broke the gloom—

> How welcome were its shade!—ah, no!
>   'Tis but a Turkish tomb.

That Turkish tomb, first glimpsed in the lightning flashes of an Albanian thunderstorm, is to be a permanent eikon of the Byronic landscape.

Poor 'Florence' makes a perfunctory appearance, remembered with dutiful devotion amid the flashes and the rumblings.

> Clouds burst, skies flash, oh, dreadful hour!
>   More fiercely pours the storm!
> Yet here one thought has still the power
>   To keep my bosom warm.

A sort of amorous cardigan. The sentiment is not convincing, and the second half of the poem has as little to do with the first as 'Glory and Greece' has to do with 'those reviving passions' in his last Greek lyric a quarter of a century later.

'Florence' spoils another good poem in 'Stanzas Written in Passing the Ambracian Gulf' (14 November 1809). The opening quatrain is superb, a faultless epigram:

> Through cloudless skies, in silvery sheen,
>   Full beams the moon on Actium's coast:
> And on these waves, for Egypt's queen,
>   The ancient world was won and lost.

Byron is looking out from the deck of the sailing *Spider* across the moonlit sea to the familiar-unfamiliar shore. His historical imagination is at once aroused. The lines reticulate past and present, space and time, in a glinting network of beams and currents. We are in a world of shifting values which are eternal in their very transience. The magisterial note, the complete finality of the statement, the classical economy, come from a mind conscious of the human oxymoron. Not just this historical event, not just Byron's observing eye, but the whole predicament of power involved with weakness, and the whole pathos of man the spectator through the ages, are concentrated in the quatrain. Byron observes, and passes on. Or should pass on—for in fact, to the ruin of his poem, he adds four feeble stanzas involving himself and 'Florence' as modern Cleopatra and Antony.

Of course she is not and he is not and the fact is later recognised. In 'The spell is broke, the charm is flown' (16 January 1810) Byron comes to his senses.

The spell is broke, the charm is flown!
  Thus is it with Life's fitful fever:
We madly smile when we should groan;
  Delirium is our best deceiver.
Each lucid interval of thought
  Recalls the woes of Nature's charter;
And *He* that acts as *wise men ought*,
  But *lives*—as Saints have died—a martyr.

Another epigram: and the best of the early Byron is found in these concise judgements: lengthier exercises betray him into diffuseness and sentiment. 'Each lucid interval of thought/Recalls the woes of Nature's charter' is pure Housman: 'But men at whiles are sober . . .'. 'Nature's charter' is Johnson's 'the doom of man', Housman's 'The troubles of our proud and angry dust', Malraux's 'la condition humaine', the existentialists' *angst*. Byron is already coming to grips with the dilemmas of 'Man's estate'. When spells are broken we are still faced with reality. The groan replaces the mad smile of our delirium; perhaps it is better, as Byron was to speculate on many later occasions, to stick to one's crazes. The thought pursues Pope's 'Where ignorance is bliss' into another dimension.

Problems are rarely solved on their own level. By transference to another level they may cease to be problems and there is nothing to solve. Byron's progress through the Mediterranean scene is a remarkable illustration of the *solvitur ambulando*. Lunes engendered among northern fogs and chills drop away of themselves. In the lyrics of transit (and much more clearly, of course, in the second canto of *Childe Harold*) we see him learning to live and function in his element. A poetry of gesture slowly replaces a poetry of protest and declamation. Byron fuses with his setting. One such gesture is the 9 May 1810 'Written After Swimming from Sestos to Abydos', a poem whose deliberate flippancy of tone has disguised its serious existential import. Here we pass from the historical recreation of the past (as in the Ambracian Gulf stanzas) to the mythological and poetical. The Troad was deeply impressive to Byron by reason of its fusion of all these elements. And who is to decide between history and myth? 'I have stood upon that place daily, for more than a month in 1810', he recalls eleven years later (in his Diary, 11 January 1821), 'and if any thing diminished my pleasure, it was that the blackguard Bryant had impugned its veracity.' Time and Schliemann have proved that Byron was right and Bryant wrong. But in 1810 Byron could do nothing about it. About another piece of the living past connected with the spot he could do something: he could re-enact it, and so, as I have suggested earlier, reinsert it in the pattern of time.

The occasion of 'Sestos to Abydos' is not a complete identification, does not approach the remarkable facsimiles of past and present he achieved in the Olympeion, the Forum and the Coliseum. Leander swam for love, Byron for glory. The poem revolves round an 'if'.

> If, when the wintry tempest roared,
>   He sped to Hero, nothing loth,
> And thus of old thy current poured,
>   Fair Venus! how I pity both!

Byron is a 'degenerate modern wretch', not, as in the Forum, 'a ruin amid ruins'. Unimpressive as poetry, the lyric marks a hinge moment in Byron's development. The tone is mature, above all in its irony. Compare it with the humorous, satiric or indignant verses of *Hours of Idleness*, and you are at once conscious of the difference. The shrillness of *English Bards* too has gone, together with the sentiment of 'The Girl of Cadiz' in *Childe Harold* I. We might already call this poem 'classical'—meaning that it has a quality we discern in Horace, Martial, Catullus: a kind of *lumen siccum*. The 'Gods' of the last stanza are real gods, accepted (for as long as Byron remains a guest in their stamping ground) as legitimate arbiters of destiny.

> 'Twere hard to say who fared the best:
>   Sad mortals! thus the Gods still plague you!
> He lost his labour, I my jest:
>   For he was drowned, and I've the ague.

This acceptance, this capacity for being 'all things to all men', which I have elsewhere connected with St Paul's own 'charity',[3] is a major 'note' of Byron's transit through the Mediterranean world.

'I would not lose thee for a world': so Byron had apostrophised 'sweet Florence' at the lame and impotent conclusion of the Ambracian Gulf stanzas. Alas for human vows! It is precisely 'for a world', this exciting new world of the Mediterranean that Byron loses not only Mrs Spencer Smith but also the memories of Mary Chaworth and the 'Paphian girls' of his juvenile effusions. He will continue to write romantic love poetry, but always with a *caveat*: this 'love' exists, we have to recognise it as a force in human lives, but it is not exactly what it seems, it draws upon a wealth of very disparate sources—glands, novel reading, boredom, custom, social status, personal insecurity. Of course *Don Juan* will be Byron's major feat of analysis: but already, in these minor poems of transit, there

are shrewd hints of test-tubes and litmus paper. Byron lets the
hints surface very rarely, and we have to look out for them, primed
by hindsight. For the Regency reader they appealed as a flattering
taking-into-the-author's-confidence. 'I am working out my problems
in this poem and you may be interested' is the approach, and the
reader was naturally delighted to participate. Here was a poet who
met them on their own level. Wordsworth, Coleridge, Keats,
Shelley were operating *de haut en bas*: teacher to pupil, great soul
speaking earnestly to little soul. Byron reverts to the civilised give-
and-take of the preceding century. And his remarkable colloquial
manner is already asserting itself. This is talk between friends. It has
Pope's urbanity, plus a Regency piquancy (Moore *flaunts* it where
Byron quietly displays it) which brings it up to date.

The tone strikes us in the notorious 'Maid of Athens, ere we part'
as an element which is detachable from the occasion, yet beautifully
adapted to it. Here Byron is parodying his own manner. The 'Emma'
and 'Caroline' poems of parting in *Hours of Idleness*, which use the
counters of 'tortured heart', 'sweet lips', 'burning cheek', 'raven
tresses' to weave a tissue of romantic nonsense, are here deflated to
an almost clinical objectivity: we do not need the evidence of the
letters[4] to detect in 'Give, oh, give me back my heart!' the note of an
unclinched bargain. 'Keep it now, and take the rest!' is almost
petulant. Or we can, if we wish, read it so: and from Byron's
situation this makes good sense, just as from the stance of the
Regency misses who swooned over the poem it made good sense to
read it as a pathetic, heartbroken lament into which they could
infuse their own love-longings. Theresa exists on two levels, as the
individual girl and as 'Maid of Athens': as sexual object which
Byron is not too keen on (*vide* letters) and as (momentary) emblem of
her divine city, upholding the Hellenic values as the caryatids of the
Erectheion (we see Byron's eye travelling up from Mrs Macri's
house to the temple not so very far above) support their crowned
and dentelated architrave. Byron's 'By those tresses unconfined,/
Woo'd by each Aegean wind' lifts us from the individual girl *down
there* in the dusty street to the divine maidens on the height;[5] when
he 'flies to Istambol' it is not the Maid of Athens but the city
('Athens holds my heart and soul') that he regrets. On this reading,
'that zone-encircled waist' is 'Athens' violet crown', the famous
cirque of mountains, Hymettus, Pentelicus, Parnes, with the southern
sea, which rings the city of Cecrops. Here resides Byron's newfound
'life', his whole new Greek existence. As always, he finds an 'objective

correlative', and usually a sexual one, for his avatars. Such correlatives are never wholly adequate, and the first Theresa is as incompetent to represent Greece, and to satisfy Byron in Greece, as the last Teresa is to represent Italy or to satisfy the Byron of Venice, Pisa and Ravenna.

The power of this little poem to move, a power which it undoubtedly has, is thus seen to depend on its ambiguities. The poem is a sustained—and concealed—paradox. Σωή μοῦ σᾶς ἀγαπῶ ('My life! I love you'). Yes, it is his *life* that Byron loves, this new life revealed to him in the Cecropian temenos of Athens.[6] Theresa is a counter, holding the antinomies of life itself, its 'alternate joy and woe' (stanza 3). Theresa's 'tresses unconfin'd, are an emblem of life untrammelled by British prejudices, of life lived in its freedom. 'Each Aegean wind' blows through the poem as the breath of life itself, Jesus' spirit blowing 'where it listeth', Rilke's 'a blowing in the god, a blast!' The rigid rhythms and the supple rhythms of the κόρη are conveyed through the structure of the poem. Two 'rigid' stanzas beginning with 'Maid of Athens' frame two 'supple' stanzas opening with 'By those . . .' evocations of physical, alluring perfections: tresses, eyelids, cheeks, eyes, lip, waist, token flowers. This almost geometrical pattern holds the thing together as a love poem, despite the sub-ironic twists. But the tidal movement is from maid to Athens, from girl to city. Who is the 'thee' of the final stanza? Theresa, or Athens? We can take our choice.

Among the minor amorous lyrics of this period most are presented as 'translations' or 'imitations' from the Greek or Turkish. Byron takes no responsibility for their sentiments. Here we have Byron the folklorist. He garners them in evening parties, or snoops on them in Piraeus tabernas. Constantly brushing up his demotic Greek, or improving his Turkish (an easy language for an Englishman), in day-to-day intercourse with Turks and Greeks, he would hardly miss the Arabic he had abandoned in Malta in the first flush of his amour with Mrs Spencer Smith. He had a fantastic turn for languages,[7] and when he set his mind to it—that is, when he was vitally interested—could achieve wonders of assimilation and adaptation. With the patriotic Greek songs which he also translates (notably 'Sons of the Greeks, arise!') the love songs attest his strong interest in balladry—a point I have emphasised elsewhere.[8] There is a reversion to the spirit of the Scottish poems in *Hours of Idleness*, an Ossianic exaltation of the bard as 'doctrinal to a nation', which is significant for Byron's growing interest in the Greek cause. The note will be repeated in *Hebrew Melodies*—'David's lyre grew mightier than his throne'—and in many a later poem. Here again Byron's taste chimes with Blake's, preferring simple melody to the artfulness of harmony. The Romaic song which he translates as 'I enter thy garden of roses,/Beloved and fair Haidée!' is taken down from the lips of

'the young girls of Athens'. . . . Their manner of singing it is by verses in rotation, the whole number present joining in the chorus. I have heard it frequently at our 'χόροι' [more correctly χοροί, dances] in the winter of 1810–11. The air is plaintive and pretty.

It is not only in writing these minor lyrics, but also for the material of the Tales, as we shall see later, that Byron depends upon *das volk dichtet*.

'Dear object of defeated care'

As poetry these 'translations' have little to commend them: they are pretty and accomplished, but no more than that. 'Lines Written Beneath a Picture' sounds a more serious note, but it is a cryptogram without any reliable key. E. H. Coleridge gives it a tentative context from 'a curious work of doubtful authority' (*PW* iii, 19). It seems to me to fall within the Edleston canon. The tone is identical with that of the Thyrza poems. If there was a 'picture', it is more likely to have been of an English boy known over two or three years than of a Georgian slave girl bought in the market at Istanbul. Portrait painting is not an Islamic vice. The poem is concentrated where the 'Haidée' lyrics are diffuse.

> Dear object of defeated care!
>   Though now of Love and thee bereft,
> To reconcile me with despair
>   Thine image and my tears are left.
>
> 'Tis said with Sorrow Time can cope;
>   But this I feel can ne'er be true:
> For by the death-blow of my Hope
>   My Memory immortal grew.

The date is 'Athens, January, 1811'. What more likely than that this is the delayed reaction to the 1810 report recorded by Hobhouse: 'the *Edleston* is accused of indecency'? 'The *Edleston*' is clearly sarcastic—'the wretched boy Byron makes an idol of and is always talking about, showing his picture, etc.'—and we can imagine

Byron having a lot to put up with from the jibes of his fellow-traveller. Now Hobhouse is proved right, and Byron wrong; Edleston is the (still) dear object of a care, an anxiety, a protective-ness which have, in the event (if the report from England is true) been defeated. 'Thine image and my tears are left.' The Edleston he has known, the pure 'Fravarshi' of his own identity,[9] is lost for ever; only the image remains. His 'hope' had been for a resumption, on his return to England, of the ideal Trinity relationship; this has now received a 'death-blow', but the memory of what had been is immortal.

If 'Dear object of defeated care' is, as I think, a Thyrza poem, it affords us an entry into the ethos of the remaining canon. There are at least ten other poems, and to their number we must add the *Childe Harold* stanzas I discuss within the context of that poem. They are all sombre, deeply moving and curiously ascetic, renouncing the gay colouring of the 'Theresa' and 'Haidée' lyrics, and indeed the conventional 'colours of rhetoric' which Byron found appropriate to the poetry of personal emotion at this period. They are almost dull: soberly imaged, subfusc, disappointing to the admirers of Byron *en panache*. There are rich rewards in them, however, for the reader who can penetrate and (above all) connect.

Connection must be inside the total canon with such *cruci* as the 'little shepherd' moment of the Zitza epiphany (*Childe Harold* II, xlviii—lii) and outside it with such ramifying Sufic 'annunciations' as Dante's *giovane vestito di bianchissime vestimenta* in the *Vita Nuova* who declares himself *Ego tamquam centrum circuli*, and the Prophet's Arab boy who scandalised the Companions, and the white-robed youth encountered by Ibn 'Arabi on his circumambulation of the Ka'ba. Edleston is indeed the key to all this later aspect of Byron's life and work which embraces and moves in and out of the two homosexual dimensions, the 'pure' and the 'impure', which Hobhouse was never able to keep separate in his mind and which Byron had an equally great difficulty in distinguishing in actuality.[10]

That 'Thyrza' is at once Edleston and an ideal youth who may take the choirboy's shape or another's at will, is unwittingly pointed out by the writer of the note 'communicated to the Editor' in E. H. Coleridge's edition (*PW* iii, 30–1). 'According to the poems', Thyrza had met Byron

> . . . many a day
> In these, to me, deserted towers

(Newstead, 11 October 1811)

When stretched on fever's sleepless bed

(Patras, September 1810)

And oft I thought at Cynthia's noon,
  When sailing o'er the Aegean wave,
'Now Thyrza gazes on that moon'—
  Alas, it gleam'd upon her grave! . . .

(Newstead, December 1811)

Exactly: he is a form who takes many shapes, now Edleston the surpliced choirboy, now the little shepherd in his white capote, now, changing sex (so that 'Thyrza' is not so much a deception as it seems), the two Leilas of *The Giaour* and *Don Juan*. He is the concentration of a whole series of nostalgic-erotic-mystic-guilty-exultant experiences, particularly where the immediate occasion of his apparition concerns death, silence or music. The memory of some early 'innocence' which is nonetheless excitingly erotic, and works like a perfume on the nostalgic nerve, invariably surfaces in Byron in response to music, birdsong, or the scent of flowers.[11] We are dealing, plainly, with a sensibility which is not very much in the English tradition, whether 'classical' or 'romantic', but which has a good deal in common with Marinism (Crashaw is the nearest English parallel) in the past and with Baudelaire, Verlaine and Rimbaud in the future.

Byron's own immediate future was to be the 'public image' of *Childe Harold* I and II. It was devastatingly successful, and Byron was to cloak himself in it for most of his allotted span, not entirely to his own advantage as man and poet. There are cracks, of course, some of them pathetically contrived by Byron—'Look at me! This is what I really am!'—some of them unwittingly revealed in moments of letting go. 'The real Byron' is situated somewhere between the public image and the exaggerations of neurosis into which he was driven by need to keep up the image. A major virtue of Byron criticism lies in the refusal to accept either extreme at face value. And at this point I would like to enter a protest against the commentators who, bewildered obscurely by the contradictions between the private and the public Byron, build up a conventional picture through reliance on gossip about him. Byron is a writer who documented himself very adequately. He is a complex being, and we shall not get easily at his mystery: but the materials are there in the voluminous verses, letters and journals. Short cuts through Medwin, Lady Blessington, and others of the 'His Very Self and Voice' crew are not really profitable. The journalist biographers can be forgiven their exploitations, but it is disturbing to find an academic critic like Professor Rutherford, for instance, opening his *Byron: a critical study* with 'Byron told Lady Blessington . . .' when what he really means is 'Lady Blessington says that Byron told her. . . .' The present book is, among other things, a plea for a re-estimation of Byron on the basis of what he himself thought and said, not of what others thought and said about him, still less of what they alleged him to have thought and said. It is the penalty of great minds to be misunderstood by lesser minds. Byron contributed to that misunderstanding by his inveterate love of leg-pulling. I cannot defend him in this, though I think I can understand his motives. We shall be safe if we stick to his own very copious passages of self-revelation, relying more on his verse than on his prose, and within the prose more on his journals than on his letters, where all too frequently he indulges his Harlequin vein.

Notes and references

1 'Byron's Greek canto: the anatomy of freedom', *Yearbook of English Studies*, iv (1974).
2 'I am not reconciled to Lord Grey, *and I never will*. He was once my *Greatest Friend*, my reasons for ceasing that Friendship are such as I cannot explain, not even to you, my Dear Sister' (letter to Augusta, 2 April 1804). Such resolutions were easily broken with Byron; and the urge to score over his mother must have been irresistible.
3 'Byron's Greek canto', *loc. cit.*
4 Cf. especially those of 23 August 1810, to Hobhouse, which show how very cynical the liaison was.
5 The *Guide Bleu* mentions, à propos of the Erectheion, 'un rhythme de lignes rigides et de lignes souples qui associe la stabilité de la colonne inerte au mouvement de la figure vivante. Du coussinet, la charge se transmet à la nuque que renforce la masse des *cheveux rejetés en arrière*' (my italics).
6 The refrain is what, actually, gives Byron's game away. A lover would not address a girl with σᾶς. The familiar σέ would be used.
7 See below, pp. 95.
8 Collections of ballads figure in his library sale catalogue (pp. 7, 9 and 12 list collections of Scottish ballads and songs, as well as Percy's *Reliques* and collections of original Scottish and Welsh airs), and Prothero notes (*LJ* i, 34) that 'Byron's taste for simple ballad music lasted throughout his life'. Compare also *Don Juan* III, xxxiv, and the 'Isles of Greece' verses in the same canto. But it is in *The*

Island II, i–vii, that Byron gives us his mature reflections on tradition and traditional song.

9   See below, p. 212.

10   The theme cannot be dealt with adequately in a general work like the present. It links up with Byron's whole 'doctrine of love', with his Sufic affinities, with his obsession with circles and towers in the domain of imagery, with the tension between his 'thalassic' and his 'oreinic' drives, with love as thrust and release; in short, with a complex of insights and image frameworks discernible in Byron's *opus* which give it an interest quite absent from the grossly simplified erotic diagrams of his contemporaries—and their successors among the Victorians. Swinburne, Morris and Patmore tried to right the balance, but deficiencies of intellect and experience betrayed them into worse follies than those committed by Tennyson, Browning and Arnold.

11   The *locus classicus* for this is *CH* III, lxxxv–xci: see below, pp. 192–7.

4

THE FIRST PILGRIMAGE

'If I do not travel now,' Byron wrote to his mother on 2 November 1808, 'I never shall, and all men should one day or other. I have at present no connections to keep me at home; no wife, or unprovided sisters, brothers, etc. I shall take care of you, and when I return I may possibly become a politician.' Writing to Hodgson from Falmouth on the eve of departure, he is more outspoken:

I leave England without regret—I shall return to it without pleasure. I am like Adam, the first convict sentenced to transportation, but I have no Eve, and have eaten no apple but what was as sour as a crab;—and thus ends my first chapter. Adieu.

Curious to think that in that one flippant sentence we have the germs of the biblical plays and the paradisal theme which runs through *Childe Harold's Pilgrimage*, the Tales, and *Don Juan*. But it is always in his flippancies that Byron is most serious.

A new chapter indeed opened in Byron's life—and in the annals of literature—with Byron's departure from England on 2 July 1809, accompanied by his Cambridge friend Hobhouse, his servant, Fletcher, and his 'little page', Robert Rushton. A new world opened upon him in the Mediterranean scene. On 6 July they reached Lisbon. Byron's sense of release from the restrictions, maternal, social, political, and personal,[1] of England comes out strongly in the 'last Good Night' song which precedes his account of the Lisbon landfall:

> Adieu, adieu! my native shore
>   Fades o'er the waters blue;
> The Night-winds sigh, the breakers roar
>   And shrieks the wild sea-mew.

> Yon Sun that sets upon the sea
>   We follow in his flight;
> Farewell awhile to him and thee,
>   My native Land—Good Night!
>
> A few short hours and He will rise
>   To give the Morrow birth;
> And I shall hail the main and skies,
>   But not my mother Earth.
> Deserted is my own good Hall,
>   Its hearth is desolate;
> Wild weeds are gathering on the wall;
>   My Dog howls at the gate.

There are eight vigorous stanzas more; these two convey the exile's
exultation. The wild sea-mew introduces that long roster of bird
images which infuse Byron's poetry to a degree unparalleled by any
other Romantic poet, and approached only by Eliot in a later period.
The sun is hailed as a recurrent eikon—and he is to be *followed*:
Byron's Apollonian avatar begins to take shape.

The conclusion of the stanza sounds the Ossianic note; in stanzas
8 and 9 a cynicism reminiscent of *Hours of Idleness* makes itself felt:

> For who would trust the seeming sighs
>   Of wife or paramour?
> Fresh feeres will dry the bright blue eyes
>   We late saw streaming o'er.

reinforced, more persuasively, by his revulsion from human contacts
to the solitude of the sea:

> And now I'm in the world alone,
>   Upon the wide, wide sea . . .

The Coleridgean echo is unmistakable, but the Childe welcomes the
desolation which fills the Mariner with dread (stanza 10):

> Welcome, welcome, ye dark-blue waves!
>   And when you fail my sight,
> Welcome, ye deserts, and ye caves!
>   My native Land—Good Night!

It is to the 'deep and dark blue Ocean', after all the deserts and
caves, physical and spiritual, of Cantos II, III and IV, that Byron
returns in his grand finale to *Childe Harold*.

Byron's 'Ancient Mariner' stance struck the novelist John Galt,
who was a fellow-passenger on the *Townshend Packet* which carried
Byron from Gibraltar to Malta on a later stage of the tour.

Byron held himself aloof, and sat on the rail, leaning on the mizzen shrouds, inhaling, as it were, poetical sympathy from the gloomy rock, then dark and stern in the twilight. There was, in all about him that evening, much waywardness. . . . Sitting amid the shrouds and rattlings, in the tranquillity of the moonlight, churning an inarticulate melody, he seemed almost apparitional, suggesting dim reminiscences of him who shot the albatross.

The 'gloomy wanderer', the Byronic hero who is already fore-shadowed in the 'Calmar and Orla' and the 'Oscar of Alva' lyrics of *Hours of Idleness*, is gaining form and substance.

'This purple land'

Lisbon disgusted Byron with its dirt, delighted him with its churches and palaces: 'I am very happy here, because I loves oranges, and talks bad Latin to the monks, who understand it, as it is like their own.' He visits Cintra, with its monastery and hermitage and its memories of Beckford. A new dimension in his understanding of Nature opens out to him with his appreciation of southern luxuriance: at the same time the painful contrast with man's destructiveness appals him:

> Oh, Christ! it is a goodly sight to see
> > What Heaven hath done for this delicious land!
> > What fruits of fragrance blush on every tree!
> > What goodly prospects o'er the hills expand!
> > But man would mar them with an impious hand. (I, xv)

This bitter dichotomy persists throughout the first three Cantos of *Childe Harold* and affords the work much of its structural resilience. With Blake, Byron was the most aware of the Romantics of the problems of what we have come to call pollution. Byron and Hobhouse rode through Portugal and Spain while the Peninsular War was still raging; their reports have the war correspondent's immediacy. 'Cintra's glorious Eden' (xviii) is the scene of the abortive Convention (political pollution), of the cave (religious obscurantism) in which the hermit 'Honorius long did dwell,/In hope to merit Heaven by making earth a Hell' (I, xx), and of Beckford's palace (moral obliquity):

> In wit, in genius, as in wealth the first
> How wondrous bright thy blooming morn arose—
> But thou wast smitten with unhallowed thirst
> Of nameless crime, and thy sad day must close
> To scorn and solitude unsought—the worst of woes!

This cancelled stanza is ironic in its projection of a vice and its punishment of which Byron himself was soon to be a notorious example.

Throughout Canto I the spectacle of man in conflict with his own happiness arouses Byron's pity and disgust. Man's artefacts, in their decay, are eikons of his impermanence. The palaces of Spain and Portugal lack the complex impact which, as we shall see, the temples of Greece and the tombstones of Turkey were to have for Byron. Nevertheless, the pathos of their past grandeur and present misery arouses that curious compassion for places which is to infuse the whole of *Childe Harold*:

> Here giant weeds a passage scarce allow
> To halls deserted, portals gaping wide;
> Fresh lessons to the thinking bosom, how
> Vain are the pleasaunces on earth supplied,
> Swept into wrecks anon by Time's ungentle tide!   (I, xxiii)

So, as he rides over the Peninsular battlefields on his way to Spain— 'a distance of nearly four hundred miles. The horses are excellent: we rode seventy miles a-day. Eggs and wine, and hard beds, are all the accommodation we found, and, in such torrid weather, quite enough' (to Hodgson, 6 August 1809)—he notes with the keenest of eyes every evidence of man's inhumanity to man and to 'maternal Nature'. The detail is vivid, impeccably presented:

> On yon long, level plain, at distance crowned
> With crags, whereon those Moorish turrets rest,
> Wide-scatter'd hoof-marks dint the wounded ground;
> And, scathed by fire, the greensward's darkened vest
> Tells that the foe was Andalusia's guest.   (I, xlix)

The vividness is secured through detail, not through rhetoric: no approach could be further from that of the 'picturesque tourist' than Byron's. He travels, as he had promised Hanson, 'to take a wider field than is customary with travellers. If I return, my judgement will be more mature' (letter of 18 November 1808). And the 'wider' includes 'deeper and more intimate'. Byron persistently engages with the day-to-day life of the places he visits. He is never contented simply to observe and pass on. He has to be 'with it'. And if the 'withness' includes and is based on the erotic, this again is what we should expect. Delighted letters home comment on the naturalness of Spanish ladies, in implied contrast to the *minauderies* of the Southwell belles and the London harlots. The same appreciation fires the stanzas of Canto I:

> Her glance how wildly beautiful! how much
> Hath Phoebus wooed in vain to spoil her cheek,
> Which glows yet smoother from his amorous clutch!
> Who round the North for paler dames would seek?
> How poor their forms appear! how languid, wan, and weak!
>
> (I, lviii)

Byron continues to 'follow', to identify himself with the sun!

Yet not with an indiscriminate admiration. Poise, balance, detachment are also Byronic virtues, nicely counterpointing spontaneity and enthusiasm: the cautious Scot in him, perhaps, tempering the ardent Norman. The virtues of Spanish women, emerging in the martial feats of the 'Maid of Saragoza' (I, liv–lvi) as well as in the amorous soft delays of the 'lovely girl of Cadiz',[2] have their darker side of callousness and frivolity, plainly to be seen in the horrific picture of the bullfight at Puerta Santa Maria, which Byron attended on Sunday afternoon, 30 July 1809 (I, lxxi–lxxx). Byron will be present at this, as any other exhibition of energy, human or cosmic, and admire it *for* its energy (as he admires 'war's magnificently stern array') while condemning it for its destructiveness. This power to stand aside to appreciate aesthetically, while immersing himself to feel with and to condemn morally, is something Byron shares with Blake and Shakespeare.

'The crowded circus', 'the silent circle's peopled walls', 'the spacious area' holds 'Young, old, high, low' within the same perimeter, while 'Full in the centre stands the bull at bay'. The bullring is thus Byron's first complete eikon of the human situation.[3] The second comes in the Coliseum stanzas of Canto IV. Both project a scenario of the lonely victim confronting his torturers. The heroism of the bull:

> He stops—he starts—disdaining to decline:
> Slowly he falls, amidst triumphant cries,
> Without a groan, without a struggle dies . . .   (I, lxxix)

enshrines Byron's permanent sense of the dignity of animal suffering, of the wolf which 'dies in silence' (IV, xxi), of 'the wild-born falcon' which tears itself to death against the bars of its cage (III, xv), and of the barbarian gladiator who falls 'butchered to make a Roman holiday':

> He leans upon his hand—his manly brow
> Consents to death, but conquers agony,
> And his drooped head sinks gradually low.   (IV, cxl)

This is real suffering. Meanwhile, in its perimeter, we have its frivolous antetype:

> Here Dons, Grandees, but chiefly Dames abound,
>   Skilled in the ogle of a roguish eye,
>   Yet ever well inclined to heal the wound;
>   None through their cold disdain are doomed to die.
> As moon-struck bards complain, by Love's sad archery   (I, lxxii)

From these mock deaths and torments our eye travels down to the ring itself and its baffled centre.

> Bounds with one lashing spring the mighty brute,
>   And, wildly staring, spurns, with sounding foot,
>   The sand, nor blindly rushes on his foe:
>   Here, there, he points his threatening front, to suit
>   His first attack, wide-waving to and fro
> His angry tail; red rolls his eye's dilated glow.   (I, lxxv)

So 'roguish eye' links with 'eye's dilated glow', 'love's sad archery' with the picador's darts, flapping fans with waving tail and threatening front. It is a masterpiece of ironic counterpoint.

Canto I is not a happy canto, nor an expansive one. We are crossing a peninsula, but after the introductory stanzas there is no sense of the sea. Even rivers fail us except for a brief allusion to Tagus (xiv) and references to other streams simply as boundaries (xxxiii, xxxiv). This is a dusty, fire-and-sun-scorched canto as remote from the legend-packed lucidities of Greece as from the rich humanities of Italy in Cantos II and IV. With Canto III it shares an obsession with war, with violence seen as *utterly* destructive (in some sense the classical heroisms and Turk-inflicted martyrdoms of Canto II, the imperial brutalities of Canto IV, are seminal, rich in promise of good to come). The powerful image of War in stanza xxxix—

> Lo! where the Giant on the mountain stands,
>   His blood-red tresses deepening in the sun,
>   With death-shot glowing in his fiery hands,
>   And eye that scorcheth all it glares upon;   (I, xxxix)

—anticipates the phrasing of the bullring stanzas and centres the whole Canto (it stands midway in the original text, the last ten stanzas being added later) in violently aggressive terms, corresponding antiphonally to the meditative

> More blest the life of godly Eremite,
>   Such as on lonely Athos may be seen,
>   Watching at eve upon the Giant Height,
>   Which looks o'er waves so blue, skies so serene,

> That he who there at such an hour hath been
> Will wistful linger on that hallow'd spot . . .   (II, xxvii)

of Canto II. We have to look out for these correspondences in *Childe Harold*; missing them, we shall fail to respond to the poem's contrapuntal structure in the same way in which, without close, intense scrutiny of phrase and image, from line to line, we shall lose its dynamic resonances.

'Daphne's deathless plant'

Iberian passions may be too insistent, too cloying. Byron must have felt this when, in full flight of praise of Spanish maidens, he turns abruptly to the remote, the classical, the unsoiled by human passion, in the shape of the famous mountain under whose shadow he is actually (16 December 1809) writing his Cadiz stanzas.[4]

> Oh, thou Parnassus! whom I now survey,
>> Not in the phrensy of a dreamer's eye,
>> Not in the fabled landscape of a lay,
>> But soaring snow-clad through thy native sky,
>> In the wild pomp of mountain-majesty!   (I, lx)

The sense of release recalls what we feel at the opening of the poem, with Byron's emancipation from England. Parnassus is projected back from Byron's actual (16 December) 'state' into the dusty, rather sticky 'state' he was in at Cadiz after his Peninsular tour, to purge and control. It is *after* this divine intervention that Byron is able to deal with the bullring. The Parnassus stanzas extend from lx to lxiii and form a brilliant indirect comment (reading them now in the framework of the Canto, not in the timelag of their composition) on the whole of what has gone before and comes after them. The effect is one of 'distancing'. Byron's personal involvement with the Spanish scene remains as great as before; but his 'bardic' relationship, now rooted in the Delphic scene, has undergone a subtle shift. It is as though Byron were saying, 'Very well, I've been writing up to now in terms of memory (though of very recent memory), but now I'm in contact with this thing, with Parnassus, with Delphi, and I have to write about this thing, and about myself and my experiences in relation to it.'

Parnassus represents Byron's first turning, in *Childe Harold*, from the immediate to the archetype. Yet the archetype is here, as always for Byron, rooted in the immediate. The approach is intensely personal. In contact for the first time with the numinous, with 'the fair humanities of old religion', his response is one of awe and of supplication:

> Now to my theme—but from thy holy haunt
> Let me some remnant, some memorial bear;
> Yield me one leaf of Daphne's deathless plant,
> Nor let thy votary's hope be deemed an idle vaunt.   (I, lxiii)

For who knows not Parnassus, 'knows not man's divinest lore'.[5] Byron's contact with Delphi means a new relationship with the 'elements' to which he had addressed his 'last Good Night' at the opening of the Canto (xiii), a relationship which, once established, will persist throughout the whole of *Childe Harold*. It is, precisely, the theme of 'this grace dissolved in place' which Byron is stating in stanza lxii:

> Though here no more Apollo haunts his Grot,
> And thou, the Muses' seat, art now their grave,
> Some gentle Spirit still pervades the spot,
> Sighs in the gale, keeps silence in the Cave,
> And glides with glassy foot o'er yon melodious wave.[6]   (I, lxii)

Cave, gale, wave project earth, air and water; the element of fire is lacking with the withdrawal of the Sun-god; yet in a real sense Byron's avatar here restores the Apollonian dimension. As late as 1821 his diary records:

Upon Parnassus, going to the fountain of Delphi (Castri) in 1809, I saw a flight of twelve eagles . . . and I seized the omen. On the day before, I composed the lines to Parnassus . . . and on beholding the birds, had a hope that Apollo had accepted my homage. . . . I have been a votary of the deity and the place, and am grateful for what he has done in my behalf, leaving the future in his hands, as I left the past.

We cannot miss the note of simple truth and trust in that. Byron may delight in bamboozling his more crass correspondents, and no reliance whatever should be placed in what his gossips report him as saying, but in his journals, intended for no eye but his own, he is consistently veracious.

'Curst Cain's unresting doom'

After the Delphi stanzas, interpolated in the Iberian narrative, the rest of Canto I (with the exception of the bullfight) comes as something of an anticlimax. Seville, where he passed 25 to 28 July, is hailed for 'Her strength, her wealth, her site of ancient days', but Cadiz is the abode of Vice:

> A Cherub-Hydra round us dost thou gape,
> And mould to every taste thy dear delusive shape. (I, lxv)

Yet the anticlimax, perhaps, is *meant*: we proceed, with an Eliot-like brutality of contrast and shock, from the remote splendours of Apollo to the all-too-immediate temptations of Venus:

> When Paphos fell by Time—accursèd Time!
> The Queen who conquers all must yield to thee—
> The Pleasures fled, but sought as warm a clime;
> And Venus, constant to her native Sea,
> To nought else constant, hither deigned to flee,
> And fixed her shrine within these walls of white;
> Though not to one dome circumscribeth She
> Her worship, but, devoted to her rite,
> A thousand Altars rise, for ever blazing bright. (I, lxvi)

Byron is still moving between the nodes of wisdom (Delphi), power (Seville), and love (Cadiz), and lines 7 to 9 of the above stanza may be raising the hetero-homosexual theme we have already noted in the Cintra section, and which will be again projected in the Albanian stanzas (later expurgated) of Canto II. It is perhaps to a conflation of the theme of sexual guilt with that of sadism (in the bullring drama) that we should ascribe the sudden and startling emergence of the murderer archetype:

> But Passion raves herself to rest, or flies;
> And Vice, that digs her own voluptuous tomb,
> Had buried long his [Harold's] hopes, no more to rise:
> Pleasure's palled Victim! life-abhorring Gloom
> Wrote on his faded brow curst Cain's unresting doom. (I, lxxxiii)

The note persists in the song 'To Inez':

> It is that settled, ceaseless gloom
>   The fabled Hebrew Wanderer bore;
> That will not look beyond the tomb,
>   But cannot hope for rest before.
>
> What Exile from himself can flee?
>   To zones though more and more remote,
> Still, still pursues, where'er I be,
>   The blight of Life—the Demon Thought.

Byron in Cadiz no longer 'whistled as he went, for want of thought'.

His education, like the Ancient Mariner's, is proceeding apace. And the final stanzas return us to the horror of death personally felt. Amidst the general carnage of the Peninsular War (lxxxvii–xcii) the death of Byron's Harrow friend John Wingfield is lamented with love and unconscious irony:

> And thou, my friend!—since unavailing woe
>> Burst from my heart, and mingles with the strain—
>> Had the sword laid thee with the mighty low,
>> Pride might forbid e'en Friendship to complain:
>> But thus unlaurelled to descend in vain,
>> By all forgotten, save the lonely breast,
>> And mix unbleeding with the boasted slain,
>> While Glory crowns so many a meaner crest!
> What hadst thou done to sink so peacefully to rest?   (I, xci)

The irony is proleptic: Byron is to suffer the same fate of inglorious death by fever at Missolonghi.

'Dearly beloved Greece'

The magnificence of 'By all forgotten, save the lonely breast', is paralleled in a number of other great lines in Canto I:

> And Mammon wins his way where Seraphs might despair   (ix)

> And traverse Paynim shores, and pass Earth's central line   (xi)

> And Tagus dashing onward to the Deep,
> His fabled golden tribute bent to pay   (xiv)

> Swept into wrecks anon by Time's ungentle tide!   (xxiii)

which serve to alert us, if we bring them into focus with those earlier felicities of phrase I have noted in *Hours of Idleness*,[7] to Byron's growing depth and richness of perception. Those lines were delicate, crystalline, lyrical, moving in their own sphere of perfection. The delicacy and the lyricism persist in Canto I, but enormously strengthened and given resonance by the external and internal experiences of the Pilgrimage. The verse is beginning to soar. And with the actual embarcation on the Hellenic theme in Canto II this soaring quality, this 'lift', makes itself unmistakably felt. The dusty, landlocked vistas of Spain and Portugal are left behind. We enter a lucid, jewelled panorama of shining coves, towering mountains, temples crumbling yet potent in dignity and eloquence, mosques and cypresses and tombstones conveying the austere ferocity of

Islam. There is an element of enthusiasm, of love as distinguished from compassion, of personal involvement replacing the war correspondent's reportage, which enters the poem only with Canto II. In the first canto Byron is still the observer, sympathetic but somewhat detached, delighting in all that is new and strange, but still unable to shake off a mask of adolescent cynicism and boyish bravado. This speaks in the poem's opening stanza, with its anti-invocation. It is a measure of Byron's artistry that this address to the Muse, though couched in terms of Delphi, and though added to the poem as late as July–November 1811, is subtly adapted in its tone to the half-flippant picture of Harold at Newstead which immediately follows. The tone is not disrespectful—Byron could never be that about Delphi—but it is ironical and slightly debunking:

> Oh, thou! in Hellas *deemed* of heavenly birth,
>   Muse! *formed or fabled* at the Minstrel's will!
> Since *shamed full oft* by later lyres on earth,
>   Mine dares not call thee from thy sacred Hill:
> Yet there I've wandered by thy *vaunted* rill;
>   Yes! sighed o'er Delphi's long deserted shrine,
> Where, save *that feeble fountain*, all is still;
>   Nor mote my shell awake *the weary Nine*
> To grace so plain a tale—this lowly lay of mine.   (I, i)

The words and phrases I have italicised convey the deprecatory stance. And if any proof were needed that this is a deliberate exercise in 'the art of sinking' in artistic conformity to what follows, I would point to that 'mote my shell'. Byron had given up his Spenserianisms and conscious archaisms long before the conclusion of Canto I; he returns to them here only, with deliberate intent.

In quoting the first stanza of Canto I thus out of context it is with the wish to place it in critical contrast not only with the Parnassan stanzas just quoted but also, and even more forcibly, with the splendid invocation to Pallas Athene which opens Canto II. This begins quietly:

> Come, blue-eyed Maid of Heaven!—but Thou, alas!
>   Didst never yet one mortal song inspire—
> Goddess of Wisdom! here thy temple was,
>   And is, despite of War and wasting fire . . .

but takes on a tinge of indignation with the thought of 'men who never felt the sacred glow' of desire for knowledge—Byron's anti-Philistinism, the hatred of commercial values and cultural narrowness

which endeared him to Goethe and Arnold. Canto II is to be
above all the canto of freedom: of freedom both external, in Byron's
support for the aspiration of the oppressed Greeks to nationhood,
and internal, in his steady progress throughout the stanza towards
self-knowledge. Now the scattered apprehensions of Canto I are
replaced by a focused vision, the great ideograms emerge and
establish themselves in terms of shattered pediment and broken
column, of light Greek and grave Muslim, of lonely cypress and
sunlit bay. By 'ideograms' I mean crystallisations of a total and
generally a paradoxical situation. They are more than figures of
speech, and less than symbols. The symbol mediates the eternal to
the temporal; the ideogram gathers up the scattered facets of the
temporal in a dramatic gesture through words, stone, music or
painting. Byron habitually thought, or thought-felt, in ideograms,
when working at his intensest:

I stood in Venice, on the 'Bridge of Sighs'   (IV, i)

There is a stern round tower of other days   (IV, xcix)

There is a tomb in Arqua;—reared in air   (IV, xxx)

Through the (generally monosyllabic) formulation of the paradox[8]
(palace and prison, stern yet round, tomb and airy soaring) an
element of shock is obtained, while the reader remains unaware of
the technical sleights that are being performed upon him. But the
complexity of the ideogram does not stop there: it entails a fusion
of Byron with his environment, and to the degree it does this we
should, perhaps, reserve the word for Byronic contexts only; there
is nothing quite like what I call ideograms in the work of other
poets. This point will become clearer as we go along.

Apart from the figure of War in stanza xxxix and the bullring in
later stanzas, there are few ideograms in Byron's opening Canto. It
needed the catalytic agency of Greece and the Levant, 'the only
place he was ever contented in' (letter to Trelawny, 15 June 1823),
the countries with which 'all his really poetical feelings begin and
end' (letter to Moore, 8 March 1816), 'that land which it is an
honour even to have visited' (letter to Edward Blaquiere of the
London Greek Committee, 5 April 1823), to unlock Byron's unique
poetic potential, and make him into a writer of European stature.
In my first 'Writers and Their Work' essay[9] I saw this revelatory
power too exclusively in terms of Greece; this I redressed somewhat
in my second essay (pp. 22–3), where a 'marriage of atoning

gestures' between mosque and temple, cypress and olive, is recognised;[10] but the full extent of Byron's 'esemplastic' role in the Middle East became clear to me only when I was studying the material I later shaped into 'Byron and Islam: the triple Eros',[11] a paper which explores the love-power-wisdom complex in its Muslim ramifications.

Behind Canto II are the schoolrooms of Harrow and the cloisters of Trinity. It is the product of a classical education, of the grind at Latin and Greek, of that Horace whom, he declares later, 'I hated so' (IV, lxxvii). You may hate Horace, but it is not so easy to wave him away, once you have been exposed to him; he is there for the rest of your life, as are Virgil, Aeschylus and Plato, the ancient world won and lost at Actium, and

> the barren spot
> Where sad Penelope o'erlook'd the wave . . .   (II, xxxix)

As the Greek light penetrated the stones, that marvellous dry light that isolates as it connects, so too it entered Byron's storehouse of mental bric-à-brac, disinfecting here, cauterising there, putting paid to a number of psychic accounts, stimulating new energic currents. 'So this is what it was all about!', we can imagine him saying, his thought going back to Harrow and Cambridge when he reached Athens on Christmas Day 1809 and stood among the fallen columns of the Temple of Olympian Jove.

Coming to Athens from the north-west, via Cephalonia, Patras, Joannina, Tepelene, Missolonghi, Delphi, and Phyle, he was to some extent prepared for what it had to offer. But the special qualities of Attica are not anticipated in any other region of Greece, and they impinged on Byron with something of the force of a revelation. Behind the wretchedness of the Turkish village which sprawled around the Acropolis he was moved to divine the 'dear city of Cecrops'[12] and the groves of Plato and Aristotle; beyond these his vision moved in ever-widening circles to Marathon and Thermopylae and the islands. The chief imagination of Europe had found its home and its theme.

The result is startling. Gothic mists, Spenserian fantasies are swept away: Canto II opens with an impassioned but classically measured appeal to the goddess of Wisdom to aid him in achieving the ultimate goal of self-knowledge. Dwelling briefly on the pre-valence of unwisdom in a commercial age (Byron's approach here is very close to Blake's), he sweeps on to a dramatic contrast between 'men who never felt the sacred glow' and those 'grand in soul' who were the glory of Athens in old days:

> The Warrior's weapon and the Sophist's stole
> Are sought in vain, and o'er each mouldering tower,
> Dim with the mist of years, gray flits the shade of power.   (II, ii)

Note the intense visualisation here: it is not just a metaphor or a personification; here is the tower, in its crumbling immediacy, and here is the grey shadow, a visible if impalpable shape, 'flitting' like a bat between its pinnacles. This connective force, possessed by no other English poet except Shakespeare, informs the whole of the *Pilgrimage* from now on. Reading this poetry, we must be ceaselessly alert. We cannot settle down into the repose which, for instance, Keats's verse invites for its full reception; a repose in which the Keatsian physiograms, densely encapsulated seeds of meaning, sink down into our muddy and fecund depths, to unfold in dark passages and to re-emerge as articulate wisdom. For Byron, the wisdom must be there from the beginning: he is a classical poet, living in bright air, the air of columns, theatres, temples brilliant in the sun. Wisdom is *there* if we can but seize it, a heritage from the past, something to be recovered, not remade. Keats works, to put it crudely, in terms of roots, Byron in terms of columns. We can come to terms with Byron only when we have come to terms with the past.

Yet in coming to terms with the past we come to terms with ourselves in ways we hardly expect, for the past is our past, the dimensions opened up to us by Byron are our dimensions. 'No poet had ever seemed to speak to men so directly', Arthur Symons wrote, 'and it was through this directness of his vision of the world, and of his speech about it, that he became a poet, that he made a new thing out of poetry.' In what way Byron 'made a new thing out of poetry', something different from what Shakespeare and Homer had made, or Wordsworth and Shelley and Keats were making, is the subject of the present study. That he 'seems to speak to men so directly' in spite of speaking to them in terms of crumbling column and Turkish tomb, more directly (Symons implies) than Wordsworth with his bare self-opening or Keats with his lavish confessionalism, must depend on his skilful relation of these counters (tomb and column) to human existence everywhere. Byron's *is* a new poetry for it works through historical-topical-personal-universal dimensions towards a new catharsis, a new dissolution of personality in space-time, in history, through which the individual disappears, swamped in the great impersonal tides, and only the Great Man lives on, rediscovering himself from generation to generation. Such a view of history, however much it may have delighted Nietszche, is totally unacceptable to our own society, and we must expect a slump in Byron's stock (once the present trend cult of *Don Juan* is over) even more vertiginous than the Victorian. They hated him for his liberalism; we shall despise him for his traditionalism.

Canto II, then, is Byron's 'self-discovery' canto, and it is filled with this exhilarating sense of the new and the unexpected. It is bound together by the unifying power of the Greek sea which I shall have more to say about when I come to discuss the Turkish Tales. Seas and mountains are Byron's major emblems. Mountains are a bit stiff, a bit portentous: they do not *move*, and for Byron movement is life. They are very grand, and the Byronic scene could not get on without them, but they represent, in the inner panorama, aspiration rather than fulfilment. In a sense they are recalcitrant to Byron's imagination. He may, like the Prisoner of Chillon,

> . . . bend
> Once more, upon the mountains high
> The quiet of a loving eye,   (II, 330–1)

but do they *respond* to that love? Wordsworth did not want them to: he wanted the father figure, rather stiff, rather remote, threatening, punishing, keeping him in order. Byron needed something different, he had already had enough of Captain Byron, and as for Mrs Byron, she was best forgotten. The sea provided a marvellous complex fulfilling his needs on the figurative plane: masculine in its power, violence, authority; feminine in its beauty, languor, fecundity. In the Turkish Tales we do not know whether Zuleika, Leila and Medora are emblems of the sea or whether the sea is the totality of Medora, Leila and Zuleika. The mountain is barren, majestic, remote; identified to some extent with the hero himself, at least an ideal he can live up to, breathing its air of freedom (*Childe Harold*, II, lxxxvii), of release from the pettiness of sea-level concerns (this was a notion Byron bequeathed to Matthew Arnold), sharing its clinical, aseptic indifference. But never a father figure as with Wordsworth.

The opening stanzas of Canto II move through architectural symbolism (notice here how the skull image expands and contracts through the 'temple' metaphor from the 'enduring bone' of the human skeleton to the ruined columns among which Byron sits as he writes) to an indignant condemnation of Lord Elgin's depredations on the Parthenon (II, xi–xv). These stanzas are a sort of prologue to the 'action' of the poem, for stanza xvi brings us back to Harold, 'the gloomy wanderer', on his seaborne way to the Hellenic shore. In a sense stanzas xvi–xix are a farewell to the purely descriptive side of *Childe Harold*. They give us a well realised, bustling, extrovert view of life aboard ship; the detail is perfect, and interesting in its own right. But from now on there will be no more such objective descriptions. Greece changes all that. Greece introduces Byron to the new dimension of a time which is also eternity, of a space in which a terrible sun burns up the distinctions of *thine* and *mine*, of *here* and *there*, on which life is the shade cast by the olive tree, and survival the oil from its berries, stored up carefully against an 'unimaginable, zero' winter. For such winters also come, in these 'Edens of the eastern wave'.

The Greek vistas of Canto II are blended of earth and water: air exists as an abstract, as the medium through which actuality is viewed, not as a part of that actuality itself, since 'air' for Byron is freedom.[13] Air enters into the Venetian scene of the fourth canto, though Venice too is enslaved, through the powers of art, through music and through painting and architecture and sculpture in a sense *as* music, and thus exists in its own right together with 'the wat'ry floor' as the double paradigm: air/water on which the great ideograms of Canto IV are to be built. In Canto II, however, air is stressed only once, in the ironic paradox of the Hymettan bee, 'the free-born wanderer of thy mountain air' flitting unconcerned over enslaved Athens. So too in the exordium to *The Giaour*: 'no breath of air' breaks the wave 'That rolls below the Athenian's grave'. The great artefacts of Venice mock her Austrian oppressors and in this sense are invulnerable, like the ghost of Hamlet's father, 'like the air': Byron did not anticipate modern bombing. But in Greece 'fire' has died into 'earth', 'air' has died into 'water'. The indifference of the Giaour to the beauty of his surroundings is the necessary indifference of air and fire (cf. Hotspur and the Dauphin in Shakespeare) to the elements they are to redeem (I return to this point in my discussion of the Turkish Tales). In Canto II and in *The Giaour, The Corsair, The Bride of Abydos* we are in a crumbling world: 'Nature still is fair', but for the Byronic humanism (again like Shakespeare's, and Blake's: 'Where man is not, Nature is barren') there is no completion outside the human-natural nexus.

Byron is thoroughly eighteenth-century in seeing nature as a landscape *with* figures.

The figures in Canto II are unheroic. *The Giaour* was to redeem this, to some extent, but the full redemption could only come with the personal commitment of 1823. The tyrannical Turks come out best: at least they have dignity: 'Unmoved the Moslem sits, the light Greek carols by' (x). Stanza xxvii introduces an archetypal figure, the monk of Athos, expressing Byron's love of solitary musing, and beyond that of his feeling for another kind of commitment, the total surrender to otherworldly values:

> More blest the life of godly Eremite,
>   Such as on lonely Athos may be seen,
>   Watching at eve upon the Giant Height . . .   (II, xxvii)

This is a figure muted in the later poems (*Lara, The Corsair, Manfred*) but potent, one feels, within Byron's imagination: one can imagine him, as one cannot imagine any other of the great Romantics, settling for orthodoxy and the monastic life—'as a refuge from insanity', to quote Blake again. Against the Monk is set, in some fascinatingly realistic-romantic stanzas (lv–lxvi), the grimly colourful Ali Pasha (whose actuality comes out even better in the letters Byron wrote at this time, to his mother and others):

> It is not that yon hoary lengthening beard
>   Ill suits the passions that belong to Youth . . .
>   But crimes that scorn the tender voice of ruth,
>   Beseeming all men ill, but most the man
>   In years, have marked him with a tiger's tooth.   (II, lxiii)

Nevertheless, there is a human immediacy in Canto II that we miss in the other three cantos.[14] Greece brought him into relationship—with the Maid of Athens, Theresa Macri, with the Turkish girl whose adventure is celebrated in *The Giaour*, with a considerable group of Philhellenes in Athens. And also with a literature: Byron learned modern Greek and was sufficiently interested in its development to draw up some 'Remarks on the Romaic or modern Greek language', written in the spring of 1811, in which one may note his attraction to Greek ballad poetry.

'Oh! where, Dodona! is thine aged Grove?'

We can trace in the second Canto the beginnings of preoccupation with the City, which was to engage Byron in Canto IV, that roll call of ruined or ruinating cities. The contrast between the 'human city' whose 'hum' is 'torture'[15] and the divine city which even in ruins still lives as a 'grace dissolved in place' starts here, in Byron's lamentation over Athens. The human city is a mere dormitory for slaves; the divine city is founded by the god, or under his aegis: drawing its physical sustenance from the surrounding countryside, it spreads its intellectual beneficence and its protection over the land in return. I have already noted how curiously this very Byronic concept—curious, that is, among nineteenth-century writers—is adumbrated in the 'Ida' sections of 'Childish Recollections'.[16]

Athens is a city in ruins, as also is Rome, but so deeply impregnated by 'grace' that even in ruins she dominates the reaches of time. Venice is a city sinking into ruin which will eventually be total because, unlike the great classical centres, she has never attained the definitive charisma. The classical city arises in Primordial Time through the union of a god and a woman, or a man and a goddess. Romulus is the son of Mars and Ilia. Theseus is the son of Poseidon and Aethra; or, in an earlier account of the founding of Athens, its first king is Cecrops, 'an earth-born, primordial being, half man and half serpent'.[17] The city is a celebration, in the Rilkeian sense, since it is a great gathering together of the scattered divinities of woods and seas and mountains, just as Man is the fulcrum of the cosmos in displaying 'the scatter'd parts of Man's immortal body': it is the place of festival, or rather is a spatial festival: Venice *is* 'the revel of the earth, the Masque of Italy'. What we can still feel, in visiting ancient sites, is a paradigmatic approximation or identification: the apocryphal saying of Jesus, 'And ye are the City' expresses this. Temples, stoas, amphitheatres are gestures, or more correctly organs, in the total drama of celebration. The theatre of Dionysus below the Acropolis is not simply the locus of the dramas performed within it, like a modern cinema, but their stony skeleton (as an insect wears its skeleton on the outside): so too with the classical hippodrome and odeon.

In Canto II we have two focal cities, Athens, politically a spent force, and Constantinople or Istanbul, a force still alive but already disintegrating. In Canto I Byron had made a linear progress through the delightful but non-charismatic cities of Spain and Portugal, a bee flitting from flower to flower. There is no identification. He tastes, and passes on. In Canto II he 'hives', establishes himself in a centre, makes his sorties, returns with his honey. And because there are *two* centres, the Hellenic and the Ottoman, Athens and Istanbul, two poles as it were, which are both *foci* of an ellipse linking two worlds and the centres of opposed, self-contained circles, the resultant intersections of curves elliptical and circular set up a series of tensions metaphysical, ethnic, religious, aesthetic and personal which make this, to my mind, the most fascinating of all the Cantos. The great intersection of the circles is at Tepelene, in Ali Pasha's palace, at approximately midpoint of the Canto (stanzas lv–lxiv). I have already contrasted the figure of the 'godly eremite' of Athos, with the sinister ideogram of Ali Pasha (see above, p. 95); the ideogram becomes all the more complex when we learn that Ali was not only a bloodthirsty tyrant but also a Baba of the Bektashi order of dervishes.[18] Here power is 'lawless law' (xlvii), wisdom is 'the Muezzin's call' (lix), love is 'the shameless torch of wild desire' lit 'for boyish minions of unhallowed love' (in a cancelled stanza). None of this is rejected by Byron: indeed, he rejoices in its intricate patterning, its violence, its existential paradoxes. 'This is life!', one can hear him saying—and life how far removed from the Southwell tea-parties, from the cloisters of Nevile's Court or the London brothels! Here passions are lived without concealment, without shame and without dilution; life and death hang on the lifting of an eyebrow, the folding of a turban, the cadence of a flattering phrase.[19] It's hell for the Greeks, of course, as the bullring was hell for the bull; nevertheless it's *alive* as England and even Spain are not, it vibrates, and for Byron vibration is life.

That is one intersection: the parallax of 'power' with 'love', a Greco-Turkish syndrome. It stands midway between the eremitical, pastoral simplicities of 'monastic Zitza' (xlviii), which Byron and Hobhouse visited after leaving Joannina on 11 October, and 'Where lone Utraikey forms its circling cove' (lxx), a scene of barbaric, even orgiastic abandon to the Dionysan element. Zitza focuses the reflective ethos of the poem, Loutraki its delight in violence and rapine. It is as though Tepelene is a prism through which Byron passes as white light to emerge on the other side as the motley monster we now know him as. This is not a book of Byron gossip, and least of all of Byron sexual gossip; nevertheless the 'white light, still and moving' of the Zitza theophany, the sense of 'pure pleasure' for 'the loitering pilgrim' to be caught from this 'small, but favoured spot of holy ground' (xlviii), his aesthetic delight in 'the little shepherd in his white capote' who 'Doth lean his boyish form along the rock' as perhaps Edleston, that 'violent but pure passion', posed

against the grey chapel walls of Trinity, and the way in which all
these things passed, after the Tepelene revelation, into what
Hobhouse at least saw as the unrestrained paederasty of the later
tour, is something which should give us pause, not as moralists, but
as interpreters of Byron's poetry in the context of his life. In this
reading Zitza was Byron's last moment of 'pure pleasure', of the
self-regardless aesthetic preception, until the moment in 1814 when
'the beautiful Mrs Wilmot' walked in beauty, like the night, at a
London ball.

Zitza is pure contemplation, or wisdom-love; Tepelene is power-
wisdom-love of a very peculiar sort; Loutraki is power-love without
a drop of wisdom. We move from circle to circle. Zitza, a mountain
retreat, focuses the circle we look down on:

> Dusky and huge, enlarging on the sight,
>   Nature's volcanic Amphitheatre,
>   Chimaera's Alps extend from left to right:
>   Beneath, a living valley seems to stir.   (II, li)

Through or under the shadow of 'Chimaera's Alps'—the delusive
overtones of 'Chimaera' would not be lost on Byron—we descend to
Tepelene, but not without a lament for Dodona, for the guidance of
ancient wisdom:

> Oh! where, Dodona! is thine aged Grove,
>   Prophetic Fount, and Oracle divine?   (II, liii)

Oddly enough, Byron and Hobhouse were upon the very site of
Dodona, excavated many years later, as these lines were conceived.
But, '*Tired of upgazing still*' (my italics) 'the wearied eye/Reposes
gladly on as smooth a vale/As ever . . .'—and one may complete
Byron's stanza with almost any parallel passage from Spenser or
Bunyan. They descend into the Bower of Bliss, where

> Richly caparisoned, a ready row
>   Of arméd horse, and many a warlike store,
>   Circled the wide-extending court below.   (II, lvi i)

The circular or circled court includes a rich diversity of types:
'Slaves, eunuchs, soldiers, guests, and santons wait' (II, lvi), and
nationalities:

> Some high-capped Tartar spurred his steed away;
>   The Turk—the Greek—the Albanian—and the Moor,
>   Here mingled in their many-hued array,
>   While the deep war-drum's sound announced the close of day.
>   (II, lvii)

It is a little world indeed; and at the centre of the web, the spider Ali.

Byron's picture of the Pasha is the paradigm of 'lawless law'. He sits as the focus of a great circle which touches Athens at one point of its circumference and the Sublime Porte at the other. His actual rule extends to a much lesser circle within that great circle. But he is always trying to extend his web. He is the Napoleon of Canto II. In any attempt to assess the nature and the scope of Byron's Titanism this first potent exemplar deserves special study.

Nor does Ali's personal aura, as distinct from his political or military, terminate with the confines of Joannina or Tepelene. It extends throughout the whole of northern Greece. His 'savage virtues' of courage, determination and hospitality are shared by 'all the sons of the mountain', and by none more than the 'dark Suliotes' into whose hands Byron and Hobhouse fell when driven by 'adverse winds' on 14 November 1809 'Full on the coast of Suli's shaggy shore' (lxvii). It is important, in reading *Childe Harold*, to keep in mind these moments of actual danger, unknown to the conventional Grand Tourist, and Byron's delighted reaction to them. His classical enthusiasm for Greece is only one side of the picture. The lover of proportion, of an elegance 'Simple, severe, erect, austere, sublime' in the Pantheon (IV, cxlvi), is constantly balanced by the lover of excess, of the unconditioned, the savage, the spontaneous, the unpredictable. Thus his regret for the past glories of Greece, his indignation at the oppression of modern Greeks, is tempered by an appreciation of the life and colour brought into the marmoreal schoolroom presentation by the urgent, violent, and creative present. Creative, for in such incidents as the dance at Loutraki (Utraikey) celebrated in stanzas lxx–lxxii, with the war song which follows them, Byron sensed the same genesis of 'traditional story' as he had noted in the schoolboy sagas of Harrow.

The natural 'circle' of Loutraki forms an antithetic frame of serenity and gentleness to the barbaric, violent circle of the Suliotes' dance:

> Where lone Utraikey forms its circling cove,
>   And weary waves retire to gleam at rest,
>   How brown the foliage of the green hill's grove,
>   Nodding at midnight o'er the calm bay's breast,
>   As winds come lightly whispering from the West,
>   Kissing, not ruffling, the blue deep's serene:—
>   Here Harold was received a welcome guest;
>   Nor did he pass unmoved the gentle scene,
> For many a joy could he from Night's soft presence glean.

> On the smooth shore the night-fires brightly blazed,
>   The feast was done, the red wine circling fast,
>   And he that unawares had there ygazed
>   With gaping wonderment had stared aghast;
>   For ere night's midmost, stillest hour was past,
>   The native revels of the troop began;
>   Each Palikar his sabre from him cast,
>   And bounding hand in hand, man linked to man,
> Yelling their uncouth dirge, long daunced the kirtled clan.

(II, lxx–lxxi)

'The kirtled clan' carries us unmistakably back to the Highlands.
And if we ask why Byron reverts at this late stage in *Childe Harold* to
the Spenserian archaisms of the early Canto I, the answer cannot,
plainly, be in terms of a failure of original impulse: here, if anywhere in the poem, Byron is writing from an experience deeply felt.
To understand what he is doing we have to turn to that later poet
with whom I have had so frequently to compare him, and remember
in 'East Coker'

> The association of man and woman
> In daunsinge, signifying matrimonie—
> A dignified and commodious sacrament.
> Two and two, necessarye coniunction,
> Holding eche other by the hand or the arm . . .

With the Loutraki dance and the Suliote warsong this second
Canto ended, in Byron's original MS. But so abrupt a conclusion
is alien to the reconciling ethos of the whole poem; the great threnos
on Greece, 'sad relic of departed Worth', is an indispensable coda
to this extraordinary 'quartet' of classical, modern, Muslim and
Christian themes. As always with Byron, we return not nostalgically
but positively, creatively, to a past which *still lives* in its natural and
artistic matrices, and which can be revitalised by self-sacrifice and
understanding. Across his MS of stanza lxxiii—

> Fair Greece, sad relic[20] of departed Worth!
>   Immortal, though no more; though fallen, great!
>   Who now shall lead thy scattered children forth,
>   And long accustomed bondage uncreate?
>   Not such thy sons who whilome did await,
>   The helpless warriors of a willing doom,
>   In bleak Thermopylae's sepulchral strait—
>   Oh! who that gallant spirit shall resume,
> Leap from Eurotas' banks, and call thee from the tomb?

—Byron three times scribbled his own name. The gesture may be
seen as one of megalomania, or of dedication. The proof of the

pudding was very definitely in the eating. Byron died for his scrawl.

'Unmoved the Moslem sits, the light Greek carols by'

From enslaved Greece Byron moves on, in stanzas lxxvii–lxxxii, to a rapid evocation of enslaving Istanbul, where he spent two months with Hobhouse from 13 May to 14 July 1810. As always in his contrasts of Greek and Turk, it is the Hellenic levity which he stresses, the acceptance of servility so long as conditions are not too harsh. Since *Childe Harold* is self-discovery through self-criticism as well as through expansion, we may suspect a shrewd bit of psychiatry here: in the Greco-Turkish antithesis Byron is exposing the hidden nerves of his own agon. The second 'great Lent' of the Orthodox Church, beginning on the first Monday after Trinity, and ending on the 29 June, is preceded by a carnival:

> Loud was the lightsome tumult on the shore,
>   Oft Music changed, but never ceased her tone,
>   And timely echoed back the measured oar,
>   And rippling waters made a pleasant moan:
>   The Queen of tides on high consenting shone,
>   And when a transient breeze swept o'er the wave,
>   'Twas, as if darting from her heavenly throne,
>   A brighter glance her form reflected gave,
> Till sparkling billows seemed to light the banks they lave.
>
> (II, lxxx)

Note the closeness of the phenomenal observation there—not detached and dramatised as Wordsworth, or Shelley, would have presented it, but playing its ironic role among the human contexts: 'The Queen of tides on high *consenting* shone'; and under that aegis 'the *lightsome* tumult on the shore', the *changing* Music, the *measured* oar, the *rippling* waters, and the *transient* breeze, all combine into a synaesthetic symphony to which one might give the programme note of 'Disgrace dissolved in place', a velleity which is almost excused by its charm: but not quite:

> But, midst the throng in merry masquerade,
>   Lurk there no hearts that throb with secret pain,
>   Even through the closest searment half betrayed?
>   To such the gentle murmurs of the main
>   Seem to re-echo all they mourn in vain.
>
> (II, lxxxii)

For the conscious of slavery the echoes persist, but with a mournful, not a merry resonance. 'Even through the closest searment',[21] the scars of wellnigh four hundred years, they feel the secret pain of lost liberty, of ancient shrines standing but usurped by an alien faith. Once again we note Byron's uncanny quality of self-identification, of empathy with the here-and-now in its contrapuntal anguish or delight. Patterns are never imposed: the poet opens himself to the here-and-now as simple recorder or resonator. As recorder he gives us the facts, as resonator he gives us his responses to the facts—but his responses as poet, never as 'philosopher', never in terms of a 'system'.

The transition now is inevitable to the poem's grand finale, the Hymettan apocalypse which occupies stanzas lxxxiv–xciii. I have discussed this part of the Canto in considerable detail elsewhere[22] and my present remarks can be no more than a summary with some filling-up of gaps. Byron is back in Attica (on his own now, having parted from the England-bound Hobhouse on 17 July 1810, off Keos) and the great music of the first fifteen stanzas is resumed. But with a difference. Those opening stanzas were nostalgic, bitter, despairing, lifted to sublimity only by the memory of past glories. These closing stanzas are also mournful, but at the same time curiously buoyant and filled with light and life. The opening stanzas were city-bound, reflecting Byron's mournful sense of the decay of cultures:

> Ancient of days! august Athena! where
> Where are thy men of might? thy grand in soul?
> Gone—glimmering through the dream of things that were:
> First in the race that led to Glory's goal
> They won, and passed away—is this the whole?
> A schoolboy's tale, the wonder of an hour?
> The Warrior's weapon and the Sophist's stole
> Are sought in vain, and o'er each mouldering tower,
> Dim with the mist of years, gray flits the shade of power.   (II, ii)

The men of might, the ancient warriors, and the grand in soul, the sophists or philosophers, are no longer to be found in enslaved Athens. The shade of power flitting batlike over the mouldering towers reintroduces the Ossianic note. In the sustained meditation on the skull that follows (iii–viii) Byron recalls Hamlet and his own early skull poem (above, p. 62), expanding his Newstead intuitions of death and time to take in the whole panorama of history revealed to him by his travels:

Remove yon skull from out the scattered heaps:
  Is that a Temple where a God may dwell?
Why ev'n the Worm at last disdains her shattered cell!

Look on its broken arch, its ruined wall,
  Its chambers desolate, and portals foul:
  Yes, this was once Ambition's airy hall,
  The Dome of Thought, the Palace of the Soul:
  Behold through each lack-lustre, eyeless hole,
  The gay recess of Wisdom and of Wit
  And Passion's host, that never brooked control:
  Can all Saint, Sage, or Sophist ever writ,
People this lonely tower, this tenement refit?   (II, v–vi)

Standing in the *temenos* of the great Temple of Olympian Jove,
looking up to the even more central Temple of Pallas Athena which
crowns the Acropolis, caught between horizontal and vertical
dimensions of power and wisdom in decay, Byron brilliantly extra-
polates from the skull he holds in his hand to the shattered towers and
pillars he sees above and around him. From this despairing stance
he flows out into the highways and byways of enslaved Greece,
tasting the perversions of power and love in the court of Ali Pasha
and the mountain strongholds of the wild Suliotes, the decay of
wisdom in the Orthodox monasteries and the *tekkes* of dervishes, but
coming finally to rest in the Hymettan stanzas which bring the
Canto, in its original form, to a close.

It is from the Constantinopolitan evocation that we swing into
this marvellous epiphany, from 'the lightsome tumult on the shore',
human life at sea-level, up to the wild crags of Hymettus and its
humming bees. Enslaved Athens lies below, but the soul of Greece
persists in its 'heroic earth' (lxxxv) and its still existent monuments—
'some solitary column', 'Tritonia's airy shrine', 'some warrior's
half-forgotten grave'

Where the gray stones and unmolested grass
Ages, but not Oblivion, feebly brave   (II, lxxxvi)

—and how Byronic that *concern* for the grass and the grey stones, that
recognition of strength in weakness, the Pauline paradox, in the
oxymoron 'feebly brave'! But better still is to come in the complex
semantics of stanza lxxxvii. The lines are penetrated by an admiring
compassion:

Yet are thy skies as blue, thy crags as wild;
  Sweet are thy groves, and verdant are thy fields,
  Thine olive ripe as when Minerva smiled,
  And still his honied wealth Hymettus yields;

> There the blithe Bee his fragrant fortress builds,
> The free-born wanderer of thy mountain-air;
> Apollo still thy long, long summer gilds,
> Still in his beams Mendeli's marbles glare:
> Art, Glory, Freedom fail, but Nature still is fair.   (II, lxxxvii)

It is the Greek earth itself which now functions as the repository of ancient and the matrix of modern heroism; the blithe Bee, symbol of Apollo's solar benevolence, hives the golden essence of Hymettan flowers, the honey of health and wisdom; love glows in the self-giving of Minerva's olive, offering her abundant oil out of the rocks and stony soil.

In stanzas lxxxvii–xciii we slowly descend from the mountain—which may be called, in Christian terms, Byron's Mount of Transfiguration—to the plains and their human problems. These problems are indigenous, rooted in Hellenic history, and to Byron and Hobhouse in 1810 appeared virtually insoluble. But each traveller brings his own problems with him, and may find them resolved in 'this consecrated Land', this 'magic waste' (xciii). Greece is the homeland of the soul:

> He that is lonely—hither let him roam,
> And gaze complacent on congenial earth.
> Greece is no lightsome land of social mirth:
> But he whom Sadness sootheth may abide,
> And scarce regret the region of his birth,
> When wandering slow by Delphi's sacred side,
> Or gazing o'er the plains where Greek and Persian died.   (II, xcii)

Thus Delphi rounds off the whole Canto (the original MS closes here) with a reassertion of 'this grace dissolved in place'. A 'waste land', yes, but 'Come in under the shadow of this red rock': for the lonely heart Greece offers the benediction of her solitude, her divine austerity.

Ironically, it was outside the healing region of Greece, back in what I have called 'the glooms and glumpiness of Newstead, Cambridge and London',[23] that Byron was to suffer the series of hammer-blows which reduced him from the poised, compassionate witness and participant of *la condition humaine*, the vatic role of the representative poet, to the shattered 'Baby Byron' who turned in his anguish to Hobhouse, Scrope Davies, Augusta—and finally, and most disastrously, to Annabella—for sympathy and support. All this belongs to my next chapter, and so too, in the order of time, do the four anguished stanzas on the death of Edleston which bring the

Canto to its close. Yet artistically their fitness to end Canto II is unassailable: it is with consummate art that Byron modulates from the threnos over his great topical to his great personal love—

> Thou too art gone, thou loved and lovely one!
>   Whom Youth and Youth's affections bound to me;
>   Who did for me what none beside have done,
>   Nor shrank from one albeit unworthy thee.
>   What is my Being? thou hast ceased to be!
>   Nor staid to welcome here thy wanderer home . . .

Edleston is 'Eden Lost' (the anagram cannot have failed to register in Byron's inveterately punning brain), Penelope's web finally woven by the hand of death, and Byron already anticipates a resumption of his Odyssey:

> Nor staid to welcome here thy wanderer home,
>   Who mourns o'er hours which we no more shall see—
>   Would they had never been, or were to come!
> Would he had ne'er returned to find fresh cause to roam!
>
> (II, xcv)

The extent to which Byron felt-thought Greece through the Edleston prism is made abundantly clear in the later interpolations he makes into the text of threnodic passages connecting the inner with the outer loneliness and dereliction. This is the last of them; the earlier

> There, Thou!—whose Love and Life together fled,
> Have left me here to love and live in vain—   (II, ix)

fixes the Edleston focus as firmly on the initial Minerva/Athens situation as this does on the Apollo/Hymettus.[24] The central episode of 'monastic Zitza' with its white walls 'glistening fair on high' and its 'little shepherd in his white capote' was conceived before he knew of Edleston's death, but it is as potent and as revealing as the others.

Notes and references

1   It is from 'an abyss of Sensuality' that Byron flees in 1808 (letter of 27 February 1808 to Hobhouse).

2   This lyric, coming after stanza lxxxvi, is replaced in the published version by the mournful 'To Inez' (after stanza lxxxiv).

3   For Byron's imagery of circles, see below, p. 163.

4   Byron began writing *Childe Harold* at Joannina (Yannina) on 31

October 1809. The second Canto was finished on 28 March 1810, at Smyrna.

5   Cf. Callimachus, *Hymn to Apollo*: 'Whoever has seen Apollo, he is great; who has not seen him, he is of low condition.'

6   Cf. Callimachus again: 'Hushed as is even the sea when the minstrels celebrate the lyre or the bow.'

7   See above, p. 28.

8   It is fashionable to talk of Byron's 'rhetoric', but even if we free the word of its pejorative associations, it is still important to note how many of the greatest of his effects are secured by a phraseology as austere as Dante's.

9   *Byron: Lyric and Romance*, Longman, 1970.

10   See above, pp. 58–60, where these pages are incorporated.

11   *Journal of European Studies*, December 1974, pp. 325–63.

12   Quoted by Marcus Aurelius (*Meditations*, iv, 23) from an unknown source.

13   It is in Canto II that the Heraclitean structure of *Childe Harold* first becomes apparent. The quadripartite schema of the poem has curious affinities with Eliot's *Four Quartets*, which is based on Heracleitus' thesis of the 'dying' or transmutation of elements the one into the other. Byron's Cantos are as definitely, though probably not as consciously, Heraclitean. The poem has a cyclic structure. 'Fire lives the death of air, and air lives the death of fire; water lives the death of earth, earth that of water' (*On the Universe*, XXV). Thus in Canto I the dominant elements are earth and fire. Fire dies into earth, in war and the bullring. In Canto II, predominantly earth and water, fire is 'dead', but reappears together with water in Canto III, while Canto IV gathers up the whole quartet into fiery, airy, earthy and liquid patterns of art, architecture and human life hitherto unattempted. Both Byron's and Eliot's poem mediate that 'grace dissolved in place' focused in the latter's 'Marina', 'The point of intersection of the timeless/With time' of 'The Dry Salvages' at certain climactic *loci*, 'places which are also the world's end' ('Little Gidding'). It is odd that Eliot, who did something to reinstate the prestige of Byron's 'Tales', should have turned a cold shoulder on *Childe Harold*.

14   Byron in 1816 preferred the third to the first two Cantos (*LJ* iv, 46. See also *LJ* iv, 49).

15   Arriving at Ali's court in Joannina on 5 October 1809, Byron may well have remembered that speculation in Rycaut's *The Present State of the Ottoman Empire* (1668), which he had read before he was ten, that without terror and the constant menace of the death penalty 'this mighty body would burst with the poyson of its own ill humors, and soon divide itself into several Signories, as the ambition and power of the Governours most remote from the Imperial Seat administred them hopes and security of becoming absolute' (ch. 2). In terms of one of the themes of the present book, that of integration/disintegration, this reference has its relevance.

16   See above, p. 35.

17 Cf. C. Kerenyi, *The Gods of the Greeks* (Thames & Hudson, 1951), p. 124.

18 See my 'Byron and Islam', *loc. cit.*, for the facts establishing this.

19 R. A. Davenport's *The Life of Ali Pasha*, London 1837, gives an exhaustive account of the vizier and his peculiar *moeurs*.

20 Byron originally wrote 'sad mother', but probably his memories of an actual mother prompted him to substitute 'relic'. It is not until the writing of the Rome stanzas of Canto IV, long after the recollection of Mrs Byron had receded into the kindly mists of time, that Byron can address a metropolitan matrix as 'City of the soul!'

21 E. H. Coleridge notes that 'It has been assumed that "searment" is an incorrect form of "cerement" . . . but the sense of the passage seems rather to point to "cerecloth", "searcloth", a plaster to cover up a wound' (*PW* ii, 154n). The form 'searcloth' is not listed in the Oxford dictionary; I take Byron to be intending a pun on 'cere/sear', on the cauterisation which seals off areas of pain which still continue to exist under the surface—Eliot's 'inveterate scars' in 'Burnt Norton' which appease 'long forgotten wars'.

22 *In Yearbook of English Studies* vol. iv, 1974, pp. 172–189.

23 See above, p. 54.

24 This interpolation is conveyed in a letter of 14 October 1811 to Dallas.

Part Two

THE GULF
AND THE FOUNTAIN

5

THE
TURKISH TALES

Byron returned from the Levant on 14 July 1811, to plunge almost at once into a scene of doubt and despondency. His mother died on 1 August, before he had time to reach Newstead; bitterly as he resented her tyranny, his memory of her had become mellowed by time and travel, and he remembered Cowper's words, 'We have only one mother'. This blow was followed swiftly by another, the death of his Cambridge friend Charles Skinner Matthews, drowned in the Cam on 3 August. In October he received the news of Edleston's death in the preceding May. A letter to his cousin Dallas is eloquent of his state of mind at this time:

I have been again shocked with a *death*, and have lost one very dear to me in happier times; but 'I have almost forgot the taste of grief', and 'supped full of horrors' till I have become callous, nor have I a tear left for an event which, five years ago, would have bowed down my head to the earth. It seems as though I were to experience in my youth the greatest misery of age. My friends fall around me, and I shall be left a lonely tree before I am withered. Other men can always take refuge in their families; I have no resource but my own reflections. . . . I am indeed very wretched, and you will excuse my saying so, as you know I am not apt to cant of sensibility.

We note the *Macbeth* references here: more and more in this transitional period of his life does Byron turn to Shakespeare,[1] and particularly to the four great tragedies, as though to a pre-existent pattern of his own suffering which affords him both self-expression and catharsis.

Byron's state at Newstead was desolate indeed in the late summer of 1811. For the first and last time in his life we find him calling out for help. 'Some curse hangs over me and mine', he writes to his friend Scrope Davies on 7 August, 'My mother lies a corpse in this house; one of my best friends is drowned in a ditch. . . . Come to me, Scrope, I am almost desolate—left almost alone in the world—I had but you, and H[obhouse], and M[atthews], and let me enjoy the survivors whilst I can.' He makes his will, quotes the Greek original of 'Whom the gods love die young' in a letter to Francis Hodgson of 3 September, and doubts the immortality of the soul. Nevertheless, the fact that he has recovered sufficiently to argue with Hodgson about the respective merits of Mussulmans, Talapoins and Bonzes as against an Anglican 'fox-hunting curate' is a sign of returning good spirits. His complicated financial affairs engross him, and there is the fate of *Hints from Horace*, which he had handed over to Dallas for publication, to be considered. Dallas read it and was disappointed. It lacked, he thought, the vigour and the wit of *English Bards and Scotch Reviewers*. Had Byron nothing else to show for the fruits of his travels? Diffidently, according to Dallas, Byron gave him the MS of *Childe Harold's Pilgrimage*. Dallas read it and was delighted.

As every schoolboy knows, Byron awoke on a March morning of 1812 to find himself famous. He stepped at one stride into the position of pre-eminence in not only English but European letters which he was to maintain to the end of his career. The literary, psychological and personal causes for this triumph have been endlessly analysed, and need not detain us here. The social consequences for the desolate and insecure young lord were cataclysmic: he became at once the idol of London high society. At Holland House, the centre of Whig society at this time, he was accepted into a brilliant circle not only of the great Whig families but also of a literary cenacle which included Moore and Rogers. At yet another social centre, Melbourne House, Byron first met Lady Caroline Lamb, with whom he was to have the most notorious of his London affaires, and Annabella Milbanke, the cousin of Lady Caroline's husband William Lamb, whom he was to marry in 1814. These data belong to the field of Byron biography—I had almost said Byron gossip—and concern us no further than they provide a frame for his writing.

Despite his literary and social success, Byron was not happy. I have given reasons in 'Byron and Islam'[2] for thinking that Byron had made resolutions while in the Levant for a radical reform of his way of living which were unfortunately frustrated by the success which came to him almost unsought, certainly unexpected. The 'fashionable dissipation' which he had rejected on leaving England for the East, the 'abyss of sensuality' from which he had extricated himself, return upon him now in double measure.[3] His turning to marriage, and especially to marriage with a woman so obviously unsuited to him as Miss Milbanke, was a desperate remedy for what he considered to be his disease of inconstancy and unrooted-ness.[4] A postscript in a letter to her of 20 October 1814 is ominous:

Those who know me most intimately can tell you that I am if anything too childish, with a greater turn for the ridiculous than for anything serious,— and, I could hope, not very ill natured off the stage, and, if angry, never loud. I can't say much for these qualifications, but I have such a regard for yours, that I am sure we shall be a very happy couple. I wish you had a greater passion for governing, for I don't shine in conducting myself, and am very docile with a gentle guide.

An invitation to disaster if ever there was one! The stiff and starchy Miss Milbanke would take the concluding 'wish' very seriously indeed, and pay no attention whatever to the opening confession of childishness, in which Byron is saying 'At least with you I shan't have to go on being Childe Harold!'

There was one being on whom Byron could always count to guide him 'gently' and laugh him out of his fits of spleen and his egotistic absurdities. Augusta, the half-sister he had scarcely met in his boyhood, and who was now married to the unsatisfactory and irresponsible Colonel George Leigh, re-entered Byron's life in 1813 and became thereafter its emotional centre. A perfect understanding existed between the two: while revering her brother's intellectual and poetic eminence, he was always 'Baby Byron' for her as she was 'Goose' for him: they would joke together, quarrel, make it up, and in the end Byron would always find himself being 'guided' by her shrewd but never obtrusive common-sense. What he is saying to Annabella in the letter quoted above is 'Be an Augusta to me!', but of course she couldn't. No one could: but among the scores of brainless debutantes who thronged around Byron in those 'years of fame' he would not have found it difficult to choose a bride better suited to him than the mathematical Miss Milbanke.

Byron married Annabella on 2 January 1815, but before this a number of events significant for his life and work occurred. He made his maiden speech in the House of Lords on 27 February 1812, a brilliant and violent diatribe on behalf of the Nottingham weavers against the Framework Bill which sought to impose the death penalty for frame-breaking. This, with his second speech of 12 April on the Catholic Claims Bill, established him as the 'radical peer', deeply committed to the defence of liberty. The immense success of *Childe*

Harold's Pilgrimage and the ensuing financial profits for its publisher, John Murray, meant that anything he might now care to write was certain of publication provided it did not infringe the recognised code of political and religious conformity. What he did write and publish were the 'Turkish Tales', between 1814 and 1816, which had an even greater success than *Childe Harold*, and brought even greater rewards financial and reputational. The Tales project a medley of personal and impersonal, Oriental and English experiences whose exact proportions must always, probably, remain a mystery. We know that at the time of their writing he had entered an almost certainly incestuous relationship with Augusta; his affaires with Lady Caroline Lamb, Lady Oxford and others continued; and his nights were made hideous by a series of nightmares whose scenario seems to have been laid in the Levant of 1809–11. Typical entries in his 'Journal, Begun November 14, 1813' are these:

No more reflections.—Let me see—last night I finished 'Zuleika', my second Turkish Tale. I believe the composition of it kept me alive—for it was written to drive my thoughts from the recollection of

> *Dear sacred name, rest ever unreveal'd.*

At least, even here, my hand would tremble to write it. (14 November)

It ['Zuleika', later called *The Bride of Abydos*] was written in four nights to distract my dreams from—Were it not thus, it had never been composed; and had I not done something at that time, I must have gone mad, by eating my own heart—bitter diet. (16 November)

I awoke from a dream!—well! and have not others dreamed?—Such a dream!—but she did not overtake me. I wish the dead would rest, however. Ugh! how my blood chilled—and I could not wake—and—and—heigho!

> Shadows tonight
> Have struck more terrors to the soul of Richard,
> Than could the substance of ten thousand ———s,
> Arm'd all in proof, and led by shallow ———.

I do not like this dream—I hate its 'foregone conclusion'. And am I to be shaken by shadows? Ay, when they remind us of—no matter—but, if I dream thus again, I will try whether *all* sleep has the like visions.[5]

I must not dream again;—it spoils even reality. I will go out of doors, and see what the fog will do for me. (23 November)

No dreams last night of the dead, nor the living; so—I am 'firm as the marble, founded as the rock', till the next earthquake. (24 November)

Went to bed, and slept dreamlessly, but not refreshingly. (7 December)

I am too lazy to shoot myself—and it would annoy Augusta. (10 December)

A wife would be my salvation. (16 January 1814)

Went to Waites [his dentist]. Teeth are all right and white; but he says that I grind them in my sleep and chip the edges. That same sleep is no friend of mine. (19 February)

Heighho! I would I were in mine island!—I am not well; and yet I look in good health. At times, I fear, 'I am not in my perfect mind';—and yet my heart and head have stood many a crash, and what should ail them now? They prey upon themselves, and I am sick—sick—'Prithee, undo this button—why should a cat, a rat, a dog have life—and *thou* no life at all?' Six-and-twenty years, as they call them, why, I might and should have been a Pasha by this time. 'I 'gin to be a-weary of the sun.' (27 February)

Hobhouse told me an odd report—that *I* am the actual Conrad, the veritable Corsair, and that part of my travels are supposed to have passed in privacy [piracy?]. Um!—people sometimes hit near the truth; but never the whole truth. H. don't know what I was about the year after he left the Levant; nor does any one—nor—nor—nor—however, it is a lie—but, 'I doubt the equivocation of the fiend that lies like truth!' (10 March)

My heart begins to eat *itself* again. (28 March)

There is ice at both poles, north and south—all extremes are the same. . . . To be sure, I have long despised myself and man, but I never spat in the face of my species before—'O fool! I shall go mad!' (19 April)

And there the Journal ends. It should be read in its entirety for this crucial hinge period of Byron's life. I have extracted only the shortest and most telling entries: piece them together, and some sort of story seems to emerge. It is a warp and woof, made up of terror of the dead and remorse for the living (entry of 24 November). The living victim is certainly Augusta—*Manfred* is to make that clear; but the dead is projected for us only in a series of fictional heroines in the Tales—Leila, Medora, Gulnare, Kaled, Zuleika, Francesca, Parisina—who seem to combine features of Augusta with bolder traits of some Levantine girl who died in circumstances of horror for which Byron holds himself responsible. Byron was a dab hand at red herrings, and his own carefully tailored 'revelations' about the episode, including the solemn affidavit he obtained from the un-suspecting Lord Sligo,[6] must have afforded him some amusement in the intervals between the nightmares. The Tales themselves tell a story we can only partly decipher.

'The Mind, that broods o'er guilty woes'

The original Turkish Tales are five in number: *The Giaour* (1813), *The Bride of Abydos* (1813), *The Corsair* (1814), *Lara* (1814), *The Siege of Corinth* (1816). They were followed by three more Tales which are not linked to the Eastern scene: *The Prisoner of Chillon* (1816), *Parisina* (1816), *and Mazeppa* (1819). They are all extrapolations of what we might call the energic component of Byron which could not find expression in the meditative structures of Cantos II and IV of *Childe Harold*. For Byron, poetry is basically a projection, the verbal sloughing off of what cannot be put into action; yet such a projection can itself be a new life form, a creation existing alongside the poet, as it were (cf. *Childe Harold* III, vi). These Tales embody a 'romantic' element which Byron sensed had to be eliminated before he could pass on to the 'metaphysics' (his own word) of Canto III and the 'hypostatics' (my word, meaning a fusion of human and non-human *personae*) of Canto IV.

In the Tales we are in Nietzsche's world, not Spinoza's: here power is law, and the satisfaction of passion brushes every other consideration aside. The surface effect is melodrama. As characters, the *dramatis personae* of these Tales can hardly be said to exist, and the plots are extravagant. Yet the total effect is not negligible. All the Tales express obsession with the Fall; all the heroes are variations on Adam, Cain, the Scapegoat, the Wandering Jew. In these melodramas 'The wandering outlaw of his own dark mind' works out his complex destiny. Freedom is the apple with which Gulnare tempts Conrad in *The Corsair*; in *Lara*, its sequel, the guilty pair are exiled from their eastern Eden. The Cain–Abel drama is re-enacted in the murder of Ezzelin. A Fall–Redemption pattern links all the Tales, though it is inconclusive: we may see it as bliss-danger-disaster-rescue-counterperil, Byron's 'cynicism' rejecting a happy ending. And though all these dramas except *Lara* are sited in the Greek scene (and even *Lara* is related to it), we miss certain of the resonances of *Childe Harold*, what I might call the eternity dimension. We are given brilliant and indeed moving descriptions of landscape and seascape, but these are emotionally unrelated to the human action, which is seen as incompatible with its setting (*The Giaour*, lines 46–67). These 'Edens of the eastern wave' have been desecrated by human guilt, and the gates to their enjoyment are closed, 'With dreadful faces thronged and fiery arms'. The ethos of *Paradise Lost* is pervasively present, curiously combined with that of Dante— 'that gentleness in Dante beyond all gentleness', as Byron perceptively notes in his Journal for 29 January 1821—'who *but* Dante could have introduced any 'gentleness' at all into *Hell*?' Here too, in the Tales, are adumbrations of those Dantesque circles, 'bolges', whirlpools of narrowing and deepening guilt, which are to constitute the very structure of *Don Juan*. That the fiery vortex is the basic Byronic ideogram is a point I have already made: in a celebrated passage of *The Giaour* which is strikingly similar to section IV of 'Little Gidding', the 'whirling gulf of phantasy and flame' of *Childe Harold* III, vii, is the prison of the scorpion, Remorse:

> The Mind, that broods o'er guilty woes,
>   Is like the Scorpion girt by fire,
> In circle narrowing as it glows,
> The flames around their captive close,
> Till inly searched by thousand throes,
>   And maddening in her ire,
> One sad and sole relief she knows,
> The sting she nourished for her foes,
> Whose venom never yet was vain,
> Gives but one pang, and cures all pain,
> And darts into her desperate brain.   (422–32)

A suicide motif is here, and in the rest of the Tales, superimposed on the *weltschmerz* lamentation which runs through *Childe Harold*. Reading the Tales simply as narrative, it is not always easy to appreciate, unless on this supposition, the fatality which drives the Byronic hero to cast away what the situation offers of simple love and goodness. Of course there are classical pressures active too: the idea of *hubris*, of a happiness coveted by mortals but beyond their reach, frowned on by the gods.

> With shivering hearts the strife we saw
> Of passion with eternal law . . .

One finds one's thoughts returning to Matthew Arnold's brilliant assessment. Law and passion are indeed the poles around which the action of these Tales gyrates, antitheses established by a variety of rhetorical devices. The first of course is the sea symbolism: storm/ tide: passion/law. The interpenetration of sea and land had been gentle in Canto II of *Childe Harold*, the music of the Mediterranean's miniature tides flowing into quiet coves, but in *The Giaour* a fiercer harmony begins. The opening is calm, but it is the calm of death:

> No breath of air to break the wave
> That rolls below the Athenian's grave.

This deathlike slumber of Greece under her oppressor is broken, within the limited circuit of *The Giaour*, by formidable storm rhythms projected into the *human* action of the poem:

> Who thundering comes on blackest steed,
> With slackened bit and hoof of speed?
> Beneath the clattering iron's sound
> The caverned Echoes wake around
> In lash for lash, and bound for bound;
> The foam that streaks the courser's side
> Seems gather'd from the Ocean-tide.   (180–6)

Indeed we must note, in the Tales, how little the sea values are presented in their own right (contrast *Childe Harold* and *Don Juan*): these narratives are obsessive presentations of certain 'romantic' aspects of the human dilemma, and Byron is going to allow no tincture of the 'picturesque' to blunt their existential impact.

'They exhibit rather passions personified, than persons impassioned.' This comment by a contemporary critic, Henry Taylor, is justified: yet the passions are real enough, and personal. It is significant that in despatching part of his Memoirs (later destroyed) to Tom Moore in 1821 Byron calls it a *'Giaour*-nal' (*LJ* v, 356). Writing in his 1813 Journal (27 November) about a portrait he has just sent to Augusta, he comments:

—— has received the portrait safe; and, in answer, the only remark she makes upon it is, 'indeed it is like'—and again, 'indeed it is like'. With her the likeness 'covered a multitude of sins': for I happen to know that this portrait was not a flatterer, but dark and stern,—even black as the mood in which my mind was scorching last July, when I sat for it.

Late summer of 1812 was the time when *The Giaour* was shaping itself in his mind, and the 'dark and stern' portrait of Byron is also a portrait of that poem's hero. The poem is based on fact.

This remains a constant. The Tales attracted, and still attract, by their authenticity. However brilliant the colours, however *outré* the action, however unbridled the passions, Byron is able to convince his readers that what he is writing about is based on what he himself has seen and experienced. No wonder that Walter Scott's verse romances, located most of them in an idealised Middle Ages, and lacking the note of passion, declined in popularity. This note of immediacy is struck in the first of the Tales, *The Giaour*, where the nub of the plot, the drowning of the Turkish girl, derives from a real life episode in which Byron was directly involved. 'To describe the *feelings* of *that situation* were impossible—it is *icy* even to recollect them', he wrote in his diary some three years later.) This is Byron the man of action, a role in which he always preferred to see himself.

The plot of *The Giaour* is not easy to follow. Byron uses a deliberately cinematic technique, involving flashbacks in time and close-ups in focusing. And 'this snake of a poem', as he calls it himself, is the end result of an interminable succession of afterthoughts, revisions and additions. Within the narrative itself we have to be alert to who is the narrator: sometimes Byron himself, commenting and moralising, sometimes an old Turkish fisherman, presenting his very unsympathetic point of view; and finally, towards the close, the Giaour's own voice or that of the monk with whom he is speaking. The poem is an experiment; it is a collection of fragments, but these fragments are the foundation stones of all the later Tales—the foundations and the germs, and as 'germs' presenting a concentration of Byronic essences which make the later narratives seem a little diluted, a little watered down. I wish I had space to linger over the great moments of the poem: the scorpion passage which I have already touched on, the lyrical description of the Greek islands (to receive an even more powerful apotheosis in the Haidée episode of *Don Juan* and its attendant song, 'The isles of Greece'); the meditation on death beginning 'He who hath bent him o'er the dead' (lines 68–91); the great celebration of liberty beginning 'Clime of the unforgotten brave!' (lines 103–41); and, in an entirely different mood from these (Byron's endless versatility!) the sombre meditations of

> The steed is vanish'd from the stall;
> No serf is seen in Hassan's hall;
> The lonely Spider's thin gray pall
> Waves slowly widening o'er the wall;
> The Bat builds in his Haram bower
> And in the fortress of his power
> The Owl usurps the beacon-tower . . .   (288–94)

and of

> A Turban carved in coarsest stone,
> A Pillar with rank weeds o'ergrown,
> Whereon can now be scarcely read
> The Koran verse that mourns the dead.   (723–6)

This has always seemed to me one of the most marvellous of Byronic visualisations, catching as it does, without rhetoric, this facet of Islam which, while remaining purely Islamic, can say something to the traveller of another faith and culture. From his letters too we understand the depth of Byron's feelings for the cypress-circled Turkish graveyards: places of slanting, turban-topped tombstones which seem uncared for but are never allowed to run to waste, where the hemlock reaches to the height of the turban and the cedar bends down to touch it too, and both are kept in bounds by an intervention which is never seen but is constantly (or perhaps sporadically) active. Who can tell? I think Byron liked this feeling of a human activity which was indistinguishable from the slow processes of nature: this too passes into the Tales and modulates the brightness of the Greek scene. Here again we are close to the Eliot of *Four Quartets*, turning

> behind the pig-sty to the dull façade
> And the tombstone. And what you thought you came for
> Is only a shell, a husk of meaning . . .   ('Little Gidding', I)

The sense of *spent* force, of an action which has been caught up into time, which crumbles, is ineffective, whose ineffectiveness is its essence, is conveyed in the later addition 'The browsing camels' bells are tinkling', and of course points forward to Tennyson and *The Lady of Shalott*: we meet it again in 'Little Gidding' II:

> Ash on an old man's sleeve
> Is all the ash the burnt roses leave.
> Dust in the air suspended
> Marks the place where a story ended . . .

and it is Yeats's finale too:

> An old house
> Where nothing stirs but a mouse.

Ultimately, this indoor world (for the grave too is indoors) is not Byron's world. He touches it from time to time, and I think he might have touched it more but for his mother and all the dreadful memories of his youth; *they* drove him outwards, denied him a focus, made him dilate himself where his pressing need was for concentration.

Each Tale is a new metrical experiment. *The Bride of Abydos* opens with a tidal surge of anapaests which demonstrate that this measure can be as languorous in one context as it can be vigorous in another ('The Destruction of Sennacherib' for instance). Later sections give us Coleridgean deviations from the strict octosyllabic couplet—interlaced rhymes, expanded lines, a wealth of triplets. The action is more close-knit than *The Giaour*'s, and better sustained: the dominant Fall theme, overtly presented in the pentameters of section VI (Byron's sense of decorum leads him to drop the octosyllabics)—

> Fair, as the first that fell of womankind,
>   When on that dread yet lovely serpent smiling,
> Whose image then was stamp'd upon her mind—
>   But once beguiled—and ever more beguiling   (158–61)

—provides the groundnote of the poem. The sea is feminine here, seductive and betraying, though the betrayal is unconscious. The hero, Selim, is androgynous, a pawn almost in the fierce subterranean battle between Zuleika and Giaffir. There is an inward-looking, enclosed feeling to the poem which is quite absent from *The Giaour*, a sense of intrigue and stifled passion, a Harem atmosphere which oppresses, but gives Byron the opportunity to demonstrate that his gift for interior description is not inferior to his genius for landscape:

> And by her Comboloio lies
> A Koran of illumined dyes;
> And many a bright emblazoned rhyme
> By Persian scribes redeemed from Time;
> And o'er those scrolls, not oft so mute,
> Reclines her now neglected lute;
> And round her lamp of fretted gold
> Bloom flowers in urns of China's mould;
> The richest work of Iran's loom,
> And Sheeraz' tribute of perfume;
> All that can eye or sense delight
>   Are gather'd in that gorgeous room.
>   But yet it hath an air of gloom.
> She, of this Peri cell the sprite,
> What doth she hence, and on so rude a night?   (II, v)

What this passage owes to *Christabel* it repays, and in full measure, in its contributions to 'The Eve of St Agnes' and 'The Eve of St Mark', and beyond them to Morris and Tennyson.

The Corsair (1814) returns us to the outdoor world of *The Giaour*, but with a difference. The poem was begun and completed in the last fortnight of December 1813, an extraordinary feat of composition. The difference resides in the growing importance of the feminine element, which Byron now begins to weave contrapuntally, rather than antiphonally (if I may so express it) with the masculine. *The Giaour* was a Tale in which the hero had failed to rescue the heroine; in *The Bride* the heroine causes the death of the hero. In *The Corsair* the heroine rescues the hero, but does so in such a way as to destroy his honour. In *The Giaour* the landscape dominates the human pair, in *The Bride* heroic landscape is balanced by seductive interior, in *The Corsair* there is an interpenetration of feminine 'interiority' with the outdoor masculine scene. This is beautifully conveyed in the diptych of the setting sun and rising moon which opens Canto III. This passage is borrowed—'I scarce know why', Byron said—from the as yet unpublished 'The Curse of Minerva': indeed, it is possible to see *The Corsair* as a transposition into narrative terms of the sun-moon counterpoint of this splendid passage, which impresses by its immediacy ('written on the spot, in the Spring of 1811', as Byron notes). It also affords us a glimpse into the workings of Byron's mind, from landscape into life and from life back again into landscape. Here was something Byron had felt so deeply that it had become a part of his being and had to be re-expressed in lyric, in narrative, and in dramatic terms at each new stimulus. Who, he asks, can ever forget the magic of Greece?

> Not he—whose heart nor time nor distance frees,
> Spell-bound within the clustering Cyclades!   (*The Corsair* III, ii)

To this extent—and it is wide enough—we may see the Turkish Tales as the extrovert rendering of Byron's long love-affair with Greece. They are also the extroversion of the fire element in Byron, providing a vent for the aggressive and passionate stresses which could not be fused into the melancholy, meditative earth-and-air pattern of Canto II of *Childe Harold*.

I have suggested that the Tales are variations on the theme of peril, disaster, rescue, counterdisaster. In *The Corsair* Conrad is captured in rescuing Gulnare, and is then rescued by Gulnare at the price of honour. The counterdisaster comes in *Lara* (1814) which is the sequel to *The Corsair*: a sombre, somewhat featureless and obsessively guilt-racked narrative which takes us away from the Mediterranean scene (Lara, the former Corsair, returns to his ancestral home, apparently in some inland region of Spain) and thus from the sea; in so doing the poem forfeits a dimension and a resonance which the other Tales had possessed. We miss the sea voices. It is the most complex of the Tales, and the most obscure. As counterdisaster, it fuses certain features of *The Corsair*: Medora, Conrad's 'pure' love, interacts with the 'guilty' Gulnare to evolve the 'page-boy' Kaled; Gulnare's treachery enters Conrad's soul to render him capable of the assassination of Ezzelin (who himself has a mysterious relationship with Medora). The main interest of the Tale lies in its elaboration of the Byronic hero. But this I must leave for discussion in a later chapter.

'Where life is lost, or freedom won'

Between *Lara* and the rest of the Tales came the *Hebrew Melodies* (1815). These are reflective lyrics which I shall discuss shortly; they had their influence on the sequence of the Tales. They are boldly experimental in their manipulation of poetic forms and metres, and the possibilities here explored are exploited in the next of the Tales, *The Siege of Corinth* (January 1816). We are listening to a new music, which has learned much from *Christabel* and *Kubla Khan* yet preserves its own masculine drive and stress. We return to the tetrameter, but a tetrameter infinitely more flexible than that of *The Giaour*. The sea too returns:

> 'Tis midnight: on the mountains brown
> The cold, round moon shines deeply down;
> Blue roll the waters, blue the sky
> Spreads like an ocean hung on high . . .
> The waves on either shore lay there
> Calm, clear, and azure as the air;
> And scarce their foam the pebbles shook,
> But murmured meekly as the brook.
> The winds were pillowed on the waves;
> The banners droop'd along their staves,
> And, as they fell around them furling,
> Above them shone the crescent curling;
> And that deep silence was unbroke,
> Save where the watch his signal spoke,
> Save where the steed neighed oft and shrill,
> And echo answered from the hill,
> And the wide hum of that wild host
> Rustled like leaves from coast to coast,
> As rose the Muezzin's voice in air
> In midnight call to wonted prayer.   (xi)

This is Byron's 'central realm'. The isthmus of Corinth stands for Pope's 'isthmus of a middle state' which is the condition of man. Byron excels at these moments of suspense, of the poised wave, the tottering column: what in the *Monody on Sheridan* he calls the 'breathing moment on the bridge where Time/Of light and darkness forms an arch sublime'. This breathing moment comes as the midpoint of an action which is easily seen as triple: Day–preparation (i–x); Night–pause (xi–xxi); Day–assault (xxii–xxxiii). Byron liked to present himself as a careless writer, but structurally the *Siege* is the best-knit of the Tales; and nowhere more so than in this central pause of section xi, which is itself organised along a triple sequence.

To begin with, we are central in time ('Tis midnight) as we are central in space (on the isthmus connecting two seas). In the course of the movement from 'midnight' in the first line to 'midnight' in the last we move through a series of vertical and horizontal transformations which connect the world of Nature (the first nine lines), the world of Man (the second nine lines), and the world of God (the last couplet). We begin with a downward movement penetrating a horizontal. Ruskin's comment is valuable here:

> Now the first eleven words are not poetry, except by their measure and preparation for rhyme; they are simple information, which might just as well have been given in prose—it *is* prose, in fact: It is twelve o'clock—the moon is pale—it is round—it is shining on brown mountains. Any fool, who had seen it, could tell us that. At last comes the poetry, in the single epithet, 'deeply'. Had he said 'softly' or 'brightly' it would still have been simple information. But of all the readers of that couplet, probably not two received exactly the same impression from the 'deeply', and yet received more from that than from all the rest together. Some will refer the expression to the fall of the steep beams, and plunge down with them from rock to rock into the woody darkness of the cloven ravines, down to the undermost pool of eddying black water, whose echo is lost among their leafage; others will think of the deep heaven, the silent sea, that is drinking the light into its infinity; others of the deep *feeling* of the pure light, of the thousand memories and emotions that rise out of their rest, and are seen white and cold in its rays. This is the reason of the power of the single epithet, and this is its *mystery*.[7]

Now however 'Victorian' that comment may seem in its rather plush exuberance, its refusal to separate what Richards has called 'stock responses' from relationships clearly definable in the paragraph context, it is nevertheless a valuable exercise in 'close analysis' in its focusing of the word, the epithet, and its attempt to get at what the word is saying. My own reading is closest to Ruskin's second suggestion: 'deeply' is a nexus binding the three worlds of Man, God and Nature. 'Spreads like an ocean hung on high' itself connects the 'starry shore' of the sky with 'the watery floor' of the sea (Blake's 'Hear the Voice of the Bard' is not irrelevant here); the effect is similar to that gained in the Brenta stanzas of *Childe Harold* IV, xxvii–xxix, 'Where the Day joins the past Eternity'. Here, the *waves* are as 'Calm, clear and azure as the *air*'; they are 'unshaken' by foam; and the winds are asleep. Nature, in short, is at her usual task of trying to rescue senseless man from his 'lunes'. Note how the 'turn' from Nature's world to man comes in the middle of a couplet:

> The winds were pillowed on the waves;
> The banners drooped along their staves.

The banners are emblems of war; the crescent which 'shines' above them in the next couplet is the emblem of Turkish might and domination, but it is also a figure of the moon, the mild and reconciling deity of 'The Ancient Mariner' and so much of Byron's own poetry. Atop of the flagpole the crescent will be horizontal (as it is when it crowns the dome of a mosque): this presents us with another image, the cradle shape which is also that of the Ark in a well-known design of Blake's. We are moving in and out of warlike/ pacific imagery in a sinuous pattern woven with immense if unobtrusive virtuosity. The phallic upward thrust of the 'staves' is met with the womblike response of the 'crescents'; the rigid weapon by the 'curling', growing thing. And even the eternity dimension seems to add its voice for peace

> As rose the Muezzin's voice in air
> In midnight call to wonted prayer.

But here of course all Byron's irony is unleashed: the 'wonted prayer' in its declaration that there is only one God, and that Muhammad is his Prophet, excludes other faiths and other races; Islam is a fanatical, warlike religion; and it is on the Jihad, the Holy War, that the muezzin invokes the blessing of Allah. What had seemed a moment of true suspense, of possible truce, is broken by that arrogant cry.

But sea responds to land in a harmony unheard before in Byron's verse, in what one can only call a kind of compassion, a fellow-feeling which links man too with his dust:

> The silent pillar, lone and grey,
> Claimed kindred with their sacred clay;
> Their spirits wrapped the dusky mountain,
> Their memory sparkled o'er the fountain;
> The meanest rill, the mightiest river
> Rolled mingling with their fame for ever.
> Despite of every yoke she bears,
> The land is Glory's still and theirs!
> 'Tis still a watch-word to the earth:
> When man would do a deed of worth
> He points to Greece, and turns to tread,
> So sanctioned, on the tyrant's head:
> He looks to her, and rushes on
> Where life is lost, or Freedom won.   (xv)

The later narratives (*Parisina*, *The Prisoner of Chillon*, *Mazeppa*) seem to me less successful. Divorced from Greece, indeed from the classical scene in general, they have lost a nerve, a dimension; here

Byron's weaknesses show themselves without his strength: senti-
mentality, melodrama, frigidity, and occasionally bombast. *Parisina*
(1816) was published along with *The Siege of Corinth*; the reviewers
attacked it on moral grounds ('the guilty passion of a bastard son for
his father's wife') while our *caveats* are likely to be otherwise directed:
the insipidity of the heroine, the supineness of the hero, and indeed
the whole unreality of a situation which could hardly arise nowadays.
The versification is in no ways an advance on the earlier Tales.
The Prisoner of Chillon is in another category: here Byron was fired
by direct access, and in company with Shelley (who always brought
out the best in Byron), to the scene he was writing of: the result is a
very superior tear-jerker, but could one say more for it than that?
There are great lines, certainly:

> . . . to bend
> Once more, upon the mountains high,
> The quiet of a loving eye   (329–31)

and

> With spiders I had friendship made,
> And watched them in their sullen trade,
> Had seen the mice by moonlight play,
> And why should I feel less than they?   (381–4)

but to gauge the remoteness of all this from the multi-dimensional
world of the Turkish Tales we have only to remember

> The steed is vanished from the stall;
> No serf is seen in Hassan's hall;
> The lonely Spider's thin gray pall
> Waves slowly widening o'er the wall;[8]
> The Bat builds in his Haram bower
> And in the fortress of his power
> The Owl usurps the beacon-tower.   (*Giaour*, 288–94)

The 'Sonnet on Chillon' (in spite of Byron's dislike of the form, one
of the supreme sonnets of our language) distils in its fourteen lines
the essence of *The Prisoner*'s fourteen strophes.

Mazeppa, finally, extracts the extrovert maximum from all these
stories. Let us note that in them the masculine energy, supreme in
The Giaour, has been steadily subordinated to the feminine. *Parisina*
is an almost complete emasculation. In *The Prisoner of Chillon* the hero
is submerged *beneath* the lake in a sealed dungeon, a passive sufferer
watching his brothers die as the Ancient Mariner had watched his
shipmates, and at length shrinking from deliverance. Dante's

Ugolino and the Mariner meet in Byron's Bonnivard. In *Mazeppa* there are other resonances, chiefly from *Kubla Khan*; but there is no imitation—Byron's uncanny power of assimilating the essence of another mind's 'message' and transposing it into his own ideograms was never more convincingly at work. Here 'the royal madman' Charles XII is the Khan, to whom 'ancestral voices prophesying war' sound together with 'the mingled measure' of Mazeppa's narrative, while Coleridge's 'woman wailing for her demon lover' is evoked by 'the first moonrise of midnight' shining on the mad passion of Theresa and Mazeppa; and the Abyssinian maid finds her counterpart in the Cossack maid, who in her gentleness befriends the exhausted hetman. The frenzied gallop of the wild horse through a wolf-infested wilderness recalls the turbulent passage of the river Alph through the 'caverns measureless to man' of *Kubla Khan*: both are emblems of unconscious, instinctual forces.

The wild horse (which since Freud we have come to recognise as a blatant sexual symbol) acts as the medium between the hero's sense of guilt and his impulse towards self-punishment; yet Mazeppa is saved by this same energy, though not released—liberation is achieved only through the innocent tenderness of the Cossack maid. *Mazeppa* is *The Corsair*'s mirror image, a transposition of action into suffering. And it is the Mercator's projection of *Kubla Khan*, Coleridge's vertical and vortical patterns being flattened out, as it were, into a linear, horizontal diagram which shows nevertheless the same love/war and action/suffering contours. Byron, with the rapid glance of genius, has divined the interiority of *Kubla Khan*, the 'meaning' over which critics have been quarrelling for a century and a half, and his exegesis in *Mazeppa*. Whatever we may think of the success of Byron's experiments in psychological narrative in the Tales, we ought to abandon once for all the notion that they can be dismissed as irrelevant to his total *oeuvre*.

Notes and references

1   Whose works he seems to have had almost by heart, despite his constant and I think deliberately provocative denigration of Shakespeare. Professor G. Wilson Knight's *Byron and Shakespeare* (Routledge, 1966) gives an account which cannot be bettered.

2   *Journal of European Studies*, June 1974.

3   See above, p. 105.

4   The full story may be read in Malcolm Elwin, *Lord Byron's Wife* (Macdonald, 1962).

5   A very late reference, authenticated by the *Richard III* quotation, comes in *Don Juan* XV, xcvi: 'I say I do believe a haunted spot/ Exists—and where? That shall I not recall,/Because I'd rather it should be forgot,/"Shadows the soul of Richard" may appal.' Byron often identifies himself with Richard III in guilt as in deformity.

6   Letter to Byron of 31 August 1813 (*LJ* iii, 257n).

7   *Works*, ed. Cook and Wedderburn, vol. i, 441–3.

8   Cf. T. S. Eliot's 'East Coker' I, 9–13, and 'Little Gidding' II. The phrases, images and rhythms of Byron's Turkish Tales are pervasively present in *Four Quartets*.

6

'HEBREW MELODIES'

Hebrew Melodies (1815) is a collection of lyrics with a mainly biblical background which Byron began composing before his marriage and which he continued to work on through the honeymoon (or 'treaclemoon'), with Annabella as his amanuensis. The poems served a typically Byronic triple purpose. A Jewish composer, Isaac Nathan, had approached Byron with the request that the 'first poet of the present age' would provide the lyrics to 'a considerable number of very beautiful Hebrew melodies of undoubted antiquity' (letter to Byron of 30 June 1814). Nathan's request was supported, on 15 September, by Byron's old Cambridge friend, the Hon. Douglas Kinnaird, who solicited Byron's help for Nathan as 'a composer of Music, whose very singular merits, both as a composer and a man, have interested me in his behalf'. Byron's aid in such causes was rarely asked in vain, and he agreed at once, sending Kinnaird a number of poems by return of post. We may guess that not only Nathan's worthiness as man and composer, but also his position as member of a long-persecuted race, would sway Byron to a favourable decision. Moreover, there were those 'very beautiful Hebrew melodies'. Byron was all his life a fervent reader of scripture on the one hand and a lover of tradition—old ballads, legends, songs and tunes—on the other.[1] We find him writing to Annabella as early as 20 October:

Kinnaird . . . applied to me to write words for a musical composer who is going to publish the *real old undisputed Hebrew melodies*, which are beautiful & to which David & the prophets actually sang the 'songs of Zion'—& I have done nine or ten on the sacred model—partly from Job &c. & partly my own imagination; but I hope a little better than Sternhold & Hopkins.

It is odd enough that this should fall to my lot, who have been abused as 'an infidel'. Augusta says 'they will call me a *Jew* next'.

Other reasons for Byron's compliance with Nathan's request are suggested by Thomas L. Ashton in his study and edition of the *Melodies*.[2] 'The lamentation for lost freedom', says Mr Ashton, 'might serve as a means for the expression of his personal melancholic sense of lost innocence and his nostalgia for what had been.' Mr Ashton rightly links this melancholy to his love for the choirboy John Edleston. I would also link it to Byron's sense of frustration in the London society of 'the years of fame', and in particular to his haunting sense of regret that the possibilities of self-transformation, even of realisation, which had been offered to him during his Eastern tour had been dissipated. The hope of renewal through drinking 'from a purer fount, on holier ground' (*Childe Harold* III, ix), that is, by relinquishing the Caroline Lambs and the fair Florences for Annabella Milbanke, has proved a mirage. The image of the ideal woman remains, a being virginal yet maternal, protective yet remote, so remote that like Wordsworth's Lucy she passes outside the human context to inhabit a world of tides and starry spaces and elemental dance. But now she is unattached to any human correlative. And because this is so, Byron takes his revenge, during the honeymoon and after, on Annabella. Even the *Melodies* are a subtle form of revenge, of mockery. Annabella makes meticulous fair copies of them as they flow from Byron's pen, not grasping in the least their cryptic significance.[3]

Only about half the 'Melodies' can be called 'Hebrew'. Some, including the famous 'She walks in Beauty, like the night . . .', had been written before Byron was even approached by Nathan; others are lyrics of nostalgia or reflection unconnected with biblical themes.[4] The collection falls into two main groups: 'the terrific numbers', as Blake would have called them (*Jerusalem*, 'To the Reader'), and the 'mild and tender' lyrics. The first group is largely concerned with power and its downfall, with war, and with the occult. The poems of the second group express more personal themes, often touching on love, regret for the past, or the mystery of death. Poems belonging to the two groups are mixed indiscriminately: there is no discernible order or progression. Following 'She walks in beauty . . .' we have a spirited ode on the power of music, a favourite eighteenth-century theme, in 'The Harp the Monarch Minstrel Swept'. The power of David, 'the King of men', was concentrated in his harp—it was a spiritual as well as a material or warlike power. Now (with the downfall of Jerusalem, a motif which even when not mentioned is pervasively present throughout the *Melodies*) 'its chords are riven'. Both aspects of power are eclipsed. Yet 'Devotion and her daughter Love/Still bid the bursting spirit soar' to the sound of music. There are frequent references in Byron's letters and journals to the pleasure he took in music, and this short ode has the stamp of veracity. Probably the association with Edleston was also in Byron's mind. The situation at Trinity was very much that of the gloomy Saul soothed by the voice of the young David. This Saul–David nexus is continued in 'My soul is dark . . .', and here the David addressed may perhaps be Annabella. A moment of spiritual crisis is suggested: Annabella, and no one but she, can save him now:

> My soul is dark—Oh! quickly string
>> The harp I yet can brook to hear;
> And let thy gentle fingers fling
>> Its melting murmur o'er mine ear.
> If in this heart a hope be dear,
>> That sound shall charm it forth again:
> If in these eyes there lurk a tear,
>> 'Twill flow, and cease to burn my brain.

Under the image of music, Byron is asking for Annabella's understanding and sympathy. The moment is urgent—'quickly string . . .', and the issue is in doubt—'If in these eyes . . .': Annabella is called upon to reveal Byron to himself.

> But bid the strain be wild and deep,
>> Nor let thy notes of joy be first:
> I tell thee, minstrel, I must weep,
>> Or else this heavy heart will burst;
> For it hath been by sorrow nursed,
>> And ached in sleepless silence long;
> And now 'tis doomed to know the worst,
>> And break at once—or yield to song.

The strain must be 'wild and deep', the understanding, and therefore the therapy, radical. Annabella has to accept and be ready to forgive his anguished, guilty past: then perhaps Byron will be able to forgive himself, wash away his guilt in a flood of healing tears. All depends, the last two lines seem to say, on Annabella's response.

The implicit Byron–Annabella dialogue which seems to me to run through the *Melodies* takes a new turn in 'Were my bosom as false as thou deem'st it to be'. Mr Ashton discusses this poem in the context of another lyric, 'On the Day of the Destruction of Jerusalem by Titus', with rather less than his usual assurance. 'On the Day of the Destruction', he rightly sees, belongs to the group of poems, including 'On Jordan's banks' and 'By the Rivers of Babylon', which exploit the exilic theme. Exile is one of Byron's great topics, intimately linked to his own career: he was a willing exile in 1809–1811, he is to be a half-reluctant, certainly a furious one, from 1816 onwards. The theme of exile, of the displaced hero, runs through the Turkish Tales. In England now, in 1815, Byron is again an exile, this time from the Levant, the homeland of his choice.[5] There has been a radical reversal. Byron's identification with the Levant, and specifically with an *Islamic* Levant, is clear from his own 1811–16 journals and letters and from Annabella's separation affidavits. Annabella was convinced that Byron had actually 'turned Mussulman' in 1810, had renounced the faith and the moral code of his country. She refers to his 'dark predestinarianism', to his veiled hints of 'a crime without a name'.

Byron's own words suggest a moment of choice. The publication of *The Bride of Abydos* on 2 December 1813 recalls him to 'a country replete with the *brightest* and *darkest*, but always the most lively colours of my memory' (5 December Journal). And on 27 February 1814: 'I might and should have been a Pasha by this time.'[6] We tend to dismiss such comments as flippant. The tone may be flippant ('I am always flippant in prose', Byron remarked) but the sense is serious. Byron felt out of place, unrooted, in England. The pull to the East was almost irresistible. But it meant a complete break with the traditions of his house and his class and his race. He hesitates, as who would not? Is there an alternative? He sees a possible salvation in Annabella. She will be his Medora, his Egeria: she will 'guide' him, 'manage' him, save him from himself. He marries her, but the hoped-for salvation does not eventuate. He appeals to her for understanding (in 'My soul is dark') but she responds with horror at his moral deviations, with accusations that he has abjured his faith. He replies with 'Were my bosom as false . . .':

> Were my bosom as false as thou deem'st it to be,
> I need not have wandered from far Galilee;
> It was but abjuring my creed to efface
> The curse which, you say'st, is the crime of my race.

'If I were a complete renegade to Western codes of thinking and acting', Byron is saying, 'I could easily have remained in the Levant. All that was needed was to "turn Mussulman", and then what in Western eyes are the crimes of the Byrons (Mad Jack, Byron, Augusta) would have been readily accepted in the tolerant moral

code of Islam.' 'Galilee', in short, is set down for 'Levant' in the
continued cryptogram which *Hebrew Melodies*, on one of its levels, is.
The reviewer in *The British Critic* who wrote 'Let the noble Lord
maintain his station upon Turkish ground, the hill of Zion alone is
forbidden ground!' might have saved his ink: Byron's Turkish ties
were unbroken.

Did Annabella, as she copied out the poems, understand what
Byron was trying to say to her? Perhaps not entirely. She was an
intelligent woman, penetrating though devious, herself given—
though along different lines—to the love of 'mystification' with
which she charges Byron. Byron's mystification was the agonised
intellectual, emotional, strategic play of a 'wounded falcon' beating
himself against the bars of the cage he has constructed for himself
(*Childe Harold* III, xv); Annabella's devious incomprehension is the
protective barrier thrown up by an acute but limited mind against
the reception of totally new and outrageous ideas. Her attitude is
that of the 'holier than thou'; but, says Byron,

> *If* the bad never triumph, then God is with thee!
> *If* the slave only sin, thou art spotless and free!
> *If* the Exile on earth is an Outcast on high,
> Live on in thy faith, but in mine I will die.[7]

Byron is an exile on earth: Annabella tells him he is also an outcast
in heaven. Perhaps so, and here comes the ironic twist: perhaps in
not 'turning Mussulman', in not accepting the true faith of Islam,
Byron has forfeited his chance of Paradise. But let Annabella live on
in *her* faith, her unforgiving version of Christianity, and Byron will
continue to follow *his*, the Christianity of Blake, the 'mutual forgiveness of each vice' which Jesus came to teach.

> I have lost for that faith more than thou canst bestow,
> As the God who permits thee to prosper doth know;
> In his hand is my heart and my hope—and in thine
> The land and the life which for him I resign.

In not abjuring Christianity Byron has lost a happiness (in the
Levant) greater than any Annabella can give. This may simply be
the Islamic way of life, but perhaps there is a more personal,
emotional involvement which Byron renounced when he rejected
Islam. 'The God who permits thee to prosper' is bitterly ironic, and
the phrase chimes with a score of others referring to Annabella and
her advisers in the post-separation letters. The irony is intensified
and complicated in the concluding couplet. Byron's heart and hope
is in the hand of the Christian God. Like Blake, I think, Byron

believed that 'All religions are one': the Father of Christianity and
the Allah of the Muslims are one and the same. The monolithic
simplicity of Islam appealed to Byron, at this period of his life, above
the doctrinal and ritual complexities of Christianity: nevertheless,
he has sacrificed his preference and remained faithful to the creed
of his fathers. That is the doctrinal sacrifice—the renunciation of a
congenial creed. The material and spiritual sacrifice—the 'resignation' of a gipsy life, moral permissiveness, a wonderful climate,
incomparable landscape—has been placed in the hand of Annabella
when he married her.

The unsoothed, unannealed Saul reverts to his true David,
Edleston, and to his real Iphigenia, Augusta. The treaclemoon is
over.[8] The songs of Zion lamenting captivity in a strange land are
echoes of those earlier strains heard and loved in the chapel of
Trinity. That 'Edleston' anagrammatises as 'Eden lost' is a velleity
which would not be overlooked by Byron's incorrigibly punning
mind, as I have noted elsewhere: his death becomes the archetype of
all deaths, his loss is the epitome of the loss of a whole early world
of passionate innocence. I am sure Professor Marchand is right when
he refers 'There be none of Beauty's daughters' (considered briefly
at p. 157 below) to Edleston: the 'none' cuts out the entire female
world, though if he had been challenged Byron would have denied
it. No doubt too that the exquisite 'Oh! snatched away in beauty's
bloom', and 'Bright be the place of thy soul', are elegies for Edleston.
The first is in the mode of Collins, but transcends the uncomplicated
pathos of 'How Sleep the Brave!':

> Oh! snatched away in beauty's bloom,
> On thee shall press no ponderous tomb;
> But on thy turf shall roses rear
> Their leaves, the earliest of the year;
> And the wild cypress wave in tender gloom:
>
> And oft by yon blue gushing stream
> Shall Sorrow lean her drooping head,
> And feed deep thought with many a dream,
> And lingering pause and lightly tread;
> Fond wretch! as if her step disturbed the dead!
>
> Away! we know that tears are vain,
> That Death nor hears nor heeds distress:
> Will this unteach us to complain?
> Or make one mourner weep the less?
> And thou—who tell'st me to forget,
> Thy looks are wan, thine eyes are wet.

Byron's effects here are gained by subtle metrical shifts; the inter-lacing rhymes follow the fluctuations of emotion, generating in cross-currents of the two couplets a tension which is released in the lengthened fifth line. The introduction of 'thou' in the last stanza effects the opening from Byron's personal grief to the universality of sorrow, and this demands the extension of the stanza by the added sixth line which so magnificently diverts Byron from preoccupation with his own grief to a realisation that the spectator can feel with him. The whole poem is couched in a tone of hushed lamentation: we begin reading with the feeling that nothing can be more subdued than the mood of stanza one, but Byron's metrical virtuosity, like that of a great violinist, continues to lower the volume to the pianissimo of the final lines.

Note too how the antithetic imagery contributes its structural counterpoint: the evanescence of 'snatched away' is balanced by the ponderous pressure of the second line, 'bloom' by 'tomb'; soaring motifs assert themselves again with the springing turf, with 'roses rear their leaves'. The final exotic cypress adds a touch of mystery, lifts the scene out of the English into an oriental landscape. In the second stanza it would not be difficult to demonstrate the superiority of Byron's single personification over Collins's collection (Fancy, Honour, Freedom) by pointing out the work it has to do, and how well it does it. Here Byron has learned from and improved on Collins (though, as the late Professor A. S. P. Woodhouse has pointed out,[9] Collins's use of personification is far more 'organic' than that of most of his contemporaries). The earlier Romantics—Wordsworth, Southey, Coleridge—began by outlawing the personification, but it forced its way back into currency to fill a need their own practice engendered. It returned rich and revitalised. Shelley's 'Eternal Hunger' in *Adonais*, Byron's 'Sorrow' here, and Wordsworth's own 'Fear and trembling Hope, Silence and Foresight' in 'Yew-trees', are potent beyond the mode of Thomson or Gray.

Edleston's ghost continues to sing the songs of Zion. 'On Jordan's banks . . .', 'The wild gazelle . . .', 'O weep for those . . .', 'By the rivers of Babylon . . .', are variations on the exilic theme. This is at once historic and biblical—the plight of the Diaspora; mythological and psychological—man's estate, *la condition humaine*, the error of the Lost Travellers; and personal—Byron's own plight, the drama of the displaced person. Byron feels his displacement all the more bitterly because he has failed the test imposed upon him by his Eastern tour: the possibility of self-transcendence is rejected, as Manfred rejects it

when he calls for paper 'tablets' to set down his experience instead
of the fleshly tablets of his heart.[10] These exilic laments belong to the
'mild & tender group', but there was an energetic side to Byron
which could not be satisfied with mere melancholy: action is also
needed, however ineffective it may prove to be. Saul returns in the
'terrific numbers', which include the 'Song of Saul before his Last
Battle', 'Saul', 'The Destruction of Sennacherib', 'On the Day of the
Destruction of Jerusalem by Titus', 'Vision of Belshazzar', and 'A
Spirit passed before me'. These blend the martial and the prophetic-
horrific, the occult (always a major interest of Byron's). 'Saul' is a
thrilling evocation of the Witch of Endor's raising of Samuel's
ghost:

> Thou whose spell can raise the dead,
>   Bid the Prophet's form appear.
> 'Samuel, raise thy buried head!
>   King, behold the phantom Seer!'
> Earth yawned; he stood the centre of a cloud:
> Light changed its hue, retiring from his shroud.
> Death stood all glassy in his fixéd eye;
> His hand was withered, and his veins were dry;
> His foot, in bony whiteness, glittered there,
> Shrunken and sinewless, and ghastly bare:
> From lips that moved not and unbreathing frame,
> Like caverned winds, the hollow accents came.
> Saul saw, and fell to earth, as falls the oak,
> At once, and blasted by the thunder-stroke.

The stark visualisation here surpasses most things in Byron's earlier
writing. Samuel is presented as an inhuman force of punitive
prophecy: that 'From lips that moved not' is a brilliant stroke.[11]
The deadly words which follow are channelled through him like
winds through a cave:

> 'Why is my sleep disquieted?
> Who is he that calls the dead?
> Is it thou, O King? Behold
> Bloodless are these limbs, and cold:
> Such are mine: and such shall be
> Thine tomorrow, when with me:
> Ere the coming day is done,
> Such shalt thou be, such thy son . . .'

The fall of kings theme runs through the *Melodies*, and is closely
linked to the power of prophecy, to warlocks and to ghosts. In Saul,
Belshazzar and Sennacherib, tyrannic power manifests in its most

violent guise: such men, Byron implies, always come to grief, defeated by spiritual forces which use their own inner deficiencies to destroy them.

The same dramatic instancy is heard again in 'The Destruction of Sennacherib' and 'The Vision of Belshazzar'. The first of these, too well known to quote, is a brilliant metrical and theatrical *tour de force*. Cosmic imagery—stars on the sea, the blue wave rolling nightly, the leaves of the forest, the winds of Autumn, the rock-beating surf, the dew, the melting snow—emphasises the ironic contrast between the Assyrian's wolfish might, apparently invincible, and the awesome power of 'the Angel of Death' who makes use of the winds to bring about the tyrant's destruction. This is a perennial biblical theme (we remember 'The stars in their courses fight against Sisera') and was highly congenial to Byron.

'The Vision of Belshazzar' projects a cryptic warning: its significance is interpreted by the captive prophet, Daniel. Here the divine Mover and his servant work in close harmony. Belshazzar at his impious feast is transfixed, as it were, between the upper and the nether millstones of avenging wrath. The power of the nether millstone is asserted in the mere fact of Daniel's captivity, a 'power made strong in weakness', as Paul was later to express it in his Christian context.[12] Here Byron achieves a barebone intensity hardly to be met with again before Hardy and Housman:

> In that same hour and hall,
>   The fingers of a hand
> Came forth against the wall,
>   And wrote as if on sand:
> The fingers of a man;—
>   A solitary hand
> Along the letters ran,
>   And traced them like a wand.   (ii)

The implicated repetition emphasises the eeriness of the event and conveys the sense of incredulous shock. 'The monarch saw, and shook': earthly power is impotent in face of the divine wrath. Perhaps earthly wisdom will come to his aid? He summons 'the men of lore . . . the wisest of the earth', but they cannot read 'the unknown letters'. Only Daniel, 'a captive in the land', can interpret the message, and it proves to be a fatal one:

> 'Belshazzar's grave is made,
>   His kingdom passed away,
> He in the balance weighed,
>   Is light and worthless clay.

> The shroud, his robe of state,
>   His canopy, the stone;
>   The Mede is at his gate!
>   The Persian on his throne!'   (vi)

The 'clay' of this last stanza responds antiphonically to the 'gold' of the first, the gold of the sacred vessels of the Temple which Belshazzar is desecrating. This theme of sacrilege is constant in Byron. It runs through *Childe Harold*—the violation of Nature's purity and generosity by war in Cantos I and III, the spoliation of Greece's ancient fanes in Canto II, the insults offered to genius (Blake's 'Holy Ghost') in Canto IV—and, as my illustrations show, is not confined to strictly religious profanation. The theme returns in the companion poem, 'To Belshazzar', but the desecration now is inflicted not on the 'thousand cups of gold,/In Judah deemed divine', but on the King's own soul, on the promise of his youth, his possibilities of spiritual greatness. I suggest that Byron was thinking of his own life story when he wrote:

> Youth's garlands misbecome thee now,
>   More than thy very diadem,
>   Where thou hast tarnished every gem:—
>   Then throw the worthless bauble by,
>   Which, worn by thee, ev'n slaves contemn;
>   And learn like better men to die!

Byron's letters and journals of this time are full of complaints that his own 'soul expired ere youth decayed' (stanza iii): it is he who has 'tarnished every gem' life had to offer him: his rank, his genius, his 'pure passion' for Edleston, his love for Augusta, the trust reposed in him by Annabella.

Writing to Annabella on 20 October 1814, Byron remarks that the 'nine or ten' songs he has already written are 'partly from Job &c. & partly my own imagination'. I have discussed the more important of the '&c' poems: let us glance finally at those 'from Job ... & ... imagination'. There is one with the specific title 'From Job', but the influence of the Book of Job is pervasively felt in a number of others. 'From Job' versifies the vision of Eliphaz the Temanite (Job 4:13–21) and belongs to the category of the prophetic occult. A comparison with the related 'Saul' is instructive. Samuel rises from the dead at man's call, and appears as human in shape, though dehumanised in function. The 'spirit' appears uncalled for and unannounced. It has no form, human or otherwise:

A spirit passed before me: I beheld
The face of Immortality unveiled—
Deep Sleep came down on every eye save mine—
And there it stood,—all formless—but divine;
Along my bones the creeping flesh did quake;
And as my damp hair stiffened, thus it spake:

'Is man more just than God? Is man more pure
Than he who deems even Seraphs insecure?
Creatures of clay—vain dwellers in the dust!
The moth survives you, and are ye more just?
Things of a day! you wither ere the night,
Heedless and blind to Wisdom's wasted light!'[13]

The 'formlessness' of the Spirit recalls Shelley's Demogorgon:

> —a mighty darkness
> Filling the seat of power, and rays of gloom
> Dart round, as light from the meridian sun.
> —Ungazed upon and shapeless; neither limb,
> Nor form, nor outline; yet we feel it is
> A living spirit. . . .

'The deep truth', Demogorgon declares, 'is imageless'. In both Byron's miniature and Shelley's full-length drama we enter the Cloud of Unknowing, the approach to wisdom by the *via negativa* which Byron will essay again, though just as tentatively, in *Manfred*, the later *Childe Harold*, and the biblical plays. In 'From Job' Byron bypasses the metaphysical aspect of the vision in favour of a questioning of human 'purity', 'justice' and 'security': again one wonders if Annabella, as she wrote out the fair copy, took these questions to herself. The insecurity of the Seraphs connects decisively with Annabella's later declaration that Byron thought of himself as a fallen angel, and points onward to *Heaven and Earth*. *Lara*, with its metaphysical hero—

> He stood a stranger in this breathing world,
> An erring Spirit from another hurled   (xviii)

—had been written in the summer of 1814, immediately before Byron made a start on *Hebrew Melodies*. The Tale poses several of the themes which are raised again in the *Melodies*. Lara, like Belshazzar, like Sennacherib, like Saul, is 'Lord of himself;—that heritage of woe'. He is the mixed being who appeals to Annabella for understanding:

> In him inexplicably mixed appeared
> Much to be loved and hated, sought and feared.   (xvii)

He consults the occult:

> Why gazed he so upon the ghastly head
> Which hands profane had gathered from the dead,
> That still beside his opened volume lay,
> As if to startle all save him away?   (ix)

In similar fashion all save Eliphaz are thrown into deep sleep, unable to face the revelation from the spirit world.

The spirit world of Job lies behind the world of ethical and existential values which made that book so congenial to Byron. Mr Ashton[14] comments on Byron's declaration, 'Of the Scriptures themselves I have ever been a reader & admirer as compositions, particularly the Arab-Job—and parts of Isaiah—and the song of Deborah', as follows: 'The selection is significant: 'Arab' Job for the infidel Calvinist, Isaiah for its nationalism, and Deborah for its defiance and archaic expression.' I would emend this to: 'Arab' Job for its Arabness, its proto-Islamic flavour, Isaiah for its spirit of prophecy, and Deborah for its projection of the feminine component in terms of lyrical ecstasy. Until we recognise Byron's deep commitment to Islam the weight of that word 'Arab' must escape us. Islam is pre-eminently a masculine faith, and Byron puts Job as the first term of a trilogy of which the song of Deborah is the feminine third. In between comes the spirit of prophecy which plays above and between 'the sexual strife'. Job, a book which Byron recognised as being outside the Judaic canon proper, expresses a 'fatalistic' and ultimately submissive creed which is close to that of Islam (the word means 'submission'). Jephtha's daughter, in the *Melody* of that title, submits to her fate, and in submission achieves her triumph and Israel's. The same 'faith which looks though death' inspires the song 'Thy days are done'. The end of days is the beginning of fame; the death of the individual ensures the freedom of the race. The 'generous blood' of the fallen warrior circulates in the veins of those who survive him. I have called attention elsewhere[15] to this Byronic theme of the cyclic process of man 'commingling slowly with heroic earth' to re-emerge in the circlings of history.

> Thy fall, the theme of choral song
>   From virgin voices poured!

links up with the song of Deborah, but it is not very far from the Islamic

Yet died he as in arms he stood,
And unavenged, at least in blood.
But him the maids of Paradise
    Impatient to their halls invite,
And the dark heaven of Houris' eyes
    On him shall glance for ever bright.   (*The Giaour*, 737–40)

This hope of immortality, the resonance of another aspect of the Book of Job, the 'I know that my Redeemer liveth' which Byron would remember from chapter 19 and from that performance of *Messiah* which he had scrambled through a window in Great St Mary's to hear in his Edleston days, pervades the '&c.' poems. There is a 'high world' which is created by and is of love: a world of unselfish devotion centred on sacrifice: and here, as in Handel's oratorio, the ethos of the Old Testament meets that of the New, Job the guiltless victim and the suffering servant of Isaiah meeting in the spotless lamb of Calvary. Deborah's song, to bring in the third term of the syndrome, anticipates at once the lament of Mary and the triumph song of the suffering Church.

Our last group of poems, 'If that High World', 'All is Vanity, saith the Preacher', 'When coldness wraps this suffering clay', 'Sun of the sleepless', 'They say that Hope is Happiness', and 'Bright be the place of thy Soul', are a set of variations on the immortality theme which casts a curious light on Byron's religious beliefs at this time. One surmises that Job's declaration, 'Yet in my flesh I shall see God', with Handel's accent on the 'shall', must have deeply impressed Byron, the most psychosomatic of English poets. To see God in and through the flesh is a Tantric ideal which could not fail to appeal. These are poems of time, and of the divisions of time, past present and future, *sub specie aeternitatis*: time reaching out into eternity, eternity interpreted in the fluxes of time. 'Time', Blake said, 'is the mercy of eternity': it is the mode by which eternity arrests the consequences of the Fall, substituting a temporal for a spatial collapse which would have been absolute. 'Sun of the sleepless! melancholy star!' stretches back into the past, with its memories of what has been:

So gleams the past, the light of other days,
Which shines, but warms not with its powerless rays;
A night-beam Sorrow watcheth to behold,
Distinct, but distant—clear—but, oh how cold!

The coldness is that of interstellar space; the sorrow is that of Dante's '*Nessun maggior dolore . . .*' 'If all time is eternally present',

says Eliot, 'all time is unredeemable.' The coldness of the star is
the coldness of light arriving over infinities of years, making nonsense
of our earthly clocks. In 'They say that Hope is Happiness', it gathers
together the delusions of time future, past and present:

> Alas! it is delusion all:
>   The future cheats us from afar,
> Nor can we be what we recall,
>   Nor dare we think on what we are.

But in 'Burnt Norton' we find an answer:

> Time present and time past
> Are both perhaps present in time future,
> And time future contained in time past.

There is a dimension in which 'past and future are gathered'. This is
Byron's 'high world', what Mircea Eliade calls 'Great Time'. It
'lies beyond/Our own' ('If that High World', 1–2): note that Byron
chooses 'beyond' rather than 'above'. It is a dimension of the
eternal present, not a 'future state', though Byron will bow to
religious tradition in using the phrase 'that future' in his concluding
lines. In terms of the Christian mythos, and of our everyday thinking
which is bound by time, the 'high world' is future, since we are not
in it here and now; death releases us from the trammels of time and
space, so that it is true to say that 'after death' we enter that world;
but Byron, like Blake, was aware that there is 'a little death in the
Divine Image' which effectively releases us from 'Being's severing
link' (a powerful oxymoron) into the light of Eternity (lines 12, 8).
This is the death to self brought about by unselfish love.

> It must be so: 'tis not for self
>   That we so tremble on the brink;
> And striving to o'erleap the gulph
>   Yet cling to Being's severing link.
> Oh! in that future let us think
>   To hold each heart the heart that shares,
> With them the immortal waters drink,
>   And soul in soul grow deathless theirs!

No sensitive reading could see this as a poem about mere physical
death. The dying man does *not* 'strive to o'erleap the gulph'; on the
contrary, he clings with all his remaining forces to life. But the
spiritual death of the Sufi, the Zen adept, the Christian ascetic, *is*
a struggle between aspiration towards the light of Eternity and a
clinging to the known goods of this life, of which the greatest is love.
The highest flights of the *via negativa* present 'realisation' as a divorce

from all passion, all emotion as unregenerate man knows it. 'A condition of complete simplicity', in Eliot's words ('Little Gidding' V), 'Costing not less than everything'. Does this everything include love? Christianity seems to say yes: Sufism has a different answer, cogently formulated in *The Giaour*.

The rather too jaunty anapaests of 'Bright be the place of thy soul' attack the problem in personal terms; in all probability the poem again refers to Edleston. In 'If that High World' Byron was speaking from his Sufic centre, and the poem's grave but far from ponderous harmonies have a tradition behind them. Here one feels that Byron is forcing the tone. He is trying to cheer himself up. 'On earth thou wert all but divine'—this is exaggeration, self-spoofing: one can understand and sympathise with Byron's need for such an 'objective correlative' to his metaphysical insight, but the poem's limp clichés give the lie to his enthusiasm. 'No lovelier spirit . . . the orbs of the blessed . . . all but divine . . . thy God is with thee . . . the spot of thy rest . . .': these are phatic disasters which stand in strong contrast not only to the 'Being's severing link . . . grow deathless theirs . . . the eye the same, except in tears'[16] of the earlier poem, but also to the equally taut phrasing of 'When coldness wraps this suffering clay', the poem which in its austerity stands as a counterpoise to the hopeful aspiration of 'If that High World'. Here we are neither in the Sufic nor the Christian world, but in the bleak afterlife of classical and neo-Platonic speculation.

> When coldness wraps this suffering clay,
>   Ah! whither strays the immortal mind!
> It cannot die, it cannot stay,
>   But leaves its darkened dust behind.
> Then, unembodied, doth it trace
>   By steps each planet's heavenly way?
> Or fill at once the realms of space,
>   A thing of eyes, that all survey?

'*Animula, vagula, blandula!*', Hadrian's Address to his Soul when Dying, translated by Byron with this title during his Harrow years, stands behind 'When coldness wraps . . .' The speculation here is metaphysical. Does the 'immortal mind' adapt itself gradually to its disembodied state? That is, does it remain an individual mind, still bound to a *seriatim* acquisition of knowledge, or is it merged at once in and identified with the Newtonian 'sensorium', becoming 'a thing of eyes' immediately cognisant of 'the All'? Blake's 'One Thought fills Immensity'[17] springs to mind as we read this and the next stanza:

> Eternal—boundless—undecayed,
> A thought unseen, but seeing all.

If this is so, then it is able to surmount the divisions of time:

> Before Creation peopled earth,
>   Its eye shall roll through chaos back;
> And where the farthest heaven had birth,
>   The Spirit trace its rising track.
> And where the future mars or makes,
>   Its glance dilate o'er all to be,
> While Sun is quenched or System breaks,
>   Fixed in its own Eternity.

This is the science fiction world of 'Darkness', which I discuss a little later. The 'it' which is the immortal mind to begin with has now become one of those pitiable instruments of knowledge which carry a grain of human longing and fear into the desolation of the interstellar spaces. The text denies this:

> Above or Love—Hope—Hate—or Fear,
>   It lives all passionless and pure.

But does it? Even the seraphs, 'Who are, or should be, passionless and pure' (*Heaven and Earth*, 715), fell from their high estate through human longing. This 'thing of eyes' may also fall.

Or so Byron implies. With 'When coldness wraps this suffering clay' he moves out of the comparatively cosy Hebraic-Islamic world of *Hebrew Melodies*, a world still of matrimonial compromises, into the exilic solitudes of the Alps, the Manfred world of inhuman elements and frozen whirlpools. A competent psychiatrist, had such existed in Byron's day, might have foretold his future progress from this one poem alone. We are prepared, now, for the world of the fallen angels and humans which are *Cain* and *Heaven and Earth*, the vertiginous abysses of *Manfred*, the equally suicidal 'dark declivities' of Venice, the descending *bolges* of *Don Juan*.

Notes and references

1   On his projected tour of the Hebrides in 1807 Byron planned 'to collect all the Erse traditions, poems, etc., etc., and translate, or expand the subjects, to fill a volume' (letter of 11 August 1807 to Elizabeth Bridget Pigot).

2   T. L. Ashton, *Byron's Hebrew Melodies* (Routledge & Kegan Paul, 1972). This book is invaluable for anyone wishing to follow the order of composition of the poems and to get an insight into the way Byron's mind was working as he wrote them.

3   *Hebrew Melodies* was not the only instrument of his revenge at this time. Annabella was also set to copying out *Parisina*, a Tale whose incest motif she must have found most distasteful. Byron wrote sarcastically to Murray: 'I am very glad that the handwriting was a favourable omen of the *morale* of the piece' (letter of 3 January 1816).

4   I prefer to leave comment on 'She walks in Beauty . . .' until a little later (p. 153) when I can better draw it into comparison with other poems of its kind.

5   See 'Byron and Islam', *loc. cit.*

6   See above, p. 115, for the full entry.

7   My italics.

8   I am not (to stress a point already made) prejudging the order of composition of the *Melodies*. No doubt the ebb and flow between Edleston–Augusta and Annabella was a recurrent tidal movement in these two crucial years.

9   'The poetry of Collins reconsidered', in *From Sensibility to Romanticism*, ed. F. W. Hilles and H. Bloom (Oxford University Press, New York, 1965).

10   See below, p. 234.

11   This, then, is another 'skull poem', to be grouped with the early 'Lines' and the various *Childe Harold* passages (see pp. 62–65, 102–103 above, and below pp. 222–223).

12   I discuss this aspect of Pauline influence on Byron in my paper 'Byron's Greek Canto: the anatomy of freedom', *Yearbook of English Studies*, 1974, vol. iv, pp. 172–189.

13   This line reintroduces the wisdom theme dropped since the *Childe Harold* II presentation, except (cryptically) in *The Corsair*. What I have to say below of the *via negativa* links up with this theme: I have no space to develop it here.

14   *Byron's Hebrew Melodies*, pp. 67–8.

15   See below, p. 189–190

16   The line is not self-explanatory, and Mr Ashton's normally instructive commentary fails us here. The reference is to Revelation 6:17, 'And God shall wipe away all tears from their eyes'.

17   Cf. also Donne's 'Second Anniversary', lines 185ff. And Byron's 'Detached Thoughts' No. 96 (1821): 'How far our future life will be individual, or, rather, how far it will at all resemble our *present* existence, is another question; but that the *Mind* is *eternal*, seems as probable as that the body is not so.' The possibility of reincarnation is raised in a letter of 11 April 1817 to Moore.

7

POEMS OF
THE SEPARATION

The more powerful the mind, the more liable it is to explosions from the dynamic centre; the more subtle it is, the more vulnerable to disturbances of balance and harmony. Byron's mind was both subtle and powerful, but it lacked a steadying influence. What wonder if he imagined he had found one in Annabella? Mixed with the exilic and martial songs of the *Melodies* we note these more nostalgic strains: the theme of the faultless, remotely perfect woman ('She walks in beauty'), the Iphigenia ('Jephtha's Daughter'), the *ewig weibliche* moving between smiles and tears ('I saw thee weep'). These are ideal projections upon an as yet little known Annabella. If in the end she did not come up to that ideal figure, the blame hardly rests with her. Byron could never have become 'fixed'. The 'prospect of rational happiness' which he anticipated in his letter to Annabella of 25 August 1813 rapidly revealed itself as 'a state of sameness and stagnation' (letter to Moore, 2 March 1815). But in his famous (or notorious) 'Fare thee well! and if for ever . . .' (17 March 1816) Byron was saying goodbye not merely to Annabella but to any hope of an Iphigenia figure in his life. His despair and resentment for this were expressed, unworthily, in the even more notorious 'A Sketch' which pours bitter scorn on the lady's maid, Mrs Clermont, whom he suspected of poisoning his wife's mind against him. Neither of these poems, though they made much stir at the time, merits our attention as poetry.

From Annabella, Byron's emotional revulsion was to an earlier Iphigenia figure, his half-sister Augusta.[1] The Augusta–Byron relationship and the Dorothy–Wordsworth one are oddly similar, even down to the hints of incest, itself a major Romantic theme.

This is the 'all nameless' guilt which is the mainspring of *Manfred*, but in these transitional lyrics we hear only of the Egeria side of the relationship, the tenderness and understanding that led Wordsworth to write his 'She gave me eyes, she gave me ears', and Byron his 'Stanzas to Augusta':

> When Fortune changed—and Love fled far,
>   And Hatred's shafts flew thick and fast,
> Thou wert the solitary star
>   Which rose and set not to the last . . .   (iii)
>
> Thou stood'st, as stands a lovely tree,
>   That still unbroke, though gently bent,
> Still waves with fond fidelity
>   Its boughs above a monument.   (vii)

This is the elegiac pathos of 'Oh! snatch'd away . . .!' The second set of 'Stanzas to Augusta' is less successful: jaunty anapaests hardly fit this theme: but the 'Epistle to Augusta', written in 1816 (Byron is by now on the Continent), but not published until six years after the poet's death, reinforces the love-childhood-nature motif:

> I feel almost at times as I have felt
> In happy childhood; trees, and flowers, and brooks,
> Which do remember me of where I dwelt
> Ere my young mind was sacrificed to books,
> Come as of yore upon me, and can melt
> My heart with recognition of their looks;
> And even at moments I could think I see
> Some living thing to love—but none like thee.   (vii)

We are witnessing a revulsion and a regression; from the disappointment of his marriage back to Augusta, back to childhood, to Scotland, even to the dark watershed of the streams of birth and death, the prenatal state where, in his father's loins, he and Augusta are united.

> Could I remount the river of my years
> To the first fountain of our smiles and tears,
> I would not trace again the stream of hours
> Between their outworn banks of withered flowers,
> But bid it flow as now—until it glides
> Into the number of the nameless tides.

These lines open a 'fragment' (Diodati, July 1816) which we may regret Byron's failure to complete, since it is of an intensity rarely met with in reflective verse and it begins to touch on themes—the

meaning of death, the identity of absence with death, the possibility
that the dead enjoy some kind of shadowy consciousness:

> . . . do they in their silent cities dwell
> Each in his incommunicative cell?
> Or have they their own language? and a sense
> Of breathless being?—darkened and intense
> As Midnight in her solitude? . . .

on which we would gladly hear Byron further. But of course these
were to be the themes of *Manfred* and of the group of reflective
poems we have now to consider.

'The starlight of his boyhood'

> . . . To keep the mind
> Deep in its fountain . . .

This intense aspiration, first voiced in *Childe Harold* (III, lxix), lies
at the core of Byron's reflective—or, as it might better be called,
intuitive—verse. For Byron is not a poet of reflection as is Wordsworth, Coleridge or even Keats. T. S. Eliot, in a famous passage of
criticism, talked of the Romantics 'ruminating'. Byron does not
ruminate, chew the cud of recollected experience, nor does he
ratiocinate, building systems on glimpses of 'reality' or 'truth'.
I have already written of Byron's capacity for reacting with his
whole being to an immediate experience; there was thus no 'space'
left over for him, as it were, to dwell on memory data, he is too
busy with the here-and-now, and the intersection of the here-and-
now not with the stream of recollection but with the shaft of eternity.
Byron's problem is the complexity and insistence of sense data; he
recognises in himself the danger of being submerged and carried
away by the torrent of events, and his 'reflective' poetry focuses a
constant effort to anchor himself in the inner source of his being.
This possibility of anchorage in his own centre (the 'my fountain-
mind undisturbed' of the Zen story) was something which sustained
Byron through all his external dissipations and explosions. It
sustained in the two senses of the word, as anchor and as source, the
hidden fountain of joy, strength and peace. A *hadith* of the Prophet
is relevant: 'Everything shall return to its origin.'[2] Those who
knew him in his early years, or accompanied him on his travels,
remark again and again on his habit of withdrawing suddenly and
unexpectedly from 'the hot throng' to sit alone for hour upon hour

on some rock overlooking the sea, plunged deep in the exploratory and revitalising contact with his innermost self.[3] The same note often sounds in the private Journals, though tinged even here with the mocking self-depreciation which runs through his letters and reported conversation:

> I do not know that I am happiest when alone; but this I am sure of, that I never am long in the society even of *her* I love,[4] (God knows too well, and the devil probably too,) without a yearning for the company of my lamp and my utterly confused and tumbled-over library. . . . I have sparred for exercise (windows open) with Jackson an hour daily, to attenuate and keep up the ethereal part of me. The more violent the fatigue, the better my spirits for the rest of the day; and then, my evenings have that calm nothingness of languor, which I most delight in. (10 April 1814)

'Hobhouse rhymes and journalises; I stare and do nothing', he writes to Francis Hodgson from the Salsette frigate as it lies off Abydos on 5 May 1810. Byron's *wei wu wei* is very close to Wordsworth's 'wise passiveness' and even closer to the Keatsian 'indolence' on which I have commented at length in my book *The Consecrated Urn*; what I have had to say there (especially on pp. 56–66) may very largely be applied to Byron too. But we must be careful to distinguish Byron's 'indolence' from his 'speculation' or reflection. This is the creative 'idleness' of which his first volume of verse celebrates the canonical 'hours'.

A division similar to 'indolence'/'speculation' may be of use in categorising Byron's later lyrics: we might see it as 'calm nothingness of languor'/'metaphysics' (one of Byron's favourite words, as his letters and journals show). The mood of 'all passion spent' suffuses the lyrics of the first category. 'All things remount to a fountain, though they may flow to an ocean', he remarks in his 'Detached Thoughts' (No. 101), thus neatly summing up the inner and outward movements of his thought which I dwelt upon in an earlier chapter. If this final sentence of Thought 101 represents his 'calm nothingness' side, the 'speculation' with which the Thought opens: '. . . I sometimes think that *Man* may be the relic of some higher material being, wrecked in a former world, and degenerated in the hardships and struggle through Chaos into Conformity . . . as the Elements become more inexorable . . .' belongs to his 'metaphysical' thinking: such a retraction from the cosmic to 'the mind deep in its fountain' is characteristic of Byron. Speculations on the origin, nature, and destiny of Man are of course important factors in his biblical dramas (discussed in chapter 10) but they also motivate a number of non-dramatic and non-lyrical poems. Of these 'Darkness' is the best-known example.

This poem, one of Byron's very rare excursions into blank verse outside the dramas, was originally called 'A Dream'. It was written during Byron's residence at Geneva, and is dated July 1816. Jeffrey's comment will serve both as a summary and as an indication of how it was received by contemporary opinion:

'Darkness' is a grand and gloomy sketch of the supposed consequences of the final extinction of the Sun and the heavenly bodies; executed, undoubtedly, with great and fearful force, but with something of German exaggeration, and a fantastical solution of incidents. The very conception is terrible above all conception of known calamity, and is too oppressive to the imagination to be contemplated with pleasure, even in the faint reflection of poetry. (*Edinburgh Review*, xxvii, Feb. 1817.)

Sir Walter Scott, usually one of Byron's most appreciative critics, found the poem obscure and 'feverish'. 'The waste of boundless space into which they lead the poet, the neglect of precision which such themes may render habitual, make them, in respect to poetry, what mysticism is to religion.' But in fact there is nothing obscure or feverish about the poem itself. It is a fragment of science fiction in verse (the theme of the Last Man was interesting many writers at this time) written with an almost clinical precision of statement which makes the horror of the subject even more intense. And it is of course much more than a thiller: it is a presentation of the end of one of the aeons in cyclic time, the revelation of the chaos 'without form and void' shown to Cain in Byron's later drama, the interval before the inauguration of a new 'aeon'.[5] It is interesting to remember that *The Ancient Mariner* too had been greeted (by Southey) as 'a Dutch attempt at German sublimity'. The opening lines of 'Darkness' give the gist of the theme:

> I had a dream, which was not all a dream.
> The bright sun was extinguished, and the stars
> Did wander darkling in the eternal space
> Rayless, and pathless, and the icy Earth
> Swung blind and blackening in the moonless air;
> Morn came and went—and came, and brought no day,
> And men forgot their passions in the dread
> Of this their desolation; and all hearts
> Were chill'd into a selfish prayer for light:
> And they did live by watch-fires—and the thrones,
> The palaces of crownéd kings—the huts,
> The habitations of all things which dwell,
> Were burnt for beacons . . .

The writing is notably firm and controlled. There is no plot, and little emotional development, though the fidelity of a dog guarding the corpse of its master provides a moment of Byronic pathos.

Also dated July 1816 is another blank verse poem, 'The Dream', which is a mournful celebration of his love for Mary Chaworth and at the same time a sort of emotional 'Tintern Abbey', presenting Byron's inner progress from warm idealism to desolation and despair. This is a longer and more personally interesting poem than 'Darkness'. The opening section explores one of Byron's deepest preoccupations, the relationship between sleeping and waking, and of both with the creative act. Note the greater lightness and flexibility of the verse; this is Byron's speaking voice:

> Our life is twofold: Sleep hath its own world,
> A boundary between the things misnamed
> Death and existence: Sleep hath its own world,
> And a wide realm of wild reality . . .   (1–4)

The nature of dreams is discussed:

>   . . . they speak
> Like Sibyls, of the future; they have power—
> The tyranny of pleasure and of pain;
> They make us what we were not—what they will,
> And shake us with the vision that's gone by,
> The dread of vanished shadows   (11–17)

One such dream occupies the remainder of the poem. In section ii the mournful confessional music begins:

> I saw two beings in the hues of youth
> Standing upon a hill, a gentle hill,
> Green and of mild declivity . . .
>   —the hill
> Was crowned with a peculiar diadem
> Of trees, in circular array, so fixed,
> Not by the sport of nature, but of man: . . .
> The Maid was on the eve of Womanhood;
> The boy had fewer summers, but his heart
> Had far outgrown his years, and to his eye
> There was but one belovéd face on earth,
> And that was shining on him.   (iv. 27–49)

Here, plainly, we have a further regression from the mortifying fiasco of his marriage, beyond Augusta, now, to boyhood dreams and hopes; but they too had issued in frustration and humiliation. 'Do you think I could care anything for that lame boy?', Mary Chaworth is reported to have remarked to her maid; and Byron overheard her, or was told of the remark. No wonder his first title for 'The Dream' was 'The Destiny', Byron's lifelong destiny of frustration, from the initial lameness right up to the final tragicomedy of Missolonghi.

> Time taught him a deep answer—when she loved
> Another; even *now* she loved another,
> And on the summit of that hill she stood
> Looking afar if yet her lover's steed
> Kept pace with her expectancy, and flew.   (ii. 70–4)

Byron never wrote better blank verse than this; the last two lines have a Dantesque bareness and shudder.

The remaining seven short sections trace Byron's life in its stages as an emotional drama rooted in this primal trauma:[6] an Oresteia, as it were, reduced from dynastic to personal terms. Section iv shows him 'a wanderer' in 'the wilds/Of fiery climes . . ./And his Soul drank their sunbeams':

> —and in the last he lay . . .
> Couched among fallen columns, in the shade
> Of ruin'd walls that had survived the names
> Of those who rear'd them.   (iv. 114–18)

In section vi his marriage is briefly touched on:

> The Wanderer was returned.—I saw him stand
> Before an Altar—with a gentle bride;
> Her face was fair, but was not that which made
> The Starlight of his Boyhood.   (vi. 145–9)

In section viii he is 'alone as heretofore':

> The beings which surrounded him were gone,
> Or were at war with him; he was a mark
> For blight and desolation, compassed round
> With Hatred and Contention; Pain was mixed
> In all which was served up to him, until,
> Like to the Pontic monarch of old days,
> He fed on poisons, and they had no power,
> But were a kind of nutriment; he lived
> Through that which had been death to many men,
> And made him friends of mountains: with the stars
> And the quick Spirit of the Universe
> He held his dialogues; and they did teach
> To him the magic of their mysteries;
> To him the book of Night was opened wide,
> And voices from the deep abyss revealed
> A marvel and a secret—Be it so.   (viii. 186–201)

Already, here, is emerging the figure of the Magus, the wizard endowed through guilt and suffering with powers to probe the secrets of the universe, 'the book of Night', the *Anima Mundi*, who is to dominate *Manfred* and the other metaphysical dramas.

'All that's best of dark and bright'

Byron may plausibly be presented as a vortex moving through a space-time continuum, encountering historical vortices, reactivating and being reactivated by them. The ideogram of the vortical hero is fully active in the Ossianic imitation of *Hours of Idleness*, 'The Death of Calmar and Orla':

He looks down from eddying tempests: he rolls his form in the whirlwind, and hovers on the blast of the mountain . . . his yellow locks . . . streamed like the meteor of the night . . .

and persists through the varied fortunes of *Childe Harold* and the Turkish Tales. But lacking external stimulus the vortex comes, from time to time, to a standstill. The lyrics and longer poems we have just studied belong to one of these periods of calm which so rapidly degenerate into stagnation.[7] Escaping to the Continent, Byron was able once more to expose himself to time-place stimuli, as well as to exciting human contacts both sexual and intellectual.

The renewal is at once apparent in *Manfred* and the last two Cantos of *Childe Harold*, and in a handful of shorter poems as well. Of these by far the most important is the Venice poem, 'So we'll go no more a-roving', which achieves a poised synthesis of rest and motion. Before considering it in detail I should like to glance back at two well-known songs belonging to the transitional period: 'She walks in Beauty', which opens the *Hebrew Melodies*, and 'Stanzas for Music', both of which belong to the same dialectical order. We have already noted how in 'Oh! Snatch'd away in beauty's bloom' Byron's personal vortex is brought to rest on the antitheses of death: bloom/tomb, early roses/wild cypress, to be set spinning again under the torsion of these very antitheses:

Away! we know that tears are vain,
That Death nor hears nor heeds distress.

In 'She walks in Beauty' the opening antitheses, beauty/night, is developed through the stanza: cloudless climes/starry sky, dark/

bright, tender light/gaudy day, purely physical contrasts which the second stanza transmutes into terms of art. This is classical writing. The poet eliminates himself. The effect is one of total simplicity, and it is only on close inspection that we grasp its subtle personal–elemental rhetoric. The poet's anonymity, his self-effacement, stems from his exposure to a 'grace' which is itself 'nameless', ineffable. Though 'She walks in Beauty' has no causal links with the other poems that make up *Hebrew Melodies*, we cannot miss its religious tone: this is a species of catharsis through beauty. Here Byron accepts the grace which Manfred was to reject three years later. The charm of the poem depends on its below–above interfluxes, its personal–elemental, its human–cosmic tensions. We are still within the Sufic world of *The Giaour*.

The 'grace' is composed on the aesthetic level by the union of 'ray' and 'shade', on the spiritual level by the reconciliation of above/below expressed in human terms throughout the three stanzas in the aspect/eyes, tress/face, cheek/brow collocations. This is somewhat in the metaphysical style of Donne's cosmographical–erotic conceits. Marvell's 'Definition of Love' also comes to mind, with its deliberate distancing; Herrick's 'The Night-piece: to Julia' will afford some interesting comparisons. Eyes, brow, tresses compose an upper world of 'night' which is 'dark' in its interiorness: this is the realm of thought, meditation, contact with a superhuman sphere; though dark in itself, it irradiates, through its 'stars', the human world of aspect, face and cheek, evoking the virtues of tenderness, goodness, sweetness, innocence, and peace.

The first stanza posits the *elemental* diagram.

> She walks in Beauty, like the night
>   Of cloudless climes and starry skies;
> And all that's best of dark and bright
>   Meets in her aspect and her eyes:
> Thus mellowed to that tender light
>   Which Heaven to gaudy day denies.

She *walks*: this is a kind of celestial promenade, a circuit through elemental spaces, between the night of the first and the day of the final line: 'And the morning and the evening were the first day'. In a sense she creates, like Heavenly Wisdom on 'that first creating day', the silence and thus the matrix through which she functions. In Sufic terms, she is herself the space in which she moves. 'How can we know the dancer from the dance?'

This metaphysical dance is beautifully but implicitly distinguished

from the earthly dance of 'the hot throng' around her. We turn
back to the note in Wright's 1832 edition of the *Works*:

These stanzas were written by Lord Byron, on returning from a ball-room,
where he had seen Mrs (now Lady) Wilmot Horton, the wife of his relation,
the present Governor of Ceylon. On this occasion Mrs W.H. had appeared
in mourning, with numerous spangles on her dress.

This has more than a biographical interest: its three major terms,
dance, mourning and stars, are elements central to the Byron of
this period. The spangles on the dark dress are the stars in the vault
of night. Mourning and dance are linked with Byron's deformity:
'Since I am lame I cannot dance, yet dancing is in my nature, for
energy dances, and the cosmos itself is a divine dance.'[8] Since Mrs
W. H. was in mourning she would not join in the earthly dance;
and Byron could not: this forms a link between them. His biting
satire *Waltz*, with its attack on the physical implications of dancing,
had been published the previous year.

'And all that's best of dark and bright/Meets . . .'[9] Here opposites
are reconciled. Byron was as interested as Coleridge in the theme of
'extremes meet'. She is serene, yet dynamic, moving between two
worlds. She becomes a symbol, a focus, for Byron; and the agitation
which Byron felt on this occasion (noted by Wedderburn Webster)
is that of one who has received a species of shock, the *saṃvega* or
'aesthetic shock' posited by the Vedantic theorists of Beauty as the
core of every major aesthetic experience. Byron needed first that
'tumbler of Brandy', on his return to his rooms in Albany, and then
the catharsis of composing the poem, if he was to recover his calm.
The poem itself is thus something quintessential to Byron: and this
helps to explain its enduring appeal to the reader. Like the sonnet
for Shakespeare in *his* 'moment of truth', it is a spiritual alembic.

> Then were not summers distillation left
> A liquid prisoner pent in walls of glasse,
> Beauties effect with beauty were bereft,
> Nor it nor noe remembrance what it was.
>> But flowers distil'd, though they with winter meete,
>> Leese but their show, their substance still liues sweet.

Through such a moment one passes from chronological time into
Great Time; it is not a question of something remembered, but of an
eternal revelation, Boethius's *interminabilis vitae tota simul et perpetua
possessio*.

But Byron realised, with Blake ('Who binds unto himself a joy,
Doth the winged life destroy') that perpetual possession in Boethius's

sense means temporal relinquishment. There is no Byron in the
poem, no 'I'. On the temporal plane, Byron is for once *spectator ab
extra*, but he is that only because, on the eternal plane, he is very
much *participator ab intra*. The dynamics of this poem is peculiar. It is
best brought out in a comparison with Wordsworth's 'She was a
phantom of delight'. The occasions of the two poems are at once
similar and dissimilar. Wordsworth is married to Mary Hutchinson,
but Byron has no link with Mrs W. H. In noting that 'I' enters
Wordsworth's poem from the beginning we are not making a disparaging criticism but signalising the stance from which he is
writing.

> She was a phantom of delight
> When first she gleamed upon my sight.

'My sight': the poet is the recording medium, a needle swinging
from point to point in time through a wide arc. The moment comes
and, for Wordsworth, passes. The radar grasps, analyses, computes:

> A lovely Apparition, sent
> To be a moment's ornament;
> Her eyes as stars of twilight fair;
> Like Twilight's, too, her dusky hair;
> But all things else about her drawn
> From May-time and the cheerful Dawn;
> A dancing shape, an Image gay,
> To haunt, to startle, and way-lay.

The elements of Byron's poem are present, but disposed to quite
other ends. Wordsworth stresses the transience of Mary's beauty,
Byron the eternity of Mrs W. H.'s. Wordsworth's is a twilight sphere,
Byron's the deep southern night. Byron's 'every raven tress' gives
us the pure, absolute black, where Wordsworth's 'her dusky hair'
seems to be edging a little; and 'May-time and the cheerful Dawn'
destroys whatever nocturnal effects he may have been building up.
'A dancing shape, an Image gay' removes the figure into that
fairytale world of 'elfin' fancy which both Wordsworth and Coleridge
fell back on when they didn't know what to say next.

Whereas Byron's poem maintains its poise to the end, Wordsworth's
steadily deteriorates as he swings from then to now:

> I saw her upon nearer view,
> A Spirit, yet a Woman too!

The division is fatal to the unity of the experience and of the poem.
He presses on with his analysis:[10]

> A Creature not too bright or good
> For human nature's daily food.

Any transcendental significance Mary may have had is progressively devalued. Clearly it is not through the *ewig weibliche* that Wordsworth will ever make his connection with eternity! Rapture vanishes:

> And now I see with eye serene
> The very pulse of the machine;
> A Being breathing thoughtful breath,
> A Traveller between life and death.[11]

The 'machine' metaphor deals the deathblow to Wordsworth's poem and is almost unbelievable in its insensitivity.

Another poem which comes to mind in reading Byron's first stanza is Donne's 'The Autumnal'. Mrs W. H.'s beauty is not autumnal, but her 'tolerable *Tropique clyme*' unites the extremes, as Mrs Herbert's does:

> Here, where still *Evening* is; not *noone*, nor *night*
> Where no *voluptuousnesse*, yet all *delight*.

Here we are at the Byronic centre. 'There be none of Beauty's daughters' (another anthology piece, composed on 27 March 1815) is in a sense even more central. The tides move through it, tempering and deepening.

> There be none of Beauty's daughters
>   With a magic like thee;
> And like music on the waters
>   Is thy sweet voice to me:
> When, as if its sound were causing
> The charméd Ocean's pausing,
> The waves lie still and gleaming
> And the lulled winds seem dreaming.

Metrical subtleties abound. How are we to read lines 2 and 4? Their rhythm runs clean contrary to lines 1 and 2. Ocean currents cross here, move into eddies in 5 and 6, sink to rest in the quiet cove of the final couplet: it is a shorescape *felt* in its pressures and crispations more than *seen* in its moon-blanched solitude. With the second strophe we are out in mid-ocean:

> And the midnight Moon is weaving
>   Her bright chain o'er the deep.

There is a deliberate widening of the horizon, a deepening of the emotion. A favourite sleeping child image emerges, introducing the maternal element into the Virgin syndrome I have earlier noted:

we pass on, consequently, to planes of 'adoration' and 'the bowed spirit' transcending the natural 'magic' of strophe one.

'So we'll go no more a-roving'[12] belongs to another world—no longer the 'swell of Summer's ocean' or the criss cross of currents in a moonlit cove, though this is also a watery world, the intricate labyrinth of Venice's canals and slightly sinister alleys. Emotionally too we are moving through a very different spectrum. Though 'the moon be still as bright', it shines down on a subfusc world of muted gestures and responses. The scene is shadowy: human artefacts— churches, palaces, bridges—impend over slowly-moving waters. Though never mentioned, the 'fairy city of the heart' is pervasively present. Byron here has achieved a masterpiece of non-statement.

> So we'll go no more a-roving
>   So late into the night,
> Though the heart be still as loving,
>   And the moon be still as bright.
>
> For the sword outwears its sheath,
>   And the soul outwears the breast,
> And the heart must pause to breathe,
>   And Love itself have rest.
>
> Though the night was made for loving,
>   And the day returns too soon,
> Yet we'll go no more a-roving
>   By the light of the moon.

A cyclic poem, in its end is its beginning. A poem of disillusion, of weariness,[13] of ambiguities. Firm rhymes—night, bright; breast, rest; soon, moon—are intercalated with imperfect rhymes—roving, loving; sheath, breathe—of which the first pair is 'feminine', the second 'masculine'. Under the aegis of the noon, the poem is encapsulated in a feminine ambience, pressing softly on the nostalgic nerve: roving, loving, heart, moon, too soon, no more. But at its centre the male weariness, lack of resilience, the sword which cannot bend but may break, asserts itself in protest.

'So . . .' The quizzical, dry, slightly mocking tone is established at the outset. We may read it with a variety of nuances. 'So . . .': *very well*; or, *is it really true?*; or, *given that, then . . .?* We have not exhausted the possibilities. The archaism 'a roving' (about which I shall have more to say) also suggests irony, a playing down of the situation, a deliberate skirting of the absurd (for her sake, or Byron's? we don't know, but perhaps it is an echo of her voice we

hear in 'So late . . .', an echo of the flirtatious beginnings of the
attachment: 'Let's explore Venice . . .'—'But, darling, it's so late . . .')
Trivia, so far, with a touch of pathos infused from the woman's
predicament. But the pattern is suddenly disturbed, and 'So late'
takes on a darker significance with 'into the night'.[14] 'So late'
modulates into 'Too late', 'roving into the night' becomes a perilous
adventure, takes on resonances of destiny, of the human condition,
Eliot's 'they are all gone into the dark'.

Eliot comes to mind again in the hint of a popular song in line 1 of
the third stanza, where the banality adds a further ingredient to this
complex poem, as 'The moon shone bright on Mrs Porter' does to
'The Fire Sermon'. This is a side to Byron's technique which is, or
should be, acceptable to modern readers, though it made little
sense to his contemporaries. Pope knew it as 'The Art of Sinking';
indispensable in a long poem, it can be effective in a short one too.
In a sense, indeed, 'So we'll go no more a-roving' as a whole is an
exercise in the art of sinking. Is there a phrase in the three stanzas
which is 'poetic' or 'magical', anything felicitous to set side by side
with Keats's 'perilous seas' or Wordsworth's 'sovereign cry'? The
poem 'sinks' into its triple context: topical, the between-the-lines
ambience of palace-shadowed canals, looming churches; existential,
the universal human predicament; personal, the immediate man–
woman situation. Byron has achieved here that coalescence of time,
place and loved one, that 'grace dissolved in place', that he sought
through a thousand cruces in *Childe Harold* and the Tales; but he
achieves it at the point of dissolution. The extraordinary impact of
the poem, felt by every reader, depends on its being a non-poem, on
its submergence in an impersonal substrate, as the effect of the grey
column 'commingling slowly with heroic earth' in the earlier verse
depended on its sinking out of the sphere of humanity into that of
Nature.

But to discuss the poem as poetry we must return to the personal, to
the immediate situation and the means by which this is conveyed.
Deeply involved, the speaker seems to withdraw; again the 'I' is
absent, '*my* heart' is replaced, clinically, by '*the* heart'. We are
presented with a situation which is not directly described. All that
leads up to it is assumed to be understood; in this sense the poem is a
private document, an entry in an erotic journal. For understanding,
the poet relies on the reader's common humanity, his sharing in the
existential irony. The vortex has brought these two together; now it
separates them, throws them on to its outer rim, where the night is

waiting to receive them. We are at the still centre, the eye of the cyclone, watching the disruptive process. Irony permits us this double stance. It is the moment of the breaking wave, the turning tide.

The poem acts as a miniature lens, a concave mirror. Its action is by indirection, meiosis, even absurdity. Take that initial 'a roving'. The archaism isn't simply archaic, it's rustic too, belonging to the world of minor balladry from which Byron took it, hopelessly out of place in the baroque sophistication of Venice, as though one tootled a violoncello theme of Vivaldi on a bamboo pipe. This 'is at least one definite false note', as Eliot puts it in his 'Portrait of a Lady', in our Venetian symphony. Within the tiny compass of the poem we move in and out of 'irony', 'absurdity', 'sincerity', 'pathos', 'cruelty', 'detachment', 'commitment', 'personality', 'impersonality'; the miniature vortex spins to the tune of these compulsions. For this is stasis in kinesis: not stagnation, not even the poised calm of 'She walks in beauty' or 'There be none of Beauty's daughters', but a taut, coiled-spring nucleus of divergent forces. I see this poem as the hinge of Byron's gate from past into future.

Irony is implicit in the poem's circular structure.[15] We 'rove', but are trapped in the circuit of our own insufficiencies, in the maze of Venice itself and all it stands for: the unreal, the operatic, the overfluid. The initial 'So . . .' is answered by the terminal 'Yet . . .' The false rhymes, 'roving/loving', 'sheath/breathe', imply an emotional ambiguity infecting both partners. The wavering, watery rhythms, the obliquity of phrase conveying a shared experience which yet for Byron is solitary (keeping a sceptical corner to himself) the tone poised between acceptance and regret—all this is sited within the amphibious city. The sensitivity to 'this grace dissolved in place' passes here into an inner dimension. Woman and city are not distinct. Does the woman exist apart from the city? Cities, for Byron, are always feminine; for Blake and Shelley they are generally masculine, foci of tyranny. His relation to Athens (*Childe Harold* II) was filial, the impulse was to revere and protect; to Venice it is loverlike. If 'The spouseless Adriatic mourns her lord' the Doge, Byron is not reluctant to comfort her and Venice's widowhood:

> I loved her from my boyhood—she to me
> Was as a fairy city of the heart . . .

This necessity to identify himself with places, and his emotional contacts with places, may have its origins in Byron's own rootlessness, his lack of a 'background'; that time, place and loved one should not only be 'together' but fused was for him a compulsion. Hence the later 'Stanzas to the Po' and the final 'On this day . . .'.

To savour the subtle contours of a place's, a time's or a woman's identity was part of the Byronic sensitivity, which left him free to be the ironic observer—yet a *spectator ab intra*, not *ab extra*. The full irony is achieved only by the totally involved. Byron could not say, with Landor, 'I strove with none, for none was worth my strife'— almost anything which touched humanity was worth Byron's strife, and he struck at Izaak Walton in defence of fishes[16] with the same fervour with which he opposed the Turks in support of Greece. Human beings could defend themselves, however, as fishes could not; Byron is never flippant about wounded eagles or stags at bay. Women flummoxed him: the long, involved ordeal of Mrs Byron, May Gray, Mary Chaworth, Theresa Macri, London prostitutes, Annabella, Augusta, Caroline Lamb—it was all too much. 'The sword outwears its sheath.' No Freudian exegesis of the phrase is necessary to let us feel the utter sexual fatigue of the middle stanza. Here he is at the centre, the 'moment of truth'. Here human insufficiency is set against 'romantic' demands: the sword outwears its sheath, the heart must pause to breathe, love itself must rest. Was there ever a 'love poem' with such a wry admission of failure? Yet the poem exists as a love poem. Such a success could only be sustained through an equilibrium set up *in* the poem as artefact, *outside* the poem as existential drama. Its existence in the poem I think I have sufficiently demonstrated—in its close, cyclic pattern, its skeletal, almost algebraic emotional image structure. Outside the poem (while implied in it) a whole time structure is seen to be evolving. If the middle stanza, the moment of *present* truth, comes as a quiet explosion, the first and third stanzas function in terms of past and future. This is a poem of time and the heart's battle with time. Line 1 *connects* the future—'We'll go'—with the past—'no more'—and the present—'a-roving'; line 2 *comments*—'So late?— and *menaces*—'into the night'. Space adds its ironies too: the bright moon shines down with indifferent glamour on fragmented time and hearts. There is a bitter antithesis in 'bright' and 'loving'—the 'cold, lunar beam' and the warm, vulnerable heart. Anyone who has loved and lost knows that terrible brightness of the moon. It lights up, here, the Piranesi vistas of arcades receding into arcades, piazzas, alleys, canals, and the tiny human figures waving briefly to each other as the night receives them.

Notes and references

1   'At a time when all my relations (save one) fell from me like leaves from the tree in autumn winds, and my few friends became still fewer' (*LJ* v, 576) is a lament which echoes through the later letters and journals.

2   A letter to Murray of 24 September 1821 expresses Byron's urge to withdraw his mind to its fountain—keeping its 'feelings like the dead, who know nothing and feel nothing'. And here is where Nature helps: 'As long as I can retain my feeling and my passion for Nature, I can partly soften & subdue my other passions and resist or endure those of others' (Letter to Isaac Disraeli of 10 June 1822).

3   'They show a tomb in the churchyard at Harrow, commanding a view over Windsor, which was so well known to be his favourite resting-place, that the boys called it "Byron's Tomb"; and here, they say, he used to sit for hours, wrapt up in thought' (*Works of Byron*, 1832, vii, 49, footnote). What Byron experienced on these occasions is spelled out for us in *The Island* II, xvi. (The choice of a gravestone as a seat neatly inserts Byron in the melancholy tradition explored by Eleanor M. Sickels in her book *The Gloomy Egoist*.)

4   The reference is undoubtedly to Augusta.

5   'The passage from one *yuga* to another occurs in the course of a dusk, marking a decrescendo within each *yuga*, which always ends with a stage of darkness', Marcea Eliade writes (*Eranos Yearbook* iii, p. 179). A complete cycle, a *mahayuga*, ends in 'a dissolution, a *pralaya*, which is repeated more radically (*mahapralaya*, the "Great Dissolution") at the end of the thousandth cycle' (*ibid.*). At the microcosmic level one may quote Rumi. 'Dreams play an important part in the process of unification . . . Rumi views reality as a dream-like world and it is in a dream that one leaves oneself and enters another self, or in his words, "In sleep you go from yourself to yourself"' . . .' A. Reza Arasteh, *Rumi the Persian*, Lahore, 1965 p. 151).

6   'Subsequent events have proved that my expectations might not have been fulfilled, had I ever proposed to and received my idol' (*LJ* iii, 406).

7   'I am so tired,' he writes in his 19 September 1816 Journal at Diodati, 'for though healthy, I have not the strength I possessed but a few years ago': and to Moore on 6 November of the same year: 'I am subject to casual giddiness and faintness.'

8   As Sir John Davies had urged in *Orchestra*. (The words between quotation marks are of course not Byron's but my paraphrase of what might have been in Byron's mind.)

9   The received reading is 'meet' but the original (1815) has 'meets', which seems to me preferable in its unifying overtones.

10 Forgetting that wise remark of an earlier day, 'We murder to dissect'.

11 Neither one who whistles as she goes for want of thought nor one who breaks through the Traveller's dream.

12 An old Scots song, 'Sae we'll gang nae mair a-roving' is the origin of Byron's lyric (see *MLN*, Feb. 1931). The fusion of motifs from

his Highland past and his Venetian present is perhaps the most brilliant instance of what I have called his genius for connection, the 'carry-through' which extends from 'Lachin Y Gair' to *The Island* (see below, p. 264). I have to apologise here, as I do some pages later in discussing 'On This Day I Complete My Thirty-Sixth Year', for considering a poem out of its chronological sequence. My excuse is that Byron—particularly in his lyrics—is not a chronologically developing poet; and we are often better served, exegetically, by putting a lyric of 1815 employing water imagery side by side with one of 1817 using or subtly implying the same imagery, than we are by isolating the one or the other in a mass of narrative or descriptive poems. I discuss this problem at the beginning of Chapter 9.

13   Cf. letter to Moore from Venice (28 February 1817): 'Though I do not dissipate much upon the whole, yet I find "the sword wearing out the scabbard", though I have but just turned the corner of twenty-nine.' The poem carries the same date. 'I will work the mine of my youth to the last vein of the ore, and then—good night', he tells Moore in a later account of the 1818 Carnival: 'I have lived—and am content' (*LJ* iv, 198).

14   The phrase comes directly from the Scots ballad, but a line in the original MS of *The Giaour*, replaced in the printed poem by the present line 1146, supports my 'sombre' reading of this phrase: 'That quenched, I wandered far in night.'

15   Circles, diagrammatising the 'vortices', run through Byron's life and work: a circle of trees on a hill-top 'mark the spot where a story ended', his early love for Mary Chaworth; bullrings and amphitheatres are prominent in *Childe Harold*, as are 'a stern round tower of other days', and the Pantheon; the 'circus' of Bonnivard's cell in *The Prisoner of Chillon* connects with the 'amphitheatre' of the besieged Ismail in *Don Juan* VII, xxiii. Rome is 'the circus of an empire' in *The Deformed Transformed* I, ii, 282.

16   *Don Juan* XIII, cvi.

8

POEMS
OF EXILE

The tornado exists in its motion and only there. Slowing down, it disintegrates. For Byron, as we have seen, perpetually new stimuli were required to activate the poetic nerve. Not for him the Wordsworthian feeding on old experiences, or the Shelleyan delight in 'the abstract joy'. The great lyrics are moments of temporary stasis in the universal flux, and the best of these are necessarily brief. In the poems we have just considered, the spinning top betrays no wobble, the poise is perfect, the note secure. In each, we live in the moment, and the moment contains within itself the seed of its own renewal. From the momentary stalemate of 'Oh! snatch'd away . . .' the lysis comes in the last stanza: 'Away! we know that tears are vain . . .'; in the others the imagery, the evanescence of the situation itself, warn us that soon we must be on our way to fresh woods and other pastures.

But these were poems of transition, of the hinge moment of Byron's life, when many possibilities lay open to him. As the routine of his Italian sojourn closed in on him we sense a lessening of emotional and intellectual tension. More and more his themes centre in situations of checkmate or stalemate—imprisonment, exile, shipwreck, the marooned sailor, the castaway. The series begins with *The Prisoner of Chillon* and ends with *The Island* and 'On this day I complete my thirty-sixth year'; it includes *The Lament of Tasso* and *The Prophecy of Dante*. Since I have just discussed the best of his lyrics, 'So we'll go no more a-roving', I shall begin this exilic section of my survey with a glance at 'On this day',[1] a poem which has received high praise from a number of critics. It was approved of by so devout a Wordsworthian as the late Sir Herbert Read, and

Arnold included it in his anthology, while rejecting 'There be none of Beauty's daughters', to my mind a much finer poem.[2] He includes it, I think, not on a 'real' but on both a 'personal' and an 'historical' estimate[3] of its value. For Arnold, too, liked to think of himself as a warrior making a last stand against the Philistines:

> Charge once more, then, and be dumb!
> Let the victors, when they come,
> When the forts of folly fall,
> Find thy body by the wall!

This is the very accent of Byron's poem:

> Seek out—less often sought than found—
>   A soldier's grave, for thee the best;
> Then look around, and choose thy ground,
>   And take thy rest.

Or rather, let us say, one of the accents, for even a cursory reading shows us that 'On this day . . .' is a remarkably confused and ill-knit document. Perhaps the immediate circumstances of its composition have something to do with this. Count Gamba records:

This morning Lord Byron came from his bedroom into the apartment where Colonel Stanhope and some friends were assembled, and said with a smile— 'You were complaining the other day, that I never write any poetry now. This is my birthday, and I have just finished something, which, I think, is better than what I usually write.' He then produced these noble and affecting verses.

'Still let me love'

There is something pathetic about Byron's hesitant 'production' of the new poem, and something very uncharacteristic about its genesis: written to *prove* something, written for the occasion. Birthdays were things Byron usually passed over in grim silence. But now Byron is at the end of his tether. The night has closed in about him; he is irreversibly 'the castaway', with no avenue of escape save death. The vortex is immobilised, stifled in the mud and muddle of Missolonghi. Byron is frustrated at every turn, deprived on the one hand of that fruitful solitude which sustained his reflective centre, and on the other of the action, the significant gesture which would fulfil his historic destiny. 'Byron . . . Byron . . . Byron', he had scrawled over the page of *Childe Harold* which posed his own prophetic questions:

> Fair Greece! sad relic of departed worth!
>   Immortal, though no more; though fallen, great!
>   Who now shall lead thy scattered children forth,
>   And long accustomed bondage uncreate . . .
>   Oh! who that gallant spirit shall resume,
> Leap from Eurotas' banks, and call thee from the tomb?

(II, lxxiii)

And 'Byron' is still the answer in that strand of the present poem which projects the Byronic *will*, the gesture towards fulfilment in action:

> The Sword, the Banner, and the Field,
>   Glory and Greece, around me see!
> The Spartan, borne upon his shield,
>   Was not more free.

Yet even here, with all the dash and daring of the rhetoric, we discern a collapse, a contradiction. That Spartan, sad relic of departed Harrow schooldays, what is he doing here? I do not query him simply as a faded classical 'property', for which presumably Byron would have got a rap over the knuckles from Dr Drury, but as an *in any way* meaningful support of Byron's stance. The Spartan soldier, however noble, is a *dead* soldier, and what Greece needs at this juncture is living soldiers, and shields as defences, not as stretchers. The trope is not even neat: in what sense is the Spartan free—and 'more free' than whom? In what context? This collapse of meaning-structure infects the whole lyric; on inspection we find it is not one poem, but two, very clumsily glued together, and with no necessary connection with each other.

Poem I consists of verses i to iv, and viii; poem 2 of verses vi, vii ix and x. Verse v is an awkward join. The first poem is plaintively amatory:

> 'T is time this heart should be unmoved,
>   Since others it has ceased to move:
> Yet, though I cannot be beloved,
>   Still let me love!

The whine is unpleasant; the second thoughts implant a seed of disruption in the poem from the outset. Worse is to follow.

> My days are in the yellow leaf;
>   The flowers and fruit of Love are gone;
> The worm, the canker, and the grief
>   Are mine alone!

That Byron has to fall back on Shakespeare, so early in so short a poem is ominous; and now we are in full botanical spate: leaf, flowers, fruit worm, canker—'Solitary Grief' by 'Twelfth Night' out of 'Macbeth'!

> The fire that on my bosom preys
>> Is lone as some Volcanic isle;
> No torch is kindled at its blaze—
>> A funeral pile.

From fruit, worms and cankers we are wrenched into another set of clichés: fires, islands, torches, volcanoes, funeral pyres. He is plagiarising his own *Sardanapalus* and

> 'The cold in clime are cold in blood
>> Their love can scarce deserve the name;
> But mine was like the lava flood
>> That boils in Aetna's breast of flame.' (1099–1102)

from *The Giaour*. Compare the resilience of that (however 'crude' we may judge it to be) with the limp defeatism of this last poem. And the defeat is critical as well as emotional: only a year earlier Byron had laughed at his volcanoes in a witty stanza of *Don Juan*:

> I hate to hunt down a tired metaphor,
>> So let the often-used Volcano go.
> Poor thing! How frequently, by me and others,
> It hath been stirred up till its smoke quite smothers!
>> (XIII, xxxvi)[4]

That is a Byron still in possession of his faculties of humour and self-criticism. In the next stanza of 'On this day . . .' we are confronted with a Byron who has sustained the final defeat: an inarticulate Byron!

> The hope, the fear, the jealous care,
>> The exalted portion of the pain
> And power of love, I cannot share,
>> But wear the chain.

Presumably this means something; to know *what* demands a long footnote, which Byron does not give us.[5] The alliteration (and alliterations on the letter *p* are rarely effective outside a comic setting) does not reassure. We wonder what is the *un*-exalted portion of the pain and power of love—does he 'share' that? Do we (Lord Mayors aside) ever 'wear' a chain? The stanza is a muddle, and our minds may well revert to the Venice lyric with its brilliant turning to account of an unexplained situation as the polar opposite of this unfortunate poem.

Limply abandoning its cankered fruits and volcanic isles, the
lyric sags back into self-pitying complaint. Stanza v is a joiner and
a bracer, ludicrous in its determined tightening of the upper lip.

> But 't is not *thus*—and 't is not *here*—
>   Such thoughts should shake my soul, nor *now*
> Where Glory decks the hero's bier,
>   Or binds his brow.

And it's still all wrong. Italics, that bane of Byron's poetry, try to
compensate for the lack of internal stress. The counters are false
tender: shaken souls, bound brows, hero's biers. How could this
sort of thing be accepted by critics of the eminence of Arnold and
Sir Herbert Read as genuine currency? The answer, if I have got it
right, is interesting. You start off with the recognition of Byron as a
major poet, of *some* sort; you know he is a 'Romantic' poet; you do
not like the side of him that is not 'Romantic'; you ferret out the
bits that are *something* like Wordsworth or Shelley, blow them up,
turn a blind eye to their defects, and hey presto! here is your
respectable 'Romantic' Byron. Grateful anthologists bring up the
rear.

Poem 2 now begins:

> The sword, the banner, and the field,
>   Glory and Greece, around me see!
> The Spartan, borne upon his shield,
>   Was not more free.
>
> Awake! (not Greece—she *is* awake!)
>   Awake, my spirit! Think through *whom*
> Thy life-blood tracks its parent lake,
>   And then strike home!

'Awake, my spirit!', he says. But to awake it must hark back to old
dynastic arrogances, to his mother's descent from the Kings of
Scotland, and this brings him up against something much stronger
than repute, the still-living, still-torturing mother–son antagonisms
of his childhood. And once again the attempted surge outwards,
into freedom, into action, is cramped by ancient fetters.

With stanza viii we are back in poem 1:

> Tread those reviving passions down,
>   Unworthy manhood!—unto thee
> Indifferent should the smile or frown
>   Of Beauty be.

The reviving passions were homosexual, probably for Loukas, the
last of those 'little pages' who were always so picturesque a feature

of Byron's wanderings over the Mediterranean scene. War and love, his old antitheses, engage in a final tussle here: for a moment Achilles, sulking in his tent over Patroclus, focuses a fading vignette of a Harrow schoolroom. The theme affords an unconvincing modulation into poem 2. But all is poorly realised, argumentative, fussily petulant:

> If thou regrett'st thy youth, *why live*?
>   The land of honourable death
> Is here:—up to the Field, and give
>   Away thy breath!
>
> Seek out—less often sought than found—
>   A soldier's grave, for thee the best;
> Then look around, and choose thy ground,
>   And take thy Rest.

The first line seems to mean: If the urge to revert to boyhood is so strong that life as an adult is hardly worth living, why not end it all? Better perish in battle. It is not a very heroic compulsion. That a soldier's grave might be best for Byron is a personal judgement on which it is useless to comment. That a soldier on the battlefield has it in his power to look around and choose his ground, whether for fighting or dying, is so improbable as to verge on the ludicrous, and the jingle of the internal rhyme adds a music-hall touch.

Byron's final lyric[6] is an extreme case of what happens to his writing when the integrating vortex-into-vortex spin is suspended. I could bring forward other examples from among his later lyrics, but what is the point of analysing bad poems? A handful of longer poems—not bad, and meriting our critical attention—close the reflective-elegiac-prophetic roster for this penultimate epoch of his career. In these too the same suspension of energy, the same failure of nerve, may be traced. All are projections of the 'castaway' syndrome.[7] All are identifications—with Bonnivard, with Mazeppa, with Tasso, with Dante. But they are voluntary identifications; in the Missolonghi lyric the horrid reality will be forced upon him. Yet in Byron's 'circle of destiny' we may discern the Missolonghi entrapment as the lethal, negative centre of the maelstrom, exerting its pull from the beginning, a 'black hole' in 'the eternal space' into which the castaway is being sucked from the days of his earliest gyrations on the outer rim, the days of Newstead, Harrow, Cambridge, and the Pilgrimage, when 'freedom'—from his early life, from morality, from society, from himself—seemed poised on the next gyre of the vortex.

The earliest period had sought a steady centre in love or fame; the second period finds a moving centre in the self-knowledge gained in traversing the East and the inner spaces; the third period sees a clash of the vortex with the stasis of Regency society, only half resolved in the growling transit of the Low Countries, Germany and Switzerland; Italy permits a new spin through art, architecture, sex and the Ferrara-Rome vistas into the focus of the Coliseum. The final period upsets a precarious balance by its clash of opposing forces: affection for Teresa, involvement in the struggle for Italian freedom, boredom with everyday life, the pull of Greece. The lyric I have just analysed demonstrates that even Greece was not enough to solve these dilemmas.

'My soul was drunk with love'

I have already had something to say about *The Prisoner of Chillon* and *Mazeppa*, Byron's first projections of the castaway. *The Lament of Tasso* (1817) is a closer identification; Tasso himself is a poet, his imprisonment is (reputedly) for love and means a deprivation of love; he has been judged mad by his oppressors.

> Long years!—It tries the thrilling frame to bear
> And eagle-spirit of a Child of Song—
> Long years of outrage—calumny—and wrong;
> Imputed madness, prisoned solitude,
> And the Mind's canker in its savage mood,
> When the impatient thirst of light and air
> Parches the heart; and the abhorred grate,
> Marring the sunbeams with its hideous shade,
> Works through the throbbing eyeball to the brain
> With a hot sense of heaviness and pain.   (1–10)

The vortex is spinning here: the long, involved sentence gyrates through its intricacies of rhyme from the freedoms of 'eagle-spirit' and 'Child of Song' down through a narrowing funnel to the 'hideous shade', the 'throbbing eyeball' and the 'hot sense of heaviness and pain'. This is splendid, but the trouble is that it can be done, with effect, only once in a poem: the pattern suits a sonnet, but sets an impossible standard of intensity for a longer work. The rhyme scheme is admirably fitted to the feverish, involuted, semi-delirious mood of the poem: like the striations in the inner wall of a rapidly spinning funnel, the rhymes unfold, interlace, separate, come together again,

with vertiginous effect: a, b, b, c, c, a, d, e, f, f . . . and so on for the
thirty-two lines of the first section. If we are tempted, as we are in
watching the interlacing striations in such a spinning funnel, to
impose a pattern of regular rhyming (say in groups of six: a, b, b, c,
c, a) we shall find the symmetry deceptive; Byron's strophe development is genuinely long-term. Each of the nine sections of the poem
is a *bolge*, a funnel spinning at speed. If we think of the rhymes in
terms of their vowel sounds only, the use of recurrence is even more
striking: in section 1 we have only six terminal sounds, in which long
a, long and short *i*, and long and short *o* predominate. This reinforces the obsessive effect. If this could have been kept up the
result would have been a masterpiece. But the triumph is self-
destructive, like continuing to watch a sunset or smell a rose. After
strophe 1, our attention wanes.

The second section slows down, in fact, into a series of banal
couplets, losing the striated drive.

> But this is o'er—my pleasant task is done:—
> My long-sustaining friend of many years!
> If I do blot thy final page with tears,
> Know, that my sorrows have wrung from me none.
> But Thou, my young creation! my Soul's child!
> Which ever playing round me came and smiled,
> And wooed me from myself with thy sweet sight,
> Thou too art gone—and so is my delight.   (33–40)

So opens section ii; and there is no recovery. Even the favourite
'soul of my thought' theme (*Childe Harold*, III, vi) of artistic creation
fails to get the section off the ground. Section III seeks to recoup
these losses by a *coup de théatre*: the cries of madmen from another
part of the prison are suddenly heard, mixed with the brutal oaths
of their torturers. (Webster had done this better in *The Duchess of
Malfi*.) But the attempt to widen Tasso's personal suffering into a
community of pain is abortive; he knows that 'each is tortured in
his separate hell—/For we are crowded in our solitudes' (87–8).

Nevertheless, *The Lament of Tasso* makes its point as a profoundly
moving diagram of pain and frustration. If it is not a great *poem*, but
rather what Coleridge called 'Kubla Khan', 'a psychological
curiosity', the fault lies partly, as I have suggested, in the very special
skill shown by Byron in devising a structural pattern adequate to his
emotion but not to the development in verse of that emotion, and
partly in the absence from its 'world' of those elements—light, air,
sunshine, mountains, the sea—which I have already suggested.

perhaps *ad nauseam*, to be ingredients of success for Byron. For lack of outside friction, the spin slows down disastrously towards the close of the poem.

As though conscious of this, Byron introduces in section vi an excursus which removes the axis of the poem from the dungeon to the air of freedom, and in doing so opens up one of his favourite fields of speculation. Tasso is thinking of the power of love to 'foil the ingenuity of Pain':

> It is no marvel—from my very birth
> My soul was drunk with Love—which did pervade
> And mingle with whate'er I saw on earth:
> Of objects all inanimate I made
> Idols, and out of wild and lonely flowers,
> And rocks, whereby they grew, a Paradise,
> Where I did lay me down within the shade
> Of waving trees, and dreamed uncounted hours,
> Though I was chid for wandering; and the Wise
> Shook their white agéd heads o'er me, and said
> Of such materials wretched men were made,
> And such a truant boy would end in woe,
> And that the only lesson was a blow.   (149–61)

The rock and the flower combine in a Blakean passage which brings us nearer to the boy Byron at Aberdeen or Harrow than to the boy Tasso at Sorrento. And in 'drunk with love', in the connection of the erotic with 'objects all inanimate',[8] we are back with the Byron of *Childe Harold* who feels that

> All is concentered in a life intense,
> Where not a beam, nor air, nor leaf is lost.   (III, lxxxix)[9]

Significant for our understanding of Byron, the passage breaks for a moment (but only to emphasise) Tasso's bitter realisation of his predicament. The contrast between the willed solitude of childhood days and the enforced loneliness of prison, between a love expanded through the universe and a passion feeding on itself—

> Dwelling deep in my shut and silent heart,
> As dwells the gathered lightning in its cloud,
> Encompassed with its dark and rolling shroud,
> Till struck,—forth flies the all-ethereal dart!   (113–16)

—brings Tasso to thoughts of madness and suicide (sections viii and ix), the 'final solution' of Byron's tragic heroes from Manfred to Sardanapalus. He resists, upheld by the dream of fame. Within the poem's structure these conflicting motives constitute a mainspring, replace to some degree the outer thrust, keep the poem in motion, but cannot compensate, in Byron's poetry, for the fruitful intercourse of inner and outer, the cosmic dynamism.[10]

'Loved ere I knew the name of love'

The Prophecy of Dante was written at Ravenna in June 1819 on a visit to Teresa Guiccioli. 'Being deprived at this time of his books, his horses, and all that occupied him at Venice', Teresa records, 'I begged him to gratify me by writing something on the subject of Dante; and, with his usual facility and rapidity, he composed his *Prophecy*.' Byron himself described the poem, in a letter to John Murray, as 'the best thing I have ever done, if not *unintelligible*'. Byron had not much in common with Wordsworth, but a total absence of the critical faculty connects them, as far as their own writings are concerned: *The Prophecy of Dante* is not the best thing Byron ever did. Nor is it 'unintelligible'. We can read in it, all too clearly, the initial stages of Byron's lapse into the morbidities, self-pitying compulsions, and self-destructive urges which culminated in 'On this day I complete my thirty-sixth year'.

Byron's veneration for 'the great Poet-Sire of Italy', as he calls him in his Dedicatory Sonnet, was of long standing. His 'childish amour' for Mary Duff (Journal, 26 November 1813) chimed with Dante's love for Beatrice; the Italian poet's unhappy marriage and exile were a paradigm of his own.[11] Dante's popularity with his own countrymen reminded him of his own contemporary fame (Journal, 29 January 1821). Questioning Wordsworth's contention 'that *no* great poet ever had immediate fame; which being interpreted, means that William Wordsworth is not quite so much read by his contemporaries as might be desirable',[12] he points out that 'Dante's Poem was celebrated long before his death; and, not long after it, States negotiated for his ashes, and disputed for the sites of the composition of the *Divina Commedia*'. We must remember too that among modern poets it was Dante who embodied the classical and European values so essential for Byron, as for Arnold, as a counterpoise to Shakespeare.

Dante, then, is a living voice speaking from the past. Homer, Virgil, Horace, Sappho are also voices speaking from the past (and precious voices for Byron) but they are not living voices. Shakespeare is a living voice (and precious for Byron) but he does not speak from the past. Living in Italy, Byron felt himself in direct contact with this magisterial utterance, a presence linked through Virgil with the ancient world and through tradition with the modern. He can merge himself in its flux. This is important for Byron, a poet who always speaks out of a mobile context (while other poets seek to anchor themselves) of 'what is past, and passing, and to come'. That Dante is a Christian and indeed a theological poet hardly matters for Byron, who has the wit anyway to penetrate behind the doctrinal carapace (neither accepting nor rejecting it)[13] to the archetypal verities it expresses. I suspect too that he sensed Dante's other roots in the Islamic, Sufic civilisation which had come to mean so much to him in his earlier wanderings.[14] I believe that if Byron had lived he would have opened himself more and more to the influence of Dante. For here he found, disciplined, controlled, the stresses behind his own output. Here he found patterned energy.

All this being said, one records with regret that *The Prophecy of Dante* is not a success. Put crudely, there is too much Byron, too little Dante. And it is Byron in his worst, his self-pitying, world-cursing *persona*. Initially, one expects a triumph. The poem begins well, with Dante emerging from the tremendous otherworldly experience of the *Divina Commedia*:

> Once more in Man's frail world! which I had left
> So long that 'twas forgotten; and I feel
> The weight of clay again,—too soon bereft
> Of the Immortal Vision which could heal
> My earthly sorrows. . . .   (I, 1–5)

The metrical form too, the *terza rima*, with its interlacing rhymes, might be expected to give scope for what I have called the 'mobile context' of Byron's *weltanschauung*. But the trouble is that this is not a mobile Dante. This is Byron's version of a defeated, an exiled Dante. A disagreeably nagging tone swiftly asserts itself. Through the mouth of Dante, Byron voices his own frustration, bitterness, thirst for revenge. The immediacy of Tasso's situation, in the earlier poem, is absent: the dungeon, the tyrant, the lost love; and we do not feel for Dante the human sympathy we have for Tasso. A dungeon is one thing, exile another.

Tasso's dungeon is a powerful 'objective correlative' in the earlier poem; Byron attempts to give Dante as useful a one in his image of the marooned sailor towards the close of Canto I:

> For I have been too long and deeply wrecked
> On the lone rock of desolate Despair,
> To lift my eyes more to the passing sail
> Which shuns that reef so horrible and bare:
> Nor raise my voice—for who would heed my wail? (I, 138–42)

But 'deeply wrecked' is a bad phrase, and 'wail' is an insult to the stern grandeur of Dante. Self-pity is contaminated with the revenge obsession, so tiresome a feature of the autobiographical Byron:

> . . . my lone breast may burn
> At times with evil feelings hot and harsh,
> And sometimes the last pangs of a vile foe
> Writhe in a dream before me, and o'erarch
> My brow with hopes of triumph,—let them go! (I, 105–09)

This is fustian, and exploitation. And though the poem picks up somewhat in the succeeding cantos, where Dante's prophetic vision, ranging through the centuries, lists one by one the catastrophes which will afflict Italy and Europe, even here the obsessional, nagging note persists.

Even in his development of the love theme, where Byron has so much in common with Dante, at least in his early idealism, there is a failure of response the moment it touches the obsessive theme of banishment. Note how the following passage, opening with an effect of sincerity and tenderness, degenerates into a shambles both syntactical and metrical after the fifth line:

> Since my tenth sun gave summer to my sight
> Thou wert my Life, the Essence of my thought,
> Loved ere I knew the name of Love, and bright
> Still in these dim old eyes, now overwrought
> With the World's war, and years, and banishment,
> And tears for thee, by other woes untaught;
> For mine is not a nature to be bent
> By tyrannous faction, and the brawling crowd,
> And though the long, long conflict hath been spent
> In vain—and never more, save when the cloud
> Which overhangs the Apennine, my mind's eye
> Pierces to fancy Florence, once so proud
> Of me, can I return, though but to die,
> Unto my native soil,—they have not yet
> Quenched the old exile's spirit, stern and high. (I, 28–41)

The old exile Dante would hardly have described his own spirit as 'stern and high', but the young exile Byron, in full self-pitying 'wail', has no such qualms.

In his 'Stanzas to the Po', another poem of 1819 and like *The Prophecy* written at Ravenna, Byron strikes a more assured note. It was written 'in red-hot[15] earnest', he says in a letter of 8 June 1820 to Hobhouse, but there is nothing fervid about it. Indeed it is a curiously impersonal poem; it opens with a cluster of tired archaisms: 'the Lady of my love', 'perchance', 'faint and fleeting memory', but improves in its second stanza:

> What if thy deep and ample stream should be
> A mirror of my heart, where she may read
> The thousand thoughts I now betray to thee,
> Wild as thy wave, and headlong as thy speed!

It is a poem *to* Teresa, but *about* Byron, and if 'The Dream' was his 'Tintern Abbey', this is his approach to the Immortality Ode (or, more closely, to Coleridge's 'Dejection'). For it is a threnody, a lament for vanished powers, for decayed passions. These were once as tumultuous as the Po, but now

> Time may have somewhat tamed them,—not for ever[16]
> Thou overflow'st thy banks, and not for aye
> Thy bosom overboils, congenial river!
> Thy floods subside, and mine have sunk away:
>
> But left long wrecks behind, and now again,
> Borne on our old unchanged career, we move:
> Thou tendest wildly onwards to the main,
> And I—to loving *one* I should not love.   (13-20)

The Wordsworth–Coleridge aesthetic—'I see, not feel, how beautiful they are'—is here transposed into the Byronic passional: 'Such as thou art were my passions long'. But the tone is muted, Arnoldian rather than Byronic or Wordsworthian. And later stanzas present Marvellian paradoxes:

> But that which keepeth us apart is not
> Distance, nor depth of wave, nor space of earth,
> But the distraction of a various lot,
> As various as the climates of our birth.

The poem is, then, an oddity. In his one and only river poem Byron seems to be fishing, rather desultorily, for new possibilities, new bearings. But its final stanza points directly to Missolonghi:

> 'Tis vain to struggle—let me perish young—
> Live as I lived, and love as I have loved;
> To dust if I return, from dust I sprung,
> And then, at least, my heart can ne'er be moved.

That a nerve has failed, that Byron has lost his way, that a lobotomy is being operated on the complex structure we have explored in *Childe Harold*, and the Tales: these are different ways of saying the same thing. However we phrase it, it seems clear to me that Byron in his brief development goes the same road, from spiritual riches to impoverishment, trod by Wordsworth and Coleridge in their longer pilgrimage. But he covers it up. He can do this because of the reservoir of pure energy he still harbours within himself. The energy is there, but the channels in which it used to flow are silting up. In the dramas, in *Beppo* and *Don Juan*, Byron will open new channels to his daemonic drive: but they will be shallower, narrower than before.

We can push this diagnosis a bit further. The later Byron is the castaway, but he is so because he is now the fragmented Byron. At some point in the years of transition, perhaps at the moment when he clutched at the prospect of happiness with Annabella, Byron broke his link with his inclusive 'identity', with the all-sentient Byron to whom 'high mountains *are* a feeling', who lives through these stony extensions of his human senses. In the poems of exile and despair he is the outcast. In the dramas and long poems of the final period—in *Don Juan*, *The Island*, and even in *The Vision of Judgment*—he is the split man; and as such we shall go on to consider him in the next section.

Notes and references

1   The poem was written on 22 January 1824; my discussion of it here is chronologically indefensible, but there are times when dates have to bow to the claims of exegesis.

2   I suspect, though of course it cannot be proved, that Arnold's not very subtle ear was baffled by the poem's metrical complexity.

3   The three estimates listed by Arnold in his essay 'The function of poetry', which opens his *Essays in Criticism* II.

4   The apology to Shakespeare in *Don Juan* XIV, lxxv,

> I will not make his great description less,
>   And beg his British godship's humble pardon,
> If, in my extremity of rhyme's distress,
>   I touch a single leaf where he is warden;—

is also much more relevant to 'On this day . . .'.

5   Since this piece of criticism was first published in my second Byron
essay in the 'Writers and Their Work' series (1971) it has been
suggested to me that Byron meant 'portion' in the sense of 'lot',
'destiny', rather than 'part'. This reading helps to some extent, but
the stanza remains confused.

6   Or last but one. Hobhouse thought that the lines beginning 'I
watched thee when the foe was at our side' were the last Byron wrote.

7   I shall continue to use this term as shorthand for the complex of
imprisonment, rejection, abandonment, isolation and despair images
in Byron's work from now on. A re-reading of Cowper's poem
'The Castaway' may help the reader's understanding.

8   'Inanimate' meant, in Byron's day, not 'dead' but 'without a
[human] soul'.

9   See above, my *The Lost Travellers*, p. 68n.

10   A contemporary critic, John Wilson ('Christopher North'), had a
perceptive comment: 'This fearful picture is finely contrasted with
that which Tasso draws of himself in youth, when nature and
meditation were forming his wild, romantic and impassioned genius.
Indeed, the great excellence of the "Lament" consists in the ebbing
and flowing of the noble prisoner's soul;—his feelings often come
suddenly from afar off,—sometimes gentle airs are breathing, and
than all at once arise the storms and tempest,—the gloom, though
black as night while it endures, gives way to frequent bursts of
radiance,—and when the wild strain is closed, our pity and com-
miseration are blended with a sustaining and elevating sense of the
grandeur and majesty of his character.'

11   Cf. *Don Juan* III, x, xi.

12   'Observations upon an article in Blackwood's Magazine' (Ravenna,
1820).

13   Byron's religious beliefs (or superstitions) are a complex subject, to
which E. W. Marjarum's *Byron as Sceptic and Believer* (Princeton
University Press, 1938) is the best introduction.

14   Researches over the last half-century have shown the considerable
penetration of Islamic thought into *La Divina Commedia* and other
works of Dante.

15   'Red-hot' is a curious epithet to find here. The Po is the classical
river Eridanus into which Phaethon fell, and was extinguished (as
Byron sometimes felt himself to be in the embraces of the Countess
Guiccioli). Rivers were never wholly congenial to Byron: they are
images of restriction and of the irreversible flight of time.

16   I omit the semicolon printed at the end of this line; it is clearly a
mistake.

Part Three

THE MAZE
AND THE MORASS

9

THE SECOND PILGRIMAGE

A critic finds two major difficulties in writing about Byron. One is when to take him seriously: many of his deepest insights are expressed in terms of irony or farce. The other arises in trying to discuss his work chronologically, consecutively. He keeps so many different pots boiling at the same time that it is hard to develop a reasoned, sustained approach to any one facet of his output. One would have to have a mind as 'mobile' as Byron's own to assess his work on its own terms of thrust and counterthrust, shifting levels, self-cancelling alternations of the sublime and the ridiculous, the epic and the satiric. When these antitheses are combined in a single poem— *Don Juan* is of course the great exemplar—then we are forced to cope somehow; the essence of the work lies in its disparities. But when we are dealing with a 'period' of writing, some kind of compromise is forced on us. Chronology has to be abandoned in favour of sustained discussion first of one genre, then of another. We may decide to focus on the dramatic. Yet a fragment of lyrical verse which surfaces between two plays may have a decisive effect on the second of them, and though we lay it aside for the time being we may find we have to go back to it.

This problem is at its height in the final period, the period of *Don Juan*, where the fragmentation of Byron's *oeuvre* is the clearest index of the fragmentation of his personality. It is difficult to bear in mind that while he was writing his picaresque masterpiece he was also at work on those static, statuesque presentations of what Paul West has well called 'the trapped man': the plays, and in particular the Venetian plays. And that, concurrently with these, we also have *The Prophecy of Dante*, *The Lament of Tasso*, *The Age of Bronze* and 'So we'll go no more a-roving', with a number of lesser lyrics and reflective poems.

In no other major writer that I can think of do we meet with so extreme a disparity of tones within a given 'field'. Of Blake in 1800 to 1803 at Felpham, of Wordsworth in his first years at Grasmere, of Shelley in the whole of his Italian sojourn, one can say 'here and here are the subjects, the attitudes with which his imagination is engaged, a consistent and self-explanatory whole, towards which he has evolved from the preoccupations of London or Marlow', still carrying over, needless to say, this or that thread from the immediately preceding or some still earlier period. Maps of Wordsworth's, Coleridge's, Shelley's, even Keats's metaphysical journeys have been drawn up, beginning with Godwin or Hartley and ending with Plato or Berkeley: simplifications, no doubt, of much more complex patterns, but with enough veracity to make them useful as pointers. No such route maps can be drawn up for Byron. 'I am myself, alone.' What that self is has to be discovered not in progression, but in endless experiment from a centre which, while not fixed, is immutable, persistent.

The *genres* cross and clash with the life spans. We naturally take *Childe Harold* III and IV, *Manfred, The Prisoner of Chillon, Mazeppa, Sardanapalus, Cain, Heaven and Earth,* and *The Island,* as products of the 'romantic' Byron, and *Beppo, Don Juan, Marino Faliero, The Two Foscari, The Vision of Judgment, The Age of Bronze,* as formulations of the 'classical' or 'realistic'. Yet in this final span, 1816 to 1823, classical and romantic poems interlace with bewildering complexity. Within the poems themselves, and above all within *Don Juan,* the ambiguity is manifest. We cannot, or should not, complain: this is the 'metaphysical' Byron, restoring the 'unified sensibility' of Marvell, Rochester or Donne: an achievement without which the Imagist revolution would have been impossible. And Byron might well have gone Donne and Eliot's way, towards a reconciliation with the Church as the solution of his personal antinomies. But he is also the increasingly fragmented Byron, making poetic capital out of his inner disunity. 'These fragments have I shored against my ruins.'

The 'trapped' man of Mr West is at once the cause and the effect of my 'fragmented' man. He is the effect because, feeling himself to be fragmented in the crucial 1811–16 years, he searches desperately for a principle of unity first within and then outside himself: 'Marriage would be my salvation' (Journal, 16 January 1814).

Many a lesser man than Byron has fallen into this age-old trap, and either come to terms with it or else escaped from it without fatal consequences. But Byron's need was urgent and his fragmentation radical. The fragmentation itself proceeds from the first trap of childhood misery and neurosis: 'My springs of life were poisoned.' In the opening stanzas of Canto III of *Childe Harold*, Byron himself makes the revealing connection in terms of springs and fountains. I have called the second part of this book 'The Gulf and the Fountain', and the present part 'The Maze and the Morass', but these are my labels, not clearcut frontiers in Byron's life map. The mid-European transit of Canto III is an existential journey for Byron: here we see him in process of transmutation from Childe Burun to *cavalier serviente*; but the end is not yet. Canto III projects flight rather than pilgrimage: flight from the trap of marriage and the 'vortex' of social inanity which fame has brought him:

> Harold, once more within the vortex, roll'd
> On with the giddy circle, chasing Time.   (III, xi)

Why once more? To answer this question, we must glance back to the antecedents of his earlier tour. 'I am here in a perpetual vortex of dissipation', he writes to Elizabeth Bridget Pigot from London on 13 July 1807. His Eastern experiences had rescued him from the whirlpool; but the fame resulting from his poetic account of those experiences submerged him once more. And because the outer vortex corresponds to an inner gulf—

> I *have* thought
> Too long and darkly, till my brain became,
> In its own eddy boiling and o'erwrought,
> A whirling gulf of phantasy and flame

—and because that gulf in its turn is the product of the 'poison'd springs' of childhood, there is no possibility of renewal: ' 'Tis too late!' (vii). The only hope could be in a sort of spiritual transfusion, the cleansing of poisoned springs from 'a purer fount'. This is what marriage with Annabella was to have meant:

> . . . he filled again,
> And from a purer fount, on holier ground,
> And deemed its spring perpetual; but in vain!   (III, ix)

Things were not to work out like that for Byron.

The canto of transit

The opening stanzas of Canto III add up to a rather remarkable gallimaufry. The crude but sharp contours of Canto I, the classical proportions of Canto II, have vanished.[1] We are here in full spate of a creative chaos. Opening with sentiment, in the address to the infant Ada, the tone modulates immediately to defiance of 'Albion's lessening shores' and welcome to the unchartered violence of the sea (i–ii). Reflection and action, past and present, are brought together. There is an abandonment to unconscious forces:

> Still must I on; for I am as a weed,
> Flung from the rock, on Ocean's foam to sail
> Where'er the surge may sweep, the tempest's breath prevail.

The guidelines of the earlier Pilgrimage—the quest for self-knowledge, the willed immersion in *autres pays, autres moeurs*—are abandoned. The new journey is in one sense more interior, in its submission to unconscious currents; but in another sense, that of Byron's deliberate seizing on the dramatic event, landscape, artefact as a means of distracting himself from his inner woes, it is more external. There is more rhetoric in Canto III. It is very good rhetoric, and I use the term not in a pejorative sense but as descriptive; nevertheless we miss the meditative subtleties of the Greek canto.

Much of this new canto conveys Byron's bitterness at his rejection by English society after the separation; in this respect it is the most personal of all the cantos, the bitter firstfruits of exile. Indignation lends a vehement, fiery quality to his verse; travel again becomes an escape, as in Canto I, and intensity of emotion fuses 'the wandering outlaw of his own dark mind' (iii) with the scenes of past or present violence through which he passes. Tension is implicit in the opening simile, 'Though the strained mast should quiver as a reed' (ii); it is noteworthy that images of strain and release accumulate in the journals and letters of this period. There is a fear of diminished poetic power expressed in stanza iv:

> Since my young days of passion—joy, or pain,
> Perchance my heart and harp have lost a string,
> And both may jar: it may be, that in vain
> I would essay as I have sung to sing.

Certainly we miss the fresh, spontaneous, forward-and-around-looking spirit of the earlier cantos. The psychic field has narrowed, as the earlier sea vistas narrow to the 'arrowy Rhone' and the 'clear, placid Leman', eikons of tension and its release. It is forgetfulness (iv), not the self-knowledge of Canto II, that Byron now hopes to achieve.

Nor, to begin with, does the landscape inspire. There is little description in the first part of Canto III, and the reason may be found in Byron's *en route* letter to Augusta of 1 May 1816:

As the low Countries did not make part of my plan (except as a route), I feel a little anxious to get out of them. Level roads don't suit me, as thou knowest; it must be up hill or down, and then I am more *au fait*.

The lack of a viable 'correlative' to his inner landscape forces Byron into the dramatic rhetoric of the Waterloo stanzas. But the writing of verse can still be his refuge from 'selfish grief or gladness' (iv). At this point the analysis of his inner condition deepens into a remarkable evocation of the mind's cave as the dwelling-place of archetypes (v–vii), a passage Coleridgean in its images of fostering matrix and haunting shapes. The stanza (to which I return at a later point in this book[2]) takes us back to that 'impromptu' of September 1813 which is one of the most classically perfect of his early lyrics.

> When, from the heart where Sorrow sits,
>   Her dusky shadow mounts too high,
> And o'er the changing aspect flits,
>   And clouds the brow, or fills the eye;
> Heed not that gloom, which soon shall sink:
>   My Thoughts their dungeon know too well;
> Back to my breast the Wanderers shrink,
>   And droop within their silent cell.

Walter Scott's comment on this poem is interesting.

'These verses are said to have dropped from the poet's pen, to excuse a transient expression of melancholy which overclouded the general gaiety. It was impossible to observe his interesting countenance, expressive of a dejection belonging neither to his rank, his age, nor his success, without feeling an indefinable curiosity to ascertain whether it had a deeper cause than habit or constitutional temperament. It was obviously of a degree incalculably more serious than that alluded to by Prince Arthur—

> — — 'I remember when I was in France,
> Young gentlemen would be as sad as night
> Only for wantonness.'

But, however derived, this, joined to Lord Byron's air of mingling in amusements and sports as if he contemned them, and felt that his sphere was far above the frivolous crowd which surrounded him, gave a strong effect of colouring to a character whose tints were

otherwise romantic.' Scott's indefinable curiosity' might have been
assuaged by stanzas v to vii of Canto III: these elucidate Byron's
impromptu with a powerful retrospective light. 'Sorrow' now takes
on an archetypal shape, a vast brooding shadow, part *Magna Mater*,
part Our Lady of Sorrows, the image of man's fallen condition and
the darkened Eden from which he is excluded; the 'thoughts' are
the lesser, surrounding archetypes, which emerge, seeking a release
in poetry which they do not always find, and so 'shrink back' to
'the soul's haunted cell'. The systole-diastole movement of the
lyric is also an important Byronic characteristic.[3]

With these hints before us, we shall have no difficulty in de-
ciphering the course of Canto III as a series of presentations of
Byron's major archetypes: those we have already come to recognise
in the earlier Pilgrimage. Most personal of these eikons for Byron is
fire—around this nucleus he constructs ideograms expressive of a
wide variety of states. Fire indeed is of the essence of the creative
mind itself, as he declares openly at the outset of the canto:

> I *have* thought
> Too long and darkly, till my brain became,
> In its own eddy boiling and o'erwrought,
> A whirling gulf of phantasy and flame.   (III, vii)

The fiery ring of the scorpion's torment in *The Giaour* has filled the
whole circle, and the maddened victim and its 'field' are now one.
Doubtless too the fiery whirlwind of the illicit lovers in *Inferno* V
should be kept in mind. Fire in Canto III is to be both source and
material; the fluid rhythms of the Greek canto are replaced by
passionate personal stresses, rendering untenable the role of detached
observer he had sometimes assumed in the earlier cantos.

No wonder then that the first scene of the canto is Byron's
grimmest evocation of war, the field of Waterloo (xvii–xxxiii). The
connection with 'the giddy circle' is convincingly made through the
ball at Brussels on the eve of the battle,

> when Youth and Pleasure meet
> To chase the glowing Hours with flying feet—   (xxii)

and the 'glow' of love is refashioned into a 'fiery mass/Of living
valour, rolling on the foe/And burning with high Hope', soon to
'moulder cold and low'. Counterpointed with man's 'fiery' stupidities
are the cool benisons of Nature, proffered in vain (xxvii), and her
incessant efforts to restore the felicity man so wantonly destroys:

> But when I stood beneath the fresh green tree,
> Which living waves where thou didst cease to live,
> And saw around me the wide field revive
> With fruits and fertile promise, and the Spring
> Come forth her work of gladness to contrive,
> With all her reckless birds upon the wing,
> I turned from all she brought to those she could not
>   bring. (xxx)

The pathos of this rapidly modulates into the gloomy reflections
on human life (xxxiv–xlv) which centre round the antithetical
figure of Napoleon—extreme in both grandeur and misery. Byron
opens the passage with an acute observation, anticipating Freud,
on the death wish:

> There is a very life in our despair,
>   Vitality of poison, (xxxiv)

then sketches in the Emperor's character (with traits which seem to
draw somewhat on the Byronic hero), and closes with an analysis,
still in terms of fire, of the class of men to which Napoleon belongs:

> But Quiet to quick bosoms in a Hell,
>   And *there* hath been thy bane; there is a fire
> And motion of the soul which will not dwell
> In its own narrow being. (xlii)

Turning once more from human folly to the calm of Nature,
Byron begins his voyage up the Rhine. Here he cannot but be
conscious of the river's antithetic history of bloodshed, of warring
barons and the softer annals of chivalrous love, 'But still their
flame was fierceness' (xlix); and his personal history of love and
strife recurs bitterly to his mind (lii–lv). He remembers his child
Ada, and his half-sister Augusta, to whom the stirring lyric 'The
castled crag of Drachenfels' is inscribed. The martial grandeur of
Drachenfels frowning down upon the gently flowing Rhine and the
banks where

> peasant girls, with deep blue eyes,
> And hands which offer early flowers,
> Walk smiling o'er this Paradise

is one of those antithetic ideograms in which Byron delighted. His
verse habitually progresses by means of such contrasts—alternations
from fierceness to tenderness, from grave to gay, from man to nature,
from personal to impersonal. These antitheses function within the
broader pattern of alternate descriptive, meditative, and confessional

poetry which gives *Childe Harold* its uniqueness. There is a constant retraction and expansion of vistas from an intensely concentrated core, or nucleus, outwards in widening circles of descriptive and reflective data (often antithetical among themselves), and back again to 'the lonely breast'.

The lonely breast was not so lonely as the poem would lead us to believe, for Byron was accompanied by his doctor, Polidori, and was later joined at Geneva by his old travelling companion, Hobhouse. Moreover it was at Geneva that he met Shelley and Mary Godwin on 27 May 1816, the day after his arrival. So began one of the decisive literary friendships. Shelley's influence on Byron is apparent in the increasingly 'metaphysical' note in his poetry from now on. Shelley's admiration for Wordsworth led Byron to re-read him, and though I have never been able to see anything Wordsworthian in Byron's view of Nature, there are some lines along which it is profitable to draw comparisons.

Byron's 'Is it not better, then, to be alone/And love Earth only for its earthly sake?' (III, lxxi) seems a counterblast to Wordsworthian metaphysics. Byron loved to merge himself in Nature—'I become/ Portion of that around me, and to me/High mountains are a feeling' (lxxii)—rather than to brood over her and philosophise as a *spectator ab extra*. What for Wordsworth is 'a motion and a spirit, that impels/All thinking things, all objects of all thought' ('Tintern Abbey') is for Byron a shared *life* in which he is caught up, which lives itself through him: concentration, rather than diffusion or 'interfusion':

> From the high host
> Of stars, to the lulled lake and mountain-coast,
> All is concentered in a life intense,
> Where not a beam, nor air, nor leaf is lost,   (III, lxxxix)

—a conception very close to Blake's

> For every thing exists and not one sigh nor smile nor tear,
> One hair nor particle of dust, not one can pass away.
> (*Jerusalem*, pl. 13, 66; pl. 14, 1)

More than this, it is clear that for Byron Nature embodies psychic states and human situations; it is not a question of the landscape being a mere stage on which this or that action may be presented: the action and the characters emerge from the landscape, which has held them *in potentia*. In a long note to stanza c of this canto Byron asserts the 'peculiar adaptation' of the scenery around Clarens 'to the persons and events with which it has been peopled' by Rousseau; and, more than that, 'If Rousseau had never written, nor lived, the same associations would not less have belonged to such scenes'.

But this is not all: the feeling with which all around Clarens . . . is invested, is of a still higher and more comprehensive order than the mere sympathy with individual passion; it is a sense of the existence of love in its most extended and sublime capacity, and of our own participation of its good and of its glory: it is the great principle of the universe, which is there more condensed, but not less manifested; and of which, though knowing ourselves a part, we lose our individuality, and mingle in the beauty of the whole.

This conception of love as the great principle is very far from Wordsworth's 'Wisdom and Spirit of the Universe!/Thou Soul which art the Eternity of Thought!' Byron did not distinguish human, and sexual, love from the love of God or of Nature, and there is a physical quality in his intercourse with Nature—take for instance his grapplings with the sea—which would have revolted the elder poet. 'And thus I am absorb'd, and this is life', he cries in stanza lxxiii. Wordsworth's 'It is the first mild day of March' does indeed celebrate 'love' as 'a universal birth' but the poem is strangely untypical, and the 'love' very different from Byron's. It is, in fact, much closer to Thomson's 'biological' than to Wordsworth's 'metaphysical' doctrine of the Man–Nature nexus.

Byron's view is a complex one. My remarks on these Geneva stanzas obviously do no more than skim the surface of the discussion, and err by generalisation. They are, however, nearer to the truth than the determined efforts of some American critics to play down Byron's feeling for Nature as derivative from Wordsworth. There is a curious school of commentators on the other side of the Atlantic (I have just called them critics, but they are rather biographers with critical aspirations) who are determined to keep a corner in Byron the Regency rake which they feel to be threatened by any attempt to deal seriously with Byron the poet. A spokesman for this school is Professor Ernest J. Lovell, Jr, PhD, of Texas, who believes that Byron's 'preoccupation essentially with *seeing* minimised the possibility of his evolving a genuine philosophy of nature of any kind'—surely an odd remark. The professor starts back in horror from 'Byron's inability to formulate for himself an intellectual system satisfactorily relating God, man and nature'. Satisfactory to whom, one asks? His character, too, complains Professor Lovell, is 'in need of explanation and defense'; he is appalled by 'the many-sided contradictions of [Byron's] life and thought'. A valuable paper might be written on 'Unprofitable demands on Byron by North American professors', but 'let that pass', as Byron would say in his mild way, and let us return to the theme of Nature. Professor Lovell, who is sceptical of the value of giving close attention to Byron's poetry,[4] applies the same critical principle to writing *about* Byron, and so quotes as an actual confession on Byron's part that he had been working under Wordsworth's influence a suggestion made actually by Byron's editor, E. H. Coleridge.[5] Professor Lovell's book was first published in 1949. Anyone can be forgiven for committing a blunder: but when we find the book reissued in 1960 with no correction of this misleading statement (which of course is central to Professor Lovell's support of the orthodox Wordsworthian-imitator view of Byron's Nature poetry) there are liberal shepherds on this side of the Atlantic at least who will feel inclined to give the pro-fessor's blunder a grosser name. Byron's feeling for Nature, and his modes of writing about it, seem to me to stand as the antipodes of Wordsworth's. Wordsworth, that 'solemn and unsexual man', as Shelley calls him, is concerned with excluding anything suggesting the erotic from his picture of cosmic happenings: the various re-visions of *The Prelude*, among other evidence, make this abundantly clear.[6] With Byron, on the other hand, the erotic, the physically warm, vigorous, interpenetrating, fruitful, sensually exciting, is the very mainspring of the universe. His urge is to merge, to submerge (as in swimming), to co-function (using the mountains, the seas as non-individual extensions of his personal identity), to die into and resur-rect from his physical 'field', as ancient warriors and sages commingle with and arise from 'heroic earth', or as these figures of Clarens have their matrix in this particular configuration of lake and mountains. Wordsworth, however, 'worshipping' Nature, remains what Coleridge called him, the *spectator ab extra*, commenting and phil-osophising. His concern with Nature is basically with the *old*, with its permanences and rigidities. Byron's is with the perennially *new*, the Eros which like Augustine's pulchritudo is at once *tam antiqua et tam nova*:

> Love is old,
> Old as eternity, but not outworn,
> With each new being born or to be born.   (*The Island*, IV, ix)

Since Nature is a permanency for Wordsworth, he can extrapolate from her into philosophic systems just as the scholastics extrapolated from that other divine book, the Bible. But for Byron Nature is a flux incapable of predication; 'to love Earth only for her earthly sake' (*CH* III, lxxi) is to move within her currents and submit to her influences. It is only to a conceptualised Nature that Wordsworth submits: even in the apparently naive Matthew poems the marshalling mind is at work, the need to dominate intellectually, to reduce to a system.

Take one of the best-known of Wordsworth's Man–Nature conjunctions, which is also the closest to Byron's vision in its mother and child presentation. To quote it *in extenso* is impossible here, and abbreviation brings the danger of distortion. The passage comes in Book II of *The Prelude*, and traces the growth of infant sensibility to Nature. 'Nature' is at first concentred in the nursing mother. 'Gathering passion' from its mother's eye, the baby's mind

> Is prompt and watchful, eager to combine
> In one appearance, all the elements
> And parts of the same object, else detach'd
> And loth to coalesce. (245–50)

Wordsworth presents us with a *theory* of what is going on in the child's mind, couched in voluntarist terms—'prompt and watchful, eager to combine'—for which no support is likely to be forthcoming from close observation (remember that this is a child still at the breast). On the contrary, the gestures and facial expressions of a child of this age suggest a quite vague and passive relation to an environment which is hardly cognised at all. But even more dubious statements follow. The child's mind 'spreads', we are told, 'tenacious of the forms which it receives'. Working out from the 'beloved Presence' of its mother, it recognises

> A virtue which irradiates and exalts
> All objects through all intercourse of sense.
> No outcast he, bewilder'd and depress'd;
> Along his infant veins are interfus'd
> The gravitation and the filial bond
> Of nature, that connect him with the world. (259–64)

From this it is only a step to the 'Mighty Prophet! Seer blest!' of the 'Immortality Ode', which even Coleridge found it necessary to protest against; and indeed, here we have it:

> his mind
> Even as an agent of the one great mind,
> Creates, creator and receiver both,
> Working but in alliance with the works
> Which it beholds. (271–5)

Now putting aside the unverifiable doctrinal statements, we have
only to consider the *terms* of Wordsworth's presentation to realise
at what an extreme he stands from Byron. A separative framework
of seen and seer, of gravitation and the objects it acts upon, of
bondage (however 'filial') not merely restricting, in which case
there would be some hope of release, but actually 'interfusing' the
infant veins, enmeshes 'the growing boy' from his infancy. This is
'the natural man' in Wordsworth which Blake so forcibly objected
to; and Byron would object as strongly, though from another
extreme. Blake disliked Wordsworth's metaphysics from the platform
of his own metaphysics, Byron detested them from a general distrust
of 'system' and from his own close, non-mentating love of earth 'for
its earthly sake'.[7]

I suppose Professor Lovell would retort that Byron exploits the
Wordsworthian Nature-sensibility without bothering about the
Nature-metaphysics. This is really unacceptable, in a poet as alive
as Byron to every nuance of contemporary thought and in particular
to that of writers he felt to be his antagonists. Against the Lakist
'metaphysics' he asserts his own 'physics'. But there is no passage in
Byron which brings together the themes of Nature and childhood in
precisely Wordsworth's way, for the simple reason that Byron's
way is not Wordsworth's: I cannot therefore make an immediate
and telling comparison. Nature and childhood are both major
Byronic themes, but their intertwining is pervasive throughout the
oeuvre rather than dramatic and particular, as in Book II of *The
Prelude*. Three passages can however be pointed to, and they are
significant: one is the extraordinarily Blakean excursus from *The
Lament of Tasso*, and the second is to be found in the *Epistle to Augusta*,
both of which I quote and comment briefly on elsewhere;[8] the
third comes in the Geneva context we are now considering.

> Clear, placid Leman! thy contrasted lake,
>> With the wild world I dwelt in, is a thing
>> Which warns me, with its stillness, to forsake
>> Earth's troubled waters for a purer spring.
>> This quiet sail is as a noiseless wing
>> To waft me from distraction; once I loved
>> Torn Ocean's roar, but thy soft murmuring
>> Sounds sweet as if a Sister's voice reproved,
> That I with stern delights should e'er have been so moved.
>
> (*CH* III, lxxxv)

We note that Byron, as always, is in transit. He is not merely
contemplating the lake, he is sailing on it, hearing the sounds of its

'soft murmuring' like 'a Sister's voice', watching its gentle breeze fill his 'quiet sail'. There is a real give and take with his context. No philosophising, simply the openness to influence. The theme of childhood enters negatively: Byron had hardly known his sister in early years.

> It is the hush of night, and all between
>> The margin and the mountains, dusk, yet clear,
>> Mellow'd and mingling, yet distinctly seen,
>> Save darken'd Jura, whose capt heights appear
>> Precipitously steep; and drawing near,
>> There breathes a living fragrance from the shore,
>> Of flowers yet fresh with childhood; on the ear
>> Drops the light drip of the suspended oar,
> Or chirps the grasshopper one good-night carol more;
>
> He is an evening reveller, who makes
>> His life an infancy, and sings his fill;
>> At intervals, some bird from out the brakes
>> Starts into voice a moment, then is still.
>> There seems a floating whisper on the hill,
>> But that is fancy, for the starlight dews
>> All silently their tears of love instil,
>> Weeping themselves away, till they infuse
> Deep into Nature's breast the spirit of her hues.
>
>> (III, lxxxv–lxxxvii)

The movement of the initial stanza was from Nature's stillness to a stillness of the heart—the 'purer spring' which may be identified with the 'mind deep in its fountain' of a slightly earlier stanza (lxix).[9] The 'noiseless wing' is the Psalmist's 'wing of a dove' on which he longs to 'flee away and be at rest'. We are not remote from *Hebrew Melodies*. And now, in the 'populous solitude of bees and birds/And fairy-form'd and many-colour'd things' which is Leman and its surrounding shores, that inner landscape of achieved release, if only for the moment, from self, spreads out again into the context of natural objects.[10]

The landscape is presented in its dynamic contrasts not merely of light and shade but of outlines. Like Blake, Byron is a poet of 'the wiry line', the pure colour, the clearly defined mass. Wordsworth is praised, and rightly, as our supreme nature poet; but he is that in the sense of what he extracts from Nature rather than what he sees in her. There is little detail; his forms are amorphous and brooding; and it is significant that his best 'nature poetry' is written away from the scenes he describes. Byron's projection of Lake Leman is a painter's piece, rich in visual detail, while at the same time it is a deeply felt 'correlative' of an interior state. The lake in the foreground, the mountain in the rear, the littoral separating them—each area lives with its own life yet with a subtle give-and-take harmonising the whole, 'mellow'd and mingling, yet distinctly seen'. 'Darken'd Jura' rises above these horizontal textures as 'precipitously steep', an important *point d'appui*. As Byron nears the shore new senses come into play. The 'living fragrance . . . Of flowers yet fresh with childhood', the chirp of the grasshopper, the startled note of the bird, mingle in a healing synthesis. Now we feel the full force of that odd 'contrasted' in the preceding stanza. Leman is 'contrasted' with 'the wild world' in which Byron has been living; but it is also 'contrasted' in the sense of being woven out of contrasts—a vital, breathing, antiphonal entity. It opens itself to communion not only in the play of shades and contours on and around it, but in its unfolding richness of scents and sounds as the 'quiet sail' draws near to the shore.

Among the many absurdities of conventional Byron criticism the most provoking is the accusation of 'rhetoric'. Byron *is* rhetorical where rhetoric is called for (I have already called this the most rhetorical of the cantos, which does not mean that it is rhetorical through and through); where dialectic is called for he is the most compressed, the most 'metaphysical' of Romantic poets. His awkwardnesses are like those of Shakespeare in the later plays, where pressure of thought and feeling compels a species of shorthand. 'Thy contrasted lake' is not an elegant phrase; neither is 'these our interviews', at another point, to convey Byron's contacts with Nature; but close scrutiny reveals their accuracy. Byron's relation to Nature is not that of the pupil to the teacher, or the worshipper to the goddess: it is a true 'interview', in which the being who has issued out of the earth, and will return thither, and she who is the universal mother-and-grave *look at* each other in a glance of quiet and loving recognition. Bonnivard in his cell 'bends upon the mountains high/The quiet of a loving eye'. The majesty of man, the thinking reed, *connects* with the majesty of Nature, the universal flux. To read mind into Nature, as Wordsworth does, or to read mindlessness into man, as again he does with his idiot boys and old leech gatherers, upsets the classical order of things, destroys the validity of the human drama. We cannot acquit Wordsworth of a very major responsibility for the turn that drama has taken in our century. It is ironic that Blake and Byron, whose whole development was within and in defence of the tradition, should now be linked with 'permissiveness' (because they recognised and depicted its modalities in their time) while Wordsworth, whose confusion of the natural and the metaphysical, of the rational and the irrational, really opened the way to the Freudian débacle, is still respected as a moralist and a champion of human dignity.

But I digress. Moving through spaces as his boat touches the shore, Byron also moves through times. The flowers which he smells, not sees, are 'fresh with childhood'—another richly ambiguous phrase. The flowers have the freshness of childhood in their fragile beauty, their innocence, their vulnerability.[11] And these qualities, together with their evocative fragrance (memories of long childhood days in country lanes and fields) bring back the poet's own childhood, *his* time of innocence, with poignant recollection. Shelley writes in *Rosalind and Helen* of 'field smells known in infancy'.[12] This evocative power of smell creates a dimension we do not find in Wordsworth's Nature poetry, though it is keen in Byron, Shelley and Keats. The dimension of sound too—by no means absent from Wordsworth, who connects it rather with 'the ghostly music of the ancient earth' than with any personal reminiscences—opens for Byron into childhood vistas. The grasshopper, in its careless spontaneity of song, its tirelessness in music-making, 'makes/His life an infancy, and sings his fill'. The turn from the accepted 'drinks his fill' is noteworthy. Singing is an outgoing, an expansive act, but for the grasshopper it is as satisfying as the slaking of thirst. 'Careless I sing', as Byron was to write later in *Don Juan*.

The grasshopper 'makes his [whole] life an infancy'. The quality of genius, Coleridge said, lay in the power to carry the feelings of childhood into adult life. Of Juan and Haidée, in his later master-piece, Byron remarks that

> they were children still,
> And children still they should have ever been;
> They were not made in the real world to fill
> A busy character in the dull scene,
> But like two beings born from out a rill,
> A Nymph and her belovéd, all unseen
> To pass their lives in fountains and on flowers,
> And never know the weight of human hours.   (*DJ* IV, xv)

Byron's prescription is of course unfillable in 'the real world': considerations of mass and weight prevent 'beings' from passing their lives 'in fountains and on flowers'. Byron knew this, and his

frequent indictments of the Lake poets for passing their time in an
artificial retirement stem from this recognition that the world must
be taken as it is. Zen says the same. The true sage works within his
everday world, carrying his perpetual childhood within him. This
remorseless honesty of Byron, which so impressed Ruskin—the same
honesty which makes him write in the Waterloo stanzas, 'Grieving,
if aught inanimate e'er grieves', repudiating the pathetic fallacy—is
active too in this Leman passage: 'There seems a floating whisper
on the hill,/But that is fancy.' Among the varied natural voices—the
grasshopper, the startled bird, the drip of the suspended oar (note
how this 'suspension' conveys the hushed, reverential quality of
Byron's response to the revealing moment)—there is heard this
preternatural voice of the dying dews. It is heard by the inner ear,
tuned in silence of Nature to what is beyond Nature. But Byron will
not confuse it with the natural voices.

With 'a floating whisper on the hill' we are inextricably within
Byron's Sufic world of ascents and descents, of love human and
divine intermingling in an iconography of nightingales and roses.
'The dew descends', as with Herbert, 'and with the dew descends
Thy love.' Byron's doctrine of Nature cannot be separated from his
doctrine of love, and neither exists outside the target of his hits and
misses at a theology. What is the whisper? Byron's 'fancy' sees it as
the dropping of the tears of love from heaven, which are 'the
starlight dews'. At first glance as rococo as anything by Tom Moore,
the conceit opens into Byronic depths. The dews descend from the
stars, from the High World, and like the lark which is Los's messenger
in *Milton*,[13] mediate the love and forgiveness of that world to the
earth. They die, giving themselves in silence that the flowers and
birds and grasshoppers—and man—may live.

The dewdrops weep themselves away, 'till they infuse/Deep into
Nature's breast the spirit of her hues'. The 'hues' of earth are not
born on earth; colour is a gift from heaven. The 'white radiance of
eternity' is broken into an earthly spectrum. Whether we take
Nature's hues, here, to be green and blue, her predominant colours,
or the whole spectrum as revealed in the rainbow, the result is the
same. The 'spirit' of green is forgiveness, in the traditional iconography of colour,[14] or submission, in that of Islam; the 'spirit' of
blue is hope, 'blue of Mary's colour'. The rainbow (one of Byron's
most persistent eikons) is God's messenger of forgiveness and assurance to man. These divine essences, Byron is saying, descend to
earth from 'the stars' and are 'infused' into earthly Nature. Each

dewdrop is a healing crystal. Perhaps the thought had remained with him, gaining added depth as his intuition expanded, from the childhood 'sun of memory' reflecting 'the orb of day' which 'Gilds with faint beams the crystal dews of rain', and from that other etherial visitor, the snowflake of 'Lachin Y Gair'.[15] All these delicate prisms—snowflake, raindrop, dewdrop, and, one may add, the fragile Mediterranean flowers of *The Giaour*—are two-way openings: from Eternity to earth in love and forgiveness, from man to Eternity (if he pleases to 'step out' of his prison, in Blake's phrase) in love and gratitude.

Byron's universe is thus structured on the traditional two-tiered pattern of High World and Low World which Wordsworth abandoned for a monotheletic *sensorium*, very much on the Newton model, animated by 'a motion and a spirit' which 'impels' both thinking beings and the objects of their thoughts. The unity thus achieved by Wordsworth is impressive, but it is won at a cost. Austerity can degenerate into barrenness, awe into fear. Love is submerged in 'the pulse of the machine'. Byron's universe is open to the opposite danger. Crystal may easily become filigree. Delicacy of response may decay into 'sensibility'. But Byron averts these dangers by two countermeasures. In the first place, as we have seen, he never confounds the real with the fanciful. In the second place, he always provides a *punctum indifferens*, within these stanzas the 'darken'd Jura', and in the stanzas which follow, of the Alpine storm.

The complex, pastoral, lyrical world of the lake and its margin is counterpointed by the monolithic majesty of Jura, its lower slopes lost in darkness, its peaks standing out 'precipitously steep' with their mantle of snow. This is the inhuman world of 'When Coldness wraps . . .'[16] as against the High World of the stars. Byron notes its presence, but does not allow it to terrify. Perhaps the closest analogy in Wordsworth to this Leman scene is the boat-stealing episode of *The Prelude* I, 'Childhood and school-time', 372–427.[17] Here, as in the Leman stanzas, we have the guilty poet, the lake with its margin, the moving boat, the solitary peak. But the differences are as real as the similarities. Wordsworth's experience is past, Byron's present, his guilt is trivial, while Byron's is crushing, yet Nature's reproach to the boy Wordsworth is menacing, to the man Byron 'sweet as if a Sister's voice reproved'. Of course the Wordsworth passage is not about actual guilt at all, but about Wordsworth's inbuilt sense of fear; he *needs* that stern father figure of the 'huge Cliff' which 'Rose up between me and the stars', as Byron needs the gentle lake-voice of his sister. Byron's experience, wafted from distraction by the sail's noiseless wing, is emotion lived in relationship; Wordsworth's uncharacteristic fugue into distraction—the borrowing of the boat—was rebellion lived in isolation, however recollected now in tranquillity in the bosom of his family. Byron's peak, though inhumanly remote, is not frightening; his eye travels up and above it to the stars.

The boat-stealing episode is one of the most celebrated 'spots of time' in *The Prelude*. Yet, like the 'Immortality Ode', its texture is curiously uneven. The tone wavers between the sublime and the prim. The pettiness of the occasion is not consonant with the weight of the emotion and its sequel. The mechanics of this dark epiphany, the fact that Wordsworth is moving *backwards* from a 'Cavern' in 'a rocky Steep' in a stolen boat, and that the 'huge Cliff' emerges from behind the 'steep' by dint of the rower's efforts, i.e. that the harder he rows ('I struck, and struck again' suggests an almost hysterical desire to escape from something which terrifies) the huger grows the peak ('A huge peak, black and huge' in the later recension) and the only solution is tremblingly (line 412) to return to the gloom of the cavern: these elements of frustration combine into a nightmare sense of impotence. We cannot be sure that even now, so many years after the experience, Wordsworth has really faced its full implications. There are a number of 'false notes'. 'One evening (surely I was led by her)', he begins his story: the filial reverence is charming, but what, we are tempted to ask as Wordsworth's disturbing account unfolds, has he to be grateful to Nature for? What *is* the lesson? Surely not that it is wrong to take a boat on the lake without the owner's permission. And the boat itself,

> She was an elfin Pinnace; lustily
> I dipp'd my oars into the silent Lake,
> And, as I rose upon the stroke, my Boat
> Went heaving through the water, like a Swan.   (401–4)

She *was* an elfin Pinnace, Wordsworth says. We have entered the world of Fancy, but without Byron's caveat of 'seems'. The boat is not a pinnace, and 'elfin' is an epithet quite out of place in this context of brooding mountains and troubled hearts. If the boat is elfin, then its progress is not 'like a Swan': the two images cancel each other out. We are in the world of that embarrassing sky boat of the Introduction to *Peter Bell*. There is an irremediable split between the sombre hidden meaning of the episode and the attempted lightness of Wordsworth's exposition. I can only suggest that in the chatter of the opening lines Wordsworth is trying to cover up the desperation of this symbolic effort to escape from some moral imperative. 'No sooner had I sight of this small Skiff,/ Discover'd thus by unexpected chance' is in one tone; 'It was an act of stealth/And troubled pleasure' is in another; and 'my little Boat mov'd on/Even like a Man who walks with stately step' is in yet a third. It is only in the magnificent nightmare evocation of the sequel to the incident (415–27) that the full force of the experience is conveyed. Here Wordsworth is delivered from the details of that everyday world of actual events with which he so oddly thought himself equipped to deal, and is back in his own kingdom of obsessive trance.

The fear which dominates Wordsworth's lake episode is quite absent from Byron's. In *his* sequel, the great Alpine storm scene of stanzas xcii–xcvii, there is exultation, there is merging with the energies of Nature, but there is no terror. Emphasis on the inter-changes of heaven and earth, on delight, and on creation are continued from the lake epiphany into this new dimension of violence.

> And this is in the Night:—Most glorious Night!
> Thou wert not sent for slumber! let me be
> A sharer in thy fierce and far delight,—
> A portion of the tempest and of thee!
> How the lit lake shines, a phosphoric sea,
> And the big rain comes dancing to the earth!
> And now again 'tis black,—and now, the glee
> Of the loud hills shakes with its mountain-mirth,
> As if they did rejoice o'er a young Earthquake's birth
>
> (*CH* III, xciii)

Byron places his readers at the centre of the storm; we share its moment to moment fluctuations with him. As Byron empathises with his object, so the reader is able, almost forced, to empathise with Byron. With the 'fierce' lightning flashes our view fixes first on the near, the lit lake and the big rain, then on the 'far delight' of the circling mountains, expressed in gleeful thunder: there is a constant systole and diastole.

As the storm recedes over the mountains, there comes the moment of reflection. *Among* 'Sky, mountains, river, winds, lake, lightnings . . . night, and clouds, and thunder', and not detached from them as observer, Byron includes 'a soul/To make these felt and feeling'. His soul is the soul of the phenomena surrounding him; they feel through him as he feels through them (xcvi). And so he is moved to speculate on the cosmic purpose, within himself and without.[18] Had he the power of lightning, he would express all that is within himself.

> But as it is, I live and die unheard,
> With a most voiceless thought, sheathing it as a sword.
>
> (III, xcvii)

This sense of the impotence of human speech, a Romantic despair unknown to previous generations, receives its most frequent and most eloquent expression in Byron.

The thought leads into the final section of Canto III with its portraits of Rousseau, Voltaire and Gibbon, three masters of the written word who have changed the course or brilliantly described the changing course of the world. Here the themes of love and wisdom and power are drawn to a literary nexus in the circuit of Lake Leman. It is worth pausing at this point to observe how cunningly our guiding themes are disposed throughout the cantos of *Childe Harold*. There is something of all three in each of the cantos, but Canto I, with its horrors of war, has more of Power, Canto II, under the aegis of Apollo, Pallas Athene and Socrates has more of Wisdom, while Canto III, framed between the twin addresses to Ada and concentring on 'Clarens! sweet Clarens, birthplace of deep Love!' is the apotheosis of Love. Canto IV, finally, knits all three together in a unique synthesis. But within each Canto we have witnessed the interweaving of the triple theme. Here, in Canto III, Love is displayed in its natural analogues on the shores of Lake Leman; Wisdom is implicit in Byron's own willingness to accept the epiphany and escape into 'a purer spring' than 'Earth's troubled waters'; Power is released in the majestic violence of the storm. Now, in the concluding stanzas, after the long and impassioned apostrophe of love (xcix–ciii), which established Clarens as the very home of Eros as Delphi is of Apollo, Byron passes into a new venture, the attempt to express his values in terms of literary genius. Rousseau, Voltaire and Gibbon, all denizens of Clarens and other lakeside villages at some time or other, are all in some way or other under the influence of its guiding principle, love. Rousseau's is human, sexual but idealised love; it is also concern for freedom and the destiny of the human race. Voltaire's is a passion for intellectual honesty, for the freedom of the human mind. Gibbon's ardour for truth is scholarly, factual, historical, tracing in the long power struggles of the Roman Empire the external correlative of the twistings and turnings of that same human mind. But Byron remains aware, even in full spate of eulogy, that truth is antithetical. Thus Gibbon is the *ironic* historian of power, Voltaire is the *sceptical* exponent of wisdom (intellect) untrammelled by superstition or convention, Rousseau is the *self-centred* teacher of human-cosmic love.

> His love was Passion's essence—as a tree
> On fire by lightning; with etherial flame
> Kindled he was, and blasted; for to be
> Thus, and enamoured, were in him the same.
> But his was not the love of living dame,
> Nor of the dead who rise upon our dreams,
> But of ideal Beauty, which became
> In him existence, and o'erflowing teems
> Along his burning page, distempered though it seems.
>
> (III, lxxviii)

Rousseau, then, is the fulfilment of Byron's desire to be 'lightning' (xcvii). His love is not a single, individual passion, but a quintessence. It is not even tied to the dead past, as Byron's is to Leila (line 6). It is a kind of madness, which nevertheless gives life to his pages. This madness, this dissatisfaction with ordinary life, turned Rousseau into a neurotic (lxxx), fighting against human kind; nevertheless from the violent workings of this 'frenzy'

> he was inspired, and from him came,
> As from the Pythian's mystic cave of yore,
> Those oracles that set the world in flame,
> Nor ceased to burn till kingdoms were no more.   (III, lxxxi)

The power of the exceptional individual to affect the fate of nations by sheer dynamism, of whatever kind, is a theme that always fascinated Byron as it did Nietzsche. He thought Sulla the greatest of men because he laid down his power at its apex. And that Rousseau—or Napoleon, or Caesar—is destroyed by his own inner tensions, by his neurosis, supports Byron's tendency to see individuals as forces only superficially self-controlled and controlling. Rather, they are power points through which, at destined moments, cosmic energies irresistibly flow.

This is demonstrated, Byron would say, in the vast panorama of Gibbon's *Decline and Fall of the Roman Empire*. This is a natural history of power, a clinical survey of human lust, folly, and greed. The interest of Byron's tribute to Gibbon lies in the fact that it is paid by one student and lover of the past to another student and lover whose approach was radically different. Byron immerses

himself in the past as he immerses himself in nature. Gibbon stands
apart, views 'the vanished ages' from a position of conscious superiority. If he saw the reign of the Antonines as the most delectable
epoch of human existence it is, one suspects, because he saw it less
in its own light than in that of Augustan England. And the deserts
stretched before and behind. Byron lived in a period when the
Augustan synthesis had broken down: this deprived him of Gibbon's
assurance, but left him open to whatever new 'message' the past
had to give him. But this imbues his tribute to Gibbon with a
notable detachment and authenticity. Gibbon's way of seeing
history, so close to Wordsworth's *spectator ab extra* stance, is far from
Byron's passionate identification with the past: but Byron recognises
its value, as Mrs Ramsay in *To the Lighthouse* recognises the value of
her husband's one-pointed devotion to truth. Truth is not reality:
but without truth reality is unattainable. Both Gibbon and Voltaire
are 'gigantic minds' (cv) warring against cant and superstition: like
Rousseau, such minds exercise power in the courses of history.
Voltaire was

> fire and fickleness, a child,
> Most mutable in wishes, but in mind,
> A wit as various,—gay, grave, sage, or wild,—
> Historian, bard, philosopher, combined;
> He multiplied himself among mankind,
> The Proteus of their talents: But his own
> Breathed most in ridicule,—which, as the wind,
> Blew where it listed, laying all things prone,—
> Now to o'erthrow a fool, and now to shake a throne.   (III, cvi)

Byron might be describing himself. Shelley thought of him as 'this
Proteus',[19] and 'a child' is hardly how any one would think of
Voltaire. In his portrait of Gibbon he is more detached:

> The other, deep and slow, exhausting thought,
> And hiving wisdom with each studious year,
> In meditation dwelt—with learning wrought,
> And shaped his weapon with an edge severe,
> Sapping a solemn creed with solemn sneer;
> The lord of irony,—that master-spell,
> Which stung his foes to wrath, which grew from fear,
> And doom'd him to the zealot's ready Hell,
> Which answers to all doubts so eloquently well.   (III, cvii)

'Sapping a solemn creed with solemn sneer' says the last word about
one facet of Gibbon, and the alexandrine illustrates while it comments on his use of irony.[20]

The Canto reverts to Nature in its final stanzas, and to Byron's personal stance between the world of Nature and that of men. The Alpine peaks attract him: he feels the urge to quit the lakeside for

> their most great and growing region, where
> The earth to her embrace compels the powers of air. (III, cix)

The powers of air had descended gently to earth in the dews of stanza lxxxvii; the lyrical side of Byron is expressed in the Leman idyll, but his epic-dramatic side demands the Alpine solitudes and austerities, demands a struggle of wills between the high and the low worlds, a creative interchange expressed, as in the storm scene, in conflict. The erotic note is not absent: earth 'compels' the powers of air 'to her embrace'. The high Alps are a 'growing region'; the adjective 'white' suggests that Byron is thinking of the slow encroachment of the glaciers on the fertile areas, a phenomenon that worried Shelley, but the deeper meaning of the phrase involves Byron's whole conception of a vital, pulsating, evolving Nature. The high peaks 'grow' in aspiration towards the upper world of the stars, mediated through 'the powers of air'; man's mind 'grows' in concert with them, as the Pilgrim's mind 'dilates' in his contemplation of St Peter's in stanzas clv–clix of the next Canto, (where indeed the image of 'climbing some great Alp' is used as a comparison).[21]

And the Italian vistas of Canto IV are already anticipated in stanza cx of the present Canto, just as Greece was foreshadowed in the Parnassus apostrophe of Canto I, lx–lxiv. Here Byron provides us with a short index of the themes he will be engaged with in Canto IV: 'the light of ages', Roman and modern history, 'chiefs and sages', 'the throne and grave of empires', the still-flowing 'fount . . . of knowledge . . . from the eternal source of Rome's imperial hill'.

The Canto ends as it had begun, though in reverse order, with an address to his daughter Ada and an analysis of the stresses under which he writes his poem. Again the note of diminished power is struck:

> . . .—to feel
> We are not what we have been, and to deem
> We are not what we should be,—and to steel
> The heart against itself; (III, cxi)

all this 'is a stern task of soul'. The stimulus of fame has abandoned him (cxii) along with the days of youth. Byron's bitterness is distilled into a line of superb defiance:

> I stood and stand alone,—remembered or forgot.　　(III, cxii)

But the two stanzas of explanation—or apology—which follow strike one as less successful. 'I have not loved the World, nor the world me' (cxiv) is an oversimplification. 'I have not flattered its rank breath' is true enough. 'In the crowd/They could not deem me one of such' is a vile phrase, conjuring up the lip-biting, scowling Byron. 'In a shroud/Of thoughts which were not their thoughts, and still could,/Had I not filed my mind, which thus itself subdued' (cxiii) lapses into gibberish, and the falling back upon *Macbeth* anticipates the worst excesses of 'On This Day I Complete my Thirty-Sixth Year'.[22] Byron did this sort of thing much better in the Tales and in *Manfred*, where the dramatic-narrative projection draws off the worst of the personal venom. There is a littleness in such complaints as

> I do believe,
> Though I have found them not, that there may be
> Words which are things,—hopes which will not deceive,
> And Virtues which are merciful, nor weave
> Snares for the failing;　　(III, cxiv)

(as Annabella had done, we are meant to understand) which reminds us that the great Byron can all too often show himself as the little Byron, just as the sublime Wordsworth is all too often the dull and the pompous.

It is a pity that so powerful and taut a poem as Canto III should sag in its final reaches. The concluding address to Ada—

> My daughter! with thy name this song begun!
> My daughter! with thy name thus much shall end!
> I see thee not—I hear thee not—but none
> Can be so wrapt in thee . . .　　(III, cxv)

—modulates into bathos from the whining spite of the preceding stanzas. Byron invariably employs anaphora and the simpler forms of repetition when his wells run dry. The emotion is not totally false. Byron, in some moods, liked children, though he was quickly irritated by them: and he had a strong sense of dynastic ownership and continuity. He liked them when they had emerged from the baby stage into the childhood which was for him perhaps more symbolically than actually attractive: then they became living eikons of innocence and spontaneity. But his regret for the loss of a father's duties and responsibilities and privileges strikes one as slightly false. It is difficult to see Byron in this role:

> To aid thy mind's developement,—to watch
>   Thy dawn of little joys,—to sit and see
>   Almost thy very growth,—to view thee catch
>   Knowledge of objects,—wonders yet to thee!
>   To hold thee lightly on a gentle knee,
>   And print on thy soft cheek a parent's kiss,
>   This, it should seem, was not reserved for me—
>   Yet this was in my nature:—as it is,
> I know not what is there, yet something like to this.   (III, cxvi)

'Not here, O Apollo! are haunts fit for thee!'—and the instability of Byron's stance reveals itself in the lame and impotent conclusion: once the scaffolding of repetition is removed after line 5, the rhythms degenerate towards the final collapse of the alexandrine. There is a recovery of sorts in the final stanza, where Ada is apostrophised as

> The child of Love! though born in bitterness,
> And nurtured in Convulsion! Of thy sire
> These were the elements—and thine no less.

Love, convulsion, elements, the dynastic curse—these are counters established in the course of the poem, and we accept Byron's drawing them together here, along with the sea and mountains of his blessing:

> Sweet be thy cradled slumbers! O'er the sea
> And from the mountains where I now respire,
> Fain would I waft such blessing upon thee,
> As—with a sigh—I deem thou might'st have been to me!
>   (III, cxviii)

The canto of adjustment

Byron and Hobhouse left Geneva for Italy on 5 October 1816. Their first major stop was Milan, whence Byron wrote to Augusta on 15 October:

My dearest Augusta,—I have been at Churches, Theatres, libraries, and picture galleries. The Cathedral is noble, the theatre grand, the library excellent, and the galleries I know nothing about—except as far as liking one picture out of a thousand. What has delighted me most is a manuscript collection (preserved in the Ambrosian library), of original love-letters and verses of Lucretia de Borgia and Cardinal Bembo; and a lock of her hair— so long—and fair and beautiful—and the letters so pretty and so loving that it makes one wretched not to have been born sooner to have at least seen her.

We see a new Byron taking shape, one who responds eagerly to
cathedrals and theatres, rather more cautiously to picture galleries,
and with whole-hearted enthusiasm to the human element in bundles
of old letters and manuscripts. I say 'a new Byron', though of course
we can track his footsteps in the snows of the past; the openness to
experience is the same, but the material absorbed is different, as
different as Italy's crowded past-into-present is from the brooding
present-reproached-by-past of Greece and the Troad. The chame-
leonic Byron responds, taking his colours from the life surrounding
him.

Passing through Verona and Vicenza, the travellers reached
Venice on 10 November. Three weeks later Hobhouse embarked on
a tour of the peninsula, and Byron settled down to enjoy what was
to prove a long Venetian sojourn. He was delighted with Venice.
'Here have I pitched my staff, and here do I purpose to reside for
the remainder of my life', he wrote to Rogers on 3 March 1818.
And to J. Wedderburn Webster, in September of the same year:
'The view of the Rialto, of the Piazza, and the Chaunt of Tasso
(though less frequent than of old), are to me worth all the cities on
earth, save Rome and Athens.' After the noble but slightly cramping
nature epiphanies of the warlike Rhine, the arrowy Rhone, and the
mountain-hemmed lake of Geneva, Byron once more finds himself
in a past–present, Nature–Man complex where his oddly symbiotic
genius can have full play. It is not Greece, it is not 'glory', but it is
'grandeur', and it is more in tune with the 'slightly damaged' Byron
than Greece would have been if he had after all returned there.
Those divine austerities of mountain and lonely seashore, those
Sufic demands of self-forgetfulness in a love beyond love would
have reproached him perhaps to the point of despair. So he settles
for something easier, more manageable, He settles for Venice.

But with what superb aplomb!

> I stood in Venice, on the 'Bridge of Sighs';
>   A Palace and a prison on each hand:
>   I saw from out the wave her structures rise
>   As from the stroke of the Enchanter's wand:
>   A thousand Years their cloudy wings expand
>   Around me, and a dying Glory smiles
>   O'er the far times, when many a subject land
>   Looked to the wingéd Lion's marble piles,
> Where Venice sate in state, throned on her hundred isles!
>
> (*CH* IV, i)

The Enchanter is Time, the universal illusionist. There are three supreme moments in Canto IV: the first is this, the paean of Venice; the second comes in the great Coliseum scene, and the third in the St Peter's revelation in the centre of Rome. In all three we are meshed in the trammels of time and space. The Clarens epiphany in Canto III had annihilated place and time: in that matrix of love the manifested forms—lake and mountain, man and dews and grasshoppers and bees—emerge only to vanish again in a blaze of glory. There Byron attained perhaps his most intense vision— more transfiguring even than that granted him on the Hymettan mount. But he could not remain exalted. There came the slow and painful descent—first into the labyrinth of the Annabella– Augusta fiasco, then into the morass of Venice. Morally he succumbs: artistically he triumphs. With the moral débacle we are not concerned; we can safely leave its details to the biographers. The technical triumph is immediately apparent.

The first stanza achieves an extraordinary synthesis of rest and motion, a 'happening' of great complexity. The complexity is in the personality of Byron and also in his perceptive field. Whitehead speaks of 'our bodily event'. Let us abbreviate this to 'body-event', and take it as the presence of the conscious prehender in a particular space-time context. Here, on this morning of 11 November 1816, the prehender is Byron: the context, Venice.

I have said the Enchanter is Time; but it is also Byron. The figure of Byron the magician, the Manfred avatar, emerges in this last of the Cantos with peculiar force. 'I can repeople with the past', raising the dead from their ashes, he claims in stanza xix; in the Coliseum scene he waves his wand in the centre of the 'magic circle' and evokes the awesome spirit of Nemesis. The 'body event' is complex, then: the prehender existing bodily as the Byron of this moment of 11 November, but also as the 'long body' of the Byron who stretches back to the Highlands, and the still longer body of Byron as representative European man extending through Venetian history. Byron stands on the bridge, and is the bridge.

We are from the outset in the world of the contraries. This bridge is not that of the rainbow, infusing the hues of heaven into the colourless texture of Lockeian earth. With the utmost economy, Byron makes his statement of the co-existence of grandeur and misery: the Bridge of Sighs, the Brig o' Dread, the hapless human condition spanning its 'contrary states':

> Joy & Woe are woven fine,
> A Clothing for the Soul divine.[23]

This is a theme Byron is to develop throughout the whole of the Canto, to culminate in the blood-soaked arena of the Coliseum which *still* is the focus of an irrefutable majesty. Having sounded the keynote so plangently, Byron proceeds to his immediate achievement which is to prehend the Venice past and present in all its spatio-temporal complexity. Beginning with the Composition of Place, in the first quatrain, we proceed immediately to the Composition of Time: 'A thousand years their cloudy wings expand/ Around me'. The lion is a winged lion; the years too are winged; nowhere is there permanence. History is present, but not in its clearcut Gibbonian outlines; time's wings are cloudy. Byron as enchanter, identifying himself with Time, links the local space-times as he also, by the act of prehension, raises the 'structures'. These stand, in stanza ii, 'at airy distance': thus, though speciously permanent, they do not weigh on the spirit (cf. 'a fairy city of the heart' in stanza xviii). Permanence merges with impermanence as the 'structures' rise from the waves. Simple location flows back into total existence, taking in the whole Mediterranean story:

> a dying Glory smiles
> O'er the far times, when many a subject land
> Looked to the winged Lion's marble piles
> Where Venice sate in state, throned on her hundred isles!

Space thus is bathed in time; a glory is restored even in its fading. This is not memory, but a breakthrough from present into past, or rather an annulment of the distinctions of past and present. Venice too is one of those cities 'at the world's end', as Eliot put it, 'where past and future are gathered': omphalic points at which the totality is seized in the instant, in a moment of vision.

I have already quoted Byron's letter of 8 September 1818 linking Venice with Rome and Athens. These three are indeed his nodal cities. If we think of Europe as a great organism, a body dying, in Byron's time, for lack of that vivifying oxygen of freedom which Byron himself was to do so much to supply, then Athens as the lungs, breathing 'mountain air' from Hymettus (II, lxxxvii), aerates the blood which nourishes the brain, Rome, the 'city of the soul' (IV, lxxviii), and Venice, the 'fairy city of the heart'. The old threefold division is useful here as scaffolding: man as body soul and spirit. Without the breathing spirit—Athens as source of wisdom, philosophy, poetry, almost divine art—no life is possible. Rome is the rational 'soul', inferior to 'spirit' in the ultimate analysis, and fed from spirit as the brain is fed by the oxygen provided by the lungs, but pre-eminent in the human values of power, government, practical philosophy and civic art whereby Mansoul stands above the beasts and the barbarians. *Spiritus intus alet,* as Virgil says; but *anima* and indeed *animus* keep the organism in working order.

Venice is 'heart', love, and not least in her seductiveness. This is emphasised by Byron throughout stanzas i–xviii. Her mythological deity is Cybele, the Great Mother, rising from the thalassic depths.

> She looks a sea Cybele, fresh from Ocean,
>   Rising with her tiara of proud towers
>   At airy distance, with majestic motion,
>   A Ruler of the waters and their powers. (IV, ii)

Here Byron opens his personal-historic-past-present vistas into the mythic dimension, and the elemental world of 'powers' he has already approached at the end of Canto III.[24] This is also the world of the archetypes, and the Venice overture moves immediately (v) into a fugal movement on 'the beings of the mind' which recalls the very similar modulation in Canto III, v, from 'ocean's foam' to the 'airy images' of 'the soul's haunted cell'. Looking back to Canto II, we note that it is again precisely at stanza v that Childe Harold picks up the 'shattered cell' of the skull and elaborates his Hamletish meditations on worms and sepulchres, Wisdom and Wit. The 'Eremite's sad cell' of the final line of stanza iv in the first Canto initiates a very similar series of reflections and actions. Here the 'cell' image is absent, perhaps significantly.

Canto IV is the most 'extravert' of the four, and in a sense the most compensatory. 'The mind/Deep in its fountain' of Canto III is now projected outwards, into works of art, 'picturesque' comment on scenery and history, identification with heroes of the past. This compensatory quality of the Venetian years is a point I shall have to make more forcibly later, in discussing *Don Juan*;[25] its expression here strikes a keynote for the whole of this last Canto:

> The Beings of the Mind are not of clay;
>   Essentially immortal, they create
>   And multiply in us a brighter ray
>   And more beloved existence: that which Fate
>   Prohibits to dull life, in this our state
>   Of mortal bondage, by these Spirits supplied
>   First exiles, then replaces what we hate;
>   Watering the heart whose early flowers have died,
> And with a fresher growth replenishing the void. (IV, v)

This seems to me a decline from, and to some degree a vulgarisation of, the 'airy images' of the corresponding Canto III passage. There, 'creation' produced 'a being more intense', and the 'Soul of my thought!' was an actual alter ego, a kind of guardian daemon, with whom the poet 'traversed earth'. Meanwhile, in 'the soul's haunted cell', the 'airy images' of the subconscious world keep their customed state. The poet moves in divided and distinguished worlds, drawing sustenance from and restoring vitality to each and all. Now, everything is out in the open. The airy images have left their cell and act as nurses and compensators. The first four lines are un-exceptionable; they *say* much the same as lines 7–10 of stanza v plus lines 1–6 of stanza vi of Canto III, but the reader has only to turn back to those lines to feel the immense difference. And the last six lines of our present stanza give the game away. Poetic creation is no longer an opening, through the physical world, into the unknown, but a compensation for lost powers. Byron's phrasing is obscure, and a paraphrase may be welcome: 'Our present life is dull and restricted; art (the ideal) opens another world to us, first by driving unpleasant realities out of our mind, and then by replacing them with ideal forms, thus compensating for the inevitable deter-ioration of vision which comes with the passing years.'

The Canto, then, may be called compensatory. The 'picturesque' element is more to the fore. Yet to note that it is Byron who himself gives us the caveat should make us pause. This acutely intelligent mind analyses its own momentary limitations. We must not forget that it is also supremely inventive. Resistance to the horrors of childhood and the frustrations of the treaclemoon and its sequel have given it a toughness and resilience not easily defeated, and able in some instances to supply the want of that early morning freshness of response we welcomed in Canto II. Our initial tough/tender dis-tinction, somewhat lost sight of in the complexities of love/wisdom/power and Heraclitean elements dying into elements, which served us well in discussing the earlier cantos of *Childe Harold*, receives a new validation:

> But from their nature will the Tannen grow
>   Loftiest on loftiest and least sheltered rocks,
>   Rooted in barrenness, where nought below
>   Of soil supports them 'gainst the Alpine shocks
>   Of eddying storms; yet springs the trunk, and mocks
>   The howling tempest, till its height and frame
>   Are worthy of the mountains from whose blocks
>   Of bleak, gray granite, into life it came,
> And grew a giant tree;—the Mind may grow the same.   (IV, xx)

So the snowflake of 'Lachin Y Gair' continued to exist on the exposed
peak of the mountain; and, indeed, could exist nowhere but there.
Minds like Byron's need the same savage fostering.

> Existence may be borne, and the deep root
>   Of life and sufferance make its firm abode
>   In bare and desolated bosoms: mute
>   The camel labours with the heaviest load,
>   And the wolf dies in silence.   (IV, xxi)

Images from Byron's Anatolian past and his Italian present come
'in aid' here[26]—that dying wolf is to generate a whole poem by De
Vigny. But that is not the point. What is the point, within the total
structure of Canto IV, is the extreme subtlety with which Byron
conducts us from the warm Venetian vistas of stanzas i–xix, via this
confessional interlude, into the austerities of the Roman *temenos*.
Not at once, of course, not without a preliminary tour of Italian
cities; but the keynote is struck here, in the tannen stanzas. 'Savage
fostering' is a phrase I had set down on paper before I realised how,
with the wolf of the succeeding stanza, it exactly projects the genesis
of the Roman state.

So we move from tender into tough. The quality of 'prehension'
does not cease with the Venetian overture: it is strong throughout
the Canto. Byron 'takes hold' of his body-event, as it were, while at
the same time he is grasped by it. There is an element of apprehension in the prehension. Fame has brought Byron one sort of
confidence while robbing him of another. He now feels the necessity
of being in control of his material, of moulding it to the likeness of
his own inner pattern, rather than merging intuitively with it. The
spiral movement of Byron's successive stances is interesting. In
Canto I he was the indignant but detached reporter, the war
correspondent. He moves through Canto II on quite a different,
indeed an Apollonian level, responding to and eliciting the grace
dissolved in place of heroic earth, living his myth. Canto III is a
canto of merging; the mythic dimension is withdrawn, but that of
virgin nature is more powerfully felt. The Canto contains no living
characters,[27] as Canto I had contained Wellington and the Maid of
Saragoza, and Canto II Ali Pasha and the Suliotes. It is an exercise
in withdrawal from the world of men. Now, in Canto IV, we return
to the world of men and their works: the reportage is resumed from
Canto I, though on a higher level, enriched by experience and
meditation. Canto IV, with 186 stanzas, is exactly twice the length
of Canto I: the difference is not merely quantitative. A quality of

packed reflection expands the limits of reportage: the somewhat
skeletal outlines of Canto II enclose a relatively simple species of
perception.

And of course Byron as the enriched personality is now to the
fore, standing boldly as 'I' at the entrance to his poem: 'I stood in
Venice, on the "Bridge of Sighs".' 'On each hand' is an awkward
phrase, and we may ponder the unconscious motives for its choice.
Hands are the prehensive organs, and the enchanter's wand is
wielded by a hand. Hands build prisons and palaces, erect structures,
grasp the sceptre of state in the last line. The exhaustless East 'pours'
gems into Venice's lap, and monarchs 'partake' of her feast. We are
in a prehensive, manipulating world, and we sink deeper into it in
the succeeding episodes of the Canto as we move through the realms
of painting, sculpture, architecture, and man's handling of man in
politics and society.

Childe Harold himself, the poem's hero, is dropped from the
Canto until stanza clxiv when he is recalled to the stage for his last
bow. 'The fact is,' Byron tells Hobhouse in his dedicatory Preface,

I had become weary of drawing a line which every one deemed determined
not to perceive: like the Chinese in Goldsmith's 'Citizen of the World', whom
nobody would believe to be a Chinese, it was in vain that I asserted, and
imagined that I had drawn, a distinction between the author and the
pilgrim; and the very anxiety to preserve this difference, and disappointment at finding it unavailing, so far crushed my efforts in the composition,
that I determined to abandon it altogether—and have done so.

It is interesting that Byron is so definite about this. Modern critics
agree with the reviewers of Byron's day that the distinction was a
fiction: that Childe Harold *is* Byron, and that his abolition is a gain
to the poem. But notice the strength of Byron's denial: 'anxiety',
'disappointment', 'crushed' are not light terms. Byron is an inveterate
spoofer, but there is no reason for spoofing here. It is not as though
Byron had given the Childe all the self-revelatory outbursts of the
poem; on the contrary, these come when Byron is speaking *in
propria persona*. I believe that Byron was perfectly genuine in separating the hero of the poem from its author, and in trying to maintain
that distinction. The split between the man involved in the cares of
common life, and the ideal *alter ego*, the Zoroastrian double or
Fravarshi, was a psychological necessity for Byron and a philosophical
one for his whole metaphysics. But this is an extremely complicated
question with which I have no space to deal here. What we may
note, on the technical rather than the noetic level, is that the

abolition of the Childe robs Byron of a very valuable means of distancing, of depersonalising the crude impact of experience. It is essentially a dramatic device. Shakespeare mastered one of his major crises in the Sonnets: their 'austere regard of control' in formal pattern of octet and sestet sufficed, but only just, as technical straitjacket. The whole apparatus of the great tragedies and problem plays is hardly sufficient to contain the final intolerable vision.

'It necessarily treats more of works of art than of Nature', Byron wrote to Murray on 20 July 1817, explaining why his new Canto would need copious notes and 'polishing'. Why 'necessarily', one asks? Italy is rich in natural beauty, and Byron might have concentrated his attention there, if he had wished. But the explanation comes, I think, when we recognise a certain disappointment in Byron's recent Nature-merging—a disappointment acknowledged in his 1816 Journal.[28] Byron's progress through life is consistently a pendulum: he had swung from the vortex of London society into Alpine solitudes, and now he swings from Nature into the labyrinth of Venice. This fluctuation of involvement is important through the Cantos—as important as what I have called the 'stances'. Byron's journey through Portugal and Spain and Malta was too rapid to admit of any real putting down of roots. Spiritual roots, of enormous tenacity, he did put down in the Levant, but he lived there after all as a foreigner, almost a being from another world among his pashas and dervishes and Greek urchins and Suliotes. Given a few more years, he would doubtless have naturalised himself. Then, in his almost Peninsular passage through Central Europe he was even more cut off—no doubt through his obsessive personal problems—from the everyday life around him: apart from the sentimental reference to 'peasant girls with deep blue eyes' there is not a touch of human contemporary life in the canto. But now, in Venice, and later in Rome, Pisa, Ravenna, he plunges into the social-political life of Italy. He seizes it—but he is also seized by it. And there is a resistance. The nature of that resistance we shall see more clearly when we come to consider *Don Juan*, his great compensatory poem. Compensatory for what? Precisely for 'the lost glory and the trailing wing', for the failure of his love-affair with Nature, the abandonment of his Apollonian identity. Even the 'Nature passages' of Canto IV, in which he clearly seeks relief from art and history, are set pieces: beautifully done, exquisitely 'polished', but lacking the spontaneity and the resonance of the great moments of Cantos II and III.

Variations on a baroque theme

We pass from the Venetian revelation to the Roman consummation through a series of 'prehensions' which, though to my mind lacking the spontaneous flow of the earlier cantos, are beautifully poised and posed in terms of elemental powers and human artefacts.

We have seen Canto IV as pre-eminently the manifestation of air and water, of water blending with air as in Canto II it penetrated the 'heroic earth' of Greece. This 'airiness' of Canto IV emerges in the frequent references to music, to wind as music (e.g. cvi), to death as somehow reanimated by air (xxx, cxi), to the rainbow (lxxii) which unites water, air and light—but one could go on indefinitely. Venice's supremacy is seen as this blending (ii), and it is precisely because of this that her greatness cannot be utterly destroyed; even under an alien tyranny (iii), she stands as an ideogram of *these* elemental values.

Canto IV is the culmination of *Childe Harold* above all in its assertion of the inclusive ideogram of the city. We have come in an enormous curve from the fragmentary cities of Canto I, unresonant, isolated by war from the total human context (earth ringed like the scorpion by fire), via Greece's heroic earth, washed by compassionate seas but resonant only of the past, and via the stifled and war-racked plains of central Europe, where for Byron cities hardly exist, to these towered, lucid panoramas in which each city is a separate ideogram alive with human values. Indeed Canto IV is the most 'human' of the cantos in its deep concern for the human condition; this sounds in the tenderness of 'Nor yet forget how Venice once was dear' (iii)—a tenderness fusing spectator, place and history.

This is also the most fugal of the cantos. Here landscape, human life, history, personal reflection, and art are interwoven with incredible dexterity. Art, which again Byron sees in terms of 'air'— Tasso's echoes (iii), the Venus de Medici (xlix), the temple of Clitumnus (lxvii), Trajan's column (cxi), the Coliseum (cxxviii)— and of 'music' in St Peter's 'Vastness which grows, but grows to har-monize—/All musical in its immensities', a 'haughty dome which vies/ In air with Earth's chief structures' (clvi), enters Byron's verse for the first time. Canto I gives us nothing of art, and Canto II presents struc-tures which, being Greek, are conceived of in existential terms trans-cending the artefact, and which in any case have been so absorbed into the landscape[29] that they are no longer distinguishable from it; Canto III, passing through Gothic scenes, is an architectural blank.

That he sees art in sexual terms will come as no surprise, after his love-and-nature assimilations in Canto III. There can be no doubt that Byron's interweaving in this canto of past and present, of the scene with art's representation of the scene (iv–vi), adds a facet if not a dimension. I suppose for most this is the greatest of the cantos: certainly it is the most complex, but I continue to prefer Canto II, where (i) Byron's cosmic perceptions are most involved and (ii) his egotism is at a minimum. By 'cosmic perceptions' I mean his capacity for penetrating the life of a scene in its relation to time and that which is out of time and reacting to it from a centre which is also out of time, and yet related. From this penetration the great ideograms arise. Cantos I and II expressed Byron's slow, hesitant emergence from the trauma of birth, of Aberdeen and Newstead; then came the second trauma of Annabella, the formidable reaction which is Canto III, and the continued though subsiding reaction which is Canto IV, leading to the final affirmation.

But since Italy is now for Byron the ancient world, it is not divorced from the great root themes of Canto II. They nourish it, in fact; and though, in the end, Byron had to respond to the gravitational pull of his spiritual motherland, these twigs and scions of Greece on a more western shore helped to sustain him. The anonymity of the gloomy wanderer of Canto II was gone, and with it his freedom of response; his liaison with Teresa Guiccioli signified his acceptance of a certain bondage, a certain role. This acceptance brought its advantages; Byron was free to take stock, to put down roots, to branch out here and there (the interest in art is an example) and laugh at himself, as in *Beppo*, as well as at society. The satiric mode returns. But the roots are in water rather than earth, the stasis cannot be permanent. Hence, I think, the emphasis on cities. Separated from Greece, where the sanctities are at their most elemental—the brilliance of light, the clarity of water, the starkness of mountain, the purity of air—Byron looks for, and finds, 'objective correlatives' to these elemental forces in the human constructs which best express them. One might define Italy as the projection of Greece in art. The projection, in the sense of the extended expression, the drawing-out of what was implicit in the Greek nucleus; or, indeed, of the interpenetration here of the present with the past, of modern man with his environment. Greece had been the great correlative of solitude: not of loneliness, which is the ethos of Canto III, for in Greece, even today, one cannot be alone, the landscape itself eliminates the human insufficiency, but one can be solitary, infinitely detached from oneself

and from one's cares and obsessions. Byron understood this: I think
it was what he meant by his use of the word 'privilege'.

So the cities of Canto IV are detached fibres of the solitary nerve.
All are antithetical, of course: Venice, 'The revel of the earth, the
masque of Italy' is the miserable victim of the Austrian oppressor;
Rome, steeped in 'The double night of ages and of her,/Night's
daughter, Ignorance'; Florence,

> Where the Etrurian Athens claims and keeps
> A softer feeling for her fairy halls;
> Girt by her theatre of hills, she reaps
> Her corn, and wine, and oil—and Plenty leaps
> To laughing life, with her redundant Horn.   (IV, xlviii)

is also the city where Dante and Boccaccio's bones do *not* lie (lvii,
lviii). Ferrara, with its 'wide and grass-grown streets/Whose
symmetry was not for solitude', is the scene of Tasso's long imprisonment.

One of the Ferrarese asked me [Byron remarks in a letter] if I knew 'Lord
Byron', an acquaintance of his, *now* at Naples. I told him 'No!' which was
true both ways, for I knew not the imposter; and, in the other, no one
knows himself.

No one knows himself: as the Pilgrimage nears its end, its goal of
self-knowledge grows ever more remote, more *diffused*—what is this
self one seeks to know? The self of Newstead? of Athens? of London?
of the Rhine? of here and now? All are different. Greece, and
Greece alone, had the power, or seemed to have the power, to fuse
them; receding from the magic centre the fibres quiver, impotently
aware. Byron was nearer to his goal on the stony slopes of Parnassus
or in the dusty streets that bordered the Choragic Monument of
Lysicrates than he ever was among the canals of Venice or the busy
highways of Rome. And he knew it.

I have said that Canto IV is the canto of splendours: of these there
is space here to point out only the major brilliances. The Byronic
spotlight falls on Venice (i–xviii); Arqua (xxx–xxxii); Ferrara
(xxxv–xxxix); Florence (xlviii–lxi); the lake of Thrasimene (lxii);
Terni (lxix–lxxii); and Rome (lxxviii–clxxii). If this were a travelogue
the achievement would be great enough, but for Byron the moment
is always 'this grace dissolved in place', and every place has its
distinct grace to inform it. Venice mediates a passionate regret for
vanished *power*, together with the charm of music, architecture, and
poetry which gave it meaning. Rome too is power, but on a longer

wavelength, as it were, of which now we can pick up only certain frequencies: empire, civilisation, brutality, vastness, austerity (lxxviii, lxxx, cxxxix, cxxviii, cxlvi), and the rest drifts back into the eddies of time. Only in Byron do we have this sense of the escaping past, of meaning and values to be salvaged. The sense of the past *as* meaning, of wisdom on its way to extinction with the stones that enshrine it; of the irreplaceable European legacy.

Between the spotlights come the moments of reflection. Canto II, with which we must constantly compare this canto, had need of no such moments: reflection is inbuilt with the parched hillside, the funeral mound, the fallen or slanting column. Man, history, philosophy are reduced to their correlatives: we live the present with the past through the worn sunwarmed stone and the scent of thyme and the wash of Odyssean seas. Silence—'No breath of air to break the wave/That rolls below the Athenian's grave'—turns its glass on the great palimpsest scratched over and over again with Mycenean, Dorian, Attic, Byzantine, Turkish and Venetian characters, a record inscribed on the parchment of mountains, seas, shores and heroic plains. 'Only connect'—and the connection must be in terms of the solid object; tombstone, beehive, architrave, cypress. So too must be its 'expansion' in the poet's tongue. If, as Eliot says, 'Only through time, time is conquered', so Byron might echo, 'Only through place, and the objects filling place, is meaning recaptured'. Byron is the first and greatest of the Imagists. Indeed, he is not far, in his major moments of elimination of the inessential, from Robbe-Grillet:

> Beneath, a river's wintry stream
> Has shrunk before the summer beam,
> And left a channel bleak and bare,
> Save shrubs that spring to perish there:
> Each side the midway path there lay
> Small broken rocks of granite gray.   (*Giaour*, 557–62)

That, as Eliot remarked of Blake, 'is the naked vision'.

Throughout his life Byron had the need to connect himself with something which would compensate for his past, and especially his childhood, deprivations. But for a being of his complexity, perverseness, oddly convoluted cybernetics, that something had to be at once very austere, very simple in its *structures* and also very warm, very satisfying—dare one say very permissive?—in its human *content*. All this Byron found in Islam, most monolithic of creeds, and in its topical context, the Greek or Albanian landscape of mountains, seas, grassless hillsides, olive trees, fig trees, cypresses growing into the blue from a parched, chalky or sandy soil. Italy provided a modified version of this: the landscape less austere, the sun less tyrannic, the contemporary human presence more insistent, the feminine component winning over the masculine. So that in his Italian vistas it is to architecture, to actual buildings, that he turns for the austerity he misses in the landscapes. Take the great moments of the progress from Venice to Rome once more, and now in terms of constructs: Venice's 'proud towers/At airy distance' (ii), 'There is a tomb in Arqua;—rear'd in air' (xxx), Clitumnus' 'Temple still,/Of small and delicate proportion' (lxvii), the 'stern round tower of other days' (xcix), the 'nameless column with the buried base' (cx), the Pantheon, 'Simple, erect, severe, austere, sublime' (cxlvi): all these are 'correlatives' of an inner need for simplification, for purgation, for identification with the 'nameless', 'buried' yet still vital thrust towards self-knowledge: a consummation he meets finally, in the St Peter's epiphany. The tourist enters the basilica:

> Thou movest—but increasing with the advance,
>> Like climbing some great Alp, which still doth rise,
>> Deceived by its gigantic elegance—
>> Vastness which grows—but grows to harmonize—
>> All musical in its immensities; . . .

> Then pause, *and be enlightened.*   (*CH* IV, clvi–clix)

The italics are mine. The 'enlightenment' is perhaps no more than momentary, no more than Manfred's achievement of the 'sought *kalon*'; but it has occurred.

The roots of the St Peter's *satori* are laid in the bloodsoaked dust of the Coliseum. Two very different structures: but both have 'the blood of the martyrs' for their foundation. Byron's Roman avatar circulates in an ellipse which has St Peter's at its centre and the Pantheon (austerity, divinity, coolness) and the Coliseum (complexity, brutal humanity, heat) as its polar foci. In a sense St Peter's reconciles the two classical extremes in its own Christian synthesis: merging divine simplicity and human suffering. Over the simplicity of the Pantheon Byron hardly pauses:

> Simple, erect, severe, austere, sublime—
>> Shrine of all saints and temple of all Gods,
>> From Jove to Jesus—spared and blest by Time;
>> Looking tranquillity, while falls or nods
>> Arch—empire—each thing round thee—and Man plods

His way through thorns to ashes—glorious Dome!
Shalt thou not last? Time's scythe and Tyrant's rods
Shiver upon thee—sanctuary and home
Of Art and Piety—Pantheon!—pride of Rome!   (IV, cxlvi)

but he has time to note, 'thy circle spreads/A holiness appealing to
all hearts'—an important observation for any discussion of Byron's
preoccupation with circles, and 'Glory sheds/Her light through
thy sole aperture' (cxlvii)—an observation equally significant when
we come to consider the starlight shining through the plural 'loops
of time' in the Coliseum.

Man aims at the stars and his approach may be through the 'sole
aperture' of sacerdotal religions, the 'domes' of the Pantheon and
St Peter's, or via 'the fury and the mire of human veins' in the
Coliseum. The 'loops of time', products of the frenzied scrabblings of
man's 'unchristened heart' at the brick and mortar of his earthly
prison,[30] are valid but unsystematised. For Byron, as for Blake,
'Time is the Mercy of Eternity': the duration which limits is also the
dimension which preserves and guards. Together with space, it
forms the continuum within which love and wisdom, at eternal odds
with mortal (death-dealing) power, work out the immortal forms of
art, which include the great Empires (political epics, as it were) as
well as the small city-states (odic or Georgic expressions of the
Man–Nature–God nexus), together with music, poetry, painting
and architecture, Blake's 'four faces' of Eternity revealed in this
world.

So, working his way towards his meeting with Nemesis in the
Coliseum, Byron, 'a ruin amid ruins' in the debris of the Forum
Romanum, reconciles the darknesses of the inner and the outer
worlds:

The double night of ages, and of her,
    Night's daughter, Ignorance, hath wrapt and wrap
All round us; we but feel our way to err:
    The Ocean hath his chart, the Stars their map,
    And knowledge spreads them on her ample lap;
But Rome is as the desert—where we steer,
    Stumbling o'er recollections.   (IV, lxxxi)

This is Byron's maze; not yet his morass. He is lost in the Forum as
he was not lost in the Olympeion; he 'stumbles o'er recollections'
(brilliant phrase!) which are recollections as much of his own
internal defeat as of the collapse of the Roman empire. Moving
through space as he circles a fallen column here and a gaping cistern

there, he moves also through times which are both personal and historic:[31] the internal screen show goes on *pari passu* with the external. (This is an aspect of Byron's *oeuvre* which only the cinema could adequately cope with, and it links up with the 'theatre of the absurd' of Byron's later Roman projection in *The Deformed Transformed*.[32])

The morass will come later: or is already entered upon, in the debaucheries of Venice which shocked Shelley. For the moment Byron, though defeated, remains in control of his guidelines. The maze, or 'desert' as he calls it here, can perhaps be negotiated. Byron has *not yet* accepted that total Pyrrhonism which informs *Don Juan*. Let us briefly summarise his progress up to now. He has approached Rome via Venice with her watery, airy vistas, via Arqua with its 'air-reared' tomb of Petrarch, via Ferrara with its sunken 'cell' of Tasso's living tomb, and via the 'fiery' spectra of Dante, Galileo and Michelangelo in Florence. Now all these elemental powers are to be gathered up and concentrated in the Coliseum. The 'ignorance' is not simple stupidity, or lack of information, or even the barbarism which followed the fall of the Roman Empire: it is man's basic condition as he now is (though not necessarily his primeval condition). Rome becomes the ideogram of *la condition humaine*, a vast palimpsest written multidimensionally in blood-soaked stone, in bloody recollections, in violent art and literature, as Greece was a palimpsest wrought from another set of scribblings. The density of what Byron has accomplished here, with apparent nonchalance, can only be appreciated if we bring ourselves to reread Dyer's *Ruins of Rome*, Thomson's *Liberty*, and the travel poems contemporary with Byron's. He moves in and out of the double night with consummate virtuosity, working here in terms of architecture dissolving into nature, there in terms of a dying gladiator avenged by the Goths, and again through 'Tully's voice, and Virgil's lay,/And Livy's pictured page' (lxxxii).[33]

A profoundly synoptic imagination finds its focus in the Coliseum (cxxviii–cxlv), which figures as the chief 'lens' in Byron's image structure, fusing positive and negative values. I have already drawn attention to the ubiquity of these circular constructs in Byron's work, from the 'peculiar diadem' of trees on the Annesley hill where he parted from Mary Chaworth, to the Spartan's shield which is his last symbol of defiance at Missolonghi. Where his constructs do not allow of circularity, as in the Gothic of Newstead and the classical of the Olympeion, he smuggles the concept in, on both occasions in the form of a skull through which he *looks at* the interiority of his 'rectangular' situation, 'circling the square' as it were. Even here, in the 'magic circle' of the Coliseum, he reintroduces the skull in the shape of 'the bald first Caesar's head' (cxliv): the grey walls wear their 'garland-forest' of wild flowers and shrubs as Caesar wore his laurel crown. That the Flavian amphitheatre postdates Julius' life-span is irrelevant: the first Caesar stands as supreme symbol of imperial power, and also, as the Historical Note xxvi to stanza xc informs us,[34] as the kind of complex character which fascinated Byron:

Nature seems incapable of such extraordinary combinations as composed his versatile capacity— . . . fighting and making love at the same moment, and willing to abandon both his empire and his mistress for a sight of the Fountains of the Nile.

Comparatively, Napoleon is only 'a kind/Of bastard Caesar' (xc); Caesar combines the extremes of love, power and wisdom in an almost supernatural degree. This supernatural quality pervades the moonlit cirque of the Coliseum as Byron stands at its centre. Significantly, Byron sees its once-murderous precinct as 'a shrine/ And temple more divinely desolate', made so by the consecrating hand of Time (cxxx), a 'still exhaustless mine/Of contemplation' (cxxviii). Here we have not simply an enhancement but an absolute transmutation of values.

Yet the Coliseum will not bear the full light of day (cxliii); it is a telescope, as it were, revealing spatial depths of meaning only at night:

> But when the rising moon begins to climb
>   Its topmost arch, and gently pauses there
> When the stars twinkle through the loops of Time,
> And the low night-breeze waves along the air
> The garland forest, which the gray walls wear,
> Like laurels on the bald first Caesar's head—
> When the light shines serene but doth not glare,
> Then in this magic circle raise the dead;—
> Heroes have trod this spot—'tis on their dust ye tread.
>
> (IV, cxliv)[35]

Four dimensions are graphed here: (1) the stars (permanent eternity or 'High World' emblems for Byron) twinkling through the loops of (2) time, and (3) the 'dead' past reinserted in (4) the present. One of the heroes whose agony has consecrated the amphitheatre is the Gladiator whom Byron celebrates in lines (cxxxix–cxlii) too familiar for quotation or comment.

The death in the Coliseum of many Christian martyrs links the amphitheatre[36] with the last and greatest of Byron's architectural constructs, the Basilica of St Peter.

> But lo! the Dome—the vast and wondrous Dome,
>   To which Diana's marvel was a cell—
>   Christ's mighty shrine above His martyr's tomb!
>   I have beheld the Ephesian's miracle—
>   Its columns strew the wilderness, and dwell
>   The hyaena and the jackal in their shade;
>   I have beheld Sophia's bright roofs swell
>   Their glittering mass i' the sun, and have surveyed
> Its sanctuary the while the usurping Moslem prayed;
>
> But thou, of temples old, or altars new,
>   Standest alone—with nothing like to thee—
>   Worthiest of God, the holy and the true.
>   Since Zion's desolation, when that He
>   Forsook his former city, what could be,
>   Of earthly structures, in His honour piled,
>   Of a sublimer aspect? Majesty,
>   Power, Glory, Strength, and Beauty, all are aisled
> In this eternal Ark of worship undefiled.   (IV, cliii–cliv)

The emphasis is at once on inclusiveness—'Behold the *Dome*!' As the dome represents the overarching sky, so the basilica is an 'eternal ark' for Byron's constant values of Power (Strength), Glory (the Majesty of Wisdom), and Beauty (the manifested form of Love). Unlike the Olympeion (symbolised by its disinterred skull), this *is* 'a Temple where a God may [and does] dwell'; it is 'undefiled' by worms (unlike the skull) or infidels (unlike St Sophia's) or jackals (unlike the Temple of Diana). Its columns *stand*, unlike those of the Temple of Jerusalem (note how, at this point, Byron's mind reverts to the major theme of his *Hebrew Melodies*). Yet there are also similarities. If we consider the third line of stanza cliii, we realise that we are still in the pattern of Byron's speaking skulls. The first of these spoke from the garden of a desecrated monastery, Newstead Abbey, and was a Christian, a monastic skull. Now St Peter speaks from his tomb under the high altar of 'Christ's mighty shrine', a church literally founded on this Rock, in architectural answer to Christ's question, 'Peter, lovest thou me?' and His command, 'Feed my sheep'. The Coliseum is also founded on the bones of the martyrs and (reversing the Newstead history) a charter of Pope Eugenius, 'long extant, granted both the ground and edifice to the monks of an adjacent convent', according to Gibbon. One of the standing

columns of the Olympeion was, for a long time, the home of a Stylite.
But while Byron's mind narrowed, in the Olympeion, from the surrounding temples to the filthy and 'shattered cell' of the sophist's
skull, here it expands:

> thy mind
> Expanded by the Genius of the spot,
> Has grown colossal, and can only find
> A fit abode wherein appear enshrined
> Thy hopes of Immortality.   (IV, clv)

The Olympeion revelation had given rise only to the doubt of any
survival (II, vii–ix). But in St Peter's Byron, identifying himself as
always with the spirit of the spot, feels the full force of the Petrine
affirmation: 'Thou art the Christ, the Son of the living God!'[37]
This faith is felt in the basilica as a force which 'dilates' the mind 'to
the size of that it contemplates' (clviii): the Byronic urge to step
outside the limits of mortality, expressed in *Manfred* and ironically
linked to a sense of human limitations, is at last satisfied. The
pilgrimage has found its goal.

Here, logically, the whole poem should have come to an end, with
a stanza or two of farewell to the reader and to the scenes through
which he has been conducted. But no, Byron—ever truthful Byron—
sacrifices the aesthetic completeness of his poem to factual truth.
The treasures of the Vatican have still to be seen: and it is interesting
to note that the two he selects, and the Promethean moral he draws
from them, stand in contradiction to the Christian ethos of St
Peter's. In the Laocoon we see 'A father's love and mortal's agony',
simple human endurance unsupported by any supernatural hopes—
'vain the struggle' (clx)—but in its very failure lies its heroism.
Victrix causa diis placuit sed victa Catoni. The unavailing self-sacrifice of
the human father stands in contrast to the availing sacrifice of the
divine Son. From this vision of mortal agony we pass to the other
pagan extreme:

> Or view the Lord of the unerring bow,
> The God of life, and poesy, and light.   (IV, clxi)

This final Apollonian avatar, running through three stanzas and
including the Promethean myth, returns Byron, after the momentary
apostasy of St Peter's, to his old allegiance: we are back at Delphi
and the oracular consecration.[38]

This clash of Christian and pagan values leads into a reflective
excursus (clxiv–clxxviii) which terminates in the famous address to

the Ocean (clxxix–clxxxiv) and the pathetic farewell to the reader (clxxxv–clxxxvi). In stanza clxiv Childe Harold is abruptly recalled:

> But where is he, the Pilgrim of my Song,
> The Being who upheld it through the past?

Perhaps he was never anything more than 'a phantasy': now 'His shadow fades away into . . . the dim and universal pall/Through which all things grow phantoms' (clxiv–clxv). The theme of immortality returns for a moment in stanza clxvi. We do not know what we shall become after death, if anything: but at least we shall not have to repeat our present wretched existence.

The six stanzas on the death of the Princess Charlotte which follow (clxvii–clxxii) are less impressive now than they must have been at the time; they serve to remind us that Byron could empathise as readily and as effectively with contemporary as with historic public events. This is occasional verse if you like, but in the mode of Pindar. 'I feel sorry in every respect', he wrote home from Venice. But for the reader today it seems an irrelevancy in the majestic sweep of Byron's thought onwards from Rome, centre of human and divine glory, through the pastoral solitudes of Nemi and its 'glassy lake', not far from 'the Arician retreat of Egeria' (as Byron remarks in a footnote) and Horace's Sabine farm, right down to 'our friend of youth, the Ocean' (clxxv). Byron takes leave here of all the long-loved objects and allegiances which have informed the fourth and indeed all the preceding cantos—of all, that is, except the desert (clxxvii) and the sea (clxxix–clxxxiv). Though he protests 'I love not Man the less, but Nature more', we must regard the close of the poem as a repudiation of human values and human achievements, and thus as a negation of the massive Empire-art-heroism-romance structures he has projected in Canto IV.

> Roll on, thou deep and dark blue Ocean—roll!
> Ten thousand fleets sweep over thee in vain;
> Man marks the earth with ruin—his control
> Stops with the shore;—upon the watery plain
> The wrecks are all thy deed, nor doth remain
> A shadow of man's ravage, save his own,
> When, for a moment, like a drop of rain,
> He sinks into thy depths with bubbling groan,
> Without a grave, unknelled, uncoffined, and unknown.
>
> (IV, clxxix)

We may detect a hint of gloating, and the facts are, even for Byron's day, incorrect: the wrecks were not all Ocean's deed, but resulted often enough from sea fights. But Byron's concern for what we now call 'the environment' is patent, and he was hardly to know that within a century and a half man would evolve means for making the sea—and in particular his 'old friend the Mediterranean'—more polluted even than the land he 'marked with ruin'; 'the vile strength he wields/For earth's destruction' being extended to the sea-bed.

This final hymn to the Ocean sums up Byron's thought along a number of channels. It expresses his contempt for man as destroyer of Nature's beneficence and peace—a thought prominent in his mind from Canto I onwards. It conveys his suspicion of empires, despite their civilising achievements, and of war as an instrument of empires. It assimilates the ocean to eternity, and thus to the un-differentiated time-space continuum for which Byron's fragmented being habitually thirsted. It thus represents a return to simplicity, to irresponsibility, in a man who felt the complexities of existence with too great sensitivity; it is a return to childhood and beyond that to the womb:

> And I have loved thee, Ocean! and my joy
> Of youthful sports was on thy breast to be
> Borne, like thy bubbles, onward: from a boy
> I wantoned with thy breakers—they to me
> Were a delight; and if the freshening sea
> Made them a terror—'twas a pleasing fear,
> For I was as it were a Child of thee.   (IV, clxxxiv)

We are not far here from the womb world of *The Island*. The ideogram of the ocean is the reverse of the inclusive ideogram of the city. The city is Apollonian, the ocean Dionysiac. The city arises from the cooperation of the gods with men: it is a celebration of their interrelationship, and as such it is the fountain of art, of philosophy, of mathematics, and of politics. It is lifted up on its acropolis, as on an altar, sacrificing and sacrificed to celestial powers. Throughout Canto IV Byron stresses the 'airy' character of the Italian cities, even of those as low-lying physically as Venice and Rome. Their towers press upwards into the depths of space; their domes and cupolas seek to enmesh the eternal values, to provide formal analogues of an unknown dimension. But the sea is its own analogue, if we regard it as the womb, the source of life and its grave; and it is the analogue of endless time, a devouring eternity, if we regard it in its destructive aspect. Byron's

Thou glorious mirror, where the Almighty's form
   Glasses itself in tempests; in all time,
   Calm or convulsed—in breeze, or gale, or storm,
   Icing the Pole, or in the torrid clime
   Dark-heaving;—boundless, endless, and sublime—
   The image of Eternity—the throne
   Of the Invisible; even from out thy slime
   The monsters of the deep are made; each Zone
Obeys thee; thou goest forth, dread, fathomless, alone

(IV, clxxxiii)

conflates the physical and the metaphysical aspects of the sea, weaving currents from first one and then the other. As the 'mirror' of God it expresses his two aspects, creative-beneficent and destructive-malign (a thought closer to Vedanta than to Christian orthodoxy). The polar and tropic detail of lines 3–5 return us to the physical realm, but 'the image of Eternity' recalls the famous 'Time is the moving image of Eternity' and we are again with Augustine, Browne, and Henry Vaughan. Finally we pass into the evolutionary, the plastic and the amorphous-morphic context, the womb world: and with 'slime' we remember that the maze of Venice is built above the morass of its lagoons.[39]

The lagoons of Venice are not exactly the sea, but in its return to the watery world Canto IV does execute a neat circuit through human back to thalassic powers. In the survey of Byron's dramas which follows, it is of course the Venetian plays which most clearly develop the maze-and-morass theme: the trappings of dignity masking human and political corruption. *Manfred* is a mountain poem, breathing the air of the heights, but even the biblical plays, and still more the psychological dramas which close the canon, are as deeply infected as the Venetian plays themselves with the miasmic, stifling, entrapped essence of the canals. It is a triumph of Byron's honesty to bring the 'slime' of ocean into its roster of aspects;[40] its corruption, gluey quality, and fecundity, spread out into the circling rivers around Nineveh in *Sardanapalus* and into the watery vistas of the biblical plays, and are not absent from 'the flooding rivers' which entrap the protagonists in *Werner*.

Notes and references

1   'A fine *indistinct* piece of poetical desolation', he calls the canto in a letter to Moore of 28 January 1817 (my italics).

2   See below, pp. 292–3.

3   See below, p. 199.

4   'It is unprofitable at times [which times?] to examine too closely the meaning of a given line or stanza in Byron' (*Byron: the Record of a Quest*, University of Texas Press, 1949; reprinted Shoe String Press, 1966).

5   *Ibid.*, p. 125; *PW* ii, 311.

6   See my paper, 'The life of things', in *Wordsworth's Life and Art*, ed. A. J. Thomson, Oliver & Boyd, 1969.

7   Swinburne is good on the nature poetry: 'Coleridge and Keats used Nature mainly as a stimulant or a sedative; Wordsworth as a vegetable fit to shred into his pot and pare down like the outer leaves of a lettuce for didactory and culinary purposes. All these doubtless in their own fashion loved her, for her beauties, for her uses, for her effects; hardly one for herself. Turn now to Byron or to Shelley. These two at least were not content to play with her skirts and paddle in her shallows. Their passion is perfect, a fierce and blind desire which exalts and impels their verse into the high places of emotion and expression' (A. C. Swinburne, *Essays and Studies*, 1875).

8   See above, pp. 147, 170–173.

9   See above, p. 148. When the mind is not deep in its fountain 'its current' may be 'soiled', by 'opinions, good, bad, or indifferent', as he tells Murray in a letter of 24 September 1821.

10   A similar mood descends on Byron at Thrasimene—another lake—and 'the finny darter with the glittering scales' of the Clitumnus is also a 'reveller' (IV, lxv–lxviii). More interesting still, it is the 'unbounded revelry' of the stars which impresses Cain in his voyage with Lucifer through space (*Cain*, II, i, 106).

11   Cf. *The Giaour*, 50–7 (above, p. 19).

12   *Rosalind and Helen* was written 1817–18; Shelley took the MS of Canto III to Murray on 11 September 1816.

13   W. Blake, *Milton*, plates 35, 36 (*Blake: Complete Writings*, pp. 526–7).

14   A good account of this is given in Huysman's *La Cathédrale*.

15   See above, pp. 16–19.

16   See above, pp. 143–4.

17   In all references to *The Prelude* I am using the 1805 text, unless otherwise stated.

18   'He came into competition with Wordsworth upon his own ground; and in the first encounter he vanquished and overthrew him. His description of the stormy night among the Alps—of the blending,—the mingling,—the fusion of his own soul, with the raging elements around him,—is alone worth all the dull metaphysics of *The Excursion*, and shews that he might enlarge the limits of human consciousness regarding the operations of matter upon mind, as widely as he has enlarged them regarding the operations of mind upon itself' (John Wilson, *Blackwood's Magazine*, June 1817). The mention of competition is silly, but the general comment is perceptive.

19   The appellation had already been given to Byron by 1814 (cf. *LJ* iii, 89n).

20   Byron recommended a reading of Gibbon to Annabella in 1813 M. Elwin, *Lord Byron's Wife*, p. 205).

21   J. J. McGann (*Fiery Dust: Byron's poetic development*, University of Chicago Press, 1969, p. 114) judges that Byron 'had carried out a fine exercise in imaginistic development' (!) in his Clarens stanzas, and praises his lines on 'Voltaire and Gibbon, who took up residence [gracious living?] in the region of Geneva', but finds that 'the first form of the poem [i.e. without the added stanza cx] did not elucidate adequately why the Alps are a "growing" region, nor did they [*sic*] illustrate the idea of a cosmic "embrace" between the natural and the transcendental orders' (p. 115). The reason why this puzzles Mr McGann is that he persistently ignores Cantos I and II, in which the cosmic-human-transcendental nexus is quietly but steadily developed.

A striking example of the carelessness with which Byron is commonly read may be found in John Buxton's *Byron and Shelley: The History of a Friendship*. Macmillan, 1968, p. 20, where after remarking that 'Byron was deriving from the same scene [Clarens] vivid suggestions of Rousseau himself', the author quotes stanza ci ('All things are here of *Him*; from the black pines,/Which are his shade on high . . ./. . . to the shore,/Where the bowed Waters meet him, and adore,/Kissing his feet with murmurs . . .'), and comments: 'Such adulation of Rousseau the man is difficult now to accept, but in the imagined perfection of Julie it was no doubt indelicate to remember the illiterate Thérèse Levasseur and her five bastards in the Foundling Hospital . . .' and so on with similar irrelevances for a whole paragraph. This kind of thing is what happens when the incorrigibly personalising mind of the biographer meets the inveterately mythopoeic mind of the poet. It is assumed that what arouses strong emotion *must* be personal, must be *a person*—and if there is a *famous* person, a V.I.P., somewhere about, what is easier and more satisfying than to set him in the centre of the stage? If Mr Buxton had troubled to read the two preceding stanzas, which introduce the Clarens idyll, he would have found that Rousseau is not mentioned; it is love, the cosmic Eros, who is the presiding deity of the place, and it is to '*Him*' that Nature's and Byron's homage is offered. This sense of the cosmic Eros dates back to a very early period in Byron's life and work; I have noted its presence on p. 12 above.

22   See above, pp. 164–9.

23   W. Blake, *Auguries of Innocence* (59–60).

24   See above, p. 203.

25   See below, pp. 290–91.

26   Not to mention, of course, the club foot which, Mary Shelley said, was not absent from Byron's thoughts for a moment. This, one may say, was his permanent 'Alpine shock'.

27   'We were divided in choice [of a new Italian home] between Switzerland and Tuscany, and I gave my vote for Pisa, as nearer the Mediterranean, which I love for the sake of the shores which it washes, and for my young recollections of 1809. Switzerland is a curst selfish, swinish country of brutes placed in the most romantic region of the world' (letter to Moore, 19 September 1821).

28   See below, p. 232.

29   Or rise from it, in the case of Mussulman architecture: the charm of many of the simpler Turkish mosques and hamams lies in this effect of growing from their surroundings, particularly in the country districts.

30   Yeats comes insistently to mind as we read Byron's Rome stanzas. The dome as disdainful of man's 'mere complexities' overshadows Canto IV. Yeats's 'Mirror on mirror mirrored is all the show' may have its origin in 'the cosmos is "a thought within a thought within a thought" ', (*khayal*^{in} *fi khayal*^{in} *fi khayal*) quoted from Rumi in Nicholson's *Studies in Islamic Mysticism*, p. 118.

31   I make the distinction in ' "The loops of time": spatio-temporal patterns in *Childe Harold*', *ARIEL*, January 1971.

32   See below, p. 258. If we can imagine a screen play in which a real-life Byron is shown 'stumbling' over a nineteenth-century Forum in a sequence which fades into a Roman Byron moving confidently through orderly ranks of temples and triumphal arches, and still a third shadowy sequence superimposed where a younger Byron at Newstead moves through cloisters of Harrow and Cambridge into Greek and Turkish and Venetian and Italian vistas, changing from boy to man as he moves—only such a surrealist fantasia could adequately project Byron's meaning in these Forum stanzas.

33   This is what Mr McGann calls 'rummaging about the museum of Italy' (*op. cit.*, p. 48) surely an inadequate response to what Byron is doing here.

34   The 'Historical Notes' to Canto IV were contributed by Hobhouse, no doubt in consultation with Byron, 'except for three or four short ones' supplied by the poet himself. Note XXVI is the shortest but one.

35   Cf. Ibn 'Arabi on the ka'ba at Mecca: 'Behold the secret building before it is too late, and thou wilt see how it takes on life through those who circle it and walk round its stones, and how it looks out at them from behind its veils and cloaks. . . .'

36   The germs of Byron's descriptions of and meditations on both the Coliseum and St Peter's are to be found in the last pages of Gibbon's *Decline and Fall of the Roman Empire*.

37   The question of the assent or otherwise of the individual Byron, in this or any of the preceding situations, is irrelevant, as is, in consequence, any ascription of sincerity or insincerity. What Byron, as universal man, is expressing is what the basilica is itself saying, and the buried Peter through the 'skull' of the basilica. In Canto II the ruined temples around the Olympeion narrowed to the rotting skull; here the rotting skull of the chief apostle expands to the temple which flowers above his bones.

38   See above, p. 86.

39   Hobhouse writes of 'the slime of her choked canals' in a Historical Note on Venice contributed to Canto IV (note VII, to stanza xv).

Lucifer, in *Cain*, describes men as 'Reptiles engendered out of the subsiding/Slime of a mighty universe' (II, ii, 97–8).

40 These include the emblematic as well as the symbolical. Only a separate thesis could do justice to Byron's complex eikon of the sea, but a passage from his January 1821 Diary will show something of its political semantics: 'I shall not fall back; though I don't think them [the Italians] in force or heart sufficient to make much of it. But, *onward!*—it is now the time to act, and what signifies *self*, if a single spark of that which would be worthy of the past can be bequeathed unquenchedly to the future? It is not one man, nor a million, but the *spirit* of liberty which must be spread. The waves which dash upon the shore are, one by one, broken, but yet the *ocean* conquers, nevertheless. It overwhelms the Armada, it wears the rock, and, if the *Neptunians* are to be believed, it has not only destroyed, but made a world. In like manner, whatever the sacrifice of individuals, the great cause will gather strength, sweep down what is rugged, and fertilize (for *sea-weed* is *manure*) what is cultivable. And so, the mere selfish calculation ought never to be made on such occasions; and, at present, it shall not be computed by me. I was never a good arithmetician of chances, and shall not commence now.'

10
THE DRAMAS
AND 'THE ISLAND'

Byron's plays are even less popular with our present critical establishment than are *Childe Harold* and the Tales, and the reason is not far to seek. Nothing could be more alien to the kitchen sink and unimpeded progress to majority rule than these obsessional probings of the Promethean nerve, these 'metaphysical' speculations on time and eternity, on kingship and the nature of man. Moreover, they are chamber drama. I have called them plays, but Byron did not intend them for the stage, though one or two, and especially *Werner*, have been acted with considerable success.

Dramas of escape

Byron subtitled *Manfred* 'A Dramatic Poem', which is exactly what it is—hardly more indeed than a dramatic monologue. It catches the hero in a moment of crisis. Byron called it 'metaphysical', a term he also applied to Canto III of *Childe Harold* which he had just finished: it expresses the same resentments and cosmic speculations. By 'metaphysical' Byron meant 'preternatural' as much as 'philosophical'; in a letter of 25 March 1817 to Murray he calls it 'the Witch Drama', and its epigraph is Hamlet's 'There are more things in heaven and earth, Horatio . . .' Byron's own summary of the action of the play, in a 15 February 1817 letter to Murray, is useful:

Almost all the persons—but two or three—are Spirits of the earth and air, or the waters; the scene is in the Alps; the hero a kind of magician, who is tormented by a species of remorse, the cause of which is left half unexplained.

He wanders about invoking these Spirits, which appear to him, and are of no use; he at last goes to the very abode of the Evil Principle, *in propria persona*, to evocate a ghost, which appears, and gives him an ambiguous and disagreeable answer; and, in the third act, he is found by his attendants dying in a tower where he had studied his art.

On the poem's own showing,[1] the 'species of remorse' which tortures Byron–Manfred arises from his relations with his half-sister Augusta–Astarte, the revelation of which broke up his marriage. In his 1816 Journal he describes himself as 'preyed on' by 'the recollections of bitterness . . . which must accompany [him] through life', and confesses his inability to 'lose [his] own wretched identity in the majesty, and the power, and the Glory, around, above, and beneath [him]'. Nevertheless, the Alpine landscape enters very forcibly into his poem. 'Around, above, and beneath': Byron's own analysis grids *Manfred's* tridimensional pattern, so different from that of *Sardanapalus*, the play with which I find it nonetheless useful to make comparisons. *Manfred* is all ups and downs, *Sardanapalus* all rounds and abouts. Yet they have much in common. Both are escapist dramas, both include the element of remorse for injury inflicted on a loved woman, both are 'metaphysical' in their *elemental* framework, exploring human–cosmic relationships.

Byron, as I have tried to demonstrate, is an elemental poet and that means we have to interpret him in close reference to his 'field'— a *gestalt* approach. In the Alps, he drew his nourishment from the Alps; in Greece, from Greece. *Manfred* is a poem of heights and abysses, as Nietzsche saw;[2] *Sardanapalus*, written at Ravenna with the waterways of Venice recently in mind, is a poem of plains and labyrinthine palaces and encircling rivers: much of its essence is drawn from Byron's Middle-Eastern experience. In both plays architecture is closely linked to surrounding landscape. Manfred's lonely tower stands in the centre of a lunar desolation of jagged peaks and dizzy gulfs, of 'the glassy ocean of the mountain ice' and the 'dead whirlpool' (II, iii, 1–10). At the centre, then, of an immobilised vortex; and the aspiration now can no longer be for fruitful union with the elements (indeed, Manfred refuses what they have to offer in I, i, 165–70), but for dominion over them and beyond them—the vertical shaft of the tower pierces the frontiers of the earth once loved 'for its earthly sake' and passes into the superhuman realm. When he quits his tower, enters into relationships —with the Chamois Hunter, with the Abbot—he shows himself inadequate to the situation, a being cut off from his kind as Harold, familiar with Pacha and peasant alike, was not. In *Sardanapalus* there is a similar yet contrasted isolation. The king revels in the innermost chamber of his palace, hemmed in by Tigris and Euphrates.[3] The palace itself is felt as a maze of concentric corridors and interconnecting passages. Outside, 'the lone and level sands stretch far away'.

Sardanapalus can no more find fulfilment in sensual pleasure than Manfred can in knowledge. These dramas are dramas of 'the scorpion', the tormented creature ringed by fire and striving desperately to burst out of its circle. If for Manfred the circle is icy rather than fiery, (note that Byron mentions only the three elements in his letter to Murray) the sensation is nonetheless that of burning,[4] and the fire element is restored in *Sardanapalus* to give the precise ideogram of the trapped scorpion. Both Manfred and Sardanapalus are trapped because they are fragmented: losing their identity, that is to say their relationship as whole personalities with the whole, they scurry from the immobilised centre to the destructive circumference and back again, seeking a final solution in suicide.

As heroes, nevertheless, Manfred and Sardanapalus are clearly distinguished. Manfred is the perfected image of the Byronic hero, Sardanapalus is almost an anti-hero. In Manfred the sombre aspects incarnate in Childe Harold, the Giaour, the Corsair, Lara, receive their apotheosis: beyond these prototypes he is guilt-ridden, darkly handsome, coldly contemptuous, autocratic, passionate, but also generous, intellectual and courageous. Much of this syndrome was taken over by Byron from his predecessors: from Milton, from the Faust legend, from the Gothic novelists, and from the archetypal figures of Cain, Ishmael, the Wandering Jew. In *Manfred* the Faustian element is now predominant, though not entirely new, for it is suggested in *Lara*. There are other differences from the earlier heroes. Childe Harold is a hero on the move, the superficially sophisticated Grand Tourist stripped of his pretences and pretensions by contact with reality, with ancient cultures and, in the last two cantos, with personal suffering. The Giaour and Alp were unsophisticated adventurers raised to heroic status by courage, by passion and by suffering again. Manfred is no tourist and no adventurer. He is a 'Childe' by birth, but a Faust by intellect; he is at home in the wilderness as the pirates were, but dominates and finally rejects it. He accepts, as they do not, the burden of guilt, striving to incorporate it in his own 'image'.

The character of Sardanapalus includes a new element of humour, of the quizzical and the tolerant, which begins to fashion the anti-hero who comes to full bloom later in Don Juan. He is more of a Regency dandy than a seventh-century B.C. Assyrian monarch, and his moral problems, including remorse for neglect of a wife, strike one as positively Victorian. Here Byron is as anachronistic as Shakespeare. But he is an attractive figure, civilised, witty, suddenly formidable. Perhaps more of Byron himself passes into him than into any of the earlier heroes. He is a sun-king, an Apollo. *Manfred* is a moon-poem, its decisive action accomplished under moon and stars: its Coliseum fantasia (III, iv, 1–45) projects the eternity values which were to be more fully expressed in the famous passage of *Childe Harold* III, cxxviii–cxlv. Significantly, the Abbot arrives immediately after this soliloquy to offer a second chance of release, through the acceptance of divine grace, from Manfred's personal dilemma. But it is too late: the even more direct intervention of grace in III, i, 6–18, has already been rejected, dismissed as illusory:

> *Manfred* [*alone*]. There is a calm upon me—
> Inexplicable stillness! which till now
> Did not belong to what I knew of life.
> If that I did not know Philosophy
> To be of all our vanities the motliest,
> The merest word that ever fooled the ear
> From out the schoolman's jargon, I should deem
> The golden secret, the sought 'Kalon', found,
> And seated in my soul. It will not last,
> But it is well to have known it, though but once:
> It has enlarged my thoughts with a new sense,
> And I within my tablets would note down
> That there is such a feeling.

Manfred rejects his 'little satori', plays the Hamlet in 'setting it down' in his tablets as an interesting emotional experience and nothing more.

It is clear that Byron–Manfred comes closer to understanding and acceptance of what I have called the eternity-dimension in the time-space context afforded by the Coliseum than in any naked beating on the Cloud of Unknowing. Viewed at midnight, the amphitheatre retains the fulness of its sun-baked, blood-soaked daylight function as 'circus' (III, iv, 27); without this it would be for Byron a relic, not a dynamic ideogram. And it is through this loop in and out of time that Byron connects his obsessively moon-and-ice context ('she is really an icicle', the Duchess of Devonshire had remarked of Annabella in 1812) in *Manfred* with the great address to the sun in III, ii, 1–30, which links up in its turn with

Beleses' soliloquy in *Sardanapalus* II, i, 1–36. For the palace of
Sardanapalus is also, in its way, a 'circus', as Bonnivard's cell was,
as Rome is to be in *The Deformed Transformed*, and as the bee's
fragrant fortress had been, in *Childe Harold* II. In these reticulated,
honeycombed, often crumbling structures which net time and space,
Byron's imagination functions as its most complex.

Superficially, however, *Manfred* is a moon poem, *Sardanapalus* a sun
poem: a solar fantasia, rich in imperial, dynastic resonances.[5]
Manfred's baronial echoes (scarcely heard, subordinated to magian
spells) are provincial in comparison. Yet they are there, and link
up with a major theme of *Sardanapalus*. Manuel's

> Ere Count Manfred's birth,
> I served his father, whom he nought resembles. . . .
>
> (III, iii, 14–15)

is the statement, in a minor key, of Salemenes' continuous denunciation of Sardanapalus as a degenerate descendant of Semiramis
(the theme, indeed, on which the play opens). These are adumbrations of the dynastic/individual, public/private dilemmas which
are brought into the open in the Venetian plays. Manfred abdicates
his role as feudal lord and therefore protector as well as exploiter,
in favour of his magian role: the separated castle and tower are
emblematic of this. Sardanapalus also abdicates: the ruler is lost
in the playboy, and the priest-king (Keats's Endymion) splits into
Arbaces and Beleses. These are fragmented, like Blake's Zoas, and
as indestructible: 'Who dares assail Arbaces?', the king cries, even
in the moment of truth (II, i, 184) when his own existence is
threatened by Arbaces; and 'all Chaldea's starry mysteries' (II, i,
251) are summed up in the traitor Beleses. For this is the dilemma
of the fragmented man: who am I? myself, or my enemy? or both?

Sardanapalus is a play of dilemmas and antitheses. The most
evident is in the character of the hero: even after declaring

> I will not see
> The blood of Nimrod and Semiramis
> Sink in the earth, and thirteen hundred years
> Of Empire ending like a shepherd's tale   (I, i, 3–6)[6]

Salemenes adds

> He must be roused. In his effeminate heart
> There is a careless courage which Corruption
> Has not all quenched, and latent energies,
> Repressed by circumstance, but not destroyed—
> Steeped, but not drowned, in deep voluptuousness.   (I, i, 9–13)

This is a more complex soul than Manfred's and a more human, and he creates around himself a more credible *milieu*: Salemenes, Arbaces, Beleses, Myrrha live as the Chamois Hunter and the Abbot did not. 'The Characters are quite different from any I have hitherto attempted to delineate', he remarks in a letter to John Murray of 30 May 1821. Nevertheless it is a more conditioned soul, and so the less free. In its dynamism *Sardanapalus* is the antithesis of *Manfred*, though both heroes are defeated. *Manfred* is a Promethean play, asserting freewill and superiority over the elements to the last. Sardanapalus accepts his doom, after a noble fight: his will finds itself impotent against chthonic disguised as dynastic forces, rough beasts slouching to Nineveh across desert sands to be born, and asserting themselves against intelligence, wit, courage, and love.

Sardanapalus is a reasonable man. But not so reasonable as his Greek slave Myrrha, who presents a devastatingly accurate diagram of the governor-governed relationship. Sardanapalus hopes that he is loved rather than feared by his people.

> *Myrrha.* And now art neither.
> *Sardanapalus.*   Dost *thou* say so, Myrrha?
> *Myrrha.* I speak of civic popular love, *self*-love, . . .
>   A King of feasts, and flowers, and wine, and revel,
>   And love, and mirth, was never King of Glory.
>
> (I, ii, 536–43)

No flower power in Nineveh!

> *Sardanapalus.* Glory? what's that?
> *Myrrha.*   Ask of the Gods thy fathers.
> *Sardanapalus.* They cannot answer; when the priests speak for them,
>   'Tis for some small addition to the temple.
> *Myrrha.* Look to the annals of thine Empire's founders.
> *Sardanapalus.* They are so blotted o'er with blood, I cannot.
>   But what wouldst have? the Empire *has been* founded.
>   I cannot go on multiplying empires.   (I, ii, 544–50)

The wry reasonableness of the retort establishes Sardanapalus as an analytic intelligence, highly perishable.

His reasonableness extends into that most sacrosanct of human illusion playgrounds, the world of words which is our everyday world, in which we live and die. 'May the king live for ever!' Pania cries (I, ii, 563) in ritual address, but Sardanapalus deritualises:

>   Not an hour
>   Longer than he can love. How my soul hates
>   This language, which makes life itself a lie,
>   Flattering dust with eternity.   (I, ii, 563–6)

And here, surely, rather than in his refusal to lead them into battle, lies the root of Sardanapalus' failure with his subjects. He is a logical positivist, pricking the bubble of pseudo-statements; his love of pleasure is not an aberration from the accepted imperial theme of gore-and-glory, but a refutation of it. He has left his subjects nothing to live on but the truth. Human kind, as Eliot says, cannot bear very much reality.

Sardanapalus is a bubble-pricker, a debunker, an enemy of cant, and as such cannot survive the brute mass of stupidity and prejudice. He feels himself hemmed in: the 'scorpion' ideogram emerges very early in the play:

> What! am I then cooped?
> Already captive? can I not even breathe
> The breath of heaven? Tell prince Salemenes
> Were all Assyria raging round the walls
> In mutinous myriads, I would still go forth.   (I, ii, 573-7)

The parallel with *Julius Caesar* is close; like Calpurnia, Myrrha succeeds in reversing the hero's decision, and for love Sardanapalus grants what neither danger nor policy can force from him: 'Well, for thy sake, I yield me' (I, ii, 613). But incarceration accepted is no less incarceration, and it is significant that the great address to the setting sun which immediately follows (II, i) is spoken not, as in *Manfred*, by the hero, but by the unheroic fragment of himself called Beleses, the soothsayer. The fragmentation initiated in *Manfred* (the baron resigning in favour of the magus) is now accelerating. Beleses as magus and Arbaces as warrior splitting off from the total image to play separate and antagonistic roles. The message of the setting sun to Manfred had been personal yet depersonalising:

> Monarch of the climes,
> And those who dwell in them! for near or far
> Our inborn spirits have a tint of thee
> Even as our outward aspects;—thou dost rise,
> And shine, and set in glory   (*Manfred* III, ii, 20-4)

—but to Beleses it is dynastic and threatening:

> The Sun goes down: methinks he sets more slowly,
> Taking his last look of Assyria's Empire.
> How red he glares amongst those deepening clouds,
> Like the blood he predicts.   (*Sardanapalus*, II, i, 1-4)

The change is ominous. Our thoughts revert to earlier Byronic sunsets—to the famous one which opens *The Curse of Minerva*, tinged

with sadness but not with blood; or to that other splendour in
Childe Harold IV, xxvii–xxix, reconciling night with day, the values
of heaven with those of earth, of time with eternity.

The obsessional dramas

Byron's subtitles for *Manfred* and *Sardanapalus* are 'A Dramatic Poem'
and 'A Tragedy' respectively; I have called them 'escapist dramas'.
Marino Faliero and *The Two Foscari* he calls 'Historical Tragedies':
I think of them as 'obsessional dramas'. They reverse the centrifugal
direction of the first pair, in which the protagonists sought deliverance, freedom, transcendence in one form or another: the scorpion's
rush to the circumference. Now, in the obsessional dramas, we have
the maddened retreat to the dark centre.[7] These are 'neurotic', as
Manfred and *Sardanapalus* were not. Not freedom from, but self-
immolating identification with the dark forces of destruction is what
is sought here: a ritual sacrifice. The closest parallel to the Venetian
plays is perhaps Milton's *Samson Agonistes*; but Samson *is* consistently
'agonistes', wrestling with himself and his persecutors, and the play
is disposed throughout to its great violent climax, the triumph of
will. Nothing of this is found in Byron's plays. His heroes are
ineffective, his *mise-en-scène* cramping. Contemporary critics saw this
at once. 'The true history of his failure', Jeffrey wrote, 'is to be
found in the bad choice of his subject in *Marino Faliero*—his selection
of a story which not only gives no scope to the peculiar and commanding graces of his genius, but runs continually counter to the
master currents of his fancy.' (*Edinburgh Review*, xxxv, Sept. 1821.)

Jacopo Foscari's violent rejection of the Aegean scene in the first
act of *The Two Foscari* is symptomatic of defeat. 'The horrid Cyclades'
can offer him nothing to compensate for the loss of Venice—to
which he *must* return, though the return involves imprisonment and
the rack. There is an insect-like automatism in both the Foscari—in
Jacopo's obsessive love for Venice, in the Doge's obsessive adherence
to the responsibilities of his office—which is inhuman, mechanical.
Gigantic insects or arthropods stilting through dark, intricate
passages which connect 'a palace and a prison'—this is how I see
the involved action of the Venetian plays. They move in a machine
world, a society purged of human values. 'Mere machines/To serve
the nobles' most patrician pleasure': so the Doge describes the plebs
of Venice. It is a world of machination, in which men are cogs in a

political engine. 'The hum/Of human cities [is] torture', Byron had noted in *Childe Harold* III, lxxii: this whirring of the political machine grows louder and centres on the ducal palace, where torture culminates in that ultimate 'engine', the rack. Human nature is wrenched from its instinctive structure to conform to insect demands, the tyranny of the ant-hill:[8]

> *Doge.* The torture! you have put me there already,
> Daily since I was Doge; but if you will
> Add the corporeal rack, you may; these limbs
> Will yield with age to crushing iron; but
> There's that within my heart shall strain your engines.
> *(Marino Faliero,* V, i, 300–4)

Natural, unnatural; human, inhuman; free, imprisoned: these are the antitheses which weave the warp and woof of the Venetian plays. The city as rack—but also the city as mistress, as the utterly adored. It is a rape on Venice herself which has been committed by her tyrants. Fresh from the torture, Jacopo Foscari is led by his guard to the open window:

> *Guard.*   There sir, 'tis
> Open.—How feel you?
> *Jac. Fos.*   Like a boy—Oh Venice!
> *Guard.* And your limbs?
> *Jac. Fos.* Limbs! how often have they borne me
> Bounding o'er yon tide, as I have skimm'd
> The gondola along in childish race.
> *(The Two Foscari,* I, i, 92–6)

The 'limbs' gambit initiates a kind of bondage-freedom word-play which Shakespeare would have enjoyed—an imaginative break-through to liberty, introducing one of the greatest of Byron's sea pieces:

>   How many a time have I
> Cloven with arm still lustier, breast more daring
> The wave all roughened; with a swimmer's stroke
> Flinging the billows back from my drenched hair,
> And laughing from my lips the audacious brine,
> Which kissed it like a wine-cup, rising o'er
> The waves as they arose, and prouder still
> The loftier they uplifted me; and oft,
> In wantonness of spirit, plunging down
> Into their green and glassy gulfs, and making
> My way to shells and sea-weed, all unseen
> By those above, till they waxed fearful; then
> Returning with my grasp full of such tokens

> As showed that I had searched the deep: exulting
> With a far-dashing stroke, and drawing deep
> The long-suspended breath, again I spurned
> The foam which broke around me, and pursued
> My track like a sea-bird.—I was a boy then.   (I, i, 104–21)[9]

The *dramatic* force of this lies in its counterpoint to the very different
sea picture presented a few lines earlier in the same scene by
Barbarigo, a Senator who has a moment of revulsion from his
allegiance to the sadistic Loredano:

> Follow *thee*! I have follow'd long
> Thy path of desolation, as the wave
> Sweeps after that before it, alike whelming
> The wreck that creaks to the wild winds, and wretch
> Who shrieks within its riven ribs, as gush
> The waters through them; but this son and sire
> Might move the elements to pause, and yet
> Must I on hardily like them.   (I, i, 56–62)

where the insect-like compulsive ethos of the play is seen as dominating the torturers equally with the tortured. But Jacopo's lines have
their *eikonic* as well as *dramatic* justification—as so many of
Shakespeare's fantasia soliloquies have—lifting the immediate situation into cosmic dimensions. The freedom of action Jacopo cannot
now exercise and is never to recover is pathetically, nostalgically
redreamed: 'I was a boy then.' The sea's antithetic essence, conveyed
in the two speeches, projects a freedom and energy which disinfects
the play's musty, dungeon atmosphere. Barbarigo's seascape of
destruction puts to shame Loredano's petty revenge obsession—and
Jacopo's equally crazy canal-lagoon fixation is irrigated by this
superbly undulant, boisterous love-play with the open sea. Line by
line the passage offers an almost tactile re-enactment of the movements of a strong swimmer in his delighted course: the first plunge
into the 'roughened' waves as they break on the shore, the pause as
he resurfaces and tosses the hair back out of his eyes, the laughing
shout back to the watchers on the shore, the resilience of the supporting waves and his command over them, the sudden dive into
'green and glassy gulfs'—it is all brilliantly, impeccably flashed on
our sight. We are not only watching him, we are experiencing with
him the sea's pressures and wayward currents. Byron is unequalled
at this kind of thing.[10] It is not, indeed, a common Romantic
capability, or a Victorian; and because it 'taught us little' I
presume, this splendid passage was not included in Arnold's *Poetry of
Byron*.

There is no moment in *Marino Faliero* which breaks physically out of the Venetian labyrinth as does Jacopo's speech in the later play. The exquisite night scene of Venice in IV, i, comes from Lioni, a minor character, not from the Doge, and is static; yet serves something of the same purpose of distancing in time which Jacopo's speech effected in space:

> Around me are the stars and waters—
> Worlds mirrored in the Ocean, goodlier sight
> Than torches glared back by a gaudy glass;
> And the great Element, which is to space
> What Ocean is to Earth, spreads its blue depths,
> Softened with the first breathings of the spring;
> The high Moon sails upon her beauteous way,
> Serenely smoothing o'er the lofty walls
> Of those tall piles and sea-girt palaces,
> Whose porphyry pillars, and whose costly fronts,
> Fraught with the Orient spoil of many marbles,
> Like altars ranged along the broad canal,
> Seem each a trophy of some mighty deed
> Reared up from out the waters, scarce less strangely
> Than those more massy and mysterious giants
> Of architecture, those Titanian fabrics,
> Which point in Egypt's plains to times that have
> No other record. . . .　　　　　(*Marino Faliero*, IV, i, 68–85)

The sudden reference to the Pyramids opens up archaic vistas; but the passage as a whole contains satiric and ironic elements (lines 69–70, and 79: Lioni is just back from a ball; the palaces are altars to *what* deity?) absent from the pure dynamism of Jacopo's speech. Both plays are in any case (apart from these moments of release) eminently solipsist, retreating from community to the 'selfish centre' and pressing hard on the destructive nerve. The only outlets are through memory or imagination. 'My own sepulchre, a walking grave'—Marino Faliero and the two Foscari embody Samson's self-definition even when they move in sunlight; they are obsessed, Dostoevskian figures, wounded scorpions seeking the dark.

> This love of thine
> For an ungrateful and tyrannic soil
> Is passion, and not patriotism; for me,
> So I could see thee with a quiet aspect,
> And the sweet freedom of the earth and air,
> I would not cavil about climes or regions.
> This crowd of palaces and prisons is not
> A paradise; its first inhabitants
> Were wretched exiles . . .

Marina tells her husband (*The Two Foscari*, III, i, 141–9). Feminine reasonableness is indeed the only counterbalance, in these later plays, to masculine manias. 'I have . . . attempted to make a play without love', Byron says of *Marino Faliero*, 'and there are neither rings, nor mistakes, nor starts, nor outrageous canting villains, nor melodrama in it.' And of the later play: 'What I seek to show in "the Foscaris" is the *suppressed* passions, rather than the rant of the present day.' Romantic love is certainly absent, and we may be grateful for that; but conjugal and unselfishly clearsighted love upholds the whole series of more or less crazy heroes from Faliero to Werner, and provides an essential *punctum indifferens* in the plays.

Tested by the touchstones which have served us well in our survey of the pre-dramatic *oeuvre*, the resonances of man as centre to environment as volume and circumference, these Venetian plays remain unsatisfactory, impoverished. They function within a restricted framework of diminished values. What is Venice to its Doge, who commits treason to save it (or so he says)—a sea Cybele fresh from ocean, as in *Childe Harold*? No, but 'this precarious commonwealth' (*Marino Faliero*, II, i, 183), 'this scorpion-nest of vice' (*ibid*, 300) or 'the wariest of Republics', in Angiolina's more measured assessment (*ibid*, 113). Faliero is in his own estimation 'a poor puppet' supported only by 'self-esteem' (I, ii, 374)—a startling contrast to Manfred and Sardanapalus in their complementary though diverse assertions of dignity. The status of love likewise shrivels: if not 'a foolish dotard's vile caprice' (II, i, 310) it is a 'patriarchal' affection anticipating the horrors of *Middlemarch*. The attempted link with Othello's 'To be free and bounteous to her mind' fails, because neither the Doge nor Angiolina has much of a mind to be bounteous to or with; and there are no 'moving accidents by flood and field' apart from the shameful episode at Treviso with which to ensnare her (I, ii, 310), no significant past-into-present inflows; this is a static world. An insult can stand between the sun and a nephew of the man who has suffered the insult (I, ii, 246–7): an unparalleled stroke of paranoia. The indoor character of the whole drama is implicit in its palace-prison structure and in the image framework of dull, leaden refusal of participation with life's flow: 'blighted old age' (II, i, 456), 'the deep vale/Where Death sits robed in his all-sweeping shadow'. Israel Bertuccio's

> Your fiery nature makes you deem all those
> Whose are not restless, cold: . . .   (II, ii, 63–4)

suggests Byron suspected he was going too far in filling his play with zombies; but the damage by this time is done.

The Two Foscari plumbs even more sadistic, more perverse depths. Nothing arrests time more neatly than torture, that black eternity. Brutus' gigantic error, the rejection of the real, of human love, for the fictitious, for political theory, is compounded here in the father's grotesque immolation of his son. The theme has, indeed, already appeared fleetingly in *Marino Faliero*. Israel Bertuccio's casual reference to 'son' provokes the curious outburst—

> *Doge.* Wretch! darest thou name my son? he died in arms
>   At Sapienza for this faithless state.
>   Oh! that he were alive, ere I be in ashes!   (I, ii, 556–8)

—and the lines introduce that father–son theme which is to persist through the works of the final period: through *The Two Foscari*, *Cain*, *Heaven and Earth*, *Werner*, *Don Juan*, and *The Island* (the quasifilial link of Christian with Bligh) right into *The Deformed Transformed* where it provides the dynamism (Caesar–Arnold) for a breakaway from the ultimate trauma, never faced till now, of the Arnold–Bertha, mother–son relationship. We may trace it back to the priest–penitent (or rather impenitent) liaisons of *The Giaour* and *Manfred*, hovering upon but never surrendering to an acceptance of the need to

> Die of the absolute paternal care
> That will not leave us, but prevents us everywhere.[11]

When one says that Byron 'failed', in these dramas, to do this or that, it is of course in the sense one says Shakespeare failed in *Hamlet*, or Blake failed in *Jerusalem*, or Joyce failed in *Ulysses*, to do what he set out to do—or what we judge him to have set out to do. We have to bear in mind the complexity and the originality of what he was trying to accomplish. The epigraph to *The Two Foscari* (Byron's epigraphs, always significant, have not been enough considered) poses an antithesis, and admits a fragmentation: 'The *father* softens, but the *governor's* resolved', from Sheridan's *The Critic*. Sheridan's play is a comedy, Byron's a tragedy; but leaving aside this point, let us consider the antithesis in itself, with its opposition of the tough to the tender already evident in the triple epigraphs of *Hours of Idleness*. It sounds a note of irony, of detachment, absent from the feverish nightmare of the play. We revert to Billy Bunterish school-days, the 'guv'ner' failing to remit the hoped-for postal-order. But the governor is also (*a*) the helmsman and (*b*) the censor, the interior escapement mechanism. As a schoolboy, Byron had no 'governor', and the fact was no doubt noted by his Harrow class-mates. The mechanism works in the play as machination on the political level and as the rack on the physical, a meshing of cog-wheels, a Kafkaesque nightmare. Byron is projecting the totalitarian state. We wrong the play if we read it on one level only, just as we habitually wrong Byron when we read him along a linear rather than an areal spectrum.

The theological dramas

The biblical plays, which Byron called 'Mysteries' in allusion to medieval drama and which I think of as 'theological',[12] are soundings into doctrinal deeps. Byron read his Bible seriously, critically. As a poet the sublime rhythms of the Authorised Version moved (and moulded) him as they did Bunyan and Blake; but little of this passed into *Cain* (July–Sept. 1821) or *Heaven and Earth* (Oct.–Nov. 1821). Formally these plays are as remorselessly neoclassical as *Sardanapalus* and *Marino Faliero*, except for some slight relaxation of the Unities.

Cain is a refutation of that 'first lesson of Monosyllables—"God made man, let us love him"' which Byron learned by rote at Bodsy Bowers's school at the age of five. Its theme is equally monosyllabic: 'God made man, let us hate him.' God made man, but to live under a tyranny, and then to die. Made him with the thirst and capacity for immortality, the sense that he is greater than he knows. Cain is the first rebel, the delinquent, immensely conscious of the 'generation gap'. He revolts as did Blake and Shelley against the son–father relationship, whether the father is seen as God or Adam.

The setting is 'The Land without Paradise', pinpointing the exilic theme. The lost Garden is still visible, its gates 'With dreadful faces thronged, and fiery arms'. Adam, Eve, Abel, Adah, Zillah, cling together in a society of acceptors, the guilty and the repentant. Cain alone rebels, asserts the right of the human spirit to be itself in all its plenitude. 'Content thee with what is', Eve's injunction and (for Byron) the eighteenth century's, cannot be accepted. Nor can the chronic curse of work:

> And this is
> Life?—Toil! and wherefore should I toil?—because
> My father could not keep his place in Eden.

What had *I* done in this?—I was unborn:
I sought not to be born; nor love the state
To which that birth has brought me.   (I, i, 64–9)

The whole speech of which this is the beginning is a powerful
presentation of the intellectual difficulties of the Mosaic-Christian
theology of the Fall. It follows upon an opening scene in which the
rest of the family unite in morning prayers and thanksgivings. Cain
only abstains, and after a painful argument with his parents he is
ready for the confrontation with Lucifer.

Lucifer has much in common with Milton's Satan and is thus a
type, also, of the Byronic hero. But he has much in common too with
Gabor in *Werner*, the drama Byron was to begin writing some five
months later. He is a psychological tempter, an analyst, and his
treatment of Cain's trauma has all the marks of depth therapy. The
sort of situation we find in Thomas Mann's *The Magic Mountain* and
Eliot's *The Cocktail Party* and *The Family Reunion* is prefigured in
Cain: there is a sense of analysis within analysis.[13] In revolting from
his natural father, Adam, Cain fixates on the antithetic father figure
of Lucifer. Unlike Adam, Lucifer pities Cain and says '[I] would
not have made thee what thou art'. He refutes Adam and Eve's
assurance that 'all the fruit is Death!'

> *Lucifer.* They have deceived thee; thou shalt live.
> *Cain.*   I live,
>   But live to die; and, living, see no thing
>   To make death hateful, save an innate clinging,
>   A loathsome, and yet all invincible
>   Instinct of life.   (I, i, 109–13)

Here Byron touches on issues raised in our century by Heidegger and
Sartre.

Blake reacted to *Cain* with the Dedication of his own *Ghost of Abel*
'To LORD BYRON in the Wilderness: What doest thou here,
Elijah?' Blake recognised Byron's twin function as prophet and
scapegoat, and his presentation of Los and Orc in the later Prophetic
Books may owe much to this recognition. In Byron's 'Omnipotent
Tyrant' he would see many of the icy and solitude-making features
of his own Urizen. 'He is great', Lucifer reports of Jehovah,

> But, in his greatness, is no happier than
> We in our conflict! Goodness would not make
> Evil; and what else hath he made? But let him
> Sit on his vast and solitary throne—
> Creating worlds, to make eternity

> Less burthensome to his immense existence
> And unparticipated solitude;
> Let him crowd orb on orb: he is alone
> Indefinite, Indissoluble Tyrant.[14]   (I, i, 145–53)

Lucifer presents Jehovah to the eagerly attentive Cain as the restrictive, sadistic 'demon', himself as the Promethean benefactor of mankind. Milton, Blake had said, 'was a true poet and of the Devil's party without knowing it'. Byron is also of the Devil's party and knows it, and his readers knew it, hence the howl of execration which arose when it was first published, and hence Shelley's raptures:

What think you of Lord Byron now? Space wondered less at the swift and fair creations of God, when he grew weary of vacancy, than I at the late works of this spirit of an angel in the mortal paradise of a decaying body. . . . Lord Byron's last volume . . . contains finer poetry than has appeared in England since the publication of *Paradise Regained*—*Cain* is apocalyptic—it is a revelation not before communicated to man. (Letters to John Gisborne, 12 and 26 January 1822.)

Re-echoing Milton's 'the mind is its own place' (the first echo had been in *Manfred*) Byron gives Lucifer the Promethean words:

> Nothing can
> Quench the mind, if the mind will be itself
> And centre of surroundings things—'tis made
> To sway.   (I, i, 213–16)

But whereas Milton's 'mind' *is* a place, a still centre which abides and comprehends, Byron's is a moving centre, a vortex spinning with 'sway' through a universe of infinite possibilities. This is the ruling theme of the drama, and we are reminded again of Blake's conception of an 'ever-growing' eternity. Jehovah's is a 'sullen, sole eternity' (I, i, 239) enclosed and rigid; Lucifer presents the diagram of a 'participative', contrapuntal *Sat-Chit-Ananda*. My use of the Vedantic term may appear wilful, but we can justify it through a glance at the second great theme of *Cain*, the approach to fulness of being by the twin paths of love and knowledge, the *bhakti-marga* and the *jnana-marga* which are the contrasted devotional and contemplative 'ways'. Byron uses, naturally, the Judaeo-Christian equivalents, cherubim and seraphim:

> *Adah.*   I have heard it said,
>   The seraphs *love most*—Cherubim *know most*—
>   And this should be a Cherub—since he loves not.
>   (I, i, 419–21)

Here Adah unwittingly probes the chink in Lucifer's armour, and

his rather waspish reply shows how the innocent, ignorant comment
has struck home:

> And if the higher knowledge quenches love,
> What must he be ye cannot love when known?
> Since the all-knowning Cherubim love least,
> The Seraph's love can be but ignorance.   (I, i, 423–6)

In terms of *bhakti-marga* and *jnana-marga Cain* is the sciential,
Heaven and Earth the devotional side of the same medal, the failure
of both love and the thirst for knowledge to pierce through the
Cloud of Unknowing which envelops man from his birth.

Cain's flight with Lucifer through 'the Abyss of Space' which
occupies Act II is a brilliant extrapolation of Byron's inner distances.
A modern physicist-philosopher has noted that 'the scale of observation creates the phenomenon'; as Cain wings his way into outer
space the relevance of 'his little world' and 'his little life' (i, 14, 15)
diminishes, and he attains a cosmic freedom of insight. He is introduced to the majesty of disinterested thought (49) and taught that
the all too 'sweet degradation' (179) of sexual love distorts that
intellectual purity. But the rational argument which forms the basis
of Lucifer's temptation in Act I is here replaced by the visual
evidence of relativity: in view of these cosmic distances can man's
petty drama be so significant after all? (153–66). Yet the *beauty* of
'ces espaces éternels' (99–117) sets a countercurrent going in Cain's
mind. The development of this first scene is extremely subtle, with
Lucifer functioning now as tempter, now as exegete, now as analyst;
the material is too compressed for presentation within a single play
of the tiny dimensions of *Cain*.

Descending into Hades in scene ii, into the world of things past
and dead, Cain exclaims: 'Curséd be/He who invented life that
leads to Death!' (II, ii, 18–19). 'Dost thou curse thy father?'
Lucifer replies. The father–son conflict in Byron is thus brought into
the open in theological terms: the long brother–sister ganging up
(Byron–Augusta against Mrs Byron) is at last undermined, and the
diabolical analyst probes into the poisoned springs. Cain's reply is a
revelation straight from the psychiatrist's couch:

> Cursed he not me in giving me my birth?
> Cursed he not me before my birth. . . .

to which Lucifer returns:

> Thou say'st well;
> The curse is mutual 'twixt thy sire and thee.   (22–6)

The descent into Hades, which is the descent into the womb, releases Byron from his dynastic compulsions. But 'the curse is mutual' between the father/son lust/power/possession drives; for the moment 'for the womb the seed sighs': the guilt of the womb itself will be left over for consideration in *The Deformed Transformed*. For the moment, then, we remain in the womb, a place 'Of *Swimming* shadows and enormous shapes' (my italics), without further comment; our concern is with the shapes and their observers, Cain and Lucifer. Byron is working on a number of levels: on the psychological-dynastic, as I have just suggested, but also on the theological-metaphysical and the geological-historical. A note in his diary ('Detached Thoughts', no. 101) of this same year 1821 sums up some of these speculations:

If . . . you could prove the World many thousand years older than the Mosaic Chronology, or if you could knock up [i.e. disprove] Adam and Eve and the Apple and Serpent, still what is to be put in their stead? or how is the difficulty removed? Things must have had a beginning, and what matters it *when* or *how*?

I sometimes think that *Man* may be the relic of some higher material being, wrecked in a former world, and degenerated in the hardships and struggle through Chaos into Conformity—or something like it; as we see Laplanders, Esquimaux, etc., inferior in the present state, as the Elements become more inexorable. But even then this higher pre-Adamite suppositious Creation must have had an Origin and a *Creator*; for a *Creator* is a more natural imagination than a fortuitous concourse of atoms. All things remount to a fountain, though they may flow to an Ocean.

And No. 102 reads:

What a strange thing is the propagation of life! A bubble of Seed which may be spilt in a whore's lap—or in the orgasm of a voluptuous dream—might (for aught we know) have formed a Caesar or a Buonaparte: there is nothing remarkable recorded of their Sires, that I know of.

The speculation is close to the 'filthy cheat' outburst of Lucifer's in sc. i, 50–60. This sexual motif is expanded in sc. ii to cover the whole theme of generation and degeneration raised in Detached Thought No. 101: the juxtaposition of the diary entries suggests we shall not go astray in connecting the two scenes of the drama. The pre-Adamites Cain is privileged to observe are

> Living, high,
> Intelligent, good, great, and glorious things,
> As much superior unto all thy sire
> Adam could e'er have been in Eden, as
> The sixty-thousandth generation shall be,

In its dull damp degeneracy, to
Thee and thy son.   (II, ii, 67–71)

After viewing further wonders of the lost worlds—prehistoric animals, phantasms of ancient oceans, the mysteries of space—and opening his mind to all the insidious arguments of Lucifer against the supposed goodness of Jehovah, Cain is returned to the earth in Act III and to its tender and not-so-tender domesticities. There is only one scene in this final act: it opens with Cain and Adah bending over their sleeping child, and ends with Cain and Zillah bending over their murdered brother. The ominous note is struck immediately with the shadowing cypress:

> *Adah.* Our little Enoch sleeps upon yon bed
>   Of leaves, beneath the cypress.
> *Cain.*   Cypress! 'tis
>   A gloomy tree, which looks as if it mourned
>   O'er what it shadows.   (III, i, 3–5)

The dialogue centres in Adah's plea for family life, for parental joys, for contentment with simple human satisfactions, as against the vast and disturbing speculations which throng Cain's mind after his cosmic journey. The exchanges here are not on the level of interest of those between Cain and Lucifer; Adah's is a very limited intelligence, acceptable only by its loving faithfulness. Her cue is always to draw Cain's attention back—when the argument gets out of hand—to the sleeping Enoch:

> Oh Cain! look on him; see how full of life,
> Of strength, of bloom, of beauty, and of joy—
> How like to me—how like to thee, when gentle—
> For *then* we are *all* alike; is't not so, Cain?
> Mother, and sire, and son, our features are
> Reflected in each other; as they are
> In the clear waters, when *they* are *gentle*, and
> When *thou* art *gentle*. Love us, then, my Cain![15]   (III, i, 140–7)

The argument, if it can be called such, is a levelling one: 'Let us all be loving and 'gentle' together in an unthinking, bovine 'alikeness'.

Adah is coming near to calming Cain's troubled mind when Abel intrudes with his insistence on a joint sacrifice to Jehovah. If Adah is a zombie, Abel is a bore, pompous and persistent. What Cain clearly needs after his terrific experience is solitude in which to assimilate it; but Abel insists on plaguing him first with enquiries

and then with demands. Cain *must* conform, must follow the established pattern of behaviour, including the slaughter and sacrifice of
animals. The question of the involvement of animals in Adam's fall
had already been raised theoretically in the cosmic journey (II, ii,
200–10); and Cain had expressed his compassion for 'the hopeless
wretches' in burning words. Now Abel clumsily and brutally assails
this compassionate nerve with his unfeeling slaughter of 'the firstlings
of the flock'. The climax comes when Jehovah graciously signifies
his approval and acceptance of Abel's blood sacrifice and his
rejection of Cain's offering of fruits. At this point all Lucifer's
accusations against the 'sole tyrant', the Maker-Destroyer, seem fully
justified; and it is with an emotion of generous indignation that
Cain rushes to overturn Abel's altar. Here he stands for life—not
just his own life, but that of the planet—against the death-principle,
and his action is Promethean.

Heaven and Earth is a more complex drama than *Cain* and all is not on
the surface. The setting is biblical, but with an odd infusion of
'elementals', earth spirits, magic spells which belong to an extra-
Judaic tradition. Coleridge's symbolism is interwoven with that of
Genesis to form a singularly effective psychological structure. His
sunlit dome, expressing the conscious level of experience, is here
seen as 'yon exulting peak/Whose glittering top is like a distant star'
(I, iii, 22–3). His 'caverns measureless to man' are here the abodes
of those chthonic forces which emerge from their underground
labyrinths with 'shouts of laughter' to mock poor Japhet's attempts
at rational discourse. 'Ancestral voices prophesying war' are
paralleled by written records:

> The scroll of Enoch prophesied it long
> In silent books, which, in their silence, say
> More to the mind than thunder to the ear . . .   (I, iii, 275–7)

—books stored through the millennia, like the Hermetic fragments,
within 'the long-neglected holy cave'.[16]

   Heaven and Earth may thus be seen as a commentary on 'Kubla
Khan' as much as a sequel to *Cain*. What happens, Byron is asking,
when the barrier between Heaven and Earth is lowered? Cain's
journey with Lucifer through the cosmic spaces had been the upward
thrust of knowledge, exciting but emotionally barren. The descent
of the Sons of God to the Daughters of Men initiates frightening
consequences. 'The same day were all the fountains of the great

deep broken up.'[17] Chthonic forces invade the sphere of the celestial-terrestrial, the sunless sea overflows the world of the shining dome and the girdled garden. The play is thus an assertion of the unity of being, of Blake's doctrine that the physical cannot be separated from the spiritual, that 'The body is that portion of the soul discerned by the five senses', and that 'All that lives is holy'. The very coordinates of time and space, Byron insists, cannot be imagined apart from the mind that conceives them, any more than Eternity has a meaning apart from the God whose attribute it is. If man disappears the universe disappears with him:

> Aye, day will rise; but upon what?—a chaos,
> Which was ere day; and which, renewed, makes Time
> Nothing! for, without life, what are the hours?
> No more to dust than is Eternity
> Unto Jehovah, who created both.
> Without him, even Eternity would be
> A void: without man, Time, as made for man,
> Dies, with man, and is swallowed in that deep
> Which has no fountain.   (I, iii, 300–8)

Very similar conjectures had engaged Cain on his cosmic journey.[18] Worlds, Lucifer declares, have come and gone, and with worlds their times and spaces (*Cain*, II, i), and Hell itself is opened to him in scene ii, where the shadows of the gigantic pre-Adamites deflate his conceptions of human dignity and uniqueness. Much of this comes from Cuvier, but Byron's power to clothe scientific speculation in poetic form is impressive, and his picture of world after world destroyed by cosmic explosion seems more authentic in our age of atomic power than it did to the nineteenth century, intent on its dream of inevitable progress.

As a work of art, *Heaven and Earth* is disappointing. It is of course unfinished, and therefore resistant to final criticism; but from what we have it is difficult to imagine a triumphant completion. Swinburne praised the long choral passages for their 'magnificent lyric measures', while condemning (rightly, I think) the insertion of 'short lines with jagged edges'. The play proceeds, indeed, from 'hymn' to 'hymn': it is essentially a play of voices where *Cain* was a play of gestures. E. H. Coleridge, in his introduction (V, sc. 281) calls attention to Byron's acquaintance not only with the Bible but also with 'The Book of Enoch'.[19]

'In the Beginning was the Word'—in thus turning, in his second biblical play, to the word, to voices, to prophecy and 'The Book of

Enoch', to ancient scrolls, Byron is making his last cast *outward* before the catatonic stasis of *Werner* and the manic-depressive seesaw of *The Deformed Transformed*. What is at issue here is the question of intercourse, or communication. How is the heaven–earth nexus to be achieved? Or, if it cannot be achieved, what are the impediments? These are the problems Byron will go on to investigate in his final plays.

Heaven and Earth serves to remind us that one of Byron's major issues was this problem of communication. The enormous variety of forms he essayed in his career—more, surely, than any other Romantic poet—and the final attempt to blend them all into a new kind of 'epic', is symptomatic of a dissatisfaction with existing media. Blake had the same problem. He solved it as little as Byron, artistically speaking; but because the very awkwardness and gigantism of his attempt impress, modern critics are ready to take Blake seriously as a 'symbolic thinker'. Byron, always the nonchalant improviser, is less acceptable. He doesn't attempt to create a new mythology. He works with the materials he has to hand: travel poems, sentimental/ironic lyrics, comedy, satire, but along lines and through dimensions which often give the lie to their surface purposes. He is a Dali of poetry, juxtaposing heterogeneous values. This has been noted and accepted in *Don Juan*, which is Byron's trend poem for the latter half of the twentieth century. But its beginnings, and in some respects its more complex expression, in the later dramas have been overlooked.

The psychological dramas

Towards the end of 1821 Byron wrote to John Murray begging him not to send 'any modern, or (as they are called) *new*, publications in *English whatsoever*' apart from those of a few favourites (Scott, Crabbe, Campbell, Rogers) and books of travels *not* relating to countries he has himself visited. He also rejects all periodicals and reviews; and requests 'that you send me *no* opinions whatsoever, either *good*, *bad*, or *indifferent* of yourself, or your friends, or others, concerning any work, or works, of mine, past, present, or to come'. All these he has found to be distractions. Reviews 'tend to increase *Egotism*; if favourable, I do not deny that the praise *elates*, and if unfavourable, that the abuse *irritates*'. As for 'opinions', these 'do not interrupt, but they soil the current of my Mind'.[20] A remarkable letter, in which we see Byron clearing the decks for action. If we ask 'what action', the answer lies in the final plays, where Byron comes to grips at last with his deepest springs of being. His mind must be kept *'free* and *unbiassed* . . . to let my Genius take its natural direction, while my feelings are like the dead, who know nothing and feel nothing of all or aught that is said or done in their regard'.

This 24 September letter is an index to the dimensions in which Byron's mind was moving as he gathered himself for the final assault of self-analysis in *Werner* and *The Deformed Transformed*. Here, in dramatic terms, he works out the sources of his 'poisoned springs' and the patterns of the dried-up water-courses into which he later stumbled (*Childe Harold* III, iii and vii). Outside Shakespeare's final plays, it is difficult to think of a drama which more incisively and agonisingly projects an inner conflict of self-appraisal, or one couched in such heroically self-negating terms. Sardanapalus, Manfred, Cain, can all be assimilated to the Byronic image; Faliero and the Foscaris less so; now in Werner and Arnold, even though Byron is approaching the nuclear nerve of his own trauma, the hero becomes less heroic, less 'Byronic', more complex, weaker, questioning, bewildered. To write such a drama the playwright has to be 'like the dead, who know nothing and feel nothing of all . . . that is said or done in their regard', i.e. have to be like the patient hypnotised on the psychiatrist's couch. Here Byron is his own patient and his own analyst. Hitherto the father/son confrontation has been progressively 'expansed'. It is continued in *Werner*; but *The Deformed Transformed* at last brings the basic mother/son relationship to the surface. Significantly, the play is left unfinished.

Byron took the plot of *Werner* (which he subtitles 'The Inheritance: A Tragedy') from a story called *Kruitzner* by Harriet Lee. He had read the tale when he was a boy of thirteen and tried to turn it into a drama; that the interest persisted to the last years of his life is an indication of the hold this theme had on his imagination.

Werner is a play of disguises and counterdisguises, plots and counterplots. Characters are ill-defined, like figures in a dream, moving in and out of conflicting personae as do the Zoas in Blake's Prophetic Books. Werner, the original Kruitzner, is also the Count Siegendorf; he is pursued by a kind of *doppelgänger*, called Stralenheim, who seeks to deprive him of his inheritance. Werner's son, Ulric, who has been separated from his father and his mother Josephine for twelve long years, is the energic component, the Orc (in Blakean terms) of the fragmented Albion whose other components are

Urizen-Stralenheim and his 'emanation' Josephine, and Tharmas-
Idenstein, the comic earth figure who deflates most pretensions in the
play. A further figure, Gabor, whom early critics found 'inexplicable
. . . he is always on the point of turning out something more than he
proves to be' (as the *Eclectic Review* complained), functions in the
play as the psychiatrist—very much like Reilly in Eliot's *The
Cocktail Party*. The initial setting of the drama, 'a decayed Palace
near a small Town in the Northern Frontier of Silesia', seems a far
cry from the sungirt grandeurs of *Sardanapalus*, and of course we are
in a diminished world, as the adjectives suggest; nevertheless the
geometry is strangely similar, the besieged palace, full of twists and
turns; the surrounding flats; the restricting rivers. Everything is
horizontal, implicated; mountains, gulfs have ceased to exist as
objective correlatives, and depths are discovered only (under Gabor's
probings) in the heart of man.

Werner is *l'homme moyen sensuel* who will not look into the depths.
He is pursued by his *alter ego*, Stralenheim, and teased by his censor,
Gabor, who refuses to allow him to take refuge in evasions. In the
very early draft of 1815 we find the significant lines 'My father's
wrath extends beyond the grave,/And haunts me in the shape of
Stralenheim' (I, i, 18–19). We approach a moment of truth (the
old bullring, Coliseum pattern reasserting itself) within the 'decayed
palace' which is Byron's final 'circus'. Converging forces—
Stralenheim, Ulric—mass here for explosion. Unwilling to acknow-
ledge that he and Stralenheim are 'travelling the same way' (I, i,
536), Werner also questions the integrity of Gabor, whom he takes
for 'a mere tool and spy of Stralenheim/To sound and to secure me'.
Pressed in thus upon himself, 'begirt too with the flooding rivers'
of the rising unconscious forces (578), his 'Now I am master of
myself at least' (621) rings ironically.

Josephine, Werner's wife, is like all the women characters of the
dramas a restorer of sanity, an anchorage in reality. Her responses
to Gabor are sensible and straightforward, contrasting with
Werner's evasions. She is the eikon of feminine warmth and balance
mitigating Werner's icy manias. A long soliloquy (I, i, 697–734)
projects the familiar Blake/Byron antitheses of North–South, ice–
sunshine, death–life in terms of feudal oppression and existential
misery. How can Werner, she wonders, wish to lord it in a land where

> the despots of the north appear
> To imitate the ice-wind of their clime,
> Searching the shivering vassal through his rags,

To wring his soul—as the bleak elements
His form . . . ?   (719–23)

'What a state of being!', she exclaims.

> In Tuscany, my own dear sunny land,
> Our nobles were but citizens and merchants,
> Like Cosmo. We had evils, but not such
> As these; and our all-ripe and gushing valleys
> Made poverty more cheerful, where each herb
> Was in itself a meal, and every vine
> Rained, as it were, the beverage which makes glad
> The heart of man.   (708–14)

Her plea is for that integration of man with his environment under a healing sun which mitigates, if it cannot abolish, social injustice. This was the symbiosis Byron recognised even in the enslaved land of Greece. In *Werner* we have retracted from this to conditions pointed out in the 'setting' as 'decayed', 'small', 'on the Northern Frontier': this is a 'Land without Paradise'. We are far indeed from the sea and mountain vistas of *Childe Harold*, or the queen-city of the 'Ode to Venice'.

The communion of earth and air was the basis of the flower-and-rock relationship which underlay the compassionate, meditative structures of the early verse, and suggested a title for the first part of the present book. Now this communion is shattered by the element of fire, by the eruption of 'the fount of fiery life', the 'whirling gulf' of the opening stanzas of Canto III.[21] A passage in *The Corsair* which formed no part of the original narrative, but was added in January 1814, is precise in its connection of the Byron/Conrad 'poisoned springs' with this supersession of the flower-and-rock nexus:

> His heart was formed for softness—warped to wrong,
> Betrayed too early, and beguiled too long;
> Each feeling pure—as falls the dropping dew
> Within the grot—like that had hardened too;
> Less clear, perchance, its earthly trials passed,
> But sunk, and chilled, and petrified at last.
> Yet tempests wear, and lightning cleaves the rock;
> If such his heart, so shattered it the shock.
> There grew one flower beneath its rugged brow,
> Though dark the shade—it sheltered—saved till now.
> The thunder came—that bolt hath blasted both,
> The Granite's firmness, and the Lily's growth:
> The gentle plant hath left no leaf to tell
> Its tale, but shrunk and withered where it fell;
> And of its cold protector, blacken round
> But shivered fragments on the barren ground!   (III, xxiii)

Whether we interpret the 'one flower' as Augusta,[22] or 'Thyrza', or 'Leila', or a combination of all three, or, more abstractly, as his own potentiality for goodness, there can be no doubt of the poignantly remorseful note of this passage. On the 'abstract' reading, Medora, the Egeria-figure who is also the betrayed flower, dies in the tower which is always for Byron the eikon of wisdom,[23] and with her dies the possibility of enlightenment for Byron, the 'tender secret' of her song:

> Deep in my soul that tender secret dwells,
>   Lonely and lost to light for evermore,
> Save when to thine my heart responsive swells,
>   Then trembles into silence as before.
>
> There, in its centre, a sepulchral lamp
>   Burns the slow flame, eternal—but unseen;
> Which not the darkness of Despair can damp,
>   Though vain its ray as it had never been.
>
> Remember me—Oh, pass not thou my grave
>   Without one thought whose relics there recline. . . .
>
> (I, xiv, 347–56)

The vortices of *Childe Harold*—the hero, and those of the continuum in which he moved as 'an equal among mightiest energies'—now shrink to painfully small proportions; as Wordsworth's, along his very different gamut, subsided to Anglican mutterings. The plays are a series of constriction patterns. Sardanapalus finds himself in the straits of the scorpion 'ring'd with fire'; Werner is hemmed in by the dull Silesian rivers; the Venetians are prison-and-torture bound; Cain, borne by Lucifer through blank, meaningless spaces, comes close to losing his identity:

> I am sick of all
> That dust has shown me—let me dwell in shadows.
>
> (*Cain*, II, ii, 108–09)

The human vortex, in the plays and perhaps particularly in *Werner* is both immobilised and fragmented; the existential field of vortices is annulled, and we are confined to frustrating enclosures: the prison cell of *The Two Foscari*, where Bonnivard's friendship with the 'spiders at their sullen trade' is reduced to a kinship with 'a strange firefly, which was quickly caught/Last night in yon enormous spider's net' (III, i, 104–05)—the ducal cap of *Marino Faliero*, also a snare; Cain's Eden, 'with dreadful faces thronged and fiery arms', excluding humankind. Instead of moving at speed within luminous, life-giving spaces, the new line of Byronic heroes wastes its strength in the futile effort to break into or out of obsessedly loved or hated enclosures.

Werner breaks out of the 'decayed palace' on the Silesian border to find himself trapped in the 'inheritance' he has at last gained for himself and his son, the 'large and magnificent Gothic Hall in the Castle of Siegendorf, decorated with Trophies, Banners, and Arms of that Family'. His son, Ulric, has prepared this triumph by duplicity and finally murder: his ironic response to Stralenheim's dismissal of his father (the play's Adam, as Ulric is the play's Cain):

> *Ulric.* And this sole, sick, and miserable wretch—
> This way-worn stranger—stands between you and
> This Paradise?—(As Adam did between
> The devil and his)—[*Aside*]   (*Werner*, II, ii, 384–7)

sums up the whole Fall-ethos of the later dramas. *Werner* is a play of wrong decisions and their consequences. The scenes move in narrowing circles, from 'the Hall of a decayed Palace' to 'a secret Passage', thence to 'a Garden' adjacent to the Palace where a temptation scene takes place; thence, in the second part of the action, to the 'Gothic Hall in the Castle of Siegendorf' where the final confrontation is held, and thence again through a secret passage to 'the interior of a Turret' in the final scene: 'Exit Werner into the Turret, closing the Door after him'.

All this is Byron's presentation of the same basic parent–son drama projected by Blake in his Prophetic Books. The Orc–Los–Urizen–Enitharmon syndrome is Byron's own early life pattern. His frequent assertions that he was proud of his father, together with his equally frequently expressed longings for a guiding hand in childhood and young manhood, build up tensions to be released only in the letting-go of *Beppo*, *Don Juan* and (in its different mode) *The Island*. *The Island* is the fantasy fulfilment which could not be realised; *Beppo* and *Don Juan* are very workable alternatives, from the centre of which Byron lived as he wrote.

The Deformed Transformed (1822) is a surrealist fantasia of mask and countermask in which Byron seems, at times, to be parodying himself. His personal involvement is evident. Mary Shelley wrote on the flyleaf of her copy that 'No action of Lord Byron's—scarce a line he has written—but was influenced by his personal defect'. The play is peculiarly relevant to our era in its grasp of the importance of the 'image': this is stressed in the whole image/anti-image involvement of the opening scenes (Part I, sc. i) and the 'The Bourbon! the

Bourbon!' propaganda ethos of the rest of the drama. Byron is coming to grips here with a number of interrelated problems. First, his own childhood trauma, and its extension into later life; second, the problem of his own fame; and third, the increasing emptiness of modern values. The drama is satirical in a way *Werner* was not. Many shibboleths are questioned. The play moves around the poles of man and his masks—transformation, renewal, the formidable allurements of illusion and power. It must be assessed in its relation to *Werner*. *That*—the analysis; *this*—the therapy? Werner's rejection of Ulric left us with a problem, not a solution. Mad Jack's 'For my son, I am happy to hear he is well; but for his walking, 'tis impossible, as he is club-footed' was an earlier rejection, never forgotten. In *The Deformed Transformed*, Byron catches up all these themes into a crazy, slap-stick scarcely viable mélange of 'sick' comedy, history and psychedelic mythology which leaves us gasping. Ancient history moves into modern and out again, supernatural meshes with all-too-human, and the scene where Olimpia hurls herself, to escape rape, from the high altar on to the marble floor of St Peter's might have been written for the modern 'Theatre of Cruelty' or 'Theatre of the Absurd'.

As therapy, the technique is 'occupational'—Byron's projection of himself into various dominating roles—and anticipates the real-life drama of Missolonghi. As analysis, it takes us back beyond the *Werner* situation to the original mother trauma:

> *Bertha.* Out, Hunchback!
> *Arnold.*   I was born so, Mother!   (I, i, 1)

reverts to the boy Byron and his 'amiable Alecto'.[24] Yet the play is, in contrast to *Werner*, an open-air one. Its dynamism is war, not intrigue; death in battle, not assassination. This fantasy world is a field of choices, however unreal. There are fountains, forests, birdsong. Noble phantasms are presented to Arnold: Caesar, Alcibiades, Socrates, Antony, and Demetrius Poliorcetes who embodies solar values forgotten in Byron's drama since *Sardanapalus*:

> Who is this?
> Who truly looketh like a demigod,
> Blooming, and bright, with golden hair, and stature,
> If not more high than mortal, yet immortal
> In all that nameless bearing of his limbs,
> Which he wears as the Sun his rays—a something
> Which shines from him, and yet is but the flashing
> Emanation of a thing more glorious still . . .   (I, i, 246–53)

A wealth of seemingly positive, creative values is offered to Arnold for choice: power, charm, wisdom, love, radiance. He opts, in Achilles, for physical prowess. It is perhaps, in all the circumstances, the inevitable choice (bearing in mind Byron's own 'Achilles' heel'); but in terms of *Werner* it is the preference of Ulric to Gabor. Sea values, however, disinfect and illuminate:

> *Stranger.*   I must commend
> Your choice. The godlike son of the sea-goddess,
> The unshorn boy of Peleus, with his locks
> As beautiful and clear as the amber waves
> Of rich Pactolus, rolled o'er sands of gold,
> Softened by intervening crystal, and
> Rippled like flowing waters by the wind.   (I, i, 266–73)

A release, then, from the dungeons of Foscari and Faliero and the labyrinths of Werner, a release into a curious Renaissance world of Gothic-classical values. *Manfred* and *Childe Harold* IV meet here in uneasy partnership.

Manfred is recalled in the Faustian mainspring of the drama—the diabolic temptation motif. And Arnold falls as Manfred did not. Byron acknowledges his debt to Goethe, but the farcical character of part of the action brings Marlowe more forcibly to mind. The play falls constantly between two stools, achievement and satire; like *Don Juan*, in Hazlitt's penetrating phrase, 'it is a poem written about itself'. We may see it as the product of a 'double bind', the outgoing movement to heroic achievement constantly checked by the sceptical intelligence whose Hamletish self-analyses have again to be ballasted by positive action . . . and so on *ad infinitum*. This feedback system of self-stultifying forces is presented in the opening scene of the drama. First we have the maternal rejection, self-pityingly accepted by Arnold:

> Oh, mother!—She is gone, and I must do
> Her bidding;—wearily but willingly
> I would fulfil it, could I only hope
> A kind word in return. What shall I do?
> [*Arnold begins to cut wood: in doing this he wounds one of his hands.*]
> My labour for the day is over now.
> Accursèd be this blood that flows so fast;
> For double curses will be my meed now
> At home—What home? I have no home, no kin,
> No kind—not made like other creatures, or
> To share their sports or pleasures. Must I bleed too,
> Like them? . . .   (I, i, 28–38)

The blood theme links up with earlier expressions in the dramas; here it finds a special application in sealing the pact with the devil which shortly follows. The flowing blood merges with the flowing spring in which Arnold washes his hand: the two forces of life and death, the upspringing and the downflowing, image Arnold's double bind as hatred of life as it is, thirst for life as it might be. He seeks death 'in the high Roman fashion' by falling on his dagger; but the place of death is beside a well, a 'spring', which Arnold calls 'Nature's mirror'; and it is so in a double sense, as being the slaking of his thirst for life and the horrid reflection of his deformity. The two images, dagger and spring, constitute an antinomy which is yet a complement: at the moment he falls upon the dagger (total resignation to death) he looks into the well (existential vision), or, as the stage direction puts it,

> [*As he rushes to throw himself upon the knife, his eye is suddenly caught
>   by the fountain, which seems in motion.*]
> The fountain moves without a wind: but shall
> The ripple of a spring change my resolve?
> No. Yet it moves again! The waters stir,
> Not as with air, but by some subterrane
> And rocking power of the internal world.
> What's here? A mist! No more?—
> [*A cloud comes from the fountain. He stands gazing upon it; it is
>   dispelled, and a tall black man comes towards him.*]   (I, i, 76–82)[25]

The tall black man, with his aura of tea-leaves and silver-crossed palms, is something of a comedown; and indeed the play never quite picks up again from this Coleridgean moment. Farce takes over. Arnold barters his soul for the noble form of Achilles, while the Stranger mockingly assumes Arnold's cast-off shape and the name of Caesar. Asked where he would prefer to exercise his new-found powers, Arnold chooses Rome:

> *Arnold.* I have heard great things of Rome.
> *Stranger.*   A goodly choice—
>   And scarce a better to be found on earth,
>   Since Sodom was put out. The field is wide too;
>   For now the Frank, and Hun, and Spanish scion
>   Of the old Vandals, are at play along
>   The sunny shores of the World's garden.[26]   (I, i, 502–7)

The reader too may expect much of Rome, after the splendours of *Childe Harold*; but there is disappointment in store for him. To begin with, we are (in scene ii) *outside* Rome (for this is eminently Byron's drama, the drama of the outsider); and we are in the thick of a siege.

Note the reversal from *Werner*, where all the effort was to break out:
in *The Deformed Transformed* it is a break-in which is attempted and
ultimately accomplished. But what Byron is really after is a break-
through. And this sadly, inevitably, does not occur. Byron is too
honest a poet to pretend. The sack of Rome is a desecration of
ancient sanctities. And the ethos of the play itself is a desecration of
the Rome presented to us in *Childe Harold* and the Coliseum monologue of *Manfred*. Classical values have been silted over by the
detritus of Christian centuries: it is the Popes' Rome, but also the
martyrs' Rome, with voices crying from under the altar. Not least
of the antinomies of this curious play is the counterpoint of the
Papal with the Imperial City.[27] The Apocalypse is pervasively
present. The Lutheran soldier's

> proud Babylon's
> No more; the Harlot of the Seven Hills
> Hath changed her scarlet raiment for sackcloth
> And ashes!   (II, iii, 25–8)

uses St John's very phrases. But the consonances are more than
verbal. This is Byron's 'Mystery Play' in a sense deeper than *Cain*'s
or *Heaven and Earth*'s: a true Apocalypse, rounding off the sequence
of Scripture-slanted dramas which begins with Manfred's Fall,
skirts the borders of Eden in the Biblical plays, gives us a Captivity
interlude in *Sardanapalus*, and presents Pauline theology in *Werner*.

Rome stands, in its siege, as an emblem of the ancient world, of
human as against technological values. For the Romans, in their
monstrosities of cruelty as in their imperial greatness (the Coliseum
imaging both) were human in a sense which Byron, with his uncanny
insight into times and places, felt to be passing. As in the Venetian
plays, a machine ethos (here active in the 'engines' of siege as, in the
earlier plays, in the 'engines' of torture) is taking over. Arnold
pleads for a reprieve for the City:

> And those scarce mortal arches,
> Pile above pile of everlasting wall,
> The theatre where Emperors and their subjects
> (Those subjects *Romans*) stood at gaze upon
> The battles of the monarchs of the wild . . .
> For a sole instant's pastime, and 'Pass on
> To a new gladiator!'—Must it fall?   (I, ii, 49–53; 61–2)

The Stranger's reply is ambiguous. In the central scene of the
desecration of St Peter's the later values of Christianity are likewise
repudiated. Here is the womb of Rome, the Rome Byron had hailed

in *Childe Harold* as 'my country! city of the soul! . . . lone mother of
dead empires' to whom 'the orphans of the heart must turn' in
forgetfulness of self, finding in this mighty ideogram the resolution
of their 'petty miseries' (IV, lxxviii). Now devalued, spurned by
Arnold as matrix, the once creative centre where, for Harold,
architecture had flowed into sound, sound into history, history into
understanding (IV, clv, clvi), has become a cockpit of opposing
forces. The split Harold, who is Arnold/Caesar, debates the modern
world.

> *Caesar.* Thou art a conqueror; the chosen knight
>   And free companion of the gallant Bourbon,
>   Late constable of France; and now to be
>   Lord of the city which hath been Earth's Lord
>   Under its emperors,—and—changing sex,
>   Not sceptre, an Hermaphrodite of Empire—
>   *Lady* of the old world.
> *Arnold.*   How, *old?* What! are there
>   *New* worlds?
> *Caesar.* To *you.* You'll find there are such shortly,
>   By its rich harvest, new disease, and gold.   (I, ii, 4–12)[28]

The theme is not developed, but it is interesting to see the razor-sharp
mind of Byron racing ahead into the Century of the Common Man.

Arnold, then, is an anti-Harold: not now the creative vortex
moving among dormant vortices to reanimate and connect, but a
destructive void feeding on ancient sanctities. Rome, which for the
Childe had been a native country, is now a shambles, a pawn in a
discreditable game. The ideogram of the city is devalued. We are
witnessing a species of matricide, a trampling on the 'lone mother'
who for Harold had been the focus of so many nostalgias. In terms
of the metaphor which has sustained us hitherto, the spin is arrested
in a frantic countermeshing of gears. The smooth integration of
Harold-within-the-Coliseum is negated. The man-environment field
has fallen irretrievably apart. You may say, of course, that this is
Byron's coming-of-age, and no doubt it is; but it is a coming of age
Shelley was never in sight of in his thirty years nor Blake in his
seventy. Here Byron passes into the field of the defeated poets, with
Wordsworth and Coleridge. And it is precisely in this mood of
defeat, of disgust with 'what man has made of man', that Byron
embarked in January 1823 on the writing of his last and longest
Tale, *The Island*.

'The Island'

Climbing thankfully into Sir John Colquhoun's carriage at the close of their three months' tour of the Hebrides, Johnson and Boswell acknowledged 'a pleasing conviction of the commodiousness of civilisation, and heartily laughed at the ravings of those absurd visionaries who have attempted to persuade us of the superior advantages of a *state of nature*'. The year is 1773, just half a century before the writing and publication of *The Island*. Byron's last Tale is probably the most powerful expression in English verse (and by one whom no one has ever called an 'absurd visionary') of the cult of the noble savage and the discommodiousness of 'civilisation'. The Highlands were Johnson's taste of primitivism, an experience he enjoyed intellectually but repudiated as a way of life. Between his day and that of Byron (whose earliest primitivism had also been Scottish, as he reminds us in the poem) a whole new order of revolutionary values had come into existence. Visionaries had sprung up on every side, in France and Britain and Germany; a literature of dream and nostalgic quest for a lost Eden had swept away the last traces of Augustan complacency. The bastions of what Johnson called 'subordination' had begun to crumble.

The Island is Byron's little epic of insubordination, and if he had known more about the horrors of Captain Bligh's rule he would no doubt have given us some initial flogging scenes on *The Bounty* to balance the later lotus-eating on the island, as the shipwreck balances the Haidée idyll in the greater epic. This would have been a dramatic gain. Byron himself felt the difficulty. 'I have two points to avoid', he writes to Leigh Hunt on 25 January 1823,

—the first that of running foul of my own *Corsair* and style, so as to produce repetition and monotony—and the other not to run counter to the reigning stupidity altogether, otherwise they will say that I am eulogising *Mutiny*. This must produce tameness in some degree.

The degree is slight, and *The Island* remains a spirited and complexly fascinating work, furnishing co-ordinates whereby we can map the course of Byron's inner navigation in *Don Juan* and the last plays.[29]

'Man cannot be on a level with the Beasts,' Coleridge wrote to H. J. Rose in 1816, 'he must be above them or below them.' But neither, Byron would reply, can men endure to have their natural instincts crushed, to be compulsory 'hermits of the brine' (92). Under stress, they will revert to the rights which no 'Social Contract' can take from them—a fact recognised by both Hobbes and Rousseau. *The Island* is Byron's own apologia for a revulsion from the stifling domesticities and cavalier serventism of Italy. He is the original 'man who loved islands', spots of land which concretise spots of time cut off from mainland conditioning. Here he finds his ultimate refuge and his ultimate defeat: womb poem is also doom poem. We revert to the origins. Neuha is the perfect mother-maid image, affording both protection and gratification. Torquil is the boy, the innocent, who splits off from the older, responsible Christian whose guilt is inevitably punished. (Byron seeks to have his cake and eat it.) Revenge is taken by Byron-Christian on the Captain-Bligh/Captain-John ('Mad Jack') who is the initial author of all his woes;[30] returning to 'the Mothers', Byron returns to childhood, discarding adult values. Here we pass beyond the permissive but still classically ordered confines of the *hellenikos kosmos* accepted in the Turkish Tales into a dream-world of gratified desire.

> Like coral reddening through the darken'd wave,
> Which draws the diver to the crimson cave   (II, vii, 139–40)

—this is a womb world, suffused with blood in the dark amniotic streams.[31]

The primitivism is plainly autobiographical. Torquil is a 'boy' born and bred in the Orkneys, an idealised *Hours of Idleness* figure; speaking in his own person, Byron confesses that 'The infant rapture still survived the boy,/And Loch-na-gar with Ida look'd o'er Troy'. Byron's *connective* imagination is powerfully at work here. Interest in oral tradition, in balladry, is a permanent element in his make-up and whole stretches of Canto II of *The Island* are devoted to a version of an actual song of the Tonga Islands and an enthusiastic comment on the power and beauty of traditional art.

Bligh (the father figure) is rejected, a castaway; but he survives and returns with all the power of avenging civilisation in the British warship. Christian (the son) escapes, but not for long: his guilt, admitted in the 'That—Captain Bligh—that is the thing—I am in hell—I am in hell!' of Bligh's *Narrative*, catches up with him. Torquil is also a castaway, but as the guiltless aspect of Christian (which is also the mindless aspect) he survives, 'closing the door after him'[32] as he enters the subterranean cave, the secret passage into primeval satisfactions. Now the prison becomes the palace, reversing the moral of the dramas. The womb image, crimson-hued, excludes the outside world of values and responsibilities. Tidal rhythms, mindlessly pulsing, counterpoint with softly rounded shell-fruit-guitar shapes to weave a pattern of compulsive euphoria.

> How pleasant were the songs of Toobonai,
> When Summer's Sun went down the coral bay!   (II, i, 1–2)

It's almost a pop song, as relaxed and as meaningless:

> The wood-dove from the forest depth shall coo,
> Like voices of the Gods from Bolotoo . . .   (II, i, 5–6)
> Again bestow the wreaths we gently woo,
> Ye young Enchantresses of gay Licoo!   (II, iii, 57–8)

The sea now, after its long series of metamorphoses in Byron's poetry,[33] is reasserted as the mother, the protectress. The reversion to boyhood which we noted in the lyrics of the separation is fixed as an ultimate value.[34] And with the *turning back* of Christian to the womb world, Byron's Pilgrim's progress is reversed. The old goal of knowledge, essentially the Socratic self-knowledge, is abandoned. We have seen it eroded little by little in the dramas: we shall shortly see it cynically rejected in *Don Juan*. As the boat 'makes her liquid way' to the cave of 'some soft savage' the bright Aegean light of *Childe Harold* II is softened to a tropical haze, warm, comforting but unrevealing. Forms flow into one another, and outlines are ill-defined.

> For food the cocoa-nut, the yam, the bread
> Born of the fruit; for board the plantain spread
> With its broad leaf, or turtle-shell which bore
> A banquet in the flesh it covered o'er;
> The gourd with water recent from the rill,
> The ripe banana from the mellow hill.   (IV, viii, 169–74)

A lotus-eaters' paradise, rich in rounded, voluptuously inviting satisfactions: even the hill is 'mellow'. But of course this is not to be Byron's last word. *The Island* is one solution to a loss of faith in what Yeats has called 'the abstract joy,/The half-read wisdom of daimonic images': it is the solution of sinking below the images to the daimons who project them, of preferring mergence to interpretation. But there is another, providentially offered to Byron at the moment of collapse by the resurgence of 'dearly beloved Greece': the way of action, the *karma-marga*.

Notes and references

1   Cf. Act II, iv, 121–56.

2   'I must be profoundly related to Byron's *Manfred*: of all the dark abysses in this work I found the counterparts in my own soul—at the age of thirteen I was ripe for this book. Words fail me, I have only a look, for those who dare to utter the name of *Faust* in the presence of *Manfred*' (*Ecce Homo*).

3   E. H. Coleridge cogently quotes Nahum 2, 1—'The gates of the rivers shall be opened, and the palace shall be dissolved'. The theme of the dissolution of 'the palace' (cf. S. T. Coleridge's 'dome' in *Kubla Khan*) by chthonic forces is to be a major motif in the dramas.

4   Like Coleridge, Byron was impressed by the 'Extremes meet' paradox (cf. Coleridge's 1803 Notebook, with the illustration from *Paradise Lost*, 'The parching Air/Burns frore, and cold performs th' effect of Fire').

5   'I *have* resumed my "majestic march" ', he writes in response to a plea from John Murray, 'in Sardanapalus' (letter of 14 June 1821).

6   Cf. Blake, *The French Revolution*: 'Shall this marble built heaven become a clay cottage, this earth an oak stool, and these mowers/ From the Atlantic mountains mow down all this great starry harvest of six thousand years?' (Blake, *Poetical Works*, ed. G. Keynes, Oxford University Press, 1966, p. 138.))

7   The effect is helped by Byron's approximation to the Unities. Of *Sardanapalus* he had already noted (in his 30 May 1821 letter to Murray): 'You will remark that the *Unities* are all *strictly* observed'; and in a later letter to Moore, 'Writ according to Aristotle—all, save the chorus—I could not reconcile me to that.'

8   We remember that Byron's maiden speech in the Lords was for men against machines. 'We must not allow mankind to be sacrificed to improvements in mechanism', he remarks in a letter of 25 February 1812, to Lord Holland, two days earlier.

9   Ferenczi points out how 'the sensations of swimming, floating and flying express at the same time the sensations in coitus and those of existence in the womb' (*Thalassa: A Theory of Genitality*, New York, 1968, p. 42). With reference to Byron, and especially to the sequence *Sardanapalus*, *The Two Foscari*, *Cain* (all 1821), *Heaven and Earth*, *Werner*, *The Island* (1823), we may note how the inundation/swimming and the flying/floating motifs express the divergent urges to escape and to regress which culminate in the final work.

10   Cf. the similar eikon of physical energy in the dash of the wild horses in *Mazeppa*, 671–708. This is pure animal energy. At another point in the scale we have the description of the waterfall in *The Island*, which Ruskin so much admired, calling it 'the loveliest description of a shore waterfall, probably, in European literature'.

11   T. S. Eliot, 'East Coker' IV.

12   I note that M. K. Joseph has anticipated me in using this label in his very perceptive account of the biblical plays (*Byron the Poet*, pp. 116ff).

13   Manfred's 'The tree of knowledge is not that of life', a doctrine re-echoed in *Cain*, is restated by Mann: 'Knowledge as the enemy of life, as the tempter to death, as the ally of disease—this is an ever-recurring theme in Thomas Mann's works' (Erich Heller, *The Ironic German*, Secker & Warburg, 1958). Nietzsche had already praised this statement of Manfred's.

14   This last line is extraordinarily Blakean.

15   Cf. the 'Clear, placid Leman' stanzas of *Childe Harold*, canto II (above, p. 192–9), and the other Augusta/lake passages cited. The nexus brother-sister/lake/reflection/physical likeness suggests an occasion or occasions when Byron and Augusta had watched their reflections in the lake at Newstead.

16   Coleridge, 'A Tombless Epitaph'. For 'the scroll of Enoch', see over-leaf, and for the cavern theme my *The Lost Travellers*, pp. 1–50.

17   Byron cites this passage from Genesis in a footnote, placing the emphasis of his poem on that 'Marriage of Heaven [and Earth] and Hell' which was occupying, around this time, the greatest of his contemporaries. (Blake's *Jerusalem*, 'The Everlasting Gospel', and *For the Sexes: The Gates of Paradise*, all belong to the opening decades of the century. *The Marriage of Heaven and Hell* had been written as long ago as 1790–93.)

18   Cf. Jili, *Insanu 'l-Kamil*: 'The world will not cease to be living so long as humankind continues there. When humankind departs, the world will perish, and collapse, as the body of an animal perishes when the spirit leaves it.' This is dervish doctrine, and is complemented by its opposite in a *nefes* which Birge says (*The Bektashi Order of Dervishes*, London, 1937, p. 121) is the most universally known among the Bektashis: 'When there was no Adam and Eve in the world,/We were really existent with the Divine Reality in the impenetrable mystery./ For a night we were the guest of Mary;/We are the real father of Jesus the exalted.' I have argued for Byron's acquaintance, through Ali Pasha, with Bektashi circles, in my paper 'Byron and Islam' already referred to. For Cain's cosmic journey, cf. Birge p. 119, and for the unity of being theme, *ibid.* p. 117ff. Byron often reads his Bible through Islamic spectacles. Lucifer's teaching in *Cain* I, i: 'Thou livest, and must live for ever: think not/The earth, which is thine outward cov'ring, is/Existence—it will cease, and thou wilt be/No less than thou art now', belongs to the same tradition.

19   Translated by Richard Laurence, LL.D., Oxford, 1821. Those commentators on Byron who like to trace any and every 'meta-physical' interest of his to 'the influence of Shelley' might ponder these and other implications of the fact noted by Ruskin (*Praeterita*, ch. viii) that 'Byron's early power was founded on a course of general reading of the masters in every walk of literature, such as is, I think, utterly unparalleled in any other young life, whether of student or author'.

20   Adding in a postscript: 'I have taken these resolutions not from any irritation against *you* or *yours*, but simply upon reflection that all reading, either praise or censure, of myself has done me harm. When

I was in Switzerland and Greece, I was out of the way of hearing either, and *how I wrote there!*' Byron's underlining evidences at least *one* judgement of his regarding the relative merits of *Childe Harold* and his later works.

21   It can also be shattered by Byron's second preoccupation of the 'gulf-and-fountain' period: the dungeon, the man-made gulf. In Chillon 'the goodly earth and air/Are banned and barred—forbidden fare' (9–10).

22   'I hope you will consider me not only as *a Brother* but as your warmest and most affectionate *Friend*, and if ever Circumstances should require it your *protector*. . . . Trust to your Brother, and be assured he will never betray your confidence . . .' (Letter to Augusta 22 March 1804. Byron's italics.)

23   Mr Gleckner, in his interesting analysis (R. F. Gleckner, *Byron and the Ruins of Paradise*, 139–53), confounds the tower with the cave as types of love-Edens (143), whereas they strike me as clearly distinguished eikons of wisdom and sensual love. Medora's tower is the abode of love-wisdom, Zuleika's cave of irrational passion.

24   Letter to John Pigot, 9 August 1806.

25   E. H. Coleridge (*PW*, V, 480) rightly draws attention to the consonance of this passage with the raising of Eros and Anteros from their fountain-dwellings, in *Manfred* II, ii, 93; we may also remember the 'mind deep in its fountain' of *Childe Harold* III, lxix, and the whole systole-diastole dynamism of Byron's poetry as we have traced it up to now. See also *The Giaour*, 299–319.

26   Cf. Burton, *Anatomy of Melancholy*, II, iii, 4: '*Italy* or *Greece*, the Gardens of the world.' Burton was a favourite with Byron, whose views of human nature, travel, and exile often echo those of the *Anatomy*.[27]

27   A point taken up by Nietzsche in *The Genealogy of Morals*.

28   'A discovered world has brought little to the old one, except the p[ox] first and freedom afterwards—the latter a fine thing, particularly as they gave it to Europe in exchange for slavery' (1821 Diary). Cf. De Quincey's very similar prognostication: 'No memory now of the great poets, those true philosophers, whose golden words have so often yielded oracular truth in behalf of ancient monuments, and ancient institutions. No room for Cicero! No ear for the profound harmonies of Plato!—All will now wear the gloss of American novelty, and will be supported with American insolence.' (Richard H. Byrns, 'Some unpublished works of De Quincey', *PMLA* lxxi, no. 5, 990–1003.) De Quincey's expression is clumsy, but perhaps we hear an echo of Byron's Forum Romanum

> where the immortal accents glow,
> And still the eloquent air breathes—burns with Cicero!

and yet

> Tully was not so eloquent as thou
> Thou nameless column with the buried base!

> (IV, cxii, cx)

The juxtaposition of 'oracular truth' in 'ancient monuments' and 'no room for Cicero' is suggestive here.

29 Chapter 7 of my *The Lost Travellers* (Longmans, 1962) deals with *The Island* at some length, and perhaps I may refer the reader to those pages. Even so I shall not be able to avoid some repetition of conclusions arrived at there.

30 Captain Byron sinned in his repudiation of responsibility and desertion of the newborn George Gordon. Byron's mother would certainly not have omitted to tell Byron of his father's heartless dismissal (see above, p. 9). In the twin womb worlds of ship and island walking is minimised, and cancelled out in the cave.

31 Cf. Ferenzci, *op. cit.* p. 47 ff.

32 *Werner*, see above, p. 257.

33 I discuss this in *The Lost Travellers*, pp. 188–97.

34 Cf. also 'On this day I complete my thirty-sixth year' and such stanzas of *Don Juan* as IV, viii–xv.

11
SOCIAL AND POLITICAL SATIRE

The satirical side of Byron's genius contributed little to his contemporary fame. His first satire, *English Bards and Scotch Reviewers*
helped that fame to get off the ground, but aroused small delight in
its readers. *Hints from Horace* and *The Curse of Minerva* were still less
popular. The wit was enjoyed, but the 'philosophy' was deprecated.
Byron's satire had an even dustier reception in the Victorian age,
when wit itself was rejected as inimical to 'poetry', and Arnold
declared Dryden and Pope to be 'classics of our prose'. Arnold's
famous volume of selections from Byron contains, in its 276 pages,
thirty-nine which are labelled 'Satiric': most of these we should
not consider satiric at all, but mildly humorous. Exactly one page is
given to a gentle paragraph from *English Bards*. And the editorial
fate of *Waltz: An Apostrophic Hymn* (1813) is yet more revealing.
John Wright's 1832 edition of the *Poetical Works*, the first to approach
completeness and to include extensive annotation, prints the poem
but with only two short editorial footnotes. The index has four
references to the poem, all of them erroneous. The 1879 reprint of
Wright's edition[1] has no reference whatever to *Waltz* in its index,
though the poem is to be found in vol. iii. The progress in British
morality over that half century is neatly summed up in this quiet
sepulture. A recent American critic[2] still refuses to discuss the
poem!

Yet if *Waltz: An Apostrophic Hymn* has never been a favourite,
even for Byron's admirers, the reasons are moral and political
rather than literary. Byron published it anonymously; the fictional
author, 'Horace Hornem, Esq.', is a country gentleman who
contributes a Prefatory Epistle 'To the Publisher' which is a

masterpiece of Regency wit in the direct line from Congreve and Wycherley:

Sir,
  I am a country gentleman of a midland county. I might have been a parliament-man for a certain borough; having had the offer of as many votes as General T. at the general election in 1812 [Byron's footnote: State of the poll (last day), 5.] But I was all for domestic happiness; as, fifteen years ago, on a visit to London, I married a middle-aged maid of honour. We lived happily at Hornem Hall till last season, when my wife and I were invited by the Countess of Waltzaway (a distant relation of my spouse) to pass the winter in town. Thinking no harm, and our girls being come to a marriageable (or, as they call it, *marketable*) age, and having besides a Chancery suit inveterately entailed upon the family estate, we came up in our old chariot—of which, by the bye, my wife grew so much ashamed in less than a week, that I was obliged to buy a second-hand barouche, of which I might mount the box, Mrs H. says, if I could drive, but never see the inside—that place being reserved for the Honourable Augustus Tiptoe, her partner-general and opera-knight. . . .

This is prose in the great colloquial tradition. The squire reveals his personality in a few telling strokes, at the same time suggesting a social background which expands, as the Letter continues, into wide areas of absurdity: 'Judge of my surprise, on arriving, to see poor, dear Mrs Hornem with her arms half round the loins of a huge, hussar-looking gentleman I never set eyes on before'—a picture which is pure Rowlandson. The satire itself lives up to the standard of this prose prologue, though it is less humorous; the prologue lets us see Regency society through the myopic, bewilderedly indignant, country-cousin eyes of good Squire Hornem, but the satire proper is Byronically incisive and virulent.[3] The squire's indignation is personal and sexual:

By-and-by they stopped a bit, and I thought they would sit or fall down:—but no; with Mrs H.'s hand on his shoulder, '*quam familiariter*' (as Terence said, when I was at school), they walked about a minute, and then were at it again, like two cockchafers spitted on the same bodkin.

Byron's revulsion introduces wider issues:

> Hail, nimble Nymph! to whom the young hussar,
> The whiskered votary of Waltz and War,
> His night devotes, despite of spur and boots;
> A sight unmatched since Orpheus and his brutes.   (15–18)

—a theme to be taken up later in the love-and-war diatribes of *Don Juan*. Squire Hornem's prologue employs Byron's favourite tactics of 'distancing through division', a technique of *divide et impera* which separates hero-subject and cynic-commentator: the

effect is first achieved in *Childe Harold* and *The Curse of Minerva* and
brought to perfection in *Don Juan.*

The attack develops from the Invocation (1–38) with its sexual
innuendoes, to political satire on the waltz as a German invention
introduced into England along with so many other Teutonic
blessings:

> Oh, Germany! how much to thee we owe, . . .
> We bless thee still—for George the Third is left!
> Of kings the best—and last, not least in worth,
> For graciously begetting George the Fourth . . .   (39, 44–6)

then back to the sexual theme, this time in its social and pedigree
ramifications, in the two amusing paragraphs beginning with yet a
third invocation:

> To you, ye husbands of ten year! whose brows
> Ache with the annual tributes of a spouse. . . .   (93–4)

The repetition of the word 'Waltz' at the end of four consecutive
paragraphs creates the effect of a refrain, or of the circling movement
of the dance itself. The waltz is compared with other dances, ancient
and modern, Irish and Scotch, modern Greek and Spanish (109–
132); and 'Shades of those belles whose reign began of yore' (133)
return to their scenes of former triumph, like Pope's 'ghosts of
beauty', to admire and envy:

> Back to the Ball-room speed your spectred host,
> Fool's Paradise is dull to that you lost.   (137–9)

Byron's satire becomes more outrageous as the ball proceeds (it is a
major triumph of the poem that we feel ourselves caught up as we
read into the dance itself, with the hussars getting steadily tipsier,
the ladies more complacent) but does not lose sight of the political
overtones:

> From where the garb just leaves the bosom free,
> That spot where hearts were once supposed to be;
> Round all the confines of the yielded waist,
> The strongest hand may wander undisplaced;
> The lady's in return may grasp as much
> As princely paunches offer to her touch.
> Pleased round the chalky floor how well they trip,
> One hand reposing on the royal hip!
> The other to the shoulder no less royal
> Ascending with affection truly loyal![4]   (190–9)[2]

Political cant is associated with moral cant; and 'the modest Turk' of Byron's Levantine acquaintance who asked if 'nothing follows all this palming work' (300–1) is brought in as a shrewd counterblow to English hypocrisy. *This* is social and political satire as the other early lampoons are not, and is thus properly considered outside its chronological context along with *Beppo*, *The Vision of Judgment* and *Don Juan*.

Waltz links too, thematically, with 'the coxcomb Czar,/The autocrat of waltzes and of war' of *The Age of Bronze*, section x; and, on its Squire Hornem side, with

> Alas, the country! how shall tongue or pen
> Bewail her now *un*country gentlemen?

of that poem's section xiv. But *The Age of Bronze* interests us less as satire (which it is in only a feeble, rather repetitive sense) than as an index to what was occupying Byron's mind in early 1823. As the title suggests, the poem voices disillusion with modern times: 'All is exploded—be it good or bad' (ii), and the age of intellectual giants is over. Perhaps the most interesting part of *The Age of Bronze* comes in the second section: a sustained meditation on death almost in the manner of Sir Thomas Browne:

> How peaceful and how powerful is the grave
> Which hushes all! a calm, unstormy wave
> Which oversweeps the World. The theme is old
> Of 'Dust to Dust'; but half its tale untold:
> Time tempers not its terrors—still the worm
> Winds its cold folds, the tomb preserves its form,
> Varied above, but still alike below;
> The urn may shine—the ashes will not glow—
> Though Cleopatra's mummy cross the sea
> O'er which from empire she lured Anthony.   (21–30)

Alexander's weeping 'for worlds to conquer' is briefly and scornfully touched on; and we note the renewed concern with Greece, 'his native Greece/Hath all of desolation, save its peace'. It is a theme we return to in section vi, which is concerned with movements of liberation throughout the world:

> Where Greece *was*—No! she still is Greece once more   (271)

—a verdict which reverses that of *The Giaour* (1813):

> 'Tis Greece, but living Greece no more!   (91)

Another reversal of judgement—this time at a much shorter interval—comes in the long passage on Napoleon (iii–v) which represents Byron's final thinking on the man who had fascinated him since his Harrow days. Here Bonaparte is once more presented as a fire-figure (iv), above ordinary humanity and not to be judged by its laws. His antithetic nature, stressed in *Childe Harold* III, is again evoked:

> Yes! where is he, 'the champion and the child'
> Of all that's great or little, wise or wild . . .?   (50)

He is judged superior to Alexander, and even to Caesar (v) (we remember that he was 'a kind of bastard Caesar' in *Childe Harold* IV, xc, written six years earlier). What we seem to be witnessing in *The Age of Bronze*, below the surface of its disillusionment, is a recrudescence of the hopes in great causes and great personalities, men of destiny, which had been long submerged in the morass, lost in the maze, of the Italian sojourn. Elemental forces enter the imagery of the poem, detracting from its satiric, but buttressing its dynamic impulse. Fire opens section iv; section v begins with an invocation of heaven and earth, and returns to fire in its close. Frost is powerfully invoked midway in section v:

> Thou other Element! as strong and stern,
> To teach a lesson conquerors will not learn!—
> Whose icy wing flapp'd o'er the faltering foe,
> Till fell a hero with each flake of snow;
> How did thy numbing beak and silent fang
> Pierce, till hosts perished with a single pang!   (185–90)

This is not satiric writing; it seems to me to represent a movement of resurgence in Byron towards a new identification with cosmic forces.

> Hear! hear Prometheus from his rock appeal
> To Earth, Air, Ocean, all that felt or feel
> His power and glory, all who yet shall hear
> A name eternal as the rolling year.[5]   (227–30)

This Promethean motif, endemic in Byron's poetry and concentrated in the *Prometheus* ode of July 1816, is to find fulfilment in the sacrificial happenings of 1823–4. Its influence not only over everything Byron wrote but over everything of importance that he did deserves a separate study.[6]

Summing up the total effect of these initiatory social satires (before we turn to the magisterial three which close Byon's career) we note first the congruence of their *moral* attitudes with those of the early 'literary' satires. Byron's sense of human limitation, in a

scheme of cosmic complexity, his intuition of the extreme waywardness of destiny and of man's incapacity to anticipate its moves
or confront them at all adequately, remains strong. From this
proceeds a kind of despair. Under the surface flippancy, the razor-
edged wit, lies the Kierkegaardian *angst*, microcosmic analogue of
those 'black holes' in space which Cambridge scientists are identifying, as I write, as enormous concentrations of force for ever
devouring themselves. If he had rested there, Byron would have been
simply an Ur-Kafka or-Strindberg. But, because his apprehension
of the human condition was wide as it was deep, spanning centuries
and continents, rejecting both 'cant' and the anticant of 'commitment' in all their sad varieties of humbug, he functions within a
traditional framework of proven values. Tyranny is bad; democracy
is also bad, 'an aristocracy of blackguards' ('My Dictionary', May
1821). For Byron, what is good is what works, and what allows man
the individual to breathe with maximum freedom in the curious
prison called society he has constructed for himself. Here he diverges
on the one hand from the physiocrats and on the other from an
idealist like Shelley with his faith in future freedom cut off from the
shackles of a restricting past. Byron saw that this concept of a segmented time—past/present/future—led to absurdities comparable to
the segmented space absurdities of 'Achilles and the Tortoise'. Man's
life is lived through a space-time continuum in which 'past and future
are gathered' into the Now, and only the deficiencies and limitations
of our human perceptory mechanism divide experience into the
distant and the near, the racial and the individual.

Byron's early satire had been normative and critical in the Popean
sense—concerned with the assertion and maintenance of standards.
The criticism is basically literary or 'cultural'. It looks to models
and respects authorities. Since culture cannot be isolated from the
social scene, moral judgements are implied and frequently expressed.
We are conscious of a background of accepted, and largely
eighteenth-century, values. But the later satire moves away from the
critical to a permissive and mocking presentation of human
absurdities. We are now in Shakespeare's world, not Jonson's—nor
Johnson's. The Shakespeare, that is, of the comedies, and usually of
the 'tragi-comedies': of *Measure for Measure* and *The Tempest*.
Anomalies are presented, investigated, laughed at, but seldom
condemned. Even Southey, in *The Vision of Judgment*, is accepted
with a wry smile as part of the literary landscape—a clown figure

who would have to be invented if he did not exist. *Beppo*, *The Vision*, *Don Juan* are virtuoso exercises in technique and dialectic, rich in knowledge of the world, tolerant and all-embracing. The technical mastery was acknowledged by contemporary critics who shook their heads over the permissiveness. Here is a representative paragraph from *Blackwood's* 'Remarks on Don Juan' (August, 1819):

It has not been without much reflection and overcoming many reluctancies, that we have at last resolved to say a few words more to our readers concerning this very extraordinary poem. The nature and causes of our difficulties will be easily understood by those of them who have read any part of *Don Juan*—but we despair of standing justified as to the conclusion at which we have arrived, in the opinion of any but those who have read and understood the whole of a work, in the composition of which there is unquestionably a more thorough and intense infusion of genius and vice— power and profligacy—than in any poem which had ever before been written in the English, or indeed in any other modern language. Had the wickedness been less inextricably mingled with the beauty and the grace, and the strength of a most inimitable and incomprehensible muse, our task would have been easy: but SILENCE would be a very poor and a very useless chastisement, to be inflicted by us, or by any one, on a production, whose corruptions have been so effectively embalmed—which, in spite of all that critics can do or refrain from doing, nothing can possibly prevent from taking a high place in the literature of our country, and remaining to all ages a perpetual monument of the exalted intellect, and the depraved heart, of one of the most remarkable men to whom that country has had the honour and the disgrace of giving birth.

Similar but less extreme judgements were passed on *Beppo* (1818), Byron's earlier model, so to speak, for *Don Juan*, and the poem in which he flexed his metrical muscles in the *ottava rima* stanza, and displayed his mastery of the colloquial mode. Not a few good critics, such as Jeffrey, concentrated their attention on the poem's technical side, and showed an appreciation of Byron's conversational style which has left little new for modern critics to contribute. It is interesting to compare Jeffrey's comments on the Third Canto of *Childe Harold* in the December 1816 number of *The Edinburgh Review* with what he has to say in February 1818 about the anonymous *Beppo*. Here is part of his 1816 critique.

'Words that breathe and thoughts that burn', are not merely the ornaments, but the common staple of his poetry; and he is not inspired or impressive only in some happy passages, but through the whole body and tissue of his composition. It was an unavoidable condition, perhaps, of this higher excellence, that his scene should be narrow, and his persons few. To compass such ends as he had in view, it was necessary to reject all ordinary agents, and all trivial combinations. He could not possibly be amusing, or ingenious, or playful; or hope to maintain the requisite pitch of interest by the re-citation of sprightly adventures, or the opposition of common characters. To produce great effects he felt that it was necessary to deal only with the greater passions—with the exaltations of a daring fancy, and the errors of a lofty intellect—with the pride, the terrors, and the agonies of strong emotion —the fire and air alone of our human elements.

This is both subtle and sensible, and establishes a distinction between the modes of poetry—a distinction radical to classical rhetoric—which Rosamond Tuve has done much to reassert in our own day against critics who would make the colloquial a basic condition of *all* good poetry. When he came to review *Beppo*, Jeffrey intelligently changed his stance, praising its 'constant ease and amenity' and 'the simplicity and naturalness of the language . . . with the exclusion of all scholastic or ambitious eloquence, all profound views, and all deep emotions'.

The unknown writer before us . . . has furnished us with an example, unique we rather think in our language, of about one hundred stanzas of good verse, entirely composed of common words, in their common places; never presenting us with one sprig of what is called poetical diction, or even making use of a single inversion, either to raise the style or assist the rhyme— but running on in an inexhaustible series of good easy colloquial phrases, and finding them fall into verse by some unaccountable and happy fatality. In this great and characteristic quality it is almost invariably excellent. In some other respects it is more unequal. . . . Some passages are rather too foolish, some too snappish, and some run too much on the cheap and rather plebeian humour of out-of-the-way rhymes and strange sounding words and epithets.

At the close of his review Jeffrey suggests that in stanzas xlv and xlvi (on the charms of Italian women) the anonymous writer

seems to have caught a spark from the ardent genius of Byron. . . . [He is] betrayed into something too like enthusiasm and deep feeling for the light and fantastic strain of his poetry. . . . [This is] the only passage in which the author betrays the secret (which might, however, have been suspected) of his own genius, and his affinity to a higher order of poets than those to whom he has here been pleased to hold out a model.

I surmise that when Jeffrey began writing his review he was as much in the dark as anyone else about the poem's authorship, and that enlightenment came as he read on. *Beppo*, in its gaiety and freedom from rhetoric, marked a complete break from the dark Byron who 'could not possibly be amusing, or ingenious, or playful' in *Childe Harold*, or *Manfred*; yet that Byron's chameleon talent held these colours also in its spectrum might have been guessed from *Childe Harold* I, from the early satires, and of course from his conversation and letters.

Beppo, A Venetian Story was an immediate success. It established the *ottava rima* as the stanza for Byron's narrative satire—a stanza coming down to Byron from Pulci and in his own day from John Hookham Frere's 'Whistlecraft' (1817–18).[7] On Byron's indebtedness Arthur Symons comments judiciously:

> Taking a hint from Frere, who had nothing to say, and did but show how things might be said, Byron gave up oratory and came nearer than he had yet come to poetry by merely talking. . . . In *Beppo*, in *The Vision of Judgment*, and in *Don Juan*, words, style, language, subject, are at one; the colloquial manner is used for what is really talk, extraordinarily brilliant talk, and at the same time, as Goethe saw, a 'classically elegant comic style'; the natural man is at last wholly himself, all of himself, himself not even exaggerated for effect.[8]

This is true. The wit is subtler than Frere's, the personal involvement greater. Frere writes about a mythical King Arthur's court, Byron about the Venice he knew so well. The story matters little, though it points onward to the 'unexpected return' theme which dominates Canto II of *Don Juan*; what is striking and engaging is the brilliant picture of early nineteenth-century Venice, conveyed in an off-beat, deliberately provocative North/South England/Italy antiphony whose *tragic* harmonies we have already heard in *Werner*.

This translation of the tragic into the comic mode is indeed the major achievement of the post-dramatic period (and, as the dates show, the process is going on *pari passu* with the dramas). *Beppo* is *Marino Faliero* projected on to the stage of farce; Laura's apology (xci–xciii) is what Angiolina might have said if Steno's accusation had been true. George III's hovering on the outskirts of the heavenly paradise is a farcical re-enactment of Cain's dilemma before the angel-guarded gates of Eden. Don Juan's pilgrimage is Childe Harold's in reverse: the direction is from sunshine to snow, from freedom to confinement, from the Alhambra to Newstead. What is deflated in these last poems is a world and the spirit that had moved through that world, interpreting and adunating.

Beppo belongs to that category of poetry, including the greatest lyrics, which seems meant exclusively for enjoyment and not for analysis: one can make comments on it, but they are rather of the order of butterfly-breaking. *Don Juan* is different, because of its epic magnitude and the large number of human figures it contains. Here the critic has room to move about without smashing things. *Beppo*

is *Don Juan* in miniature; I shall not quote from it, as it is short
enough for the reader to enjoy at a sitting, and any excerpt would
be irretrievably damaging to its total, gossamer-light texture. Nor
shall I comment further on it: what I shall have to say at some length
about *Don Juan* will be found to apply, *mutatis mutandis*, to the earlier
comic fantasia.

Byron's opinion of Robert Southey, now (since 1813) the
Laureate, had been sketched in *English Bards* and amplified in
succeeding satires.[9] A stinging 'Dedication' of Cantos I and II of
Don Juan (1819) did not appear ('As the Poem is to be published
anonymously, *omit* the Dedication. I won't attack the dog in the
dark. Such things are for scoundrels and renegadoes like himself'),
but its contents were widely known. But when Southey, in the
Preface to his *Vision of Judgment* (11 April 1821), attacked Byron as
the presiding genius of 'the Satanic School', he played directly into
Byron's hands. One thinks of some lumbering sheep dog with a
mountain lion making circles round him. Southey's attack was
cautious, preferring the plural to the singular pronoun:

Men of diseased hearts and depraved imaginations, who, forming a system
of opinions to suit their own unhappy course of conduct, have rebelled
against the holiest ordinances of human society, and hating that revealed
religion which, with all their efforts and bravadoes, they are unable
entirely to disbelieve, labour to make others as miserable as themselves, by
infecting them with a moral virus that eats into the soul! The school which
they have set up may properly be called the Satanic school; for, though
their productions breathe the spirit of Belial in their lascivious parts, and
the spirit of Moloch in those loathsome images of atrocities and horrors
which they delight to represent, they are more especially characterised by a
Satanic pride and audacious impiety, which still betrays the wretched
spirit of hopelessness wherewith it is allied.

The virulence of this excuses Byron's personal satire in *The Vision of
Judgment*, which is directed much more against Southey than against
the mad old king whose death had 'inspired' the Laureate to his
'spavined dactyls'.

Southey's limping hexameters—a metre alien to English versification but no doubt adopted to gain dignity—remove the poem still
further from the world of reality. Byron's parody, in its use of
flexible, idiomatic English, the real speaking voice, pricks Southey's
prosodic as well as his personal and political bubbles. I have no
space for lengthy quotation, but a glance at Southey's ornate
description of 'the house of the dead', with its splendid coffins—

> Around it were coffins
> Each in its niche, and palls, and urns and funeral hatchments,
> Velvets of Tyrian dye, retaining their hue unfaded;
> Blazonry vivid still, as if fresh from the touch of the limner;
> Nor was the golden fringe, nor the golden broidery, tarnish'd

—will suffice to show his naive admiration of surfaces. This Byron cruelly deflates with a razor slash at the corruption beneath:

> It seem'd the mockery of hell to fold
> The rottenness of eighty years in gold.

Or take Southey's awestruck announcement of the arrival of George III at the heavenly gates:

> O'er the adamantine gates an Angel stood on the summit.
> Ho! he exclaim'd, King George of England cometh to judgment!
> Hear, Heaven! Ye Angels, hear! Souls of the Good and the
>   Wicked,
> Whom it concerns, attend! Thou Hell, bring forth his accusers!
> As the sonorous summons was utter'd, the Winds, who were
>   waiting,
> Bore it abroad thro' Heaven; and Hell, in her nethermost corners,
> Heard and obey'd in dismay.

How Byron must have enjoyed that wonderful '*Whom it concerns*, attend!' and 'the Winds, *who were waiting*' (Winds-in-Waiting, as it were). His glee is evident in his alternative picture:

> But ere he could return to his repose,
>   A Cherub flapped his wing right o'er his eyes—
> At which Saint Peter yawned, and rubbed his nose:
>   'Saint porter,' quoth the angel, 'prithee rise!'
> Waving a goodly wing, which glowed, as glows
>   An earthly peacock's tail, with heavenly dyes:
> To which the saint replied, 'Well, what's the matter?
> Is Lucifer come back with all this clatter?'
>
> 'No,' quoth the cherub; 'George the Third is dead.'
>   'And who *is* George the Third?' replied the apostle:
> '*What George*? *what Third*?' 'The king of England', said
>   The angel. 'Well! he won't find kings to hustle
> Him on his way; but does he wear his head?
>   Because the last we saw here had a tussle,
> And ne'er would have got into Heaven's good graces,
> Had he not flung his head in all our faces.'   (xvii–xviii)

Here St Peter is brought to life as the most irascible of the apostles, now grown old and still more crusty in his long service at the gates of heaven. *Nihil quod tetigit non animavit*, one might say of Byron. He cannot deal in counters, however venerable; flesh and blood has to pulse under his fingers.

As, we may remember, Minerva's owl had to be seen and heard as a real owl in *The Curse of Minerva*. And this too, his last great satire, is a vision poem. The 'unity of place' is first established, with the setting before Heaven gate. St Peter, fumbling with his keys, is cast as a comic but still formidable figure (i–vii), lamenting the boredom of his office in an impious age. Few present themselves for admission in the opening decades of the nineteenth century. But suddenly—the date is 29 January 1820, and the whole action of the poem is completed on this day, thus preserving the unity of time—the soul of King George III presents itself for judgement. The unity of action is as strictly kept: there are no sideshows. But who is the hero? George III hardly qualifies: he does nothing, and says nothing. St Peter is the most fully realised character, but his office debars him from the major role. Satan dominates the action, but it is *ab extra*, as a *diabolus ex machina*, condescending to appear. We must, I think, conclude that the hero of this minature epic, or epic fragment at least, is Bob Southey himself. We are in the world of irony and farce, not of satire. And the deadly urbanity of Byron's tone, throwing the reader's mind inevitably back to the puerile vindictiveness of Southey's 'Satanic' Preface, is the poem's major achievement.

The whole action of the poem leads up to the appearance of Southey in person in stanzas lxxxv–cv. It is a triumph of anticlimax, prepared first by the impressive encounter of Michael with Satan (xxiv–xxxvii) in which Byron shows his power of sustaining dignity, indeed sublimity, without sacrificing irony. I can think of no other poet who can poise disparate tones in fruitful apposition as Byron does here.

> But bringing up the rear of this bright host
>   A Spirit of a different aspect waved
> His wings, like thunder-clouds above some coast
>   Whose barren beach with frequent wrecks is paved;
> His brow was like the deep when tempest-tossed;
>   Fierce and unfathomable thoughts engraved
> Eternal wrath on his immortal face,
> And *where* he gazed a gloom pervaded space.
>
> As he drew near, he gazed upon the gate
>   Ne'er to be entered more by him or Sin,
> With such a glance of supernatural hate,
>   As made Saint Peter wish himself within;
> He pottered with his keys at a great rate,

> And sweated through his apostolic skin:
> Of course his perspiration was but ichor,
> Or some such other spiritual liquor.   (xxiv, xxv)

Here then is the Satan whom Southey has so incautiously invoked
in his Preface! Against the entry of George III into Paradise he
summons the evidence of those 'unvirtuous', such as Wilkes and
Junius, whom Southey consigned to perdition. The human characters
which throng the middle section of the *Vision* are varied enough but
do not break the 'unity of action' established by the strictly episodic
nature of the poem. I use the word episodic deliberately. The effect
created by the *Vision* derives from a wider context than itself. It
forms part of a great narrative-dramatic-satiric structure which
includes *Beppo* and *Don Juan*. It shares with these works the same
world of abounding human interest, as it shares the same metrical
form, and the same destructive energy directed against what
Goethe and Arnold called 'Philistinism'.

It is this Philistinism, as embodied in Southey, which is the real
'hero' of *The Vision of Judgment*. The whole of Byron's later work
can be regarded as a set of variations on the theme enunciated by
Schiller: *Mit der Dummheit kämpfen die Götter selbst vergebens*. The
earlier work has been an *agon*, a real wrestling with bad poetry and
worse critics (*English Bards and Scotch Reviewers*) ruthless archae-
ologists (*The Curse of Minerva*) hypocritical morality (*Waltz*): but
vergebens. The only answer is irony. The image of Satan in the *Vision*
projects what might be called *absolute* values. The image of Michael
is impressive, but on a somewhat lower plane: his values are
political, belong to the Establishment. Satan respects him, but takes
sly advantage of his embarrassment (xxxv–lxi) in their encounter;
as Michael's senior in the celestial hierarchy he permits himself a
little condescension:

> Satan met his ancient friend
> With more hauteur, as might an old Castilian
> Poor Noble meet a mushroom rich civilian.   (xxxvi)

Satan combines the attributes of Milton's hero—dignity, beauty,
courage, might—with Byronic traits—humour, analytic intelligence
(shown in his opening indictment of George III, xxxix–l) and
detachment (lxiv). Michael is 'A beautiful and mighty Thing of
Light' in stanza xxviii; in stanza xxx there is a slight devaluation:

> Michael flew forth in glory and in good;
>   A goodly work of him from whom all Glory
> And Good arise

—the implicated repetition and the quizzical tone initiate a down-grading which is emphasised in the legalistic quibbling he later engages in (li, lxii–lxiii). He emerges finally as an admirable civil servant. His job is to smooth things down, to avoid extremes (lxxxiii) and any kind of confrontation (xci).

Satan, then, is in Blake's terms *energy* and *freedom* as against Michael's *politeness* and *compromise*. The setting, outside the gates of heaven, analogises the *mise-en-scène* of *Cain*. Poor old George III is Adam, a thoroughly defeated representative of the human race, neither terribly good nor terribly bad. Just stupid. Just made use of by the disruptive forces—democracy, egalitarianism—projected by Wilkes (who has the grace not to bear witness against the king—indeed without such a figurehead where would anarchy find its target?) and by Junius, the 'liberal' demagogue whose 'shape' cannot even be seen.

Comparing *The Vision of Judgment* with *Cain* (and such comparisons are vital in dealing with such an all-of-a-piece poet as Byron) we find ourselves linking theological, political and social fields of discourse. Southey's absurd panegyric served to focus within an eighteen-twentyish context all the hard-won insights Byron had gained since 1810 into his imperial theme of human greatness and littleness. His knowledge of the Italian scene over five years deepens his social and political references. His lapse into a comfortable, quasimarital relationship with Teresa tends towards a deflation of certain 'Romantic', Corsairish bubbles, while giving a closer insight into how women feel and think: all this comes out in *Beppo* and *Don Juan*. *The Vision of Judgment* is unique among Byron's poems in omitting the sexual interest; but its very absence warns us what we may and may not expect from the poem.

For here again (as in the Venetian plays) we are not within the completely 'natural world'. George III is not least a *victim* of his age in being deprived of his right to extinction, of reduction to his elements. Even after death he is forced into a role.

> So mix his body with the dust! It might
>   Return to what it *must* far sooner, were
> The natural compound left alone to fight
>   Its way back into earth, and fire, and air;
> But the unnatural balsams merely blight
>   What Nature made him at his birth, as bare
> As the mere million's base unmummied clay—
> Yet all his spices but prolong decay.   (xi)

This stanza, habitually overlooked by readers, forms at least *one* of the key nodes of the poem, connecting it with the 'commingling slowly with heroic earth' of *Childe Harold* and the Turkish Tales. As Adam, then he is a thoroughly modern patriarch, processed, and cellophaned: an 'Albion' desexed, debrained and denatured. He waits outside the celestial gates like a zombie. His entry or rejection depends no longer on himself, but on a species of 'grace'. We return to the Calvinist values of the child Byron.

At this point the miracle happens. After all the argument and counter-argument, all the comings and goings, involving majestic figures like Satan and Michael on the celestial plane, shrewdly persuasive figures like Wilkes and Junius on the terrestrial, there is a comic interposition. Southey appears in person. Kicking and screaming in the grip of Asmodeus, he asserts his right, as the new nineteenth-century man, to present his version of the human situation. He offers Satan a satisfactory press coverage (xcix) and an even more flattering one to Michael. And as evidence of his journalistic skill he reads them his 'Vision' (ci–cv). There is a prophetic brilliance in all this which would not be entirely apparent to the readers of Byron's own age, but to us, in the era of the adman and the image-maker, it is all too painfully clear.

Southey is the new Christ, the Redeemer of this rather seedy Adam, King George III; the opener of the gates of Paradise. Everything is brought about in a series of farcical accidents, just like 'real life'! Saint Peter, a typical reactionary, indignant at Southey's avant-garde ethics, knocks him over the brink of the celestial platform into chaos: he ends up in Windermere, but escapes drowning.

> He first sank to the bottom—like his works,
>   But soon rose to the surface—like himself;
> For all corrupted things are buoyed like corks,
>   By their own rottenness, light as an elf,
> Or wisp that flits o'er a morass. . . .   (cv)

The devils, deafened by Southey's hexameters, run 'howling . . . down to hell'.

> The ghosts fled, gibbering, for their own dominions . . .
> Michael took refuge in his trump—but, lo!
> His teeth were set on edge, he could not blow!   (ciii)

In the midst of all this confusion, George III sneaks into heaven, and in his final appearance is heard 'practising the hundredth psalm' ('Enter into his gates with thanksgiving and into his courts with praise: be thankful unto him, and speak good of his Name. For the Lord is gracious, his mercy is everlasting; and his truth endureth from generation to generation').[10]

Notes and references

1   In ten volumes, omitting the Letters and Moore's 'Life of Byron', contained in the seventeen volumes of the 1832–33 edition.
2   Gleckner, *op. cit.* p. 27, n. 21.
3   Personal prejudices are at work. 'She *waltzes*', he remarks of Miss Rawdon (*MLJ* ii, 216), '& is for many reasons the very last woman on earth I should covet', even though she has 'lived amongst the Greeks of Venice & Trieste consequently well versed in many topics which are common to her & me & would be very stupid to any one else.' And again: 'Does Annabella *waltz*?', he asks Lady Melbourne; 'it is an odd question—but a very essential point with me.'
4   The *reductio ad absurdum* kind of humour here is very close to Blake's

> 'Widows & maids & youths also,
> That lightly trip on beauty's toe,
>   Or sit on beauty's bum'

in *An Island in the Moon*. Cf. also 'the rump/of this poetic dandy' in 'Ballad', st. 5 (*PW* vii, p. 60).
5   'The first address of Prometheus in Aeschylus', to which Byron calls attention in a footnote, includes an apostrophe to the sun.
6   'The *Prometheus* [of Aeschylus] . . . has always been so much in my head, that I can easily conceive its influence over all or any thing that I have written . . .' (letter to Murray, 12 October 1817). The 'Ode' should of course be read in this context; I have not discussed it in this book because it seems to me to be negligible as poetry.
7   It should not be forgotten that it is also the stanza of *The Lusiads* of Camoẽs, an early favourite of Byron's.
8   *The Romantic Movement in English Poetry* (1909). That the later Byron was the whole Byron is of course not my view in this book, but the modern case has seldom been so persuasively put as in this early assessment.
9   See above, pp. 51–54.
10   Charles Lamb was not an admirer of Byron, but his comment in a letter of 23 January 1824 to Bernard Barton is characteristically penetrating and commonsensical: 'The decision against Hunt for the "Vision of Judgment" makes me sick. What is to become of the

good old talk about our good old King? his personal virtues saving us from revolution, etc. etc.! Why, none that think can utter it now. It must stink. And the "vision" is really, as to him-ward, such a tolerant, good-humoured thing.'

12

'DON JUAN'

The dream under the hill

At an early point in this book I remarked on the dreamlike or
Ossianic character of Byron's writing. This is something which
persists and is even more in evidence in the later work. Byron called
Childe Harold 'this protracted dream'. The Turkish Tales embody
his 1813–14 nightmares. *Don Juan* is popular today for its realism,
its extreme wide-awakeness, and on one level its character is indeed
that; but great poems exist on more planes than one, and Byron's
comic masterpiece is no exception.

At strategic points he hints at hidden meanings.

> My music has some mystic diapasons;
> And there is much which could not be appreciated
> In any manner by the uninitiated,

he remarks in Canto XIV, xxii, in a not very serious context. But
context should never be taken as a *control* in interpreting Byron.
Like Rabelais, he is an adept at the metaphysics of farce. He works
best by indirection, and flippancy is often a mask for his most
integral insights. Again, in this crucial fourteenth canto,[1] he tells us

> This narrative is not meant for narration,
> But a mere airy and fantastic basis,
> To build up common things with common places.   (XIV, vii)

'Common places' are not 'commonplaces'. The term belongs to
rhetoric, and includes the sense 'universally accepted truths'.
Byron proposes to *build up* a structure of 'common things'—everyday

happenings, quite distinct from the melodrama of his Tales, the romanticism of *Childe Harold*—with the cement of 'common places', and to see what results. Will the cement hold? Or will the weight and stress of common things be too much for it? *Don Juan* is, on this level, a laboratory experiment in the symbiosis of fact with vision, of folk-wisdom with 'the minute particulars'. Blake would certainly have approved.[2]

On one plane *Don Juan* is an ironic, picaresque narrative, on another it is an experiment in the relation of 'common places' to 'common things'. On yet a third it is a series of dream situations, ranging from the erotic to the nightmarish, strung on a single thread which, as Byron had remarked of the connecting thought of the Tales, that earlier dream sequence, 'always runs through, through . . . yes, yes, through'.[3] The thought which runs through the Tales is pretty clearly that of guilt and punishment; the thought which runs through *Don Juan* is that of escape. *The Island* conflates the two. Juan escapes from one predicament, from one temporal situation, to find himself more deeply involved in another. Not for nothing did Byron call the poem his 'Human Comedy'. It is a presentation in non-divine terms of his hero's progressive involvement in the circles of hell, purgatory and paradise. Hell in Byron's poem is the longboat and the siege of Ismail; purgatory is Catherine's court and Norman Abbey; paradise is Haidée's island, extended, in *The Island*, to Neuha's. Dante's sequence—Hell, Purgatory, Paradise —is broken, as must happen in the corrupted currents of this world. The shattered mirror is a favourite metaphor of Byron's: his poetry reflects from its fragments; as, in Eliot's 'Burnt Norton', the dry purgatorial pool 'glitters' suddenly 'out of heart of light', reflecting the dream-figures hitherto hidden 'behind us'.

In his 'Dante' essay, Eliot distinguishes between the 'high dream' and the 'low dream'. Man lives habitually in a state of dream; his contacts with reality are painful but mercifully short: 'human kind/ Cannot bear very much reality'. The dream of unregenerate man is the low dream, flowering from his animal subconscious; the dream of the saint is the high dream, the Giaour's 'light from heaven'. Poets, artists, supermen like Caesar and Napoleon and Byron, live a mixture of low and high dream, passing uneasily or with gusto from the one to the other. Some artists separate the dreams, some conflate them. A convincing conflation, such as Shakespeare's or Rabelais's or Byron's, clearly has the edge over even such brilliant reductions as Homer's, Dante's or Milton's.

Don Juan is basically Byron's bid for the low dream, but transcendentalism will keep breaking in. I have tried to suggest the lowness of Byron's approach—and incidentally to map out the terrain—by using lines from Blake's *For the Sexes: The Gates of Paradise* as my section headings. Blake's comic-strip masterpiece (look at the expressions if you doubt the 'comic') tackles the human condition on its own sexual-self-seeking terms. This is man at his weakest. But the point of the Epilogue, 'To The Accuser who is The God of This World' ('Truly, My Satan, thou art but a Dunce,/ And dost not know the Garment from the Man') is that the reductive approach will not do: the same Satan who wishes to narrow religion to 'Jesus & Jehovah' is himself 'The Son of Morn in weary Night's decline,/The lost Traveller's Dream under the Hill'.

Don Juan might be defined as a negative transcendentalism: the resisted epiphany of the high dream within the precinct of the low dream. I have tried to suggest this in the course of the following pages by another device. From time to time, within my point-to-point exposition, I have inserted lines from Eliot's 'Burnt Norton'[4] which break the positivist pattern, relating to what is going on in *Don Juan* but in a non-literal sense. The device is clumsy, but may succeed in indicating a multiplicity of levels in the poem. At the close of the chapter—and the book—I draw all these threads together by quoting the 'Garlic and sapphires' passage in its entirety.

The idea of *Don Juan* as a dream poem will find small favour with modern critics, who prefer to dwell on its realism, vigour and wit. But a contemporary reviewer commented on the first two cantos:

He has here exhibited that wonderful versatility of style and thought, which appears almost incompatible within the scope of a single subject; and the familiar and the sentimental, the witty and the sublime, the sarcastic and the pathetic, the gloomy and the droll, are all touched with so happy an art, and mingled together with such a power of union, yet such a discrimination of style, that a perusal of the poem appears more like a pleasing and ludicrous dream, than the sober feeling of reality. It is certainly one of the strangest, though not the best of dreams; and it is much to be wished that the author, before he lay down to sleep, had invoked, like Shakespeare's Lysander, some good angel to protect him against the wicked spirit of slumbers. (*The Monthly Review,* 1819.)

It is odd that the reviewer should have described this first instalment of the 'dream' as 'pleasing and ludicrous' (had he skipped the shipwreck, one wonders?) but his analysis is otherwise perceptive. Like Lysander, like the Church at Ephesus denounced by the Angel of the Apocalypse, Byron has 'forsaken his first love' (in the possibility of transcendence held out to him in his Eastern tour) and drifted into the erotic dream of Venice. Like Lysander, he finds himself surrounded by mocking phantoms, earth spirits and animal masks and loves real and unreal, philtres and antidotes. 'The crying shadow in the funeral dance,/The loud lament of the disconsolate chimera.' The pilgrimage has ended in a maze, the gulf has degenerated into a morass. His poem is veritably a *Midsummer Night's Dream* in its complexity of levels, its threading of forest by-paths into a nine men's morris filled up with mud, with its final hope, nevertheless, of 'pardon' and 'amendment', in the original matrix of Newstead. 'For where the crime's committed', as Yeats reminds us, 'the crime may be forgot.'

The crime is committed in the sexual embrace which is itself a dream and the shadow of a dream.[5] Byron's own sense of this is clear from a letter to Hobhouse of 23 August 1819:

I feel—and I feel it bitterly—that a man should not consume his life at the side and on the bosom of a woman, and a stranger;[6] that even the recompense, and it is much, is not enough,[7] and that this Cicisbean existence is to be condemned. But I have neither the strength of mind to break my chain, nor the insensibility which would deaden its weight. I cannot tell what will become of me—to leave, or to be left would at present drive me quite out of my senses; and yet to what have I conducted myself? I have, luckily, or unluckily, no ambition left; it would be better if I had, it would at least awake me; whereas at present I merely start in my sleep.

This is the voice of a man tangled in a maze. To trace that maze is the dynamics of *Don Juan*. Byron is consciously in the grip of a nightmare from which he cannot rouse himself. It is not a nightmare of the horrific kind which he suffered in 1813–14. His present state comes close to that of Coleridge in the 'Dejection Ode', 'A grief without a pang, void, dark, and drear', a 'smothering weight' on the breast. Coleridge longed for a pang to 'startle this dull pain, and make it move and live'; and we may suspect that the horrific episodes of *Don Juan*, all taken from extraneous sources, are meant to constitute that surgical intervention which will stab him into life again. In the end, of course, it took Missolonghi to do that; and then he died.

Such outcries as the letter to Hobhouse are not infrequent at this period and throughout the Italian sojourn; they are conveniently ignored by presentday admirers of *Don Juan* as Byron's mature masterpiece, the mellow embodiment of his coming to terms with life, his wise coming-of-age after the adolescent growing-pains of *Childe Harold* and the Tales. That it is a masterpiece is certain, but it strikes me as a masterpiece of despair. A Dejection Ode extended, with Byronic aplomb, through sixteen cantos of narrative, descriptive, satiric brilliance. I shall have occasion later on, in discussing the 'English cantos' XI–XVII, to describe them as 'compensatory': but in relation to Byron's previous *oeuvre* the whole of *Don Juan* is a compensatory exercise, a projection of frustrated stasis into fictional kinesis.[8] 'Garlic and sapphires in the mud/Clot the bedded axletree.' As catharsis, then, the poem stands with the earlier Tales: but in an inverse relation to 'reality'. Then, in 1813–14, the movement was from an unbearable 'reality' (Byron's repeated term for the pressure of experienced horror) into 'imagination'[9] which is fictional and therefore less acute. Now, in 1819–23,[10] Byron seeks in the sharpness of an imagined narrative the bite which is absent from his present 'reality'. Poetry is no longer 'the lava of the imagination' boiling over from the otherwise self-destructive volcano,[11] but fragments shored against the ruins of a 'reality' which is in danger of collapsing upon itself as maze, if not as morass. Venice, for Byron in 1817–19, hovers between these paradigms. *Don Juan* is compensatory, an escape where *Childe Harold* had been a voyage of discovery. Perhaps Teresa sensed the poem's function as an 'escape mechanism' when she so vigorously opposed its continuation: the moral objections she advanced rationalising her instinctive distrust of the whole enterprise.[12]

'When weary Man enters his Cave'

In a letter of 2 January 1817 to John Murray from Venice Byron declares: 'As to poetry, mine is the *dream* of my sleeping Passions', and suggest that he may abandon verse for 'some work of fancy in prose, descriptive of Italian manners and of human passions'. Yet the passions, though sleeping, are not dead, and the 'dream' that he is living is rich with archetypal shapes. This is made plain in the very first stanza of *Don Juan*.

> I want a hero: an uncommon want
>   When every year and month sends forth a new one,
> Till, after cloying the gazettes with cant,
>   The age discovers he is not the true one;
> Of such as these I should not care to vaunt,

> I'll therefore take our ancient friend Don Juan—
> We all have seen him, in the pantomime,
> Sent to the Devil somewhat ere his time.   (I, i)

Byron is doing a number of different things here. On one level he
disclaims any ambition for 'image-making', Southey's function in
The Vision of Judgment;[13] and this prepares us for the very important
function of image-breaking (the key word 'cant' makes an immediate
appearance) which is basic to the poem's satiric impact. But on a
deeper, somnambulistic level, he projects the figure of 'our ancient
friend', a figure moving through the pantomime of the dream of life.
When we read that phrase, 'our ancient friend', our mind reverts to
those profoundly revealing stanzas of *Childe Harold* III in which
Byron expresses, with unparalleled clarity, his 'philosophy' of the
creative act.

> He, who grown aged in this world of woe,
>   In deeds, not years, piercing the depths of life,
>   So that no wonder waits him—nor below
>   Can Love or Sorrow, Fame, Ambition, Strife,
>   Cut to his heart again with the keen knife
>   Of silent, sharp endurance—he can tell
>   Why Thought seeks refuge in lone caves, yet rife
>   With airy images, and shapes which dwell
> Still unimpaired, though old, in the Soul's haunted cell.
>
> 'Tis to create, and in creating live
>   A being more intense, that we endow
>   With form our fancy, gaining as we give
>   The life we image, even as I do now.
>   What am I? Nothing: but not so art thou,
>   Soul of my thought! with whom I traverse earth,
>   Invisible but gazing, as I glow
>   Mixed with thy spirit, blended with thy birth,
> And feeling still with thee in my crushed feelings' dearth.
>
> (*CH* III, v–vi)

'Our *ancient* friend . . . shapes unimpaired, though *old*. . . .' These
airy images, these shapes dwelling in the soul's haunted cell, the
inmost depths of the unconscious, are the archetypal forces upon
which Byron invariably falls back in moments of stress. They
constitute the personages of his inner 'dream'. In *Childe Harold,
Manfred, The Dream, The Vision of Minerva*, the dream moves
amongst mythological and symbolic vistas, and its hero is still a
complex, emergent character. In *Don Juan* symbol has narrowed
down to allegory, and the mythological, ranging through the

spaces of history[14] and Great Time, has become Byron's 'personal present'. The multivalent complexity of the Childe is reduced to the two-tiered, split personality of the Don. Moreover, it is no longer *with* his hero that Byron traverses earth, mixed with his spirit, blended with his birth, but as the accomplished puppet-master, directing and manipulating. Every reader of *Don Juan* must have felt the curiously zombielike character of Juan, a somnambulistic quality which gives his actions even in such a crisis as the Siege of Ismail a certain flavour of automatism.

The third Canto of *Childe Harold* was begun in early May of 1816 and finished in late June or early July. In these opening stanzas the change from the early Byron is at once apparent. Life is no longer new and full of promise. 'No wonder waits him . . .': the Socratic *thaumazein* is lost in the bitter depths of life. Byron is thrown back on the support of the archetypes, on the stimulus of unconscious forces. Thus *Don Juan* presents the paradox of a work which is apparently much more realistic, more human, more close to actual life than anything which has gone before, but which in fact is substituting a phantasmagoria orchestrated in realistic terms for the subtle, polyphonically valent movements of the earlier works. Begun two years after the completion of Canto III of *Childe Harold*, *Don Juan* is the end product of the crisis of bitterness and frustration, of near-paralysis, so vividly exposed in Canto III, in the Swiss letters and in the 1816 Journal.

Another way of describing *Don Juan* would be to say that it is a *Childe Harold* in reverse. The original Childe sets out from Newstead as a cynic, a disappointed roué, and through a growing self-knowledge and exposure to the liberating forces of nature, of ancient art and civilisation, he attains a sense of wonder, of insight into the mysteries of life and death, a new innocence. All this is plainly visible in Cantos I and II. The drama of the separation throws Byron back on himself in the opening stanzas of Canto III, and the seeds of disillusionment are sown there: but he remains open to the moulding influences of Switzerland and Italy and throughout Cantos III and IV we have the sense that the Childe's education is continuing along many complex lines. The great address to the ocean which closes the whole *Pilgrimage* brings him again into creative contact with 'the Mothers', and leaves us with an exhilarating sense of new possibilities.

Don Juan, on the contrary, starts off in innocence, though it is an animal innocence, and deteriorates steadily towards cynicism and debauchery. As I pointed out in an earlier essay,[15] his geographic progress is from the south—Seville and Haidée's Aegean island, to the north—St Petersburg and 'Norman Abbey', whereas Harold's had been from Newstead and London to the south. The distinction is important when we consider that for Byron, as for Blake, south and north, warmth and cold, are almost synonymous with good and evil. The scene is firmly set in Canto I in the sunny Seville of Byron's own 1809 experiences, so vividly described in letters to his mother and friends back in England. This was Byron's first encounter with the south, and his lines of communication run characteristically through 'oranges and women'.[16] 'Oranges' conveys the bounty of Nature with which Canto I of *Childe Harold* is persistently concerned; the 'women' are left over for the full treatment now to be given them in *Don Juan*.

'The Sexual Garments Sweet'

Don Juan is outstanding among English longer poems for the great gallery of women characters which it exhibits; here the only possible comparison is with Shakespeare in his total *oeuvre*. Each is minutely and sympathetically displayed and discriminated with all the adroitness of a man who (as Byron said in riposte to a *Blackwood's* accusation of 'treating women harshly' in the poem) could honestly affirm: 'It may be so, but I have been their martyr. My whole life has been sacrificed *to* them and *by* them.' Thus the element of autobiography enters strongly into Byron's presentation: he is remembering his wife as he paints the portrait of Donna Inez, and the Spanish girls of the Pilgrimage form the models for his detailed study of Donna Julia in Canto I, while the Haidée of Cantos II and III draws on his recollections of the Maid of Athens and the mysterious 'Leila' of *The Giaour*. Gulbeyaz and Dudu in Canto VI come straight from his Turkish days, while Aurora and Adeline in the final Canto belong to the years of fame in London.

Yet even here, and from the outset, we are conscious that the poem is proceeding on the two levels of dream and waking. The women characters come from Byron's waking life, but in the poem they are conflated in a somnambulistic phantasmagoria; 'Weaving to Dreams the Sexual strife', in Blake's phrase. Indeed, Blake's 'For the Sexes: The Gates of Paradise' (engraved in 1793, with additions in 1818, the year of the writing of *Don Juan* I and II) forms a remarkably useful 'Key' to Byron's poem on its esoteric level. 'Mutual Forgiveness of each Vice'[17] is what Byron had asked from Annabella; Blake's designs of water, earth, air, all expressing entrapment, and the final design of fire where the liberation of man is achieved only in 'endless Strife', exactly convey Byron's situation at this time. Each of the remaining 'emblems' could be shown to have its relevance: I will here mention only No. 7, 'What are these? Alas! the Female Martyr, Is She also the Divine Image?', No. 8, 'My Son! my Son!', No. 10, 'Help! Help', and No. 16, 'I have said to the Worm: Thou art my mother & my sister.' This last emblem is expanded in the concluding 'The Keys of the Gates':

> My Eternal Man set in Repose,
> The Female from his darkness rose
> And She found me beneath a Tree,
> A Mandrake, & in her Veil hid me. . . .
>
> When weary Man enters his Cave
> He meets his Saviour in the Grave
> Some find a Female Garment there,
> And some a Male, woven with care,
> Lest the Sexual Garments sweet
> Should grow a devouring Winding sheet,
> One dies! Alas! the Living & Dead,
> One is slain & One is fled. . . .
>
> Thou'rt my Mother from the Womb,
> Wife, Sister, Daughter, to the Tomb,
> Weaving to Dreams the Sexual strife
> And weeping over the Web of Life.

With almost uncanny relevance, 'The Gates of Paradise' epitomises Byron's total life pattern, from the parental conflicts of his birth to the solution 'in endless Strife' at Missolonghi; it also focuses the immediate dilemmas of 1816–19, with the mother-wife-sister-daughter agon paramount, as the letters and journals demonstrate.

This same complexity is present, if we look beneath the mocking, 'realistic' surface, in the opening stanzas of *Don Juan*, where Juan's mother, Donna Inez, is a compound of Byron's mother and wife, with some features derived from Lady Caroline Lamb and Claire Clairmont. So too, Donna Julia unites aspects of Teresa, of Augusta, of Lady Frances Wedderburn Webster, and of 'Leila'. Exactly as in a dream, these real-life characters are moulded into strange patterns and flow bewilderingly into one another. These are the 'Emanations', as Blake would put it, of the masculine archetype or Zoa who is Juan, himself a split-off piece of the universal man adumbrated in

Harold and brought to some kind of completion in *Manfred*, though the disruptive forces in Byron were from the beginning too powerful to allow a full integration.

In no respect is *Don Juan* more a reversal of *Childe Harold* than in its continuous presentation of the social order as a matriarchy. From the beginning Blake's 'shadowy Female' dominates the scene, and man, 'Woman-born and Woman-nourish'd and Woman-educated & Woman-scorn'd',[18] is scarcely more than wax in her hands. Seville is forcibly presented as a Garden, a garden 'of oranges and women'; and it was probably not absent from Byron's mind that theologians have put forward the claim of the orange rather than the apple as the forbidden fruit within the latitude of the Garden of Eden. Be that as it may, we have in the Inez–Julia nexus a curious re-enactment of the Lilith–Eve myth, with Juan–José–Alfonso as the primeval Adam 'lingering near his garden' (clxxx) in baffled *cavalier-serventism* on his women. 'Other echoes/Inhabit the garden'. Donna Inez is 'a learned lady' famed/For every branch of every science known . . . Her favourite science was the mathematical, . . . An all-in-all-sufficient self-director, . . . In short she was a walking calculation' (I, x–xvi): traits more masculine than feminine. Don José, on the other hand, is 'a mortal of the careless kind . . . a man/Oft in the wrong, and never on his guard' (xix–xxi), who is reputed to keep a mistress or two, and thus gives his wife the excuse for an inveterate campaign against him:

> . . . she had a devil of a spirit,
>   And sometimes mixed up fancies with realities,
> And let few opportunities escape
> Of getting her liege lord into a scrape.   (I, xx)

Like Annabella, Donna Inez calls on lawyers and physicians 'to prove her loving lord was *mad*'; failing in this, 'She next decided he was only *bad*' (xxvii), and is starting proceedings for divorce when Don José obligingly dies (xxxii).

Juan, the only child of this ill-assorted pair, is very like his father in temperament—spirited, careless, generous, handsome:

> At six, I said, he was a charming child,
>   At twelve he was a fine, but quiet boy;
> Although in infancy a little wild,
>   They tamed him down amongst them: to destroy
> His natural spirit not in vain they toiled,
>   At least it seemed so . . .   (I, l)

'They' are of course the women, who have taken Juan's education in hand after his father's death, and the possé of priests and school-masters with which Donna Inez surrounds him. Beside Donna Inez there is also Donna Julia:

> Amongst her numerous acquaintance, all
> Selected for discretion and devotion,
> There was the Donna Julia, whom to call
> Pretty were but to give a feeble notion
> Of many charms in her as natural
> As sweetness to the flower, or salt to Ocean.   (I, lv)

The last line leads us cunningly from the artifice of 'acquaintance, all/Selected for discretion and devotion' (Donna Julia's public face) into the dangerous tracts of 'nature', the nature of a flower's sweetness and the ocean's salt (very different from the *sal Atticum* ascribed to Donna Inez in an earlier stanza). Byron is here setting up complexities which are to accompany Juan's progress throughout the poem. Julia's 'Oriental eye' bespeaks her Moorish origin:[19] at this point Byron links up his experiences at the two ends of the Mediterranean, and fuses in Julia a feminine archetype he is to reduce to its components through the long succession of the poem's heroines. Even Inez is not so monodic as she seems. There is the suggestion (lxvi) that she had sinned with Don Alfonso, Julia's husband, before her friend's marriage. The idea comes unexpectedly, and on the realistic level of the poem's reading is not only implausible but artistically disadvantageous; it is only on the dream level, where characters and motives flow so ambiguously one into the other, that Byron's unconscious and semi-conscious compulsions become apparent. Among these we may count his sense of outrage—

> Standing alone beside his desolate hearth,
> Where all his household gods lay shivered round him
>   (I, xxxvi)

—at what the 'good' women have done to him, with the concomitant thirst for revenge (expressed in many letters of this period); and also, and of deeper import, his 'metaphysical' motif of the relativity of all human affairs and qualities, which is the basic theme of the poem. Whether Donna Inez—or Mrs Byron, or Annabella—was ever actually unchaste is irrelevant to the inbuilt antitheses of human nature—just as whether a love is 'pure' or 'impure', selfish or unselfish, Uranian or Pandemic, is irrelevant to its essential guilt. For guilt, original sin, taints all human action and in no department more clearly than the sexual. This is a point I shall return to in discussing the Haidée episode, but it is well to have it in mind here.[20]

'What might have been and what has been/Point to one end, which is always present.'

Juan and Julia fall inevitably in love and the comic-erotic action of the poem is set vigorously in motion. The rest of Canto I is devoted to this pretty piece of adultery. I have no intention of 'telling the story' of *Don Juan* here; the poem which has been called 'the most readable long poem of the nineteenth century' deserves to be enjoyed in its plenitude, not in synopsis. On the novelistic level the Juan–Julia intrigue follows what we should expect of a plot based on the old legend already exploited in the medieval play *El Atheista Fulminato*, in *El Burlador de Sevilla y Combidado de Piedra* of Gabriel Tellez in the early seventeenth century, in Molière's *Don Juan; ou, Le Festin de Pierre*, and, of course, in Mozart's opera. But from the very opening of Byron's poem some striking differences become apparent. His Juan is not a gay philanderer or sexual athlete. Far from being the exploiter of feminine weakness, young Juan is the victim of the various women who cross his path.[21] It is Julia who seduces Juan. Juan's sexual awakening at the age of sixteen, and Julia's growing attraction towards him, her struggles with her own conscience, and final capitulation—all this is drawn with great skill and verve, and the final scene, where Don Alfonso bursts into Julia's bedroom and Juan's presence is ultimately discovered, is richly comic. The undertone of existential irony, however, persists: Juan is not only the victim, but the despised victim, despised particularly by the rough common sense of Julia's maid Antonia. For Antonia, Juan is 'this pretty gentleman', 'the urchin', and his 'half-girlish face' is not worth losing a life or a place for (clxx–clxxi). Juan's first place of concealment is the bed itself, where he lies under Julia and Antonia like a piece of smuggled merchandise:

> He had been hid—I don't pretend to say
>   How, nor can I indeed describe the where—
> Young, slender, and packed easily, he lay,
>   No doubt, in little compass, round or square;
> But pity him I neither must nor may
>   His suffocation by that pretty pair.   (I, clxvi)

This double suffocation, by sense and sensibility, is relevant to the dual stresses to which Juan is exposed in the whole course of the poem: whenever he finds himself in a position to cope adequately with one, he is outflanked by the other. *Don Juan* is thus, among so many other things, a dramatic enactment of Pascal's and Pope's scenario of man on 'this isthmus of a middle state' not simply in so far as he is 'darkly wise and rudely great' but also in the sense that the dark wisdom is further obscured by the conflicting claims of passion and judgement.

This initial bedroom scene is a perfect paradigm of Juan's progress from one impasse to another in his futile gestures towards freedom. Juan is bundled from the bed, his first refuge, into the closet, his second.[22] His position is consistently undignified and, indeed, humiliating. 'I want a hero . . .', so Byron began his poem; if, in reading that first stanza, we have taken 'want' in its sense of 'wish for', we may now, looking back, accept it rather in the sense of 'lack', 'haven't got', and realise that this is a lack which Byron has no intention of supplying. In stanzas ii to iv he has given a mock-Miltonic roster of heroic names, with the rider:

> I condemn none,
> But can't find any in the present age
> Fit for my poem (that is, for my new one);[23]
> So, as I said, I'll take my friend Don Juan.   (I, v)

The nineteenth century is an unheroic age, Byron is saying; let us accept it as that, and in doing so let us ask ourselves whether there have been, after all, any heroic ages? whether the basic condition of man does not debar him from heroism, as it does from beauty, from love and from ultimate significance. The point is Johnson's, in *The Vanity of Human Wishes*, in *The Rambler*, and in *Rasselas*.

Juan's 'only garment' is torn off in the scuffle with Alfonso and he flees naked through the night to his mother's house, leaving confusion and disaster behind him. The sequel, over which Byron passes with lightning speed which however does not exclude a dig at British scandalmongering—

> The pleasant scandal which arose next day,
> The nine days' wonder which was brought to light,
> And how Alfonso sued for a divorce,
> Were in the English newspapers, of course.   (I, clxxxviii)

—ends with Julia entering a convent and Juan packed overseas 'by the advice of some old ladies' (cxc). The famous letter which Julia writes from her convent cell (a contemporary critic, Colton, found it 'quite equal, in its way, to the celebrated epistle of Eloisa') is rich in ambiguities. Among the most quoted lines in Byron are ' "Man's love is of man's life a thing apart,/'Tis woman's whole existence . . ." ' (cxciv) and the quotation is usually made with a compassionate sigh for poor woman. In the context of *Don Juan* such

an obsession reveals itself as a vampire threat[24] to the whole structure
of masculine, rational values painstakingly built up through the
civilised centuries; it is the amorphous, clinging sexual-familial
swamp to which Blake gives the name of 'storgous' in the Symbolic
Books. ' "You will proceed in pleasure, and in pride,/Beloved and
loving many . . ." ' Julia goes on, providing exquisite dramatic
irony for the reader who is reading *Don Juan* for the second or
twentieth time:

> 'My heart is feminine, nor can forget—
> To all, except one image, madly blind.'   (I, cxcvi)

It is this madness, this blindness, which constitutes the vampirish
essence of *storgè*. Eliot's contrasting 'Love is itself unmoving,/Only
the cause and end of movement,/Timeless, and undesiring' returns
us to the ethos of the Turkish Tales.

'In Time's Ocean falling drown'd'

From the cloyingly feminine world of Seville Juan is launched, in
Canto II, into the harshly masculine world of the *Trinidada*, the
shipwreck, and the horrors of thirst and cannibalism in an open
boat at sea. It is noteworthy that *Don Juan* progresses by means of
these stark horizontal antitheses. We miss the smooth modulations
of *Childe Harold*, which are largely mediated through an architectural
imagery of which *Don Juan* has virtually nothing. This is an *un-
structured* world, amorphous in the grip of forces beyond rational
control. The planned contours of the Pilgrimage are replaced by
erratic currents. If we read *Don Juan*, as I think we are bound to do,
in what Blake would have called 'its diabolical sense', linking up
the events of Byron's life, the references of his letters, the threads
which stretch backwards and forwards from his other works, to the
plot, the characters and the incidental disquisitions of this his latest
poem, we cannot but see in it the culmination of that process of
fragmentation which I have tried to trace in the Tales and the
dramas. The same scurry from the circumference to the centre of
the circle of fire is apparent in these two opening cantos of *Don Juan*.
From the circumference—the Garden, and mostly the moonlit
garden, of Seville—we retreat to the fiery centre of the longboat
becalmed under its subtropic sun. The situation is Ancient Mariner-
ish, but with a farcical dimension unknown to Coleridge. With the

byplay about who is to eat whom we return to that 'theatre of
the absurd' already noted in *The Deformed Transformed*. Agony and
death, like love, have to be deprived of their dignity if 'reality' is to
be preserved. In terms of our original love–wisdom–power syndrome,
we pass in Canto II from the sphere of predatory love to that of
predatory power, both absolute non-values undermining the basis of
civilised existence.

Existence for Byron, as for Blake—'Life feeds on life'—is very
much a matter of eating and being eaten. When the traditional
sanctions of wisdom are removed—and there is no wisdom in *Don
Juan*—we are reduced to the mouth and the vulva.[25] We know how
much Byron objected to seeing his wife eating, and while this may
have something to do with his own horror of obesity and recollections
of his mother's gormandising, there were probably moments at
which Byron saw himself as an homunculus between the steady
munch, munch of Annabella's upper and lower jaws.[26] This is
Byron eaten: Byron eating is Don Juan in his progress from Seville
to Norman Abbey. Seville is 'famous for oranges and women', and
Juan begins his career there: the rest of the poem is a tuck-shop
spree. In reverting to the schoolboy we revert to the Billy Bunter
syndrome. It is all cleverly camouflaged (with the usual Byronic
loopholes, so that the poet can riposte 'But I gave you the clue' if
we guess right) but we are not deceived: the promised postal order
has failed to arrive, the fatal compensation (financed on borrowed
cash from Bob Cherry) is near at hand.[27] Don Juan's attitude
throughout the poem is that of the compulsive eater, the eternal
enemy of the slim, aesthetic Byron.[28] Where Harold had toiled his
way along the hard track of the pilgrimage of self-knowledge, the
none-too-intelligent Don eats his way through the segments of his
orange to its non-existent centre. This explains the impression *Don
Juan* gives us of being a series of segments, in that there is no true
progression, no continued development, only a catenation of episodes.
We begin with the womb situation, the interior point of the segment,
in the Seville Inez–Julia imbroglio. From this we swing violently
through the power-eating horrors of the shipwreck with its enforced
human contacts to the idyllic solitude of the Aegean island—where
we are back again at the centre of our next segment with Haidée
and her maid Zoé, back in the love-eating complexities of a private
banquet which inevitably latches on to the public complexities of the
current Turk–Greek power-eating situation—and off we go again
with Juan to the new horrors of the Seraglio and of Ismail!

Juan and Julia, Juan and Haidée, are love-eaters: but Byron is concerned to show us, within the diagrams of the poem, that without wisdom love cannot be separated from the corruptions of power (or powerlessness). Remember that within his own private diagram Byron had sought to attain that wisdom, first through his immersion in the Islamic East, and second in his attachment to the 'wise woman' Annabella. He knew that a simple withdrawal to 'solitude', the island dream, solves nothing for a man of his kind, or for any man of energy and intelligence: you become a vegetable or break out into violence, Blake's 'endless strife'. The succumbing to the Venetian love dream was a springboard for the Missolonghian catastrophe. Even physiologically, the damages inflicted by Byron on his constitution in those years, the syphilitic self-eating, the sword outwearing its sheath, determined the fatal outcome of his fever. Without wisdom, the *tertium quid*, all the magnificence of 'sincerity and strength' which Swinburne divined in Byron availed him nothing: and of course this he had realised from the beginning. It is the whole point of the 'pilgrimage' of *Childe Harold*. The Greek adventure of 1823 was to be Byron's last cast for self-synthesis: 'the release from action and suffering, release from the inner/And the outer compulsion'.

Meanwhile, the Greek adventure of Don Juan is a further penetration into the sensual whirlpool. A tautened, cadaverous Juan (otherwise strangely unaffected by the horrors he has gone through) is washed up on the shores of an island in the Cyclades. Have we finished with Julia? Apparently: but remember her letter, 'Its seal a sun-flower: "*Elle vous suit partout*" ' (cxcviii). He may escape from the embraces of the sea, but never from 'the ocean Woman'. ('Will the sunflower turn to us, will the clematis/Stray down, bend to us; tendril and spray/Clutch and cling?') The sea enters *Don Juan* with Canto II and remains an important protagonist up to the end of Canto VI. A major element in *Childe Harold* II and IV and the Turkish Tales, it is largely absent from the dramas and the Italian poems. As the creative-devouring symbol of the eternal feminine, its presence in the first half of *Don Juan* is highly significant in establishing the work's main coordinates. In swinging from the garden of Seville into the 'murderous innocence of the sea' we pass from the theme of eating to that of being eaten, from dream into nightmare. The role of the sea as grim mother, with Juan 'rocked in the cradle of the deep' to a sleep without waking, is emphasised in the storm's lullaby—

> The high wind made the treble, and as bass
> The hoarse harsh waves kept time . . .   (II, xxxiv)

and the succeeding calm which

> Lulled them like turtles sleeping on the blue
> Of Ocean . . .   (II, lxviii)

(destined to be eaten, if caught). Juan's tutor, Pedrillo, is quietly bled to death, and the surgeon drinks 'from the fast-flowing veins', a vampire touch which is to be curiously paralleled in Haidée's maternal tending of Juan. When at last they approach land,

> Famine—despair—cold—thirst and heat, had done
> Their work on them by turns, and thinned them to
> Such things a mother had not known her son
> Amidst the skeletons of that gaunt crew.   (II, cii)

The shore is rocky, and its dangers unknown, but

> Lovely seemed any object that should sweep
> Away the vast—salt—dread—eternal Deep.   (II, ciii)

In their haste to get on shore, the four remaining occupants of the long-boat overset her, and only Juan, a skilled swimmer, survives:

> He buoyed his boyish limbs, and strove to ply
> With the quick wave   (II, cvi)

and with the aid of an oar, that 'piece of wood of small value' which here plays the part of the Ark,[29] succeeds in reaching the shore.

> There, breathless, with his digging nails he clung
> Fast to the sand, lest the returning wave,
> From whose reluctant roar his life he wrung,
> Should suck him back to her insatiate grave:
> And there he lay, full length, where he was flung.
> Before the entrance of a cliff-worn cave,
> With just enough of life to feel its pain,
> And deem that it was saved, perhaps, in vain.   (II, cviii)

And there, in front of the cave, he loses consciousness.

'Weaving to Dreams the Sexual Strife'

The situation is close to that of *The Tempest*. The Christian atmosphere, modulating guilt, prayer and forgiveness, of Shakespeare's final masterpiece has been often noted: it is here too in *Don Juan*, but with unShakespearean undertones of irony. Juan, who is

Everyman, is also the crucified Christ. The transition from Old Testament imagery—the Ark, the dove, the rainbow—to New Testament is subtly made through a pair of Pietà-like images: the first, while Juan is still in the embrace of the grim mother, has been already noted (cii): 'the skeletons of that gaunt crew' brings Michelangelo's Christ irresistibly to mind. This design is now reproduced at the entrance of the cave. When Juan recovers consciousness, he sees 'A lovely female face of seventeen':

> 'Twas bending close o'er his, and the small mouth
> 　Seemed almost prying into his for breath.　　　(II, cxiii)

Haidée—'the maid, or whatsoe'er/She was'—feeds him, watching him 'like a mother' (clviii). In his sleep he lies 'Hushed as the babe upon its mother's breast' (cxlviii); the next stanza brings in a reference to 'the sweet portraits of the Virgin Mary', and a much later stanza culminates the irony with an adaptation from Sappho:

> Oh, Hesperus! thou bringest all good things—
> 　Home to the weary, to the hungry cheer,
> To the young bird the parent's brooding wings,
> 　The welcome stall to the o'erlaboured steer;
> Whate'er of peace about our hearthstone clings,
> 　Whate'er our household gods protect of dear,
> Are gathered round us by thy look of rest;
> Thou bring'st the child, too, to the mother's breast.　　　(III, cvii)

Throughout the Haidée idyll Juan is consistently presented as a child. In swimming to shore, 'he buoyed his boyish limbs'; in the cave he 'slept like a top' (a childhood phrase), 'like an infant' (cvi, cxxxiv, cxliii): there is, in short, a return to boyhood for Juan, what I have called a regression to the central point of the fruit's segment. Haidée too is presented as very young but there is in her the mysterious essence of feminine wisdom which is, in one of its aspects, guile, and in the deepest recesses of its being, *storgè*, a force 'madly blind'.

As I have suggested in an earlier discussion of the Haidée episode, the love of Juan and Haidée is both innocent and guilty. It is innocent in its naturalness, its self-giving; but it is guilty in that it partakes of the primal guilt, the original sin, the Fall. Byron and Blake stand out amongst the Romantics in their profound conviction of this primal flaw in the nature of man: it is a 'pessimism' which contributed to Byron's downgrading by the optimistic Victorians, but as decade after decade of our twentieth century passes it becomes increasingly plausible that somehow, somewhere, some-thing went wrong in the existential drama. A false step was taken, a wrong corner turned. This is no place for theological discussion, and it matters little along which lines we care to interpret the great myth of the Fall—it need by no means be along Judaeo–Christian lines—but what does matter for our understanding of Byron is our recognition of the central place of this doctrine in his thinking. His letters and journals are full of it, and so is his verse. Long before Kafka Byron sees life as a trial, a lawsuit in which it is irrelevant whether the defendant knows or does not know what he is accused of: he is guilty by virtue of existing.

Blake's 'For the Sexes: the Gates of Paradise' may well continue to be our 'key' to the Haidée episode of *Don Juan*. Here indeed we have the sleeping 'universal man' in his cave, 'Weaving to dreams the sexual strife'. Dragging Juan into her cave, Haidée 'rescues' him as Julia had 'protected' him in the depths of her bed and the straitjacket of her 'closet'. The Haidée episode abounds in cave scenes, curiously linked to dreams and nightmares. The sea beats and washes around the caves, which are at once natural and non-natural, a Fall architecture of a ruined world:

> And thus they wandered forth, and hand in hand,
>   Over the shining pebbles and the shells,
> Gliding along the smooth and hardened sand,
>   And in the worn and wild receptacles
> Worked by the storms, yet worked as it were planned
>   In hollow halls, with sparry roofs and cells,
> They turned to rest; and, each clasped by an arm,
> Yielded to the deep Twilight's purple charm.   (II, clxxxiv)

Here, Byron's Aegean experiences of 1809–11 and his pitying sense of human destiny and the fragility of human happiness are combined. It is in the close weaving of such a wealth of apparently disparate material and tones that Byron achieves a density of utterance surpassing that of any of his contemporaries, with the exception of Blake.

The Haidée dream begins when Juan wakes out of the exposure of his shipwreck nightmare into the cosy protection of 'the lady of the cave'. He is her 'sea-treasure', her 'ocean-wreck'. The phrases carry a number of suggestions which I have discussed in that earlier essay: to those I will here add a new one, that of smuggling and 'wrecking'. Juan is salvage; is he also perhaps the fated victim of the kind of moth-to-candle attraction, which the Cornish seaboard villagers

exercised with lamp and beacon to draw the storm-tost ships on to
their murderous coasts?[30] In this reading, the witch or vampire
aspect of Haidée—'the maid, or whatsoe'er she was . . . the small
mouth . . . her eyes/Were black as death',

> Forth from its raven fringe the full glance flies,
>   Ne'er with such force the swiftest arrow flew;
> 'Tis as the snake late coiled, who pours his length,
> And hurls at once his venom and his strength[31]   (II, cxiii–cxvii)

takes on an added dimension of menace, as though the beacon
guilt-innocence in Haidée has called to the corresponding innocence-
guilt of Juan across the waste of waters. Certainly Juan is stowed
in the cave as contraband.

The coastguard turns up in the shape of Haidée's 'piratical papa',
Lambro. The name means 'shining', and his coming throws a
fierce light on the whole dream situation. Ironically he is himself a
smuggler and slave-dealer, plying among the islands for merchandise
to sell to the Turks. This is a Byronic existential complication: he
arrives on the scene just as the family poet, himself 'a sad trimmer',[32]
sings the famous 'Isles of Greece' song. We are in a world not of
make-believe but of hedgings, of provisional commitments and
rhetorical declarations in which a love so childlike as that of Juan
and Haidée has no chance to survive. Their world is a dream world
precisely because it is the natural world. In the realm of artifice
which has been man's habitat since the Fall, there is no room for
simple passion or childlike trust.

> They should have lived together deep in woods,
>   Unseen as sings the nightingale; they were
> Unfit to mix in these thick solitudes
>   Called social, haunts of Hate, and Vice, and Care;
> How lonely every freeborn creature broods!
>   The sweetest song-birds nestle in a pair;
> The eagle soars alone; the gull and crow
> Flock o'er their carrion, just like men below.   (IV, xxviii)

The natural is the abnormal. 'Here is a place of disaffection/Time
before and time after/In a dim light. . . .' In human society, only the
artificial can survive. Lambro is a curious blend of the natural and
the artificial. Byron describes him as 'an old man, who lived upon
the water'—an Old Man of the Sea, then—at a very early point in
the episode (II, cxxiv). With subtle touches here and there Byron
prepares us for his coming over three Cantos—he is 'a fisher . . . of
men,/Like Peter the Apostle' (II, cxxvi), Haidée's 'piratical papa,

'... a sea-attorney ... the best of fathers ... the good old gentleman'
(III, xiii–xv), and finally 'a dark eye ... fixed upon the pair' as
Haidée and Juan wake from their last sleep together (IV, xxxv). A
remarkable conflation of archetypes is achieved here: the fisher-king,
Ulysses, God the Father: an adult, male intrusion into the female-
orientated, childhood world of the lovers.

Juan and Haidée wake up to that remorseless eye from a sleep in
which Haidée has a nightmare. The irony of the 'Oh, Hesperus!'
stanza lies in its immediately preceding this nightmare and the
living nightmare of the homecoming of Lambro. Haidée's dream
reaches out into the past, into Juan's shipwreck, his near-death, and
the cave scene which followed it, and into the future, into the
homecoming of her piratical papa. A good deal of Byron's own 1813
nightmares seemed mixed up in it too. 'I awoke from a dream!—
well! and have not others dreamed?', he had written in his Journal
on 23 November, '—Such a dream!—but she did not overtake me.
I wish the dead would rest, however. Ugh! how my blood chilled,—
and I could not wake. . . . I do not like this dream.' Haidée's
nightmare runs:

> She dreamed of being alone on the sea-shore,
>   Chained to a rock; she knew not how, but stir
> She could not from the spot, and the loud roar
>   Grew, and each wave rose roughly, threatening her;
> And o'er her upper lip they seemed to pour,
>   Until she sobbed for breath, and soon they were
> Foaming o'er her lone head, so fierce and high—
> Each broke to drown her, yet she could not die.   (IV, xxxi)

This is dream identification: Haidée enacts her lover's ordeal as he
struggled for life before she reached him.

> Anon—she was released, and then she strayed
>   O'er the sharp shingles with her bleeding feet,
> And stumbled almost every step she made;
>   And something rolled before her in a sheet,
> Which she must still pursue howe'er afraid:
>   'Twas white and indistinct, nor stopped to meet
> Her glance nor grasp, for still she gazed and grasped,
> And ran, but it escaped her as she clasped.   (IV, xxxii)

Here we have a mixture of Byron's 1813 dream with an inversion
of the blissful 'wandering forth ... Over the shining pebbles and
the shells' quoted on p. 305 above. One suspects that Byron has
been deeply involved in some real life situation which provides the
imagery here. The 'something rolled before her in a sheet' seems to

present the 1813 'she did not overtake me' in nightmare reverse:
the shudder is worthy of M. R. James, as the final lines of the
episode, 'the sea dirges low/Rang in her sad ears like a mermaid's
song' bring to mind T. S. Eliot's waking to reality by human voices
from the chambers of the sea.

'One Dies! Alas! the living and dead!'

The harsh masculine world which Lambro brings into the epicene
fantasy of the first six cantos of *Don Juan* gradually gains the
ascendancy as we move away from the sea to the warlike foci of
Central Europe and the frozen banks of the Volga. In terms of this
present study, it is a matter of the final, or *almost* final, triumph of
power over both wisdom and love. This would not be so disastrous
for Byron as a writer if he could have gathered the theme of power
to himself, if he were celebrating some exercise of his own power, or
of some force with which he could identify himself. But it is, alas!
nothing but naked, irrational power. Naked, irrational love, in the
first four cantos, had been a difficult theme enough, though Byron
manages it with aplomb; but it has its deep creative as well as its
deep destructive sides. Naked power is nothing but destructive, and
the time has long gone by when Byron could idealise Napoleon or
Caesar. His letters and journals show his disillusion growing towards
the end of 1819—about love, politics, Europe itself ('an outworn
portion of the globe') and he even contemplates emigrating to
South America. As usual, he is fighting on a number of fronts: with
Murray and his 'committee' for the non-gelding of *Don Juan* ('Don
Juan shall be an entire horse, or none', letter of 19 January to
Hobhouse and Kinnaird), with Count Guiccioli for the possession of
Teresa (letter of 26 July to Augusta), with Teresa for the possession
of his spiritual independence (letter of 23 August to Hobhouse,
quoted above, p. 290), with Augusta for her continued affection, in
one of the most passionate of his letters (17 May):

They say absence destroys weak passions—and confirms strong ones—Alas!
mine for you is the union of all passions and of all affections—Has strengthened itself but will destroy me—I do not speak of *physical* destruction—for I
have endured and can endure much—but of the annihilation of all thoughts,
feelings or hopes.

Yet in the midst of this despondency he can defend the antitheses of
Don Juan with all his old verve and wicked wit:

. . . I will answer your friend C[ohen], who objects to the quick succession
of fun and gravity, as if in that case the gravity did not (in intention, at
least) heighten the fun. His metaphor is, that 'we are never scorched and
drenched at the same time'. Blessings on his experience! Ask him these
questions about 'scorching and drenching'. Did he never play at Cricket, or
walk a mile in hot weather? Did he never spill a dish of tea over his testicles
in handing the cup to his charmer, to the great shame of his nankeen
breeches? Did he never swim in the sea at Noonday with the Sun in his
eyes and on his head, which all the foam of Ocean could not cool? Did he
never draw his foot out of a tub of too hot water, damning his eyes and his
valet's? Did he never inject for a Gonorrhea? or make water through an
ulcerated Urethra? Was he ever in a Turkish bath, that marble paradise
of sherbet and Sodomy? Was he ever in a cauldron of boiling oil, like St
John, or in the sulphureous waves of hell . . .? (Letter of 12 August to
Murray.)

There is, finally, the fight for Italian freedom with which he is
trying to identify himself by supporting the Carbonari (a power
struggle, then, with which he *can* feel himself in sympathy, though he
has no personal ambitions) but here again he is badly let down by
the conspirators' apathy or timidity.

The transition from the sensuous-sentimental reaches of Haidée's
island to the horrific power struggle of the siege of Ismail is brilliantly
managed. The idyll begins and ends with a feast—the fried eggs,
fruit and honey of the initial cave scene, and the 'pilaus and meats of
all sorts . . . and flasks of Samian and of Chian wine' of the quasi-
nuptial banquet in Lambro's mansion. The theme is Homeric, and
this final scene of joy is suffused with an Homeric gusto. But food
implies killing, life is consequent on death, Haidée has dared to
bring Juan out of his cave into her home because of a report that
her father is dead. But Lambro is very much alive, and in the house,
though his presence is unmarked. Death, that 'gaunt Gourmand'
(XV, ix), is about to resume his sport with Juan. But first he and
Haidée are allowed to sleep, in unsuspecting happiness, when the
banquet is over and the guests have departed. It is in this sleep that
Haidée has her nightmare, and from it that she and Juan wake up to
the confrontation with her father.

The scene of somnolent, luxurious delight immediately explodes
into violence. Juan resists, and is wounded and overcome by twenty
of Lambro's men. Haidée suffers a cerebral haemorrhage, and dies
within a fortnight. That she is with child (IV, lxx) is not merely an
added touch of pathos, but a corollary of the Fall syndrome; the
child 'might/Have dawned a fair and sinless child of sin' (or, as the
MS reading runs, 'a child of beauty, though of sin', which I think is

nearer to Byron's thought) but Destiny forbids. Meanwhile Juan
resumes his career as human merchandise. Lambro's sailors rush
him down to shore immediately after the fight, 'and under hatches,/
They stowed him, with strict order to the watches' (IV, 1). Note how
his progress is relentlessly from trap to trap: Bed, closet, boat, cave,
mansion, ship, slave-market, Seraglio, bed again. The journey to
Constantinople is richly comic. Juan, now a slave, gazes out from
the ship on 'the shores of Ilion' where the mounds still marking
'many a hero's grave' meet his eye. (The irony requires no emphasis.)
His fellow-slaves are a troupe of Italian opera singers, sold to Lambro
by their own impresario while *en route* to an engagement in Sicily.
Byron here draws on his Italian experiences as in his description of
the Troad he draws upon his old Levantine pilgrimage. With jokes
about *castrati*, prima donnas, pretty lads bursting with conceit, and
the buffo Raucocanti's boundless egotism, even in chains, the point
of impotence is pressed home. As they approach the Sublime Porte,
Raucocanti is chained to his most hated rival, the tenor, and Juan
is fettered to 'a Bacchante blooming visage', a foretaste of the enforced amours of his next avatar.

The stanzas on fame which are intercalated into the narrative at
this point (IV, xcvii–cxii) bring the theme of power home to
Byron in a personal sense. The discussion is goodhumoured, ranging
through Byron's ample gamut of tones, first mocking:

> the publisher declares, in sooth,
> Through needles' eyes it easier for the camel is
> To pass, than these two cantos into families   (IV, xcvii)

—then knuckle-rapping:

> [I] recollect the time when all this cant
> Would have provoked remarks—which now it shan't   (IV, xcviii)

—then pathetic:

> Whether my verse's fame be doomed to cease,
> While the right hand which wrote it still is able,
>   Or of some centuries to take a lease;
> The grass upon my grave will grow as long,
> And sigh to midnight winds, but not to song   (IV, xcix)

—then judicial:

> And so great names are nothing more than nominal,
>   And love of Glory's but an airy lust,
> Too often in its fury overcoming all
>   Who would as 't were identify their dust

From out the wide destruction, which, entombing all,
      Leaves nothing till 'the coming of the just'—
Save change: I've stood upon Achilles' tomb,
And heard Troy doubted; Time will doubt of Rome   (IV, ci)

—then scabrously realistic, in its picture of the monument to De
Foix:

A broken pillar, not uncouthly hewn,
      But which Neglect is hastening to destroy,
Records Ravenna's carnage on its face,
While weeds and ordure rankle round the base   (IV, ciii)

—with a return to the personal in what is the most powerful apologia
Byron ever made for his life and art:

If in the course of such a life as was
      At once adventurous and contemplative,
Men who partake all passions as they pass,
      Acquire the deep and bitter power to give
Their images again as in a glass,
      And in such colours that they seem to live;
You may do right forbidding them to show 'em,
But spoil (I think) a very pretty poem.   (IV, cvii)

The theme of the first Act of *Don Juan* is eating and being eaten;
that of the second is buying and selling.[33] Exposed for sale in the
Istanbul slave-market, Juan finds himself at the side of an Englishman, a soldier of fortune named Johnson,

A man of thirty, rather stout and hale,
With resolution in his dark grey eye,   (V, x)

who treats Juan, as they wait to be bought, to an instructive discourse. He commiserates Juan's sorrow at the loss of Haidée and
freedom, but reminds him subtly that his love for Haidée was itself
a species of slavery, among the many which life brings.

'Love's the first net which spreads its deadly mesh;
      Ambition, Avarice, Vengeance, Glory, glue
The glittering lime-twigs of our latter days,
Where still we flutter on for pence or praise.'   (V, xxii)

'For pence or praise' effects a modulation from the trap motif to
that of purchase; but Byron is not content to leave the transition
there, he brings in the theme of eating as well. The merchant, who
has sold Juan and Johnson to the black eunuch, goes home to dine.
'I wonder if his appetite was good?', Byron muses: does conscience

ever ask him the 'curious sort of question . . . how far we should/
Sell flesh and blood' (V, xxx).

> I think with Alexander, that the act
>   Of eating, with another act or two,
> Makes us feel our mortality in fact
>   Redoubled . . .   (V, xxxii)

What John Johnson, a 'rough moralist' like his great namesake
(whom Byron so much admired), is in fact suggesting, is a connection
of Juan's pleasant life of love and feasting on Haidée's island with
its origins in Lambro's slave dealing: and, beyond this, with the
mercantile laws which govern all human intercourse:

> 'Tis pleasant purchasing our fellow-creatures;
>   And all are to be sold, if you consider
>   Their passions, and are dext'rous; some by features
> Are bought up, others by a warlike leader,
>   Some by a place—as tend their years or natures:
> The most by ready cash—but all have prices,
> From crowns to kicks, according to their vices.   (V, xxvii)

The stanza sums up the buying-selling episodes of the succeeding
action: the Sultana, herself a buyer, is nevertheless bought by Juan's
'features', while Juan is later bought by the leaders Lascy and
Souvaroff, and by the 'place' offered him in exchange for his sexual
services by the Empress Catherine.

Thus the Seraglio episode, coming as it does at the exact centre of
the poem as we have it, forms a species of knot or vortex into which
all the themes of the poem, past and future, are tightly woven.
Byron likes this recapitulation technique: he employs it again in the
Norman Abbey sequences at the end of the poem.[34] The palace is a
labyrinthine combination of all the earlier and later traps, a con-
catenation of caverns, corridors, closets, beds, fortresses, prisons; it
can even be seen as a slave-ship, riding high over the Golden Horn;
hemmed in by its cypresses, it is also a tomb. The first thing Juan
senses is its inhumanity, its deathlike solitude. We remember that
the claustrophobic Venetian plays are being written *pari passu* with
Cantos IV, V and VI. The 'strange firefly' caught in the 'enormous
spider's net' in *The Two Foscari* might stand for Juan entangled in
the Seraglio love–power complexities. He is here, emphatically, the
love-victim; his very masculinity is threatened when the eunuch
Baba dresses him in female garments and menaces him with
castration (V, lxxv). The Seraglio is a Lesbian world, in which

Juan's hermaphroditism offers a mild titillation to Gulbeyaz' sexual palate. The 'gigantic portal' guarding her chamber is the sexual organ itself, drawing him in as spilt spermatozoon, a dribble from the rent island intercourse: individuality is lost in the 'devouring winding sheet' of 'the Sexual Garments'.

> Some find a Female Garment there,
> And some a Male, woven with care.

The sexual strife reaches its climax in the 'address to the throne' stanzas of Canto IX, the apotheosis of the vulva: a comic extrapolation which I leave for later scrutiny in a survey of the total 'love' theme in *Don Juan*.

'Round me flew the Flaming Sword'

I opened this discussion of *Don Juan* by stressing the 'dream' aspect of the poem. But 'dream' itself has a double connotation. Man lives from a dream, the hidden world of the archetypes, but he also lives in a dream, the illusory world of his own conscious desires, drives and pretences. 'Not here the darkness, in this twittering world.' This is the world, in Canto I, of Donna Inez and Donna Julia. Juan himself is too innocent, too 'natural', to belong to this world. But as the narrative proceeds from Haidée's island to the Seraglio, from the Seraglio to the Siege of Ismail, and on into the corrupt societies of St Petersburg and London, Juan's innocence (which is a matter not of principle but of being) is gradually eroded. At the beginning of the Siege he is still a child:

> And here he was—who upon Woman's breast
> Even from a child, felt like a child . . .   (VIII, liii)

and hates cruelty 'at a distance'. But the violence he has already experienced in the shipwreck, at the hands of Lambro's men, on the slaveship, and in the Seraglio, has its corrupting effect upon him. This is the danger run by a purely 'natural' innocence without principles—the 'unorganis'd innocence' which Blake said was better called ignorance. Juan is 'A thing of impulse and a child of song', delighting in 'sensation'. At one moment it may be a sensation (Byron underlines the word) of joy and kindliness—but it can change in a flash:

And afterward, if he must needs destroy,
    In such good company as always throng
To battles, sieges, and that kind of pleasure,
No less delighted to employ his leisure;

But always without malice: if he warred
    Or loved, it was with what we call 'the best
Intentions', which form all Mankind's *trump card*,
To be produced when brought up to the test.

                                                                (VIII, xxiv–xxv)

In insisting, as he so often did in letters to his publisher and his
friends, that basically *Don Juan* is the most moral of poems, Byron
was stating no more than the truth. Its analysis of the human
condition in all its weakness and its deviousness, is immensely more
complex and far-reaching than anything we find in *Paradise Lost* or
The Excursion or *The Faerie Queene*.

    Among the major figures of the archetypal dream world, Juan is
himself the Magic Child, Inez–Julia–Haidée the Anima (the Virgin
Mother, Eve, Lilith and Mary), while the Father, the Wise Old
Man, is represented by Don José, Lambro, the Sultan and Johnson.
All these figures are awash in 'the corrupted currents of this world',
the waking dream world of obsessed passions and ambitions. 'Men
and bits of paper, whirled by the cold wind/That blows before and
after time.' Juan's father is plainly inadequate, as is the Sultan;
Lambro and Johnson are competent in the extreme, but their
competence is flawed by defects of incomprehension and ambition.
Inez, Julia and Haidée all 'love' Juan with a maternal-virginal love,
subtly infected with selfishness, with 'storgous' demands. Juan
himself is a puppet, a pipe at the mercy of 'fortune's finger, to
sound what stop she please'. He can be corrupted, but has small
possibility of growth. He learns nothing from his experiences,
except as an insect might learn, in the laboratory, to avoid channels
in the maze which are superheated, or doorways which inflict
electric shocks.

    The Siege of Ismail occupies much of Canto VII and the whole of
Canto VIII. Its horrors, like those of the shipwreck, are set out with
great spirit and with the same reliance on the actual words of
documentary sources. The battle is introduced at the end of Canto
VII with a night-piece which recalls *The Siege of Corinth* (VIII, i and
ii) and the Eve of Waterloo stanzas of *Childe Harold* (III, xxi–xxvi).
Byron is always at his best in these scenes of suspense. It is as though
the provisional, crisis-ridden texture of his own personal existence

finds a catharsis here, just as its suppressed violence emerges in the
scenes of carnage, and its compassion in, for instance, the rescue of
the little Turkish girl, Leila (VIII, xci–cii). Leila is about to be
slaughtered by 'two villanous Cossacques': the scene affords scope
for one of Byron's favourite themes, the comparison of men with
animals:[35]

> matched with *them*,
> The rudest brute that roams Siberia's wild
> Has feelings pure and polished as a gem,—
> The bear is civilised, the wolf is mild;
> And whom for this at last must we condemn?
> Their natures? or their sovereigns, who employ
> All arts to teach their subjects to destroy?   (VIII, xcii)

A rhetorical question? Perhaps: but by the skilful use of just such
marginal comments Byron constantly opens up his bustling foreground into vistas of social, political, ethical speculation.

The insufficiency of John Johnson as Wise Old Man, as guide
through the hell of Ismail, is demonstrated in this episode. Juan, the
resourceful hero, has routed the two Cossacks in the nick of time;
as he lifts the little girl from among the heap of corpses,

> Up Johnson came, with hundreds at his back,
> Exclaiming—'Juan! Juan! On, boy! brace
> Your arm, and I'll bet Moscow to a dollar
> That you and I will win St George's collar.'   (VIII, xcvii)

The motives of violence, money and ambition thrust themselves
into the momentarily tender sphere of rescue. Juan refuses to leave
the child he has saved. Johnson urges him to 'choose between fame
and feelings, pride and pity' (the alliteration emphasises the
rigidity of the choice). But 'Juan was immoveable': not until Leila
is placed in safety will he consent to press on with Johnson. Here, for
once, Juan asserts himself: and I cannot help reading the episode as
a symbolic reversal of the guilt of the Giaour. As far as I can follow
the plot of *The Giaour*, the hero of that poem arrives on the scene too
late to save *his* Leila—detained, it seems, by the prosecution of a
personal vendetta against the Turks. She is murdered; and the
Giaour's remaining years are consumed in grief and guilt. In
devising the Leila episode of *Don Juan* Byron rewrites the drama—
which in some deep sense is, as we have seen, his own drama—and
so purges his guilt. It is noteworthy that the guilt theme which has
dogged him from his Pilgrimage years now recedes from his letters,
his journals and his poetry.

Field-Marshal Souvaroff, another father figure, is John Johnson on the grand scale. He combines Johnson's practical expertise with Lambro's cool sagacity, and projects both on to the international, one might almost say the cosmic, screen. Ali Pasha, the most terrific of Byron's Wise Old Men, was simply a monster of duplicity and cruelty: there was nothing in him to admire except his completeness of evil. Souvaroff, another monster, is presented as a figure of what can only be called personal charm. He is the Readeian 'resourceful hero'[36] *in excelsis*, always alert, always competent, always *présent au présent*. He arrives on the scene in response to a letter from Prince Potemkin—surely the briefest in military history—'Vous prendrez Ismail à quel prix que ce soit'! The letter leads Byron into one of his sombre discourses on the evils of war.

> 'Let there be Light!', said God, 'and there was Light!'
> 'Let there be Blood!' says man, and there's a sea!
> The fiat of this spoiled child of the Night
>   (For Day ne'er saw his merits) could decree
> More evil in an hour, than thirty bright
>   Summers could renovate, though they should be
> Lovely as those which ripened Eden's fruit;
> For War cuts up not only branch, but root   (VII, xli)[37]

It is responsible comment such as this on the greatest of human evils which must, surely, help us to revise our estimate of Byron as a serious thinker. To readers of Byron's own day, fighting the Napoleonic wars, and of Victorian and Edwardian and Georgian days, pursuing war as a matter of Imperial policy, such attitudes as Byron, Blake and Shelley took up were simply unacceptable. How much pleasanter, how much more *poetic*, was the delicate retreatism of Wordsworth, Coleridge and Keats![38] I have already quoted Coleridge on *his* reactions to 'the taking of a city';[39] Byron himself pokes devastating fun at Wordsworth:

> 'Carnage' (so Wordsworth tells you) 'is God's daughter:'
> If *he* speak truth, she is Christ's sister, and
> Just now behaved as in the Holy Land. . . .   (VIII, ix)

and annotates:

> But *Thy** most dreaded instrument
> In working out a pure intent,
> Is Man—arrayed for mutal slaughter,—
> Yea, *Carnage is thy daughter*!   (Wordsworth's *Thanksgiving Ode*)

*To wit, the Deity's: this is perhaps as pretty a pedigree for murder as ever was found out by Garter King at Arms.—What would have been said, had any free-spoken people discovered such a lineage?

With all one's reverence for the great Wordsworth of *The Prelude* and the incomparable lyrics, and for the great Coleridge of *The Ancient Mariner* and the two or three other masterpieces, one has to recognise, I think, that where non-parochial affairs are concerned Byron is relevant and they are not; and that their isolation and rejection of involvement warped them into fatuities, or worse, whenever they felt called upon, as 'bards', to comment on the passing show. Byron saw them as renegades too: we don't have to make this judgement to recognise that he was right in his basic criticism that they were simply not *au fait* with European political or social affairs; and, what is worse, that their self-centredness cut them off from the real human agonies of their age—and any age. Wordsworth's 'Still sad music of humanity, not harsh or grating' is drowned by the howls, screams, curses of the dying at Ismail.[40]

To return to Souvaroff. Among the many eikons of power in the Byronic picture-gallery he is perhaps the most interesting. Ali Pasha was a puzzle to the young Byron: the tiger hidden beneath the lamb. Souvaroff is not disguised. He is there, frankly, as *what* he is—a daimonic energy in human form, a 'great man'. Before he arrives on the scene, morale is low. Ismail seems inpregnable. But now—

> The whole camp rung with joy; you would have thought
>   That they were going to a marriage feast
> (This metaphor, I think, holds good as aught,
>   Since there is discord after both at least):
> There was not now a luggage boy but sought
>   Danger and spoil with ardour much increased;
> And why? because a little—odd—old man,
> Stript to his shirt, was come to lead the van.   (VII, xlix)

Souvaroff is the pure professional—a type which has become commoner in our days, perhaps, than in Byron's: the executive machine, devoid of personal morals, even of personal ambition, a psyche reduced to its kinetic elements, with value judgements and the human emotions eliminated. The commissar of *Darkness at Noon*, perhaps with an enormous military competence superimposed.[41]

Souvaroff is a 'great man' but not of the order of Napoleon or Wellington. No orders, no decorations, no 'side'. Just competence. He drills his troops, sergeant-major-like, as Byron was to do at Missolonghi. His simplicity results in, or from, a kind of disruption of those elements of personality which most of us have moulded into a smooth carapace over the years:

Suwarrow chiefly was on the alert,
    Surveying, drilling, ordering, jesting, pondering;
For the man was, we safely may assert,
    A thing to wonder at beyond most wondering;
Hero, buffoon, half-demon, and half-dirt,
    Praying, instructing, desolating, plundering—
Now Mars, now Momus—and when bent to storm
A fortress, Harlequin in uniform.   (VII, lv)

This is very close to Lear's 'unaccommodated man'. Souvaroff is pure machine, a powerful servant of power, a projection into the military field of the black eunuch and the black dwarfs of the Seraglio episode. This is an imperial game of chess. The more powerful chess pieces also play multiple roles, attacking, defending, threatening, sacrificing themselves and others, feinting, 'doubling'. Souvaroff exists only in terms of his military function—we cannot imagine him as having a private life: he is the executive. As such he is clearly very interesting for Byron, always on the alert for the extremes of human character. And here too the 'extremes meet': his inhumanity as a military machine is curiously fused with his *practical* humanity as an organiser. There is nothing in the least sadistic about him; provided no military objectives are jeopardised, he can be understanding ('Right! I was busy, and forgot!'), courteous to the 'two Turkish ladies' who have helped Juan and Johnson to escape from the Seraglio ('They shall be shown/All the attention possible, and seen/In safety to the wagons, where alone/In fact they can be safe',) but finally lacking in the 'minute particulars' of compassion ('What was't to him to hear two women sob?/Nothing.') (VII, lxxvii). The love-interest of the first six cantos is now swamped in the morass of war.

'A devouring Winding sheet'

Love narrows drastically to sex in the later reaches of *Don Juan*.[42] And it is cold, calculated sex, orientated towards petty motifs of power and status, disguising itself under the various masks of sensibility, prudence, idealism and benevolence. The unbridled sexual voracity of Catherine holds a certain savage grandeur; but the English cantos introduce us to a shadow world of shifts and subterfuges. The Duchess of Fitz-Fulke is the nearest we come in Cantos XIII–XVII to Catherine's exuberance and amorality: but even she is driven to disguise in her approach to the seduction of

Juan; and that the disguise should be a religious one has its relevance.
Lady Adeline's interest in Juan is disguised even from herself.
Aurora Raby's role is dubious: the poem breaks off just as we are
getting interested. She is presented as a point of crystalline purity
and integrity within the swirling currents of intrigue and compromise
which knit the texture of these concluding Cantos: but she may be
more complex than she appears at first sight. She belongs to 'that
High World' of selfless devotion which Byron had evoked in
Hebrew Melodies:

> The worlds beyond this World's perplexing waste
> > Had more of her existence, for in her
> There was a depth of feeling to embrace
> Thoughts, boundless, deep, but silent too as Space.   (XVI, xlviii)

But is there not a touch in that 'silent too as Space' of the icy
solitudes of 'When Coldness wraps this suffering clay'? Byron, and,
perhaps we are meant to assume, subconsciously Juan also, compares
Aurora with Haidée:

> . . . each was radiant in her proper sphere:
> > The island girl, bred up by the lone sea,
> More warm, as lovely, and not less sincere,
> > Was Nature's all: Aurora could not be,
> Nor would be thus:—the difference in them
> Was such as lies between a flower and gem   (XV, lviii)

—a comparison which tells us all we need to know.

The sea which washed Haidée's island is absent from the inland
wastes of the last four Cantos. Yet not entirely so. By a subtle stroke
of his incorrigibly analogising imagination, Byron restores the sea
in its feminine aspect through an identification of this world of
women, this 'gynocracy' (XII, lxvi; XVI, lii), with the prolific/
voracious, superficially entrancing/potentially destructive powers of
the ocean. It is worth following the development of this image
through the later Cantos. The theme, dropped since the Seraglio
episode, reappears in the Catherine imbroglio:

> What a strange thing is Man! and what a stranger
> > Is Woman! What a whirlwind is her head,
> And what a whirlpool full of depth and danger
> > Is all the rest about her!   (IX, lxiv)

and is boldly amplified in the London cantos. English women may
be rather cold, 'But after all they are a North–West Passage/Unto
the glowing India of the soul', and (Byron adds ironically) 'young

beginners may as well commence/With quiet cruising o'er the ocean woman' (XIII, xxxix–xl).

'Perched on a promontory' (XV, xix) overlooking 'the ocean, Woman', Byron, now a mere spectator (XIII, vii), takes stock of its gulfs and shallows. 'There was Miss Millpond, smooth as summer's sea' (the latest projection of Annabella), who seems harmless enough, but *caveat nauta*! (XV, xli). Aurora Raby has more in common with the depths of space than those of the sea; nevertheless, her complexion is described as 'always clear,/As deep seas in a sunny atmosphere' (XVI, xciv). Adeline is concerned with her 'lord's, son's, or similar connection's/Safe conduct through the rocks of re-elections' (xcv).

About all these women there is a certain ambiguity: 'they are like virtuous mermaids, whose/Beginnings are fair faces, ends mere fishes' (XII, lxxiii). Women *are* the ocean, *express* thalassic powers as mermaids and fishes, and *carry* the ocean about with them in their wombs. This is a striking anticipation of the thesis of Ferenzci's book *Thalassa*, which sees man's sexual urge as the desire to regress, individually, to the womb and, racially, the sea: to abandon the agonising evolutionary struggle and return to the preconscious and prehuman.

A plausible exegesis of Byron's work could be made along these lines: it would conclude with a 'thalassic' interpretation of *The Island*, Byron's final and major womb poem.[43] Already, in the later *Don Juan*, we are afforded fascinating glimpses of the way his mind is moving. Beneath the factitious rationality of English 'high life', its social and political decorum (to which I shall turn shortly), the deep sexual tides are determining the distribution of the visible shoals and sandbanks. Lord Henry holds forth, boringly, by day; Fitz-Fulke glides from darkened chamber to chamber, excitingly, by night. In search of her mystery Juan, prompted by 'the rippling sound of the lake's billow' beneath his 'Gothic chamber' (XVI, xv), traverses Lara's long gallery where 'voices from the urn/Appear to wake' (xviii) and his memory reverts to a former idyll:

> And the pale smile of Beauties in the grave,
>   The charms of other days, in starlight gleams,
> Glimmer on high; their buried locks still wave
>   Along the canvas; their eyes glance like dreams
> On ours, or spars within some dusky cave,
>   But Death is imaged in their shadowy beams.   (XVI, xix)

'The dance along the artery/The circulation of the lymph/Are

figured in the drift of stars/Ascend to summer in the tree.' Death:
sea: cave—the syndrome persists. But what is Fitz-Fulke, the
ambulant mystery? Precisely that complex of life and death, of
amniotic sea and emergent individuality which is the womb.
'Voices from the urn' sound in Juan's ears, another pregnant ambiguity. They proclaim, but they also invite, entice back to the
cave—death, the womb-life. Fitz-Fulke blatantly, but also Adeline
and Haidée and Aurora in different gradations of subtlety, are
moving wombs, living organisms built around the voracious matrix.
The theme is first sounded in its starkness in the amusing address to
the vulva in Canto IX which Byron composes as a fantasia above the
ground-bass of Horace's 'O tu teterrima causa':[44]

> O thou 'teterrima causa' of all 'belli'—
>   Thou gate of Life and Death—thou nondescript!
> Whence is our exit and our entrance,—well I
>   May pause in pondering how all souls are dipped
> In thy perennial fountain:—how man *fell*, I
>   Know not, since Knowledge saw her branches stripped
> Of her first fruit; but how he *falls* and rises
> Since,—*thou* hast settled beyond all surmises.
>
> Some call thee 'the *worst* cause of War,' but I
>   Maintain thou art the *best*: for after all
> From thee we come, to thee we go, and why
>   To get at thee not batter down a wall,
> Or waste a World? since no one can deny
>   Thou dost replenish worlds both great and small:
> With—or without thee—all things at a stand
> Are, or would be, thou sea of Life's dry land!   (IX, lv–lvi)

The naughtiness of the play on 'stand' and 'fall' should not divert
us from the serious Fall theme which, running as it does through
the whole of *Don Juan*, is here narrowed to a specifically sexual
context which will persist through the remaining Cantos with little
relief from Nature's benisons or even from man's inhumanity to man.
'Elle vous suit partout.' Julia's ominous 'elle' has now caught up
with Juan, and her plaintive

> 'Man's love is of man's life a thing apart,
>   'Tis Woman's whole existence; Man may range . . .'
>   (I, cxciv)

is seen for what it is, a piece of devastating irony. Man may range;
but not very far. For wherever he ranges, it is within 'the gynocracy'. Whether he 'stands' or 'falls', it is within the ambience
of the 'perennial fountain' which is also the universal grave. The

ambiguities here remind me forcibly of the 'Lines Inscribed upon a
Cup formed from a Skull'[45] and the analogous stanzas of *Childe
Harold* II. Compare the use of 'wall' and 'waste' there with the
conceits here: wall as the ramparts of Troy and hymen, 'waste a
world' as the destruction of Troy and the death of millions of
spermatozoa. 'Life' is a dry land, a Waste Land: we plunge into
'the ocean woman' as a refuge from life, from its dry and dusty
duties, its exhausting claims upon us.[46] 'Die' is a seventeenth-
century euphemism for the sexual act: and this is one of the great
'metaphysical' moments of *Don Juan*. It is the 'low dream' and the
low world of sexual fulfilment asserted against the 'high dream' and
the 'High World' of total realisation; beneath the brilliantly funny
phrasing we detect the bitterness of defeat.

In addressing the organ Byron severs it from the woman and thus
from its total human context. At this point the poem's swing over
from 'love' to 'sex' is effected. The apostrophe ushers in the Empress
Catherine episode (IX, lvii–X, xlviii) where Juan first knows
commercial sex: commercial in the sense that beside being bought
he is himself a buyer. Catherine is 'the grand epitome/Of that great
cause of war'. She swallows lovers as she swallows kingdoms. Juan
'loves' her through 'self-love' (IX, lxviii); Catherine 'loves' him
with 'temporary passion' (lxx). The sea image re-enters the narrative
in the ignoble guise of refrigerator: Juan is 'of that delighted age'
when all women are equally attractive, that is, reduce themselves to
pure vulva:

> We don't much care with whom we may engage,
>   As bold as Daniel in the lions' den,
> So that we can our native sun assuage
>   In the next ocean, which may flow just then—
> To make a *twilight* in, just as Sol's heat is
> Quenched in the lap of the salt sea, or Thetis.   (IX, lxix)

At least four of Byron's major sanctities are desecrated here: sun,
sea, Scripture, twilight.[47] We proceed (in stanzas lxxiii–lxxvi) to an
excursus on love which for the first time in the poem stresses the
absurdity of the act, that 'trivial and vulgar way of coition' whose
folly had impressed, among others, Sir Thomas Browne. The love-
illusion itself is charming; but how uncharming the sequel.

> How beautiful that moment! and how odd is
>   That fever which precedes the languid rout
> Of our sensations! What a curious way
> The whole thing is of clothing souls in clay!   (IX, lxxv)

Byron had gone into 'the whole thing' in more detail in *Cain* (II, i, 48–60):

> *Cain.* I should be proud of thought
>   Which knew such things [as the secrets of the universe].
> *Lucifer.*   But if that high thought were
>   Link'd to a servile mass of matter, and,
>   Knowing such things, aspiring to such things,
>   And science still beyond them, were chain'd down
>   To the most gross and petty paltry wants,
>   All foul and fulsome, and the very best
>   Of thine enjoyments a sweet degradation,
>   A most enervating and filthy cheat
>   To lure thee on to the renewal of
>   Fresh souls and bodies, all foredoom'd to be
>   As frail, and few so happy . . .

The spirit/clay paradox lies behind a good deal of Byron's thinking, and in its sexual application can be traced as far back as the 1813 journal:

> It seems strange; a true voluptuary will never abandon his mind to the grossness of reality. It is by exalting the earthly, the material, the *physique* of our pleasures, by veiling these ideas, by forgetting them altogether, or, at least, never naming them hardly to one's self, that we alone can prevent them from disgusting (13 December 1813).

Part of the moral purpose of *Don Juan* was to name these ideas, to strip the veil from the face of horrid reality. And this, Byron told Murray, was what Teresa objected to when she begged him not to go on with *Don Juan*. 'The truth is that *it is* TOO TRUE, and the women hate every thing which strips off the tinsel of *Sentiment*; and they are right, as it would rob them of their weapons' (Letter of 12 October 1820).

Despite Teresa's protests, and a promise to discontinue *Don Juan* which he was not able to keep,[48] Byron proceeded to strip off more of the tinsel of sentiment. Juan's situation in Catherine's court reproduces Juan's in Haidée's cave, but in a cynical key. The successive exhaustions (X, xl) of shipwreck and love-affair are now repeated in the guise of warfare and 'royalty's vast arms' (xxxvii). 'The trilling wire in the blood/Sings below inveterate scars/Appeasing long forgotten wars.' There is an echo from even further back in the story: Julia's sentimental letter is paralleled by a letter Juan now receives from his mother, replete with hypocrisy (a deity which Juan apostrophises in stanza xxxiv) and the recommendation of dissimulation (xxxii). Donna Inez has remarried (sex has had its way with her too) and there is a new little boy to be brought up along the educational lines which have proved so effective with Juan. By a masterly stroke, Inez praises 'the empress's *maternal* love', which is not very different in voracity, Byron implies by his underlining, from his mother's 'storgous appetite'.

A survey of the sustained apostrophes which punctuate the course of *Don Juan* is a revealing exercise.[49] They are all addressed to love, and strike the keynotes of the successive episodes. Irony runs through them, and is steadily amplified up to the final 'O thou "teterrima causa" . . .!' The series begins with a quotation from Campbell:

> 'Oh Love! in such a wilderness as this,
>   Where Transport and Security entwine,
> Here is the Empire of thy perfect bliss,
>   And here thou art a God indeed divine.'
> The bard I quote from does not sing amiss . . .   (I, lxxxviii)

The fact that he *is* quoting, and that he proceeds to comment on the value of the quotation, constitutes the initial irony. This is love *in excelsis*, as it were, on which Byron feels himself unworthy to expatiate. Next comes love Platonic, in stanza I, cxvi: 'Oh Plato! Plato! you have paved the way,/With your confounded fantasies. . . .' The tone is rueful, slightly exasperated. In 'No more—no more, Oh! never more, my heart,/Canst thou be my sole world, my universe!' (I, ccxv) the two previous invocations are given a personal turn. This broadens to the historical in 'Oh, Love! of whom great Caesar was the suitor . . .' (II, ccv) and contemplates love *as* power and even wisdom: 'Thou mak'st philosophers . . .' (II, ccvii). The idyllic Haidée episode evokes a tragic apostrophe; Eliot's 'Chill/ Fingers of yew . . . curled/Down on us' are anticipated in

> Oh, Love! what is it in this world of ours
>   Which makes it fatal to be loved? Ah why
> With cypress branches hast thou wreathed thy bowers,
>   And made thy best interpreter a sigh?   (III, ii)

and the irony of 'Oh, Hesperus! thou bringest all good things . . .' (III, cvii) with its emphasis on human relationship and parental love is infused with deep pathos. The quotation from or paraphrase of Sappho here balances and corrects the Campbell complacency (note the echo of Campbell's 'wreathed' in Byron's 'entwine', 'this world of ours' in 'such a wilderness as this', and 'a sigh' in 'perfect bliss'). 'In my end is my beginning': the two apostrophes perfectly contain the first great movement of the poem, where Juan can still be seen as 'innocent'.

The second movement opens at the poem's mid-point (on a rough stanza count) with a significant collocation of Love and Glory. Love existing in its own right is no longer the theme.

> O Love! O Glory! what are ye who fly
>   Around us ever, rarely to alight?   (VII, i)

We are about to pass into the brutal power world of the siege of Ismail and its sequel, where love is corrupted to lust. In 'Oh, thou eternal Homer!' (VII, lxxix) the apostrophe implicitly recognises the right of violence to exist 'wreathed' with love, and the two siege cantos lead directly into the power-lust world in which the devouring vulva is the sardonic centre. On the 'teterrima causa' I have already sufficiently commented. This is the last of Byron's addresses to the *mater hominum et deorum*, though the poem is scarce half finished. It is followed by an apostrophe to Catherine:

> Oh Catherine! (for of all interjections,
>   To thee both *oh*! and *ah*! belong, of right,
> In Love and War). . . .   (IX, lxv)[50]

—where the identification of the empress with the vulva is undisguised, and the reflective passage (lxxiii–lxxvi) which follows sums up the themes of all the preceding apostrophes. First Campbell is confuted:

> And that's enough, for Love is vanity,
>   Selfish in its beginning as its end . . .

Next, his own 'Oh never more, my heart . . .' in

> Except where 'tis a mere insanity,
>   A maddening spirit which would strive to blend
> Itself with Beauty's frail inanity . . .

Then, the philosophers:

> And hence some heathenish philosophers
> Make Love the main-spring of the Universe.

Platonic love, divine love, marital love, even cicisbean love (poor Teresa!) are next deflated, together with the exigences of the sexual impulse:

> Besides Platonic love, besides the love
>   Of God, the love of sentiment, the loving
> Of faithful pairs . . . besides all these pretences
> To Love, there are those things which words name senses;

Those movements, those improvements in our bodies
      Which make all bodies anxious to get out
Of their own sand-pits, to mix with a goddess,
      For such all women are at first no doubt. . . .

The third sort to be noted in our chronicle
      As flourishing in every Christian land,
Is, when chaste matrons to their other ties
      Add what may be called *marriage in disguise*.   (IX, lxxiii–lxxvi)

And at this point the invocations to love terminate. In fact all apostrophes terminate, with the exception of the passing invocation to gold in Canto XII, iii, and the longer address to death in Canto XV, viii–ix, which is itself implicated in the commercial-political-social complex which encroaches like a cancer on the hitherto vigorous natural growth of Juan's life-pattern.

The real/unreal love antithesis is vigorously and brilliantly pursued through the six final cantos, which examine the Regency scene in England in the light of all that Byron/Juan has experienced in his earlier avatars. The initial excursus on Berkeley in Canto XI poses the real/unreal theme philosophically. Doubt is the 'sole prism/Of the Truth's rays' (ii)[51] but Byron begs pathetically to be allowed to drink his dram of 'Heaven's brandy', illusion, undisturbed. Of course it won't do: reality keeps breaking in.

'One is slain & One is fled'

It breaks in first, and rather oddly, in Byron/Juan's encounter with the highwayman on Shooter's Hill. Juan kills the highwayman, and in so doing kills something vital in himself. In a sense the highwayman episode is the last gasp of the old spontaneous Juan: in commanding him to 'Stand and deliver!' the robber seeks to rid Juan of his money, his worldly baggage; but Juan, who is now Catherine's Juan, shoots him down. He tries to succour him,

But ere they could perform this pious duty,
      The dying man cried, 'Hold! I've got my gruel!
Oh! for a glass of *max*! We've miss'd our booty;
      Let me die where I am!' And as the fuel
Of Life shrunk in his heart, and thick and sooty
      The drops fell from his death-wound, and he drew ill
His breath,—he from his swelling throat untied
A kerchief, crying, 'Give Sal that!'—and died.   (XI, xvi)

The Gospel story is here reversed: it is the dying thief who offers the protagonist a chance of Paradise in carrying out his last, very human, request.

> The cravat stained with bloody drops fell down
>> Before Don Juan's feet: he could not tell
> Exactly why it was before him thrown,
>> Nor what the meaning of the man's farewell.　(XI, xvii)

So Juan fails to respond. To track down 'Sal', even if he had grasped 'the meaning of the man's farewell', would have been an impossible labour, as impossible as recovering the original innocence of Haidée's island.

So Juan proceeds, 'in pleasure and in pride' (a new dimension of Julia's blessing/curse letter opens up here) to his final avatar; final, at least, as far as the epic goes before the author/hero's death cuts it short. England opens up dimensions of cant inconceivable in Spain, Greece, Turkey or Russia. His 'Chariot, rolling like a drum/In thunder, *holds the way it can't well miss*' (my italics)

> Through Groves, so called as being void of trees,
>> (Like *lucus* from *no* light); through prospects named
> Mount Pleasant, as containing nought to please,
>> Nor much to climb; through little boxes framed
> Of bricks, to let the dust in at your ease,
>> With 'To be let,' upon their doors proclaimed;
> Through 'Rows' most modestly called 'Paradise',
> Which Eve might quit without much sacrifice.　(XI, xxi)

The thundering 'chariot' rolls down chartered streets; the names of 'rows' and 'prospects' mock the reality; the Paradise theme, hitherto Byron's basic myth, is degraded. We are thus prepared for the curious sphere of masks, of make-believe, into which Juan is to be projected: 'while the world moves/In appetency, on its metalled ways/Of time past and time future'.

Even Britain's sacred places have now been devalued. Only if we have fully realised the significance of 'this grace dissolved in place' for the earlier Byron can we appreciate the bitter flavour of Byron's comments on Westminster Abbey as a repository of worthless reputations. 'Here is a place of disaffection':

> The Druids' groves are gone—so much the better:
>> Stonehenge is not—but what the devil is it?—
> But Bedlam still exists with its sage fetter,
>> That madmen may not bite you on a visit;

> The Bench too seats or suits full many a debtor;
>   The Mansion House, too (though some people quiz it),
> To me appears a stiff yet grand erection;
>   But then the Abbey's worth the whole collection.   (XI, xxv)

The sexual play on words set up in the 'teterrima belli causa' stanzas of Canto IX has by now become a major device of the poem: it counterpoints every 'serious' discussion of politics, religion, philosophy with its deflating irony.

The English cantos of Don Juan move through a series of devaluations. The word, with its monetary overtones, is exact. Byron first devalues 'the fashion,/Which serves our thinking people for a passion' (XI, xxxiii), ironically conceding the right of cerebrality (xxxiv) and of 'politicians and their double front,/Who live by lies, yet dare not boldly lie' (xxxvi). For after all what, he asks, is a lie? ''Tis but/The truth in masquerade' (xxxvii), a necessary 'leaven' to the diet of reality so unpalatable to human taste. These final cantos witness the 'stonifying' of the hero as he passes through the icy circles of near-Victorian England, adopting one by one the series of masks Byron details in a letter to John Murray, 16 February 1821, from Ravenna:

I meant to take him the tour of Europe, with a proper mixture of siege, battle, and adventure, and to make him finish as *Anacharsis Cloots* in the French Revolution. To how many cantos this may extend, I know not, nor whether (even if I live) I shall complete it; but this was my notion: I meant to have made him a *Cavalier Servente* in Italy, and a cause for a divorce in England, and a Sentimental 'Werther-faced man' in Germany, so as to show the different ridicules of the society in each of those countries, and to have displayed him gradually *gaté* and *blasé* as he grew older, as is natural. But I had not quite fixed whether to make him end in Hell, or in an unhappy marriage, not knowing which would be the severest. The Spanish tradition says Hell: but it is probably only an Allegory of the other state. You are now in possession of my notions on the subject.

Gaté and *blasé*, Juan now exists as 'our young diplomatic sinner' (XI, xxix); the phrase leads into a passage of telling satire on the Civil Service (xl–xli) which is as relevant to our day as to Byron's. We are treated to a lively survey of the London scene, swinging from 'The Blues, that tender tribe' (l), by way of ten stanzas on the fate of literary reputations (including his own and Keats's), into a brilliant evocation of London night life (lxvi–lxxxi) and *its* parallel fluctuations:

> Where's Brummel? Dished. Where's Long Pole Wellesley?
>   Diddled.

Where's Whitbread? Romilly? Where's George the Third?
Where is his will? (That's not so soon unriddled.)
And where is 'Fum' the Fourth, our 'royal bird'?

(XI, lxxviii)

All this is the social exemplar of that theme of mutability which Byron opposes philosophically to Wordsworth's theorising about nature and aesthetically to Bowles's 'invariable principles of poetry'.

Mutability is the groundnote of Canto XI, 'Driven on the wind that sweeps the gloomy hills of London'. But Canto XII reintroduces us to one of Byron's three major permanences: power. I have tried to show throughout my previous discussion how Byron's triple theme of power/knowledge/love, first stated in the three epigraphs to *Hours of Idleness*, finds interlinking expression in a variety of ways in *Childe Harold*, the Tales, the dramas, the satires, and the minor poems, yet with one function of the triptych uppermost here, another there. *Childe Harold* is primarily a pilgrimage in search of knowledge, self-knowledge. Knowledge, or wisdom, disappears from the Tales, which stress power, often in conflict with love. This love–power nexus persists through the dramas, and wisdom surfaces, only to be quickly submerged, in the incidental poems: the *Prophecy of Dante*, *Darkness*, the *Lament of Tasso*. *The Island* defeats power by the force of a love which is itself an existential wisdom, the triumph of Lawrence's dark gods. Wisdom is totally absent, I should say, from *Don Juan*; it is replaced by mockery of man's pretensions to know anything.

Canto XII sees power in terms, first, of money (i–xii). There is amusing comment on the felicity of misers—'Theirs is the pleasure that can never pall' (iii). 'Jew Rothschild, and his fellow-Christian, Baring', these and other financiers 'hold the balance of the world'— 'Are the true lords of Europe' (v, vi). We have seen the varying circle of Byron's imagery expand from the 'cirque of trees' at Annesley to the bullring of Cadiz, narrow once more to the ring of dancing Suliotes at Loutrakey, expand again to the Coliseum and St Peter's; now it narrows to 'the glittering cirque' of 'ready money', which '*is* Aladdin's lamp' (xii).

'Serpent Reasonings us entice'

With stanza xiii the 'power is love' motif (the Mansion House as 'a stiff yet grand erection') modulates into the 'money is love', or at

least money governs love, which is to be the dominant theme of the
rest of *Don Juan*. The English marriage mart had always fascinated
Byron; it is instructive to place his horrified-amused projection of it
side by side with Jane Austen's more balanced, more quizzical
criticism.

> So Cash rules Love the ruler, on his own
> High ground, as virgin Cynthia sways the tides:[52]
> And as for 'Heaven being Love', why not say honey
> Is wax? Heaven is not Love, 'tis Matrimony.   (XII, xiv)

The power of money to compel love swings over, in the married
state itself, into its opposite. The wife now takes the upper hand, and
a gynocracy ensues (lxvi) in which Byron proceeds to distinguish a
variety of power-patterns. The influence an elder woman can exert
on a young man (Byron speaks here from experience of his friendships with Lady Melbourne and Lady Oxford) is analysed in
stanzas xliii–li; next we have the power of 'report', Shakespeare's
theme in *Much Ado*, in stanzas lvii–lix; close on this follows the
power of social intimidation (lx–lxii), the power of coquetry (lxiii),
and the final sanction of the breach of promise suit (lxv–lxvi). Some
of Byron's wittiest lines come in this 'gynocracy' section:

> All matchless creatures—and yet bent on matches   (liii)

> Perhaps you'll have a visit from the brother,
> All strut, and stays, and whiskers, to demand
> What 'your intentions are?'   (lx)

> And sends new Werters yearly to their coffin   (lxiii)

> The loveliest oligarchs of our Gynocracy.   (lxvi)

Canto XIII opens a series of 'compensation' cantos which carry us
to the close of the poem as we have it. The necessity of compensations,
for Juan and for the society in which he now lives, has become
increasingly clear as the realities of existence, incarnated in Julia
and Haidée and the long-boat and John Johnson and even Catherine,
fall away from him in the impoverished English scene. 'Dessication
of the world of sense,/Evacuation of the world of fancy,/Inoperancy
of the world of spirit.' The word 'pantomime', first used in stanza i
of Canto I, now develops its full meaning. This is a world of veneers,
compromises, and dullness.

> With much to excite, there's little to exalt;
> Nothing that speaks to all men and all times;
> A sort of varnish over every fault;
> A kind of common-place, even in their crimes;

> Factitious passions—Wit without much salt—
>   A want of that true nature which sublimes
> Whate'er it shows with Truth; a smooth monotony
> Of character, in those at least who have got any.   (XIV, xvi)

A number of substitutes are found for the real thing. Indifference is cultivated, as a buttress against distress (xxxv). Glory is 'a gilded cloud' (XIII, xxxiii). Quarrels about religion and politics are welcomed as stimulants:

> The joys of mutual hate to keep them warm,
> Instead of Love, that mere hallucination.   (XIII, vi)

This is an indoor civilisation, where men and women live in a tight circle, protected against the rigours of the climate (XIII, xlii–xliii). A sea-coal fire and 'a *purchased* choice of choicest wines' (my italics) compensate for the Mediterranean sun (XIII, lxxvi–lxxviii). Boars are replaced by bores (lxxviii),[53] in 'a Paradise of pleasure and ennui'.

But the bores are nicely discriminated. 'Good company's a chess-board', Byron tells us, moved by some master-hand: but whose he will not venture to guess (lxxxix). 'Lord Henry's mansion then, in Blank-Blank Square', and later Norman Abbey, gather together a large crowd of acquaintances—'there's safety in a crowd of coxcombs'—but no friends. Lord Henry, the host, is as 'blank-blank' as the 'square' he sits on. He is

> A man known in the councils of the Nation,
>   Cool, and quite English, imperturbable,
> Though apt to act with fire upon occasion,
>   Proud of himself and her: the World could tell
> Nought against either, and both seemed secure—
> She in her virtue, he in his hauteur.   (XIII, xiv)

So far, so good; a man who can be normally cool and yet fiery on occasion is not, one would think, a mere cipher. But in developing his portrait Byron suggests that even the 'fieriness' is determined by 'principles', i.e. by prejudices:

> when once his judgment was
> Determined, right or wrong, on friend or foe,
> Had all the pertinacity Pride has,
>   Which knows no ebb to its imperious flow,
> And loves or hates, disdaining to be guided,
> Because its own good pleasure hath decided.   (XIII, xvi)

'His prepossessions, like the laws of Persians/And Medes', Byron adds, 'would ne'er revoke what went before.' In other words, he replaces intelligence by rigidity, lives by a code like the eternal public-schoolboys of Forster's novels, reacts not from the new situation but from the old stereotype.

We are in a fossilised world, remote from the fluid passions of the Mediterranean, and Lord Henry is a 'humour' hitherto unlisted in Byron's roster of male characters. Not through want of intimacy, of course; Byron has known many such stuffed dummies in his years of fame. '*Haud ignara loquor*', he remarks (XIV, xxi). But their straw personae had been burnt up in the Levantine and Italian furnaces. Now they return to the stage of his 'mental theatre'; and to play, one suspects, an increasingly significant role: the later cantos of *Don Juan*, had they ever been written, would have given us a masterly panorama of the world of cant. Lady Adeline, the spouse in whose virtue Lord Henry is so confident, is more complicated, and more likeable; but she too, 'The fair most fatal Juan ever met' (XIII, xii), is 'the Queen-Bee, the glass of all that's fair . . .' (xiii). 'Glass' robs 'fair' of its immediacy; 'Queen-Bee' implies the officinal,[54] 'factory line' hive world.

These two, in their insecure social security, surround themselves with parasites. A motley crew are assembled at the Abbey (lxxix–xciv). There is much mirth but little wit.

> Society is now one polished horde,
> Formed of two mighty tribes, the *Bores* and *Bored*.   (XIII, xcv)

Bons mots are studied beforehand and learned by heart; the skill is to 'allure the conversation/By many windings' to the point where they can be brought in (xcviii). This may serve as a substitute for genuine wit at the dinner table; but there are huge tracts of time left over in the day where nothing suffices, in a country house-party, to repel *ennui*:

> The elderly walked through the library,
>   And tumbled books, or criticised the pictures,
> Or sauntered through the gardens piteously,
>   And made upon the hot-house several strictures,
> Or rode a nag which trotted not too high,
>   Or on the morning papers read their lectures,
> Or on the watch their longing eyes would fix,
> Longing at sixty for the hour of six.   (XIII, cii)

—for the hour, that is, of dinner. 'The whole earth is our hospital', as Eliot remarks in 'East Coker', and anyone who has spent many hospitalised days recovering from an illness or an operation knows how longingly mealtimes are looked forward to as escapes from boredom. In this sense Norman Abbey figures as a kind of country sanatorium, or nursing home for disorientated persons, misfits, neurotics: Byron's vision widening out to Eliot's infinities of 'the whole earth'. Eliot's 'ruined millionaire', Adam, does not figure here: we have to look back for him to the Biblical plays, or certain passages in the 'minor' verse, *The Prophecy of Dante*, or *Darkness*, or *Hebrew Melodies*. But 'Burnt Norton' remains relevant: 'Neither plenitude nor vacancy. Only a flicker/Over the strained time-ridden faces/Distracted from distraction by distraction/Filled with fancies and empty of meaning/Tumid apathy with no concentration. . . .'

The return of the *eating* theme in this passage opens into Canto XIV with its introduction of 'the Titan's breakfast' where 'One system eats another up' (i, ii) and the all-too-physical is related to metaphysics. ('Old Saturn ate his progeny' for reasons of sexual jealousy.) An extremely subtle play of the sexual-political-poetic themes enlivens this canto. Women are ironically defended:

> Alas! worlds fall—and Woman, since she felled
>   The World (as, since that history, less polite
> Than true, hath been a creed so strictly held),[55]
>   Has not yet given up the practice quite.
> Poor Thing of Usages! coerced, compelled,
>   Victim when wrong, and martyr oft when right,
> Condemned to child-bed, as men for their sins
> Have shaving, too, entailed upon their chins,—
>
> A daily plague, which in the aggregate
> May average on the whole with parturition.—
> But as to women—who can penetrate
> The real sufferings of their she condition?   (XIV, xxiii–xxiv)

'Every Harlot was a Virgin once'

The irony in this, the juxtaposition of shaving and childbirth (ridding oneself of two excrescences, one inner, the other outer), should not blind us to the very real compassion of Byron's stance here: quite clearly he does feel for woman's lot, he does sense the cosmic injustice. Thus the later cantos of *Don Juan* effect a double *metanoia*: the romantic-erotic ethos of the Julia–Haidée situation, shading off through the Seraglio–Catherine imbroglios into stretches of eating-and-being-eaten, buying-and-being-bought in the English scene, provides one shift of attention, on what might be called the novelistic level; but on the psychological and (dare one say?) Christian level, the level of 'because she hath loved much', there is a growing appreciation of the complexity of 'the sexual strife'. It is as though the old Egeria–Circe antithesis, so adequate to the situations of the Turkish Tales, has failed Byron: it is still true as far as it goes, but it does not go far enough, there are depths and reaches of feminine–masculine relations still to be explored. And I have no doubt that in the succeeding cantos, if Byron had lived to write them, he would have anticipated Proust and Lawrence and perhaps Sartre in opening up new vistas of 'the sexual strife'.

My 'Christian' interpretation is buttressed by stanza xxxi of this Canto XIV, where Byron calls upon even so formidable a witness[56] as St Paul in aid of his 'all things to all men' stance and its extension to the man–woman relationship.

> Juan—in this respect, at least, like saints—
>   Was all things unto people of all sorts,
> And lived contentedly, without complaints,
>   In camps, in ships, in cottages, or courts—
> Born with that happy soul which seldom faints,
>   And mingling modestly in toils or sports.
> He likewise could be most things to all women,
> Without the coxcombry of certain *she* men.   (XIV, xxxi)

The final couplet reverses the intent of Paul's 'all things to all men', which advocates a saintly impersonality, by reading *andres* for *anthropoi* and supplementing it with a parallel observation on *gynaikes* and Juan's attitude to *them*. The remaining cantos initiate a survey of these 'most things' which would no doubt, had the poem been continued, have been fully implemented. But we begin, in these bridge cantos XIV–XVII, with the ways in which the 'gynocracy' assembled at Norman Abbey can be 'most things' to Juan. The charms of Lady Adeline, Aurora Raby, and 'her frolic Grace, Fitz-Fulke', are nicely discriminated. Aurora and Fitz-Fulke stand at the extremes—but they are civilised, temperate-zone extremes, lacking the subtropic fervour of Haidée or the subarctic intensity of Catherine.

We have already seen Lady Adeline (who occupies the midpoint between the voracious Fitz-Fulke and the virginal Aurora) as 'the Queen-Bee, the glass of all that's fair'. She is not a dummy, like Lord Henry; she is capable of responding to the immediate situation, and her social mask is clearly less integral than her husband's. At the great banquet (XV, lxi– XVI, viii), which occupies much the same place in *Don Juan* as Mrs Ramsay's dinner in *To the Lighthouse*, she is the perfect (and ambitious) hostess, playing guest off against guest, keeping the conversational ball rolling, while on another level she is the jealous woman, in love or half in love with Juan, alert to every whisper, every look which passes between him and the Countess or Aurora. This nucleus of real emotions forms a play within a play in the shadow world of Lady Adeline's dinner party.

The eating-eaten theme of *Don Juan* crystallises here. The banquet at Norman Abbey is the satiric antetype to the cannibal feast of Canto II. There the passions were undisguised; here they wear a variety of masks. The direct blood-lust of the banqueters has been assuaged in their day's pursuits of shooting, fox-hunting and fishing (XVI, lxxx; XIV, xxxv; XIII, cvi); now comes the satisfaction of physical hunger, in the dinner itself, and of hunger for slander, in its sequel (XVI, ci–civ). Snob-power hunger has already been gratified, round about noon, by the arraignment of 'two poachers, caught in a steel trap,/Ready for gaol, their place of convalescence', and of a pregnant 'country girl in a close cap', who 'stood in trembling, patient tribulation,/To be call'd up for her examination' (XVI, lxi, lxv), These Hardyesque vignettes flash a sudden gleam of actuality into the artificial world of Norman Abbey. Trapped poachers and snared girl are victims of that wider trap which is society. The frame of the poem is almost shattered; but Byron's art is powerful enough to contain them.[57] An extraordinarily vivid and complex tissue of appetencies (to borrow I. A. Richards's word) has been woven during the day into a pattern which only the evening and night can fully display: the dinner is a paradigm not merely of the Norman Abbey complex but of the epic as a whole.

Byron's preparation for the banquet is meticulous. We might single out XIII, lxxv, as the pre-culinary exordium:

> The mellow Autumn came, and with it came
>   The promised party, to enjoy its sweets.
> The corn is cut, the manor full of game;
>   The pointer ranges, and the sportsman beats
> In russet jacket:—lynx-like in his aim;
>   Full grows his bag, and wonder*ful* his feats.
> Ah, nutbrown partridges! Ah, brilliant pheasants!
> And ah, ye poachers!—'Tis no sport for peasants.   (XIII, lxxv)

The irony is potent enough here: the mellow autumn, rather too

mellow for the pheasants, the sweets of autumn curiously translated
into meats, the hungry rustics. But to get the full flavour of Byron's
satire we have to go further back, to the idyllic lake-picture of
stanzas lvi–lxviii, with its 'branching stag', 'the wildfowl nestled in
the brake/And sedges, brooding in their liquid bed' and the darting
fishes within 'the calmer water': a world of quiet interchange into
which the Amundeville house party erupts as irrelevant, all-
destructive turbulence. The whole of the succeeding action, and the
description, of the house party must be seen in its contrast not only
to the natural setting but to the spiritual function of the Abbey
itself. In fifteen powerful stanzas Byron projects the building first
in its architectural magnificence, which kindles

> feelings in the roughest heart,
> Which mourned the power of Time's or Tempest's march,
> In gazing on that venerable Arch.   (XIII, lix)

and next in its spiritual, as dedicated to the Virgin (lxi). Stanza lxii
conflates a Keatsian 'glass of thousand colourings' with a Miltonic
and Shakespearian evocation of 'the silenced quire'. Music deepens
into planetary resonances in stanzas lxiii–lxiv.

> We move above the moving tree
> In light upon the figured leaf
> And hear upon the sodden floor
> Below, the boarhound and the boar
> Pursue their pattern as before . . .   ('Burnt Norton', II)

The Gothic fountain closes the earth-fire-air-water tetrad (lix,
lxii, lxiii, lxv) and the elemental circle is completed.

It is into this elemental harmony that the Amundeville house-
party intrudes, as Lambro had intruded into the harmony of
Haidée's bower, and the avenging warship into Neuha's paradise.
We shall miss the total impact of these concluding Cantos of *Don
Juan* unless, while we are responding to Byron's comic brilliance in
the indoor scenes, we remain sensitive to the surrounding context of
what is not human, not contemporary, and not of this world. Byron
draws our attention to this sphere of the timeless, the non-human
and the spiritual in a score of lightly poised asides. Many are ironic,
and stand out; many are so delicately phrased as to be inaudible
unless we keep alert to their resonances. Art is called in to redress
the starchiness of Regency 'nature': the Abbey's galleries show
'Lordlings, with staves of white or keys of gold', but 'ever and
anon'

> There rose a Carlo Dolce or a Titian,
>   Or wilder group of savage Salvatore's:
> Here danced Albano's boys, and here the sea shone
>   In Vernet's ocean lights.   (XIII, lxxi)

But these examples are relatively crude in their moral, as compared with the subtler asides which counterpoint the human action of Norman Abbey against the elemental ground bass which sustains it.

'Thou'rt my Mother from the Womb'

In returning to Norman or Newstead Abbey Byron completes the cycle of his wanderings physical and metaphysical. He returns to the world of *Hours of Idleness* and to a stasis which, however brief, suffices to give a viable finale to the poem. The return is imaginary, but this doesn't matter; the brilliance of his realisation of the English scene shows how integrally Byron has identified himself with his hero's final avatar. The poem is indefinitely extensible, of course, as Byron saw; but in its existing *meaning* it ends he e. 'Home is the hunter, home from sea.' The fragment of Canto XVII which is left to us shows Byron floundering, somewhat, in search of a line of continuation, a little bored with his poem, a trifle perfunctory. No doubt he would have solved the 'problem' (XVII, xiii) with his usual aplomb; but the major problem of the whole epic has solved itself not in terms of the relations of Juan and the Countess, or Juan and Lady Adeline, or Juan and Aurora Raby, but in those of the life–death cycle to which *Don Juan* has narrowed the wider love–power–wisdom cycle of the total *oeuvre*.

For when wisdom is eliminated from the syndrome love and power become pure antagonists and as love–hate merge with each other. This has been the lesson taught in all the post-Haidée cantos. There is a constant retraction from the natural world,[58] where 'life feeds on life' but does so with a certain innocence, an absence of deliberate cruelty, a violence where pleasure taken in the pain of others is seen to stem from an inadequacy in the inflicter of suffering and in his victim. As compensation for the lost paradise, the crime of Cain is enacted over and over again.

Norman Abbey, with its idyllic setting (XIII, lvi–lxvi), should have been a refuge for Juan from the murderous scenes he has lately passed through. But he soon comes to realise that the setting is one thing and the nucleus another. The environment—lake, flowers, wildfowl, stags, rivulet, and woods—preserves its innocence. The *Hours of Idleness* ideograms reassert themselves. We return to that early image framework, with its lake, dews, flowers, nightingales. To the starkness of crags and snowflakes we cannot of course return in the Newstead context. But the cave is not forgotten.[59] Nor the lake.

> And the pool was filled with water out of sunlight,
> And the lotos rose, quietly, quietly,
> The surface glittered out of heart of light,
> And they were behind us, reflected in the pool.
>
> ('Burnt Norton', I)

The lake is one centre, the cave another. Relating Aurora Raby to Haidée (XVI, xix), the cave re-establishes the womb-refuge-prison syndrome integral to Byron's thought. So too the 'mighty window hollow in the centre', which has been 'shorn of its . . . thousand colourings', stands for an 'existential cave', if I may coin the phrase: a 'black hole' in history initiated at the point when the Catholic sun collapsed upon itself, and created a destructive maw into which the whole of subsequent history is being sucked.

Norman Abbey indeed stands as such a maw, all-voracious, all-destructive. This is not the place to go into the question of Byron's feelings of guilt over the desecration of the Abbey by Henry VIII and his own forefathers: I think they were powerful and that Byron was constantly trying to exorcise them by ribaldry or other means: *tamen usque recurrunt.* But we must recognise in his reanimation of the 'Oscar of Alva' mode—the Gothic mode—in the 'Ballad of the Black Friar' (XVI, xl ff), more than a simple technical device. The Black Friar is the human equivalent of that black hole in the mighty multicoloured window, which draws off the energies of the Amundeville house-party, turns guests to ghosts, zealots to zombies.

Thus we remain ineluctably within the sphere of eating and being eaten. The Byrons have eaten the patrimony of the monks; the sacred has become the profane. Byron tried to get over this in his witty 'Lines Inscribed on a Skull'; but guilt is not so easily exorcised. The Abbey itself becomes a species of skull, which 'yawns all desolate', and from which, 'in the noontide of the moon', there 'moans a strange unearthly sound' (XIII, lxii–lxiii). A curse falls on all who enter there. Here I am guessing, of course, but it seems probable that in his continuation Byron would have reinforced this supernatural theme (which appealed to him greatly) as a counterpoise to the Restoration comedy of the Juan–Fitz-Fulke liaison. Such a union of contraries would have been fully Byronic. He loves to work on two disparate planes at the same time.

As it is, we have the skull-like image of the Abbey, its shattered transoms and mullions grinning like broken teeth in the moonlight, its 'mighty window hollow in the centre' sucking out the vitality of its guests into space, its necrophilic guests sucking in the life of deer and fishes and pheasants and poachers and village girls in their boundless thirst for something to give them substance. This is the 'Dracula' side of Byron, which I may be accused of exaggerating, and which perhaps I do exaggerate in this particular context. But it is always there, active under the surface.[60] It was already there, in the vampire image of Haidée, in the robuster anthropophagy of the Empress Catherine. It was there in Mrs Byron, in Donna Inez, in Julia, in Gulbeyaz. It is the 'storgous appetite'. For cantos XIII to XVII are not simply a return to the origins, to *Hours of Idleness*, they are also a kind of recapitulation of everything that has gone before in Byron's life and in the fictional world he has created. 'In Time's ocean falling drown'd', Byron lives over the episodes of his life. Or, if we take Norman Abbey as a womb world, the reconceived Juan lives through, as the foetus is said to do, the episodes of *his* racial cycle. It is not accidental that *The Island*, with its blatant exploitation of the amniotic depths, is being written *pari passu* with the last cantos of *Don Juan*.

Thus we have the 'Black Friar' ballad reconstituting the Gothic side of *Hours of Idleness*, we have Juan's encounter with Fitz-Fulke reproducing on the comic level Lara's shock and fainting-fit in the Gothic Tale, the lake stanzas recreating the atmosphere of the 1816 poems to or about Augusta. There are other resonances. But this last is the most important. The lake, and the innocent creatures which inhabit or border the lake, become the centre of Byron's thought. The lake which delivers up fish and waterfowl to the insatiate maw of the Amundeville house party,[61] is Byron's permanent eikon of *relationship*. Relationship, primarily, on the brother–sister level, but by extension, as the Lake Leman stanzas[62] of Canto III show us, in the sphere of man–nature intercourse.

> Then a cloud passed, and the pool was empty.
> Go, said the bird, for the leaves were full of children . . .
>
> (*Ibid.*)

Aurora, who now stands for Augusta, is a kind of human 'lake' within the Abbey; but because she is out of place, the eikon is distorted; in her unnatural milieu she is something which 'lies between a flower and gem'. The flower is her natural character; the gem is the adamantine wall (which poor Augusta could never manage to erect against Annabella) protecting its fragility. This necessity for protection distinguishes Aurora from the perfectly 'natural' Haidée and Neuha who are altogether at home in their environments.[63]

'To close the Labours of my Day'

Byron's first great architectural construct, the ruined abbey of *Hours of Idleness*, is thus his last also. 'Why dost thou build the hall, Son of the winged days? Thou lookest from thy tower to-day: yet a few years, and the blast of the desart comes: it howls in thy empty court.' That Ossianic epigraph, prefixed to 'On Leaving Newstead Abbey', has sounded through *Childe Harold*, through the Tales, the dramas, and the comic masterpieces. It is the 'metaphysical' note of the 'ruin amidst ruins' which modulates from that first wine-filled skull in the wrecked Abbey to the earth-filled skull in the Olympeion, that 'lonely tower' which was once 'Ambition's airy hall. . . . The gay recess of Wisdom and of Wit'; and thence to the progressively 'ruined' poet standing in the debris of history in the Forum and the Flavian amphitheatre. The modalities of the presentation develop from jocular to tragic, even melodramatic, from personal to universal, but the theme, *vanitas vanitatum*, remains the constant. If in his original Newstead avatar of the pre-Tour days he sought to recreate the world of Rabelais's Thelema or Dashwood's Medmenham, the play-acting quickly palled; the sombre realities of *Rasselas* redressed the moral balance: *Fay ce que voudras* was not a motto by which he could ultimately live.

Newstead was an important paradigm for Byron because it summed up his own basic antinomies, sacred and profane, ascetic and self-indulgent, solitary and social. On the biographic level, it enshrined his dynastic pretensions on the one hand and his family squabbles on the other. Here he had first felt the pride of birth, and the submergence of that pride in affection for a social inferior.[64] Here he had known 'the pangs of disprized love' in the aura of Mary Chaworth and 'folly, doctor-like, controlling skill' in the Upas shadow of Mrs Byron, and 'strength by limping sway disabled' in the Oedipean curse of his club-foot. No wonder that 'Tired with all these, for restful death I cry!'

The emergence of the death theme is what marks Byron's juvenile poetry off from that of his contemporaries. Wordsworth has his Gothic horrors in the juvenilia he never printed, Shelley delights in worms and epitaphs, but the stress is literary, fashionable, off-beat. Byron's death-wish springs from the centre, and to escape from it is the major motive of his orgies in Newstead and London and Venice, his counterpoised immersions in *Arabic Aphorisms*, the Bible, the Mekhitarist monastery in Venice, and the whole ascetic-permissive pattern of the crucial year of 1810 in the Levant. In his obsession with death Byron belongs to the crew of the metaphysical poets and the later 'graveyard school' and to Beddoes and Housman and Powys: but what he makes of the obsession is to their presentation as his zest for and immersion in 'life' is to their eclectic tea-tastings.

> A sleep without dreams, after a rough day
>   Of toil, is what we covet most; and yet
> How clay shrinks back from more quiescent clay!   (XIV, iv)

The observation comes in the middle of the English cantos, and forms a kind of *punctum indifferens* in the busy scene of Norman Abbey. Byron has assembled his *dramatis personae*, including the old Medmenhamish crew of *Childe Harold* I, i–xi, and (in English guise of course) his Laras, Don Josés, Gulbeyazes, Medoras, Haidées and the rest of them. Like one of those old-fashioned detective stories where all the suspects are reassembled on the scene of the crime for the final revelation of guilt by the great detective, with a burly superintendent of police waiting in the wings, *Don Juan* presents in its closing scenes a paradigm of suspicion and suspense. This marks a divergence from earlier cantos, where the characters of Inez, Julia, Don José, Haidée, Lambro, Johnson, Souvaroff, Catherine, and the rest are openly presented, as also are the episodes in which they are involved. Of course the flow of episode into episode is unpredictable, and the element of suspense is preserved as in any good novel, but we miss the element of complexity in the characters which constitutes the greatness of Shakespearian drama. In these later cantos of *Don Juan* Byron is modulating into the Shakespearian world of existential flux, with Newstead and its surrounding park forming the only analogue I can think of (apart from Virginia Woolf's Skye and James Joyce's Dublin) to Lear's palace and blasted heath.

Is Don Juan going to develop as Lear develops, as Mrs Ramsay unfolds herself and Leopold Bloom exposes his complicated strata of frustrations and compensations, in the course of the cantos, no doubt brilliant, no doubt choc-à-bloc with exciting incident, which were never written? Hopeless to speculate. But the indications are in favour. The process begins in Canto XII, with Juan's heart getting 'a tougher rind', with a lessening of his 'sensibilities' (lxxxi), and continues through Canto XIII as his contacts with Lord Henry and Lady Adeline deepen into the intimacy with them and with their London 'world' which is now transferred to Norman Abbey. The English scene makes its mark on him in a negative sense: he is diminished as a human being, at the same time that he develops as a man of the world. But Juan's basic qualities of warmth, spontaneity and goodness remain untouched, and interact with his newfound knowledge of the world to produce a more complex and a more interesting personality. 'Without Contraries is no Progression.' Up to Canto XIV Juan has been essentially passive. When he has acted, the action has been forced upon him, in the longboat, at the siege of Ismail, on Shooter's Hill. Now he is to take, plainly, a more active role in the story.

There can be little doubt that Canto XIV is the hinge canto in the complete *Don Juan* which might have been. At this point the hero takes a fulcral stance, becomes the centre of interest rather than the sport of circumstance on the margin of great events. Everything that follows will rotate round him. The Canto itself moves between two abysses (i, cii) in 'great Nature' and 'the human soul'. The identification of these is Blakean and should alert us at once to Byron's existential seriousness. This is a canto of suspense in every sense: philosophical, psychological, dramatic. We may take a line from the next canto, 'Between two worlds Life hovers like a star' (xcix) as our motto: and indeed the whole of this concluding stanza of canto XV is a summing up of the 'hovering' motif of the Norman Abbey episode. Byron first hovers (XIV, l–liii) between belief and unbelief in the meaningfulness of life. Extrapolating from this to the human condition, he shows man as hanging over the abyss of nothingness, alternately fascinated and repelled (iv–vi). Returning to his own persona, he describes poetry as 'A paper kite which flies 'twixt life and death', and his own verse as a child's soap-bubble, most fragile of playthings (viii): a compensatory gesture in the no-man's-land he now occupies between youth and age:

> In Youth I wrote because my mind was full,
> And *now* because I feel it growing dull . . .

And what I write I cast upon the stream,
To swim or sink—I have had at least my dream.   (XIV, x, xi)

We end, then, as we began, with the dream. Canto XIV is the
central stasis of the Norman Abbey avatar, from which Cantos
XIII, XV and XVI radiate in their past–future extrapolations.
Here 'we return to the origins, and remain where we have always
been'. Dreams, and dreamlike action, fill the final cantos. On the
surface, the plot unfolds itself with the wealth of comic and satiric
incident Byron habitually displays; this 'no-mans-land between
heaven and earth' is the stage of the human comedy. But constantly—and never so urgently as in these last cantos—Byron directs
our attention to the archetypal currents which underlie it. Living
himself on so many different levels, all authentic though contradic-
tory, hovering 'like a star' between the two worlds of the real and
the ideal, his performance as a poet comes close to prestidigitation.
We are in the world of Hazlitt's Indian jugglers.

To catch four balls in succession in less than a second of time, and deliver
them back so as to return with seeming consciousness to the hand again, to
make them revolve round him at certain intervals, like the planets in their
spheres, to make them chase one another like sparkles of fire, or shoot up
like flowers or meteors, to throw them behind his back and twine them
round his neck like ribbons or like serpents, to do what appears an im-
possibility, and to do it with all the ease, the grace, the carelessness
imaginable.

That is one way of expressing it: in terms of technique and aplomb.
Brilliant, dazzling, yet effortless: one set of balls kept going at
Norman Abbey; another set at Toobonai, a third at Missolonghi.
Two hands only to effect the scintillating transfers. What shall we
call them? Body and spirit, spark and clay, garlic and sapphires?
Yes, we can leave the final word with the poet of 'Burnt Norton':

Garlic and sapphires in the mud
Clot the bedded axle-tree.
The trilling wire in the blood
Sings below inveterate scars
Appeasing long forgotten wars.
The dance along the artery
The circulation of the lymph
Are figured in the drift of stars
Ascend to summer in the tree
We move above the moving tree
In light upon the figured leaf
And hear upon the sodden floor

Below, the boarhound and the boar
Pursue their pattern as before
But reconciled among the stars.

Notes and references

1   See below, pp. 342–3 for a discussion of this Canto.

2   'Common things' is the *communia* of Byron's Horatian motto for *Don Juan*: '*Difficile est proprie communia dicere*'. He may also be remembering a sentence of Jeffrey's *Beppo* review, quoted above p. 277.

3   Journal, 17 Nov., 1813. Similarly, the 'one thought' that 'only through time, time is conquered', runs through Eliot's *Four Quartets*, crystallizing out of intervals in the choric octosyllabics which, as I have pointed out elsewhere, are so close in tone to the scorpion interlude in *The Giaour*.

4   'Burnt Norton' is the first of the *Four Quartets*, the one to which Eliot prefixed the Heraclitean apothegms 'The road up is the road down' and 'Though the Word is common, the many live as though they had a wisdom of their own'. In inviting the reader's attention in this chapter to Eliot's tetralogy, and to 'Burnt Norton' in particular, I am suggesting that the *elemental* link of *Childe Harold* with *Don Juan* persists and should not be overlooked; that the theme of the contraries runs through the whole of Byron's work; and that the 'wisdom of their own' to which the characters of his Juanesque gallery cling (with what devastating results!) is subtly counterpointed against a 'common Word' which runs like a ground bass through the sixteen cantos: 'Ridiculous the waste sad time/Stretching before and after.'

5   'Dream' and 'delirium' are terms he applies to his affair with Lady Caroline Lamb (*MLJ* ii, 177).

6   Perhaps all women, except Augusta, were 'strangers' to Byron?

7   An oddly commercial comment, which links up with what I have later to say about the buying–selling theme in *Don Juan* (see below, pp. 311ff, 329–330).

8   It may be objected that it is no more compensatory than the ideal *persona* of *Childe Harold*, that 'soul of my thought' in the company of which he traverses earth, and which puts a plus sign against Byron's own nothingness (*CH* III, vi). But the difference is that Harold is a positive expression of Byron's urge to transcendence: the poet is living himself through his hero.

9   'I am much more indebted to the tale [*The Bride of Abydos*] than I can ever be to the most partial reader', he notes in his 5 December 1813 Journal, 'as it wrung my thoughts from reality to imagination'; this is only one among several such comments.

10   As early as 1816 Byron sees *Childe Harold* III as a refuge 'from the weary dream/Of selfish grief or gladness—so it fling/Forgetfulness around me . . .'. Forgetfulness is Manfred's grand *desideratum* too: its conflation here with wakening from 'dream' constitutes the new Byronic paradox.

11   Letter of 10 November 1813, to Annabella Milbanke (*LJ* iii, 405).

12   Cf. letter of 6 July 1821, to Hobhouse, and of 27 August 1822, to Moore (*LJ* v, 320–1; vi, 109). Also below, p. 323.

13   See above, p. 284.

14   Juan himself may be taken as 'real or ideal' (X, xx). Mr McGann (*op. cit.*, p. 153) notes that 'Romilly, Castlereagh, Wordsworth, and Southey are attacked in his great epic because they are men possessed—incarnated avatars of timeless spiritual perversions'. Every epoch, one might add, bodies forth its own 'shapes from the cave'.

15   'Guilt and retribution in Byron's sea poems', *REL* ii, no. 7. (1961), 58–69.

16   Letters of 16 July 1809, to Hodgson, and of 11 August 1809, to Mrs Byron (*LJ* i, 233, 238; *DJ* i, viii.

17   The opening line of the Prologue to 'The Gates of Paradise'. 'The Keys of the Gates' is the subtitle given to the 24 consecutive couplets from which my section headings in this chapter are taken.

18   Blake, *Jerusalem*, III, 64 (*Complete Writings*, ed. G. Keynes, London 1957, p. 698).

19   Derived from 'her great great grand-mamma' (lvi); Haidée, in Juan's next love adventure, has a Moorish mother (IV, liv). Byron's insistence on these Eastern, Islamic ingredients is important for his whole doctrine of love.

20   I have already made it in 'Guilt and retribution in Byron's sea poems' (*loc. cit.*).

21   Also, as Karl Kroeber has well noted, of his milieu: 'Juan is victimised as much by a complicated network of social relationships [much like those Byron met in Venice] . . . as by the upsurge of his sensual appetite. He is brought into contact with Julia through his mother's offices' (*Romantic Narrative Art*, University of Wisconsin Press, 1960, p. 150). In like manner, Donna Inez approves of Juan's 'friendship' with Catherine the Great (see below, p. 324).

22   An odd thing, belonging clearly to the dream level of the episode rather than to any realistic plot structure, is that Juan's shoes are not discovered during the very thorough search at Alfonso's first entry.

23   The direct reference to *Childe Harold* here is interesting.

24   See below, p. 304. And the even earlier cannibalistic episode in the long-boat, where Julia's precious letter is torn up to make lots to decide who shall first be eaten by his famishing companions (II, lxxiv).

25   The extent of Byron's acquaintance with Zoroastrianism has yet to be assessed, but a passage like this (quoted in R. C. Zaehner, *The Teachings of the Magi*, Allen & Unwin, 1956, p. 43) seems relevant 'I created thee . . . with a mouth close to thy buttocks, and coition seems to thee even as the taste of the sweetest food to the mouth.' See also below, p. 322. I cannot at this point *prove* a connection, but the quotation may perhaps be permitted to stand as, in Coleridge's *Kubla Khan* phrase, 'a psychological curiosity'.

26 'But why will she grow fat? and you too?' he writes to Miss Mercer
    Elphinstone on 3 August 1812. 'That additional wing (with a bit of
    the breast superadded I dare say) is worse than waltzing.—But as I
    actually dined yesterday myself, I must bear these trespasses' (*MLJ*
    ii, 187). Cf. also *MLJ* ii, 219: 'I am sadly out of practice lately, except
    for a few sighs to a gentlewoman at supper who was too much occupied
    with ye *fourth* wing of her *second* chicken to mind anything that was
    not material.'

27 Readers unfamiliar with the Greyfriars saga will find their best
    introduction to it in George Orwell's essay, 'Boys' Weeklies', in
    Critical Essays, 1951.

28 'Very sulky . . . and ate in consequence a copious dinner . . . (I have
    added, lately, eating to my "family of vices")' (Diary, 4–5 January
    1821). Byron's eating habits form a reliable index to his spiritual ups
    and downs. Contrast this, to his mother en route from the Levant,
    25 June 1811: 'I must only inform you that for a long time I have been
    restricted to an entirely vegetable diet, neither fish nor flesh coming
    within my regimen. . . . I drink no wine.'

29 *The Wisdom of Solomon*: see my *The Lost Travellers*, p. 174, for a link
    with *The Ancient Mariner*.

30 References to the Cornish wreckers occur in Byron's letters of this
    period, e.g. *LJ*, v, 272.

31 The serpent image here conflates with that of Eve.

32 The MS reads 'a sad Southey', a further complication leading into
    Byron's personal resentments.

33 'A man actually becomes a piece of female property', Byron writes
    in a letter to R. B. Hoppner (31 January 1820) describing his life in
    Italy. The fifth Canto was finished in November 1820.

34 See below, pp. 340–41.

35 The 'Inscription on the Monument of a Newfoundland Dog' is the
    best known of his statements on this theme.

36 I borrow this useful term from Wayne Burns's very instructive
    Charles Reade: a study in Victorian authorship, New York, 1900.

37 Nature the renovator again (cf. pp. 81–2, 186–7 above).

38 Keats should perhaps be excepted: he died too young for us to do
    more than conjecture what his development might have been.

39 Above, p. 14.

40 The seriousness of Byron's intent is again manifest in stanza cxxxv:

> For I will teach, if possible, the stones
> To rise against earth's tyrants. Never let it
>   Be said that we still truckle unto thrones;—
> But ye—our children's children! think how we
> Showed what things were before the world was free!

where echoes of the New Testament combine with Blake's

> Children of the future Age
> Reading this indignant page,
> Know that in a former time
> Love! sweet Love! was thought a crime.

41   Hazlitt's portrait of Pitt in *The Round Table* projects the type in political terms. Byron's letters of this period are equally emphatic. 'With these things and these fellows, it is necessary, in the present clash of philosophy and tyranny, to throw away the scabbard. I know it is against fearful odds; but the battle must be fought' (Letter to Moore, 8 August 1822).

42   For purposes of exposition I pass over the Russian episode (Cantos IX–X) at this point, to take it up on p. 322.

43   This is something I half-undertook in 'Guilt and retribution in Byron's sea poems' (*REL*, ii, no. 1, January 1961), before reading Ferenzci's book.

44   If most of *Don Juan* consists of 'addresses from the throne' (III, xcvi) this is an 'address to the throne', Byron's homage as dutiful subject and vassal.

45   See above, pp. 62–5.

46   Cf. 'Detached Thoughts, 102' (1821): 'What a strange thing is the propagation of life! a bubble of Seed which might be spilt in a whore's lap—or in the orgasm of a voluptuous dream—might (for ought we know) have formed a Caesar or a Buonaparte: there is nothing remarkable recorded of their sires, that I know of.' With engaging frankness, Prof. M. K. Joseph selects the last couplet of the stanza (lvi) to sum up his indebtedness to his wife and children in the writing of his *Byron the Poet* (Acknowledgements, p. 10). Byron would certainly have approved.

47   A distinction has to be drawn between counterpointing and deflating. Byron's common technique of juxtaposing sanctities with profanities is one thing; the deliberate use of sanctities for profane ends is another. So is the offence against Latin and Greek quantity!

48   Teresa in fact released him, 'provided it [the continuation of *Don Juan*] were immaculate; so I have been as decent as need be' (Letter of 27 August 1822 to Moore).

49   These may be compared with the dramatic *invocations* which I refer to on pp. 244–50 above. *Ginevra*, published in the same year as *Cain* (1821), has 'Life's great cheat; a thing/Bitter to taste, sweet in imagining' (36–7).

50   The gasps of 'death' in its obvious sense (dying soldiers) and its metaphorical ('dying' lovers). 'Oh' may represent the indrawn breath at the onset of the orgasm, 'ah' the expiration at its finale; or more broadly the optimistic expectation at the beginning of coitus and the *omne animal triste* sigh at its ending.

51   It is worth while connecting this with the *Childe Harold* prism moments (see above, pp. 196–7) to see the shift in stance from idealism to realism.

52   A good example of Byron's integral imagery, easy to pass over on a hasty reading. The sterile 'glittering cirque' of the moon, a celestial 'sovereign', rules the tides of sexual instincts and passions.

53   'The Bores and Blues, the two great enemies, as he always called them, of London happiness . . .' (Thomas Moore, *Life*, p. 411).

54   A useful adjective, dear to Dr Johnson and adopted by Keats. It seems

a pity that Mr McGann found it necessary to emend Keats's precise 'officinal' to 'official' when quoting his 'observation on life in England' that all 'breathe in a sort of Officinal atmosphere' (*op. cit.*, p. 212).

55   Byron's use of biblical archaisms is worth investigating. I believe it will be found that where such forms as 'hath', 'doth', 'saith' etc. are found, Byron almost always intends a reference, ironic or otherwise, to religious sanctions—the Ten Commandments, the Sermon on the Mount, Old or New Testament history, and so on.

56   'That powerful apostle', he calls St Paul in a letter of 29 October 1823 to C. F. Barry.

57   Crabbe is certainly in the background, but possibly Sir Ralph Milbanke too, and a remembered episode from the ghastly pre-Wedding days at Seaham.

58   The sophistication of the food at Norman Abbey is a denaturing of 'the kindly fruits of the earth'; 'The simple olives, best allies of wine' (XV, lxxiii) seem brought in as a deliberate contrast to the Apician feast of lxii–lxxiv. They are also, of course, an important liaison with Juan's Mediterranean past.

59   I am not an avid word-frequency man, but it is of some significance to note, from Hagelman and Barnes's *A Concordance to Don Juan*, Cornell University Press, 1968) that 'flower' returns to use in Canto XIII after a nine-canto absence; that 'rose', one of Byron's most potent symbols, hardly appears between Canto II and Canto XIII; that there is a ten canto interval for 'dew' until its restoration in Canto XVI; that 'nightingale', closely associated with 'rose' in Byron's Sufic imagery, is absent between Canto VI and XIII. Even more significant is the collocation 'rose and thistle' which Byron employs in 'On Leaving Newstead Abbey' in *Hours of Idleness* and repeats in a cancelled line, 'A sort of rose entwining with a thistle', in Canto XIII, cv. I have linked this up earlier with Byron's feelings about his mother, and perhaps the nexus exists here and explains the cancellation. 'Lake' and 'cave' are deeper correlatives. 'Lake' disappears between Canto VI and Canto XIII; 'cave' figures eight times in Canto II, once in Canto IV and re-emerges only in Canto XVI.

60   There is a connection to be made with the Shelley interlude of 1816–17 with its ghost-story evenings which produced *Frankenstein* and Byron's own fragment of a Gothic Tale.

61   Byron's proper names are rarely carelessly chosen. 'Amundeville' is a kind of anagram suggesting 'a villa out of this world' enclosing a nucleus of 'devil'; other combinations could probably be found.

62   A significant castback to the Leman idyll comes in XIV, lxxxvii, where the lake and the river Rhone are projected in the mother–child relationship. But Lady Adeline's 'maternal fears' for Juan (lii) give this an ironic dimension, recalling Donna Inez and the Empress Catherine. Unsatisfactory relationships are a major theme of this Canto. Lord Henry kisses Lady Adeline ('Less like a young wife than an aged sister', lxix), and the Countess Fitz-Fulke's marital relationship is even more perfunctory.

63   Cf. above, p. 319. To exist in the artificial world of the Amundevilles
      Aurora has to turn gem instead of flower, and to exchange the
      warmth of Paradise as her setting for the icy but protective solitudes
      of space. The root thought of 'Lachin Y Gair' refinds itself here.

64   'To E —', in *Hours of Idleness*.

A SELECT BIBLIOGRAPHY

(Place of publication London, unless stated otherwise. Detailed bibliographical information will also be found in the appropriate volume of *The Cambridge Bibliography of English Literature* and *The Oxford History of English Literature*.)

Bibliography:

The Life of Lord Byron, by Hon. R. Noel (1890)
—includes *Bibliography* by J. P. Anderson, containing extensive lists of magazine articles about Byron and of musical settings.
A Bibliography of Successive Editions and Translations in *The Works of Lord Byron. Poetry*, Vol. VII (1904), ed. E. H. Coleridge
—the best general bibliography of the poems.
Byron in England, by S. C. Chew (1924)
—contains an extensive list of Byroniana.
Bibliographical Catalogue of the First Editions, Proof Copies and Manuscripts of Books by Lord Byron. Exhibited at the First Edition Club, January 1925 (1925).
A Descriptive Catalogue of ... Manuscripts and First Editions ... at the University of Texas, ed. R. H. Griffith and H. M. Jones; Austin, Texas (1924).
Byron and Byroniana: A Catalogue of Books (1930)
—an important sale catalogue, valuable for reference, issued by Elkin Mathews, the London booksellers.
A Bibliography of the Writings in Verse and Prose of George Gordon Noel, Baron Byron. With Letters illustrating his Life and Work and particularly his attitude towards Keats, by T. J. Wise, 2 vols (1932–3)
—the standard analytical bibliography. Incorporates the material of the

same author's *A Byron Library*, 1928, the privately printed catalogue of the
Byron Collection in the Ashley Library, now in the British Museum.
The Roe-Byron Collection, Newstead Abbey; Nottingham (1937)
—the catalogue of the collection at Byron's ancestral home.
Catalogue of a Collection of Books, Late the Property of a Nobleman,
Evans sale, 1816.
Catalogue of the Library of the Late Lord Byron, Evans sale, 1827
Grove's Dictionary of Music and Musicians, vol. i, pp. 1067–8, gives
a list of musical settings of Byron's works (1945).
Note: The archives of John Murray, Byron's publishers, at 50 Albemarle
Street, London, contain important manuscript material.

Collected Works:

The Poetical Works, 2 vols; Philadelphia (1813)
—the first collected edition, followed throughout the nineteenth century by
numerous other collected editions in several volumes, published in
London, New York, and elsewhere.
The Works, 4 vols (1815)
—new editions, 1818–20 (8 vols); 1825 (8 vols); 1831 (6 vols).
The Works, with His Letters and Journals, and His Life, by Thomas
Moore, ed. J. Wright, 17 vols (1832–3).
The Poetical Works. New Edition, with the Text Carefully Revised,
6 vols (1857).
The Poetical Works, edited, with a Critical Memoir by W. M. Rossetti.
Illustrated by Ford Madox Brown, 8 vols (1870).
The Works. A New, Revised, and Enlarged Edition with Illustrations,
including Portraits, 13 vols(1898–1904)
—*Poetry*, ed. E. H. Coleridge, 7 vols; *Letters and Journals*, ed. R. H. Prothero,
6 vols.
The Poetical Works. The Only Complete and Copyright Text in one
volume. Edited with a Memoir, by E. H. Coleridge (1905)
—the standard edition, often reprinted.

Separate Works:

Fugitive Pieces [Newark, 1806]
—privately printed and anonymous. Facsimile reprint, ed. H. B. Forman,
1886.
Poems on Various Occasions; Newark (1807)
—privately printed and anonymous.
Hours of Idleness: A Series of Poems Original and Translated; Newark
(1807).
Poems Original and Translated; second edn of *Hours of Idleness*; Newark
(1808)
—contains five new pieces.
English Bards and Scotch Reviewers: A Satire [1809]
—the early editions of this poem were frequently counterfeited.
Address Written by Lord Byron. The Genuine Rejected Addresses,
Presented to the Committee of Management for Drury Lane Theatre:

Preceded by that written by Lord Byron and adopted by the Committee (1812).

Childe Harold's Pilgrimage: A Romaunt. Cantos I and II (1812); Canto III (1816); Canto IV (1818); Cantos I-IV were collected in 2 vols (1819).

The Curse of Minerva: A Poem (1812).

Waltz: An Apostrophic Hymn 'by Horace Hornem, Esq.' (1813).

The Giaour: A Fragment of a Turkish Tale (1813).

The Bride of Abydos: A Turkish Tale (1813).

The Corsair: A Tale (1814).

Ode to Napoleon Buonaparte, [Anon] (1814).

Lara: A Tale (1814).

Hebrew Melodies, Ancient and Modern with appropriate Symphonies and Accompaniments (1815).

The Siege of Corinth: A Poem. Parisina: A Poem, [Anon] (1816).

[Poems on his Domestic Circumstances] (i. Fare Thee Well. ii. A Sketch from Private Life) (1816)

—these two poems had been privately printed and separately printed in the same year. Various editions of this collection with additional poems were published in 1816.

Poems (1816).

The Prisoner of Chillon and Other Poems (1816).

Monody on the Death of the Right Hon. R. B. Sheridan. Written at the Request of a Friend, to be Spoken at Drury Lane (1816).

The Lament of Tasso (1817).

Manfred: A Dramatic Poem (1817).

Beppo: A Venetian Story (1818). Anonymous

—fourth edn, with additional stanzas, 1818.

Mazeppa: A Poem (1819).

Don Juan. Cantos I and II (1819); Cantos III, IV, V (1821); Cantos VI, VII, VIII (1823); Cantos IX, X, XI (1823); Cantos XII, XIII, XIV (1823); Cantos XV, XVI (1824) originally published anonymously.

—first collected edition, 2 vols, Edinburgh 1825; ed. T. G. Steffan and W. W. Pratt, 4 vols, Austin, Texas 1957; (the fullest edition, of which Vol. I contains a detailed study of the composition of the poem). A useful one-volume edition in the *Penguin English Poets* series (1973) includes some notes and variant readings.

Marino Faliero, Doge of Venice: An Historical Tragedy. **The Prophecy of Dante:** A Poem (1821).

Sardanapalus: A Tragedy. **The Two Foscari:** A Tragedy. **Cain:** A Mystery (1821); ed. T. G. Steffan, 'Lord Byron's *Cain*: Twelve Essays and a Text with Variants and Annotations', Austin, Texas, 1969.

The Vision of Judgment (1822)

—a product of Byron's feud with Southey, first printed in *The Liberal*, 1822, an ephemeral paper promoted by Byron and Leigh Hunt. Published as *The Two Visions* with Southey's 'Vision of Judgment' in the same year.

Heaven and Earth: A Mystery, [Anon] (1823).

—first printed in *The Liberal*, 1823.

The Age of Bronze: Or, Carmen Seculare et Annus haud Mirabilis, [Anon] (1823).

The Island: Or, Christian and His Comrades (1823).

Werner: A Tragedy (1823).

The Parliamentary Speeches of Lord Byron. Printed from the Copies prepared by his Lordship for Publication (1824).

The Deformed Transformed: A Drama (1824).

Diaries, Letters, etc.

Letter to [John Murray] **on the Rev. W. L. Bowles' Strictures on the Life and Writings of Pope** (1821).

Correspondence of Lord Byron with a Friend, including his Letters to his Mother in 1809–11, ed. A. R. C. Dallas, 3 vols; Paris (1825).

Letters and Journals of Lord Byron, with Notices of his Life, by T. Moore, 2 vols (1830, revised edition 1875).

Letters and Journals, ed. R. E. Prothero, 6 vols (1898–1904).

Poems and Letters, edited from the original MSS. in the possession of W. K. Bixby, by W. N. C. Carlton; privately printed, Chicago (1912).

Lord Byron's Correspondence, chiefly with Lady Melbourne, Mr Hobhouse, the Hon. Douglas Kinnaird, and P. B. Shelley, ed. John Murray, 2 vols (1922).

Selected Letters, ed. V. H. Collins; Oxford (1928).

The Ravenna Journal, mainly compiled at Ravenna in 1821, with an Introduction by Lord Ernle [R. E. Prothero] (1928)
—printed for the members of the First Edition Club.

Byron's Letters and Journals, ed. L. A. Marchand, three volumes are so far published (1973–4), presents 'the complete and unexpurgated text of all the letters available in manuscript and the full printed version of all others'. R. E. Prothero's edition continues to be indispensable for its scholarly notes and valuable illustrations.

Lord Byron: Selected Prose, ed. P. Gunn, in *The Penguin English Library* (1972)
—a well-chosen anthology of the letters and journals.

Some Critical and Biographical Studies:

A Journey Through Albania and other Provinces of Turkey, by J. C. Hobhouse (1813).

History of a Six Weeks' Tour, by P. B. Shelley (1817).

Memoirs of the Life and Writings of the Rt. Hon. Lord Byron, with Anecdotes of Some of his Contemporaries, by [J. Watkins] (1822).

Journal of the Conversations of Lord Byron: Noted during a Residence with his Lordship at Pisa, in the Years 1821 and 1822, by T. Medwin (1824).

Notes on Captain Medwin's Conversations of Lord Byron, by John Murray; privately printed (1824)
—reprinted in *Works,* 1829.

Recollections of the Life of Lord Byron, from the Year 1808 to the End of 1814, by R. C. Dallas (1824).

The Spirit of the Age, by W. Hazlitt (1825)
—contains an essay on Byron.
A Narrative of Lord Byron's Last Journey to Greece, by Count P. Gamba (1825).
Anecdotes of Lord Byron from Authentic Sources, by [Alexander Kilgour] (1825).
The Last Days of Lord Byron: With his Lordship's Opinions on Various Subjects, particularly on the State and Prospects of Greece, by Major W. Parry (1825).
Narrative of a Second Visit to Greece, including Facts connected with the Last Days of Lord Byron, Extracts from Correspondence, Official Documents, etc., ed. Edward Blaquiere (1825).
The Life, Writings, Opinions and Times of the Rt. Hon. George Gordon Noel Byron, Lord Byron, by an English Gentleman in the Greek Military Service, and Comrade of his Lordship. Compiled from Authentic Documents and from Long Personal Acquaintance, 3 vols (1825)
—ascribed to the publisher, Matthew Iley.
Lord Byron and Some of his Contemporaries, by Leigh Hunt (1828).
The Life of Lord Byron, by J. Galt (1830).
Conversations on Religion with Lord Byron and Others, by J. Kennedy (1830).
Memoirs of the Affairs of Greece, with Various Anecdotes Relating to Lord Byron, and an Account of his Last Illness and Death, by J. Millingen (1831).
Conversations of Lord Byron with the Countess of Blessington, by Marguerite Gardiner, Countess of Blessington (1834).
Citical and Historic Essays, by T. B. Macaulay (1842)
—includes review of *Letters and Journals of Lord Byron; with Notices of his Life,* by T. Moore, 1830.
Lectures on the English Poets, by W. Hazlitt (1858).
Recollections of the Last Days of Shelley and Byron, by E. J. Trelawny (1858; ed. E. Dowden, 1906)
—see also the same author's *Records of Shelley, Byron, and the Author,* 2 vols, 1878, new editions 1887, 1905.
Lord Byron Jugé Par Les Témoins de sa Vie, by Countess T. Guiccioli, 2 vols (1868)
—English translation, 1869.
Medora Leigh: A History and An Autobiography, by E. M. Leigh, ed. C. Mackay (1869).
A Contemporary Account of the Separation of Lord and Lady Byron: Also of the Destruction of Lord Byron's Memoirs, by J. C. Hobhouse; privately printed (1870)
—reprinted in Hobhouse's *Recollections of a Long Life.*
Byron Re-Studied in his Dramas. An Essay, by W. Gerard [Smith] (1886).
'Byron', by M. Arnold, *Essays in Criticism,* 2nd series (1888).
Last Links with Byron, Shelley and Keats, by W. Graham (1898).

Journal of Edward Ellerker Williams, Companion of Shelley and Byron in 1821 and 1822. With an Introduction by R. Garnett (1902).

Astarte: A Fragment of Truth concerning Lord Byron, by Ralph Milbanke, Earl of Lovelace; privately printed (1905)
—enlarged edition, published 1921.

Lord Byron and his Detractors. *Astarte. Lord Byron and Lord Lovelace,* by Sir J. Murray; *Lord Lovelace on the Separation of Lord and Lady Byron,* by R. E. Prothero (1906)
—privately printed for members of the Roxburghe Club.

Byron: The Last Phase, by R. J. F. Edgcumbe (1909).

Recollections of a Long Life, by J. C. Hobhouse (1909–11).

The Diary of Dr John William Polidori, relating to Byron, etc.
—edited and elucidated by W. M. Rossetti (1911).

Lord Byron as a Satirist in Verse, by C. M. Fuess (1912).

Byron, by E. Colburn Mayne, 2 vols (1912, new edn 1924)
—see also the same author's *The Life and Letters of Lady Noel Byron,* 1929.

Lord Byron's Illness and Death as described in a Letter to the Hon. Augusta Leigh, dated from Missolonghi April 20, 1824, by W. Fletcher; privately printed, Nottingham (1920).

The Relations of Lord Byron and Augusta Leigh. With a Comparison of the Characters of Byron and Shelley. Four letters by E. J. Trelawny; privately printed (1920).

Byron in England: His Fame and After Fame, by S. C. Chew (1924).

Byron in Perspective, by J. D. Symon (1924).

Byron, the Poet. A Centenary Volume, edn. W. A. Briscoe (1924)
—contains essays by Haldane, Grierson and others.

The Background of English Literature, by H. J. C. Grierson (1925)
—contains 'Byron and English Society'.

La Fortuna Di Byron in Inghilterra, by M. Praz; Florence (1925)
—see also *The Romantic Agony,* translated A. Davidson, 1933.

Allegra: The Story of Byron and Miss Clairmont, by A. C. Gordon; New York (1926).

The Haunted Castle, by E. Railo (1927).

Byron, et le Besoin de la Fatalité, by C. Du Bos; Paris (1929)
—English translation by E. Colburn Mayne, 1932.

Lord Byron: Persönlichkeit und Werk, by H. Richter (1929).

Byron, by André Maurois, 2 vols; Paris (1930)
—English translation by H. Miles, 1930.

Allegra, by I. Origo (1935).

Byron: Romantic Paradox, by W. J. Calvert (1935).

Revaluation, by F. R. Leavis (1936)
—contains his influential essay 'Byron's Satire'.

From Anne to Victoria, ed. B. Dobrée (1937)
—contains 'Byron' by T. S. Eliot, reprinted in *On Poetry and Poets,* 1957.

Byron as Skeptic and Believer, by E. W. Marjarum; Princeton, N. J. (1938).

'Byron and the East: Literary Sources of the Turkish Tales', by H. S. L. Wiener in *Nineteenth Century Studies,* ed. H. Davies, W. C. de Vane and R. C. Bald (1940).

Byron's Don Juan, by E. F. Boyd (1945).

Lord Byron's First Pilgrimage, by W. A. Borst; New Haven, Conn. (1948).

The Last Attachment. The Story of Byron and Teresa Guiccioli, by I. Origo (1949).

Goethe and Byron, by E. M. Butler (1951).

The True Voice of Feeling, by Sir H. Read (1951)
—contains an essay on Byron.

Lord Byron, Christian Virtues, by G. W. Knight (1952).

Fair Greece, Sad Relic: Literary Philhellenism from Shakespeare to Byron, by T. Spencer (1954).

Byron and Goethe, by E. M. Butler (1956).

Lord Byron, un Tempérament Littéraire, by R. Escarpit; Paris (1956–1957).

'Byron as Poet', by W. W. Robson, in *Proceedings of the British Academy*, vol. xliii (1957).

Byron, by L. A. Marchand, 3 vols (1957)
—the standard life.

The Metamorphoses of Don Juan, by L. Weinstein (1959).

On Poetry and Poets, by T. S. Eliot (1959)
—contains an essay on Byron, first published in 1937.

The Style of Don Juan, by G. M. Ridenour; New Haven (1960)
—Yale Studies in English, Vol. CXLIV.

The Late Lord Byron, by D. L. Moore (1961).

The Lost Travellers, by B. Blackstone (1962)
—contains a chapter expanded from 'Guilt and Retribution in Byron's Sea Poems', in *A Review of English Literature*, Vol. II, January 1961.

Lord Byron's Wife, by M. Elwin (1962).

The Byronic Hero, by P. L. Thorster, Jr; Minnesota (1962).

The Structure of Byron's Major Poems, by W. J. Marshall; Philadelphia (1962).

Byron the Poet, by M. K. Joseph (1964).

Byron and Shakespeare, by G. Wilson Knight (1966).

Byron and the Ruins of Paradise, by R. F. Gleckner (1967)

Fiery Dust: Byron's Poetic Development, by J. J. McGann; Chicago (1968).

The Journals of Claire Clairmont, ed. M. K. Stocking; Cambridge, Mass. (1969).

Twentieth Century Interpretations of 'Don Juan', ed. E. Bostetter; New Jersey (1969)

The Blind Man Traces the Circle, by M. G. Cooke; Princeton, (1969)

'Lord Byron en España', by E. Pujals, in *Atlántida*, (1968)

Byron: The Critical Heritage, ed. A. Rutherford (1970). An indispensable collection of contemporary critical opinion.

Byron: Lyric and Romance, by B. Blackstone (1970); **Byron: Literary Satire, Humour and Reflection,** by B. Blackstone (1971); **Byron: Social Satire, Drama and Epic,** by B. Blackstone (1971): three essays in the *Writers and Their Work* Series.

'*The Loops of Time*: Spatio-Temporal patterns in *Childe Harold*', by B. Black-stone, in **Ariel** (1971).

Byron's Hebrew Melodies, ed. with commentary by T. L. Ashton, (1972).

'Byron's Greek canto: the anatomy of freedom', by B. Blackstone, in *Yearbook of English Studies* (1974).

'Byron and the Levels of Landscape', by B. Blackstone, in **Ariel,** Calgary, (1974).

'Byron and Islam: The Triple Eros', by B. Blackstone, in *Journal of European Studies* (1974).

Note: Reference should also be made to the following Nottingham Byron Foundation Lectures: *Byron's Lyrics*, by L. C. Martin (1948); *Byron and Switzerland*, by H. Straumann (1948); *Byron and Shelley*, by D. G. James (1951); *Byron's Dramatic Prose*, by G. Wilson Knight (1953); *Two Exiles: Lord Byron and D. H. Lawrence*, by G. Hough (1956; reprinted in *Image and Experience*, 1960); *Byron and Italy*, by G. Melchiori (1958); *Byron and the Greek Tradition*, by T. Spencer (1959); and *Byron's Dramas*, by B. Dobrée (1962).

INDEX

Aberdeen, 215
Abydos, 57, 70, 149
abyss, *see* gulf
Achilles, 169, 259–60, 311
Acropolis, 59, 191, 96
Actium, 69, 91
Ada, *see* Byron, Augusta Ada
Adam and Eve, 67, 79, 116, 244ff., 257, 267, 283–4, 296, 314, 327, 333, 346
Adeline, Lady, 294, 319–20, 332
Aeschylus, 91, 285
Aeneid, 32
air, 18, 94, 106, 203, 213, 225, 241, 255
Albany House, Piccadilly, 47, 155
Alcibiades, 258
Alexander the Great, 273–4, 312
Alfonso, Don, 296–7
Ali Pasha, 34, 68, 95–9, 103, 106, 211, 267, 316–17
Alps, 144, 203, 218, 228, 231ff.
Ambrosian Library, 205
America, *see* United States
Amundeville, 336, 339, 348–9
Anacharsis Cloots, 328
Ancient Mariner, The, 51, 80, 88, 125–6, 150, 300
Angiolina, 242ff., 278
animals, 14, 46, 83, 250, 315, 338
Annesley, 15, 329
antiquaries and antiquities, 56ff., 86–7, 96, 129, 261
antithesis, 17, 24, 34, 36, 38, 47–9, 58, 61, 69, 73, 99, 117, 135, 139, 153–4, 161, 169, 181, 187, 200, 207, 216, 221, 235, 239–40, 243, 245, 260, 281,

289, 297, 300, 308–9, 318–19, 325–6, 334, 340, 343
Antonia, 198
Antony, Mark, 258, 273
Apollo, 12, 80, 83, 86–7, 104–6, 200, 211, 213, 223, 225, 234
apostrophe, 324ff.
Arabic Aphorisms, 23, 36, 341
arch, 62, 103, 123, 218, 221, 261, 236
architecture, 11, 22–3, 58, 62, 81–2, 90, 92–4, 103, 106, 158, 170, 206, 208, 212, 214, 216ff., 222, 228, 232, 241, 261ff., 300, 336, 340
archetype, 85–6, 87, 95, 134, 185–6, 209–10, 291–3, 307, 313ff., 343
Aristotle, 266
Armenian monastery, 34, 341
Arnold, 258–9
Arnold, Matthew, 41, 60, 78, 90, 93, 117, 165, 167, 173, 176, 240, 270
Arqua, 216, 218, 220
art, 59, 94, 104, 106, 154, 170, 208–9, 212ff., 219, 225, 293, 336
Asia Minor, *see* Greece and the Levant
Ashton, Thomas L., 130, 140, 145
Asmodeus, 285
Astarte, 232
Athena, Pallas, *see* Minerva
Athens, 22, 55–6, 62, 72–3, 96–7, 160, 206, 208
Athos, Mount, 84, 95, 97
Attica, 53ff., 91, 102
Augustine, St., 190, 226
Augustus, Emperor
Aurora Raby, 294, 319, 320
Austen, Jane, 330

Baba, 312
Bacon, Francis
ballads and legends, 15, 26, 73, 77–8,
    95, 99–100, 129, 159–60, 264
Beddoes, Thomas Lovell, 341
Becher, The Rev. John T., 5, 29
Beckford, William, 81
Bedlam, 327
bee, 94, 96, 103–4, 202, 207, 217, 235,
    332
Bektashi, 267
Bembo, Cardinal, 205
Berkeley, George, 182, 326
'Betty' (William Henry West), 52
bhakti-marga, 246–7
Bible, 129ff., 140, 149, 190, 244ff., 267,
    304, 322, 341, 348
Billy Bunter, 301
bird, 14, 79–80, 83, 193, 196, 239, 258,
    265, 304, 306, 338
Birge, J. K., 267
Blackwood's Magazine, 276, 294
Blake, William, 11, 18–19, 24, 26, 30,
    35, 63, 74, 81, 83, 91, 94–5, 124–5,
    130, 133, 138, 141–2, 143, 155, 172,
    182, 188, 192, 194, 197, 217, 219,
    228, 235, 243–4, 245ff., 251–2, 253,
    257, 262, 266–7, 285, 289, 294, 300,
    304, 313, 316, 345–6
Blessington, Countess of, 56, 61, 76–7
Bligh, Captain, 15, 263ff.
Bloomfield, Robert, 45
bluestockings, 3, 328, 347
Boccaccio, 216
body and soul, 64–5, 251, 325–6
Boethius, 155
Bolotoo, 265
Bonnivard, 127, 169, 194, 235
Borgia, Lucrezia, 205
Bosphorus, 101
Boswell, James, 60, 263
Bourbon, 262
Bowers, 'Bodsy', 244
Bowles, The Rev. William Lisle, 41,
    50ff., 329
Brenta, 124
Bridge of Sighs, 207
British Critic, The, 133
Brougham, Henry Peter, 53
Browne, Sir Thomas, 226, 273, 322
Brummel, 'Beau', 328
Brutus, 243
Bryant, Jacob, 70
bullfight, 83, 85, 90, 97, 106, 329
Bunyan, John, 244

Buonaparte, Napoleon, 99, 187, 201,
    221, 248, 273–4, 308, 317, 347
Burns, Robert, 45, 47, 54
Burns, Wayne, 346
Burton, Robert, 268
Butler, Samuel, 48
buying and selling, 89, 298, 305ff.,
    310ff., 322, 333ff., 344, 346
Byron, Augusta, 7ff., 40, 104, 113, 115,
    118, 130, 134, 138, 146–51, 161–2,
    187, 192ff., 198, 205, 207, 232, 247,
    256, 267–8, 308, 339
Byron, Augusta Ada, 184, 187, 200,
    203–5
Byron, Mrs Catherine Gordon, 8ff., 21,
    79, 93, 107, 111, 161, 168, 247, 295,
    301, 339
Byron, Lady, *see* Annabella Milbanke
Byron, George Gordon, 6th Lord: *Works*
'A Dream', 150
'Adrian's Address to his Soul when
    Dying', 143
'All is Vanity, saith the Preacher',
    141
'Answer to a Beautiful Poem', 5
'A Sketch', 146
'A Spirit passed before me', 136,
    138–9

Beppo, 177, 215, 257, 275–7
'Bright be the Place of thy Soul'
    (Stanzas for Music), 134, 141, 143
'By the Rivers of Babylon', 132, 135

Cain, 15, 144, 150, 227, 244–50, 261,
    283, 323
'Childe Harold's Good Night', 79, 86
Childe Harold's Pilgrimage, 10, 16, 19,
    22, 34–6, 49, 54, 56, 59, 62, 63, 67,
    70, 71, 79–105, 113–14, 116–17,
    122, 124, 130, 138, 139, 148, 153,
    165, 171, 183, 184–230, 234–5, 255,
    259–60, 262, 265, 267–8, 276, 287,
    290ff., 314, 329, 340, 341, 347
Childish Recollections, 5, 16, 28, 32–9, 96
'Could I remount the River of my
    Years', 147

'Damoetas', 7, 28
Darkness, 144, 150ff., 329
'Detached Thoughts', 149, 347
Don Juan, 8, 12, 15, 45, 49, 52, 66, 71,
    76, 79, 93, 117, 119, 127, 144, 163,
    167, 177, 181–2, 195, 209, 213,
    257, 259, 265, 269, 271–2, 275,
    278–9, 287–344

'Elegy on Newstead Abbey', 22, 26
English Bards and Scotch Reviewers, 7,
43–54, 55, 57, 71, 112, 270, 282
Epistle to Augusta, 147, 192

Fugitive Pieces, 4–5

Heaven and Earth, 139, 144, 244–50,
261
Hebrew Melodies, 31, 36, 74, 123, 129–
145, 146, 154, 193, 222, 319
'Hills of Annesley, bleak and barren',
31
Hints from Horace, 28, 45, 54–6, 112
Hours of Idleness, 3–40, 43, 48, 53–4,
67, 71–3, 80, 88, 243, 264, 329, 337,
339–40

'I enter thy Garden of Roses', 74
'If that high World', 141, 143
'Imitated from Catullus', 28
'Inscription on the Monument of a
Newfoundland Dog', 346
'I would I were a careless Child', 15

'Jephtha's Daughter', 140, 146

'Lachin Y Gair', 12, 15–20, 197, 264,
349
Lara, 95, 116, 122, 139, 320, 339
Letters and Journals, 7, 44, 46ff., 61,
67, 72, 76, 114, 118, 131, 132, 138,
148, 162, 184, 232, 295, 307–8, 315
'Lines inscribed upon a Cup formed
from a Skull', 62–5, 322, 338
'Lines to Mr Hodgson', 65–6
'Lines written in an Album', 69
'Lines written beneath a Picture', 74
Loch na Garr, *see* 'Lachin Y Gair'

'Maid of Athens, ere we part', 72–3
Manfred, 15, 20, 40, 68, 95, 115, 135,
139, 144, 147, 148, 152–4, 172, 204,
207, 218, 223, 226, 231–8, 246, 259,
261, 266–8, 292
Marino Faliero, 52, 238–44, 278
Mazeppa, 125–7, 169, 266
Monody on the Death of the Right
Hon. R. B. Sheridan, 123
'My soul is dark', 131, 132

Ode on Venice, 254
'Oh! snatched away in Beauty's
bloom', 134, 147, 153, 164
'On a Change of Masters at a great
Public School', 34

'On Jordan's banks', 132, 135
'On leaving Newstead Abbey', 21, 23,
26, 340, 348
'On revisiting Harrow', 67
'On the Day of the Destruction of
Jerusalem by Titus', 131–2, 136
'On this Day I complete my Thirty-
sixth Year', 164–9, 173, 204, 269
'Oscar of Alva', 25, 81, 338
'Oh! weep for those', 135

Parisina, 115, 125–6, 145
Poems on Various Occasions, 4–5, 32, 37,
42
Poems Original and Translated, 4–5, 29
'Prometheus', 275, 285

Sardanapalus, 15, 167, 172, 226, 232–6,
254
'Saul', 136, 138
'She walks in Beauty, like the Night',
130, 146, 153–7, 160
'Sonnet on Chillon', 126
'Sonnet—to Ginevra', 347
'So we'll go no more a-roving', 30,
153, 158—61
'Sons of the Greeks, arise!', 73
'Stanzas composed during a Thunder-
storm', 69
'Stanzas for Music', 153
'Stanzas to Augusta', 147
'Stanzas to a Lady, on . . . quitting
England in the Spring', 67
'Stanzas to the Po', 161, 176
'Stanzas written in passing the
Ambracian Gulf', 69–70
'Sun of the Sleepless! melancholy
Star!', 141–2

The Age of Bronze, 273–5
'The Ballad of the Black Friar', 338
The Bride of Abydos, 94, 114, 120–1,
132
The Corsair, 15, 34, 40, 58, 94–5, 115,
121–2, 127, 255, 263
'The castled crag of Drachenfels', 187
The Curse of Minerva, 7, 54, 56–60, 237,
270–71, 281–2, 292
'The Death of Calmar and Orla',
25, 32, 81, 153
The Deformed Transformed, 9, 163, 248,
252–62
'The Destruction of Sennacherib',
120, 136ff.
The Dream, 151–2, 176

Byron, George Gordon–*contd.*
'The Episode of Nisus and Euryalus', 32
The Giaour, 76, 94–5, 116–20, 141, 143, 154, 163, 167, 186, 196, 273, 288, 315
'The Girl of Cadiz', 71
'The Harp the Monarch Minstrel Swept', 130
The Island, 15, 162, 164, 257, 262–5, 266, 288, 329, 320, 339
'The Isles of Greece', 119, 306
The Lament of Tasso, 164, 170–3, 192, 329
'The Prayer of Nature', 15, 28
The Prisoner of Chillon, 93, 125–6, 163, 268
The Prophecy of Dante, 164, 173–5, 329
The Siege of Corinth, 123–5, 314
'The Song of Saul before his last Battle', 136
'The Spell is broke, the Charm is flown', 69
The Two Foscari, 238–44, 312
'The Vision of Belshazzar', 15, 137–8
The Vision of Judgment, 53, 275–85, 292
'The wild Gazelle', 135
'There be none of Beauty's daughters', 134, 157–8, 160
'They say that Hope is Happiness', 141–2
'Thy days are done', 140
'To a fair Quaker', 31
'To a Lady', *see* 'Stanzas to a Lady'
'To a vain Lady', 30
'To an Oak at Newstead', 14, 15, 67
'To Belshazzar', 138
'To Caroline', 30
'To E—', 349
'To Edward Noel Long, Esq.', 16, 28, 38–40
'To Florence', 69
'To Inez', 87, 105
'To M—', 40
'To Mary', 29–30
'To Murray', 60
'To Thyrza', 75
Turkish Tales, 18–20, 68, 74, 79, 93–4, 111, 26, 264, 300, 329, 334

Waltz, 7, 155, 270–3
'Were my bosom as false as thou deem'st it to be', 131–3
Werner, 15, 226, 231, 245, 252–7, 278

'When Coldness wraps this suffering Clay', 141, 143–4, 197, 319
'When I roved a young Highlander', 15, 20
'Written after swimming from Sestos to Abydos', 70
Byron, Captain John, 8ff., 91, 93, 258, 264, 269

Cadiz, 83, 85, 87
Caesar, Julius, 201, 221, 248, 257–8, 260, 274, 308, 324, 347
Cain, 81, 87, 116, 150, 227, 251, 256, 267, 278, 337
Callimachus, 106
Calvinism, 140, 284
Cambridge, 7, 38, 54, 104, 141
Camoes, Luiz de, 285
Campbell, Thomas, 54, 324–5
cannibalism, 300, 335
cant, 5, 9, 15, 47, 33, 50ff., 61, 111, 202, 236, 263, 273, 275, 291, 310, 327, 332
captivity, 10, 134, 137, 164, 169ff., 219, 235, 238ff., 256, 259, 261, 268, 295, 310ff., 327, 338
Carbonari, 309
Carlisle, Earl of, 45
Carlo Dolce, 337
Carmarthen, Lady, 9, 40
carnival, 101, 163
cataract, 17, 18
Catherine the Great, 288, 312, 318, 319, 322, 324–5, 326, 330, 334, 339
Catholic Claims Bill, 39, 113
Catullus, 28, 71
cave, 11, 32, 80, 81, 86, 185, 198, 250, 255, 264, 267–8, 303ff., 309, 320–1, 323, 338, 348
Cecrops, 59, 72, 91, 96
Cephalonia, 91
Charles XII, 127
Charlotte, Princess, 224
Chaucer, 14, 55
Chaworth, Mary Anne, 12, 15, 31, 68, 71, 151, 161–2, 340
children and childhood, 5, 9, 15, 21, 28, 33ff., 39, 147, 157, 169, 172, 183, 190ff., 204, 217, 225, 257ff., 264ff., 296, 309, 314–15
Christ, 73, 96, 133, 141, 223, 267, 304
Christabel, 121, 123
Christian, Fletcher, 264ff.
Christianity, 133ff., 142, 218, 222ff., 226, 261, 303

Churchill, Charles, 43
Cicero, 27, 220, 268
Cintra, 81
circles and cycles, 18, 64, 72, 75, 78,
    83–4, 97–9, 106, 116, 117, 140, 150,
    151, 158, 160–61, 163, 186, 188, 207,
    219, 221, 233–5, 254, 257, 264, 300,
    329, 331, 337, 347
city, 95–6, 102, 148, 160, 214ff., 219,
    225, 239ff.
civilisation, 263–4, 293, 331
Clairmont, Claire, 295
Clare, Lord, 37
Clarens, 188–9, 200, 207, 228
Clarke, Edward Daniel, 34
classics, 32, 34, 37, 63, 71, 85, 91, 99,
    117, 261
clay and spark, 62ff., 125, 139, 174, 228,
    246, 322, 341, 343
Cleopatra, 69, 273
Clermont, Mrs., 146
climate, 49, 82, 134, 167, 254, 331
Clitumnus, 214, 218, 227
club foot, 9, 40, 151–2, 228, 257ff., 341
Coleridge, Samuel Taylor, 3, 14, 39,
    50, 51, 72, 135, 148, 155, 177, 195,
    227, 250, 262, 263, 266–7, 290, 316–
    317
Coliseum, 71, 170, 207–8, 214, 218ff.,
    234, 261–2, 329, 340
Collins, William, 23, 134–5
column and pillar, 14, 27, 90, 92, 94,
    103, 123, 125, 152, 159, 214, 217ff.,
    222–3, 241, 268, 311
comedy, 66, 277ff., 310, 313, 336, 339
Congreve, William, 50, 271
Conrad, 34, 115–16, 122
Constantinople, 54, 62, 65, 74, 96, 99,
    101, 103, 310
continuity, 57, 62, 65, 92
Contract, Social, 263
Corinth, 123
cosmos and cosmology, 32, 96, 149–50,
    196–7, 232, 248ff.
Cottle, Amos, 45
counterpoint, 84, 85, 102, 121, 135, 194
    214, 240, 265, 337, 347
Cowper, William, 54, 111, 178
Crabbe, George, 54, 348
Crashaw, Richard, 76
Cribb, Tom, 47, 48
Cuvier, Baron, 251
Cybele, 209
Cyclades, 122, 238
cycles, *see* circles

cynicism, 33, 48, 80, 89, 116, 265, 293,
    323
cypress, 88, 90, 91, 119, 134–5, 153, 217,
    249, 312, 324

Dallas, Robert Charles, 112
dance, 34, 54, 58, 74, 99, 130, 154–5,
    186, 270ff.
Daniel, 137, 322
Dante, 8, 14, 17, 18, 41, 75, 107, 116,
    126, 141, 152, 169, 172, 186, 216, 220,
    288
Dashwood, Sir Francis, 340
Davenport, R. A., 107
David, King, 129, 130
Davies, Scrope Berdmore, 43, 104, 112
Davies, Sir John, 162
death, 10, 19, 26, 32, 39, 62ff., 76, 83–4,
    88, 102, 104, 111, 113, 117, 119, 130,
    134ff., 142, 148, 151, 153, 155, 162,
    165ff., 201, 245, 247, 253, 256, 260,
    273, 301, 309, 322, 326, 341
De Foix, 311
De Quincey, Thomas, 268
Deborah, 140
Delawarr, Earl of, 38
Della Cruscans, 3
Delphi, 85–6, 89, 91, 104
democracy, 275, 283
Demogorgon, 139
dervish, 97, 103, 267
desecration, 21, 26, 64, 81, 138, 140,
    261ff., 322, 338
desert, 17, 23, 80, 219, 224, 340
destiny, 26, 71, 117, 152, 159, 165
dew, 28, 38, 196–7, 203, 207, 338, 348
Diaspora, 135
Dido and Aeneas, 66
diet, *see* food
Dionysus, 96, 97, 225
disguise, *see* masks
Disraeli, Isaac, 162
Dodona, 98
dome, 22, 27, 87, 103, 219, 222, 225,
    228, 250ff.
Donne, John, 66, 145, 154, 157, 182
drama and dramas, 41, 51, 52ff., 79,
    96, 139, 149, 152, 226, 231–62, 264–5,
    312, 329
dream, 32, 48, 114, 134, 150, 201, 248,
    253, 263ff., 287ff., 305, 313ff., 343–4
Drury, Dr Joseph, 35, 166
Drury Lane Theatre, 52–3
Dryden, John, 5, 6, 14, 44, 50, 55,
    270

Dudú, 294
Duff, Mary, 173
Dunciad, The, 53
Dyer, George, 220
dynasty, *see* race

earth, 18, 80, 81, 94, 103–4, 106, 188, 191ff., 202, 211, 214, 238, 255
earthquake and volcano, 114, 167, 199, 291
eating, *see* food
Eden, *see* paradise
Edinburgh Review, 43
Edleston, John, 74ff., 97, 104–5, 111, 130–1, 134, 138, 143, 145, 256
Egeria, 31, 130, 132, 147, 224, 256, 264, 334
El Atheista Fulminato, 298
El Burlador de Sevilla, 298
elements, 17, 18, 68, 86, 94, 106, 130, 144, 149, 154, 171, 214, 220, 228, 232ff., 240–1, 248, 274, 277, 283–4, 295, 336
Elgin, Lord, 56ff., 94
Eliade, Mircea, 142
Eliot, T. S., 17, 80, 87, 100, 106–7, 120, 143, 148, 159, 160, 182, 208, 217, 245, 254, 266, 288, 300, 308, 333, 343
Eliphaz, 140
Elphinstone, Miss Mercer, 346
Elwin, Malcolm, 127, 228
empathy, 102, 199, 224
empire, 60, 163, 200, 203, 216—17, 218ff., 224–5, 235ff., 261ff.
Empty Quarter, 23
enclosure, 256ff.
Endymion, 7, 40, 61
energy, 35, 48, 83, 91, 116, 127, 136, 155, 174, 177, 199, 201, 240, 266, 283, 317
England and the English, 20, 47, 51, 60, 79, 97, 132, 184, 299, 319–21, 326ff., 331, 337
Enitharmon, 257
Enoch, The Book of, 250ff., 267
environment, 14, 19, 81, 90
Ephesus, 23, 222
Erechtheion, 77
eternity, 94, 116, 124–5, 141–2, 144, 148, 156, 190, 197, 219, 225–6, 231, 234, 238, 245ff., 251
Engenius, Pope, 222
Europe, 13, 40, 91, 308, 317, 329
Eve, *see* Adam and Eve
Excursion, The, 228

exile, 67, 79–80, 87, 132, 133ff., 144, 164, 173ff., 184ff., 241
existential traits and situations, 5, 10, 13, 70, 83, 97, 118, 140, 148, 159, 161, 183, 211, 214, 245, 254, 275, 298, 305, 306, 338, 341
extremes, 115, 155, 187, 266, 283, 318, 334

falcon, 83, 113
fall of man, 116, 120–1, 141, 186, 244ff., 257, 261, 304ff., 321
Falmouth, 65, 79
Falstaff, 64
fame, 5, 26, 32, 170, 172, 173, 203, 258, 310, 328
family relationships, 9ff., 15, 19, 21, 34, 35, 37, 79, 111, 257ff., 262, 264, 267–9, 271, 295–6, 300, 304, 309, 306–7, 313, 324, 339–40, 348
fatality, *see* destiny
Faust, 233, 259, 266, 315, 325
Ferdausi, 23
Ferenczi, S., 266, 269, 320
Ferrara, 216, 220
festival, 96, 100–1
fire, 18, 29, 31, 82, 84, 89, 94, 106, 117–118, 122, 167, 186–7, 201–2, 233, 255–6, 274, 295, 300, 331
firefly, 256, 312
fish, 14, 161, 227, 320, 336, 339
Fitz-Fulke, 318ff.
flippancy, 70, 77, 79, 132, 149, 181, 275, 287
Florence, 216, 220
'Florence', *see* Smith, Mrs Spencer
flower, 14, 17, 19, 38–9, 42, 76, 121, 147, 153, 166, 172, 182, 193ff., 196, 209, 221, 227, 236, 254, 256, 297, 319, 338, 339, 348, 349
food and eating, 27, 47, 265, 301ff., 309, 311ff., 333ff., 335, 338ff., 346, 348
For the Sexes: the Gates of Paradise, 267, 289, 294ff., 305
Forster, E. M. 23, 332
Forum Romanum, 27, 219ff.
fountain, 17, 50, 86, 89, 98, 125, 130, 147–8, 149, 162, 183, 195, 203, 227, 248, 250ff., 255, 258–60, 321
Four Quartets, 17, 100, 106–7, 117, 120, 142–3, 266, 288, 343
Frame-breaking Bill, 39, 60, 113
Francesca, 115
'Fravarshi', 75, 212

fragmentation, 48, 177, 181ff., 225, 233ff., 243, 262, 300
freedom, 6, 16ff., 18, 20ff., 39, 73, 90, 93–4, 113, 116, 119, 125, 130, 166, 170ff., 200, 208, 230, 240, 273, 275, 283, 299, 306, 309, 346
French Revolution, 328
Frere, John Hookham, 278
Freud, Sigmund, 10, 13, 127, 187
friends and friendship, 5, 19, 28, 32–40, 63, 77, 111, 126, 162, 331

Galileo, 220
Galt, John, 80
Gamba, Count Pietro, 165
garden, 14, 16–17, 21, 38, 74
Geneva and Lake Leman, 12, 22, 150, 184, 189ff., 206, 267, 339, 348
George III, 274, 278ff., 329
gesture, 57–8, 70, 90–1, 165, 251
Ghost of Abel, The, 245
Gibbon, Edward, 200ff., 222, 228
Gibraltar, 54, 80
Gifford, William, 43
gladiator, 83, 220, 221, 261
Gleckner, R. F., 285
Godwin, William, 3, 182
Goethe, Wolfgang von, 41, 90, 259, 278
Goldsmith, Oliver, 212
Gordon of Gight, Catherine, *see* Byron, Mrs
Gothic, 3, 4, 11, 62–3, 65, 91, 214, 233, 257ff., 320, 336, 339
grave, *see* tomb
Gray, May, 161
Gray, Thomas, 23, 34, 63, 135
Greece and the Levant, 36, 48, 54, 56–60, 66ff., 95, 112, 114, 122, 125, 132, 166, 170, 206, 213–14, 216, 254, 265, 273, 341
Grey of Ruthyn, Lord, 68
Greyfriars School, 346
Guiccioli, Countess Teresa, 73, 170, 173, 176, 215, 283, 291, 295, 308, 323, 347
guilt, 6, 9, 10, 15, 21, 26–7, 66, 68, 76, 87, 116, 117, 122, 127, 131–2, 147, 197, 231ff., 244ff., 248, 264ff., 288, 290, 297, 304ff., 315, 338
Gulbeyaz, 294, 312–13, 339
gulf, 25, 105, 144, 152, 183, 186, 232, 239, 247ff., 251, 255, 266, 267, 290, 342
Gulnare, 115, 116, 122

Hadrian, Emperor, 59, 143
Hagelman, C. W., and Barnes, R. J., 348
Haidee, 119, 195, 263, 288, 294, 301ff., 313, 319, 327, 330, 334, 336, 339–40
Hamlet, 48, 61, 64, 102, 231, 234, 243
Handel, George Frideric, 141
Hardy, Thomas, 137, 335
Harrow, 5, 7, 15, 32, 36–9, 56, 63, 88, 91, 99, 162, 166, 169, 244
Hazlitt, William, 259, 343, 347
Heller, Erich, 267
Hellespont, 71
Henry, Lord, 320, 331
Heracleitus, 18, 106, 344
Herbert, George, 65, 196
hermit, 11, 37, 81, 84, 95, 97, 263
Hero and Leander, 71
hero, Byronic, 81, 93, 117, 122, 132, 139, 187, 233ff., 242, 245ff., 291–2, 299
Herrick, Robert, 154
Highlands, 16ff., 63, 100, 147, 207, 263
highwayman, 326–7
history, 56ff., 69–70, 92–3, 100, 102, 104, 140, 200–1, 203, 208, 217ff., 221, 258ff., 261ff., 293, 338, 340
Hobbes, Thomas, 264
Hobhouse, John Cam, 43, 46, 56, 74–5, 79, 97, 102, 112, 115, 149, 188, 205, 229, 290
Hodgson, Francis, 65, 79, 82, 112, 149
Hogg, James, 45
Holland, Lord and Lady, 52, 112, 266
Homer, 5, 6, 8, 17, 173, 309, 325
Honorius, 81
Hopkins, Gerard Manley, 19
Horace, 5, 6, 23, 55, 71, 91, 173, 224, 321
Housman, Alfred Edward, 70, 137, 341
'How sleep the brave', 134
Hucknall Torkard,
humour, 43ff., 65, 167, 234
Hunt, John, 285
Hunt, Leigh, 3, 263
Hutchinson, Mary, 156
Hymettus, 58, 72, 94, 102–4, 207–8

Ibn 'Arabi, 75, 229
Ida, 5, 32, 34, 264
ideogram, 25, 28, 38, 84, 90, 94, 97, 117, 127, 186–7, 214ff., 220, 225, 233–4, 236, 262
image-making, 257, 284, 292
imagery, 11, 16, 18, 78, 84, 93–4, 135, 137, 161, 164, 300, 304, 307, 319, 347

immediacy, 118, 122
immortality, 47, 63, 112, 139, 141, 143, 145, 148, 163, 223–4, 267
imprisonment, *see* captivity
impulse, 28, 33, 35, 38
incest, 132, 145ff., 232
India, 60
Inferno, see Dante
Inez, Donna, 296ff., 313, 323, 339
Iphigema, 134, 146
iris, 38, 196, 207, 244
irony, 3, 24, 53, 64, 71, 84, 88–9, 101, 158, 160, 181, 201–2, 241, 243, 281ff., 288, 300, 303, 310, 319, 321, 324, 328, 333, 335
Isaiah, 140
Ishmael, 233
Islam, 23, 36, 40, 42, 58, 61, 74, 88–9, 91, 112, 119, 121, 123, 125, 132ff., 140, 174, 196, 217, 222, 228, 229, 267, 297, 302, 345,
island, 15, 91, 115, 119, 167, 264ff., 301–2
Ismail, 288, 293, 301, 309ff., 314–18
Istanbul, *see* Constantinople
'It is the first mild day of March', 189
Ithaca, 91
Italy and Italians, 49, 52, 73, 84, 164, 174, 203, 205ff., 218, 225, 264, 283, 309, 310

Jackson, John, 47–8, 149
James, M. R., 308
Jami, 23, 36
Jeffrey, Francis, 50, 53–4, 150, 238, 276
Jerusalem, 130, 188
Jesus, *see* Christ
Jili, 267
jnana-marga, 246–7
Joannina, 12, 91, 97, 105
Job, 129, 138ff.
John Johnson, 311ff., 314, 330
Johnson, Samuel, 14, 17, 41, 44, 53, 55, 60, 70, 275, 299, 347
Jonson, Ben, 48, 275
José, Don, 296
Joseph, M. K., 60, 266, 347
journal, *see* letters *and* journals
Joyce, James, 341
Julia, Donna, 294, 296ff., 302ff., 313, 323, 327, 330, 339
Julius Caesar, 237
Jung, Carl Gustave, 13, 40
Junius, 282, 283, 284
Jura, 193–4, 197

Juvenal, 44, 55

Ka'ba, 230
Kafka, Franz, 304
Kaled, 115, 122
karma-marga, 265
Kean, Edmund, 53, 61
Keats, John, 3, 7, 24, 40, 72, 92, 121, 148, 149, 159, 182, 227, 235, 316, 328, 336, 346–7
Kerenyi, C., 107
Kierkegaard, Søren, 13, 275
King Lear, 115
Kinnaird, Hon. Douglas, 129
Kirke, White, Henry, 54
knowledge, 33, 34, 48, 89, 119, 233, 246ff., 250, 265, 267, 321, 329
Koran, *see* Islam
Kroeber, Karl, 345
Kubla Khan, 123, 127, 171, 250, 266

labyrinth, *see* maze
lake, 11, 22, 126, 168, 188, 197ff., 216, 227, 267, 320, 338–9, 348
Lake Poets, 51, 54, 92, 196
Lamb, Lady Caroline, 112, 114, 130, 295, 344
Lamb, Charles, 45, 285
Lambro, 316, 306ff., 336
landscape, 16, 23, 34, 36, 41, 85, 88–9, 122, 134–5, 185, 188–9, 193ff., 214–215, 217, 232
language and languages, 26–7, 55, 73, 95, 148
laocoon, 223
Lascy, 312
Laura, 278
Laurence, R., 267
Lawrence, D. H., 329
Leander, 71
Lee, Harriet, 253
legend, *see* ballads and legends
Le Festin de Pierre, 298
Leigh, Augusta, *see* Byron, Augusta
Leila, 76, 93, 115, 256, 294–5, 315
Leman, Lake, see Geneva and Lake Leman
Levant, *see* Greece and the Levant
liberty, *see* freedom
Licoo, 265
life, 10, 46ff., 66, 70, 73, 82, 87, 94, 97, 106, 187, 260, 267, 293, 301, 322
light, 58, 61, 91, 124, 214, 219, 223, 256, 258, 265, 288, 316, 338
lightning, 31, 68, 172, 199, 201, 255

Lisbon, 79, 81
'Little, Thomas', *see* Moore, Thomas
Loch na Garr, *see* 'Lachin Y Gair'
Locke, John, 48
London, 9, 48, 54, 59, 97, 104, 130, 326ff.
Long, Edward Noel, 38
Los, 257
Loutraki, 99–100, 329
love, 12–40, 62, 67–76, 78, 84, 87, 97, 127, 130ff., 141–2, 147, 158–61, 166ff., 187, 189ff., 196, 200ff., 206, 219, 221, 236, 242, 246ff., 259, 268, 271, 297ff., 300ff., 308, 311ff., 314, 318, 322ff., 329, 337, 346
Lovell, Ernest J., Jr., 14, 189
Lucifer, 245ff.
lyrics, 5ff., 28, 62ff., 129ff., 149ff., 164, 185, 251

Macbeth, 111, 114, 115, 167, 204
machine, 238, 261, 266, 317
Macri, Theresa, 72, 161, 294
madness, 114, 170ff., 201, 327
magician, magus, 51, 152, 207, 231, 237, 305
Malraux, A., 70
Malta, 62, 67, 80
man, 69–71, 80–2, 93, 96, 115, 123, 135, 149–50, 174, 194, 203, 218–19, 220, 224–5, 228, 230ff., 244ff., 248, 251, 254ff., 257ff., 266, 275, 283, 289, 298–9, 313–14
Mann, Thomas, 245, 267
Marathon, 91
Marchand, Leslie A., 40, 41
Marcus Aurelius, Emperor, 106
Marjarum, E. W., 178
Marlowe, Christopher, 259
marriage, 147, 271ff., 317, 324, 325–6, 328, 330ff.
Marvell, Andrew, 31, 154, 176
masks and masquerades, 41, 47, 101, 253, 257ff., 290, 318, 327ff., 335
matter, *see* mind
Matthews, Charles Skinner, 111
maze, 158, 160, 213, 219, 220, 232ff., 241, 250, 259, 274, 290ff., 312, 314
McGann, J. J., 228, 345
Mecca, 229
Mediterranean, 54, 70ff., 79ff.
Medmenham Abbey, 340
Medora, 93, 115, 122, 132, 256
Medwin, Thomas, 61, 63, 76
Melbourne, Lady, 112, 285, 330

memory, 32, 39, 141, 148, 241, 308, 320
merchandise, *see* buying and selling
mermaid, 11, 22, 40
Messiah, 141
metaphysics and 'metaphysical', 11, 19, 23, 64, 228, 231, 232, 267, 297, 325, 326, 333, 340–1
metrics, 16, 24, 44, 58, 66, 73, 120, 123, 126, 135, 137, 143, 147, 150–1, 157–160, 170, 174–5, 276ff.
Michael, Archangel, 281ff.
Michelangelo, 220, 304
Middlemarch, 242
Midsummer Night's Dream, A., 289–90
Milan, 205
Milbanke, Annabella, 104, 112–14, 129, 138, 139, 145–6, 152, 161, 183, 204, 207, 215, 228, 234m, 285, 294–5, 301–2, 340, 345
Milton, John, 13, 233, 238, 245ff., 282
Milton, 196, 227
mind and matter, *see* clay and spark
Minerva, 56, 89, 91, 102–3, 105, 200
Missolonghi, 88, 91, 152, 165, 176, 258, 290, 295, 317, 343
Moliere, 298
money, 60, 315, 326, 328ff., 347
monks and monastries, 11, 27, 34, 62ff., 81, 95, 103, 119, 222, 338
monument, 14, 21, 22, 26, 147
moon, 38, 39, 57–8, 76, 81, 101, 122–6, 157–8, 161, 221, 234ff., 241, 330, 338
Moore, Doris Langley, 61
Moore, Thomas, 4, 29, 46, 49, 72, 112, 118, 145–6, 162, 196
morality, 132ff., 234, 274ff., 282, 314
morass, 219–20, 226, 274, 290, 318
Morris, William, 78
mosque, 58, 88, 91, 125, 229
mountain, 11, 16ff., 58, 72, 85, 88, 93–6, 104, 123, 125–6, 152, 188, 193, 198ff., 226
Mozart, 298
Muhammad, 75, 125, 148
music, 28, 48, 74, 76–7, 81, 94, 101, 129ff., 157, 214, 216, 218–19, 265, 287, 303, 336
mutability, 24, 28, 51, 329
myth, 16, 70, 211, 258, 292, 327

Nahum, 266
Napoleon, *see* Buonaparte
Nathan, Isaac, 129–30
nature, 14, 18, 19, 34, 35, 50, 52–3, 58, 61, 70, 81–2, 94, 104, 120, 124, 138,

nature–*contd.*
  147, 152, 162, 186ff., 196, 203, 213,
  216, 220, 225, 227–8, 293, 297, 316,
  319, 331, 336–7, 339, 342
nature, state of, 263
Nemesis, 207, 219
Nemi, 224
Neptunians, 230
Neuha, 15, 264ff., 288, 336, 340
Newstead Abbey, 11, 14, 21ff., 54,
  62ff., 80, 89, 104, 111, 214, 222, 267,
  290, 294, 337, 340
Newton, Isaac, 197
Nicholson, R. A., 229
Nietzsche, 13, 46, 93, 116, 201, 232,
  266–7
night, 30, 38, 99, 123, 152–3, 148, 154,
  156, 158–9, 193, 199, 221, 241, 314,
  316
nightmare, 114–15, 199, 290, 307, 309
Nineveh, 226, 236
Norman Abbey, 41, 288, 294, 312, 331,
  332–44

occult, 130, 136, 138ff., 152, 221, 231ff.,
  250, 338
ocean, *see* sea
Ode on Intimations of Immortality, 191, 198
olive tree, 58, 61, 91, 94, 103–4, 218,
  347
Olympeion, 65, 71, 91, 103, 119, 222–3,
  340
opera, 52, 54
oracle, 98, 201
Orc, 257
Orwell, George, 346
Ossian, 3, 15, 20, 24, 26, 35, 73, 80, 102,
  287, 340
Othello, 242
Otway, Thomas, 50, 52
outcast, *see* scapegoat
Oxford, Countess of, 114, 330

Pactolus, 259
paederasty, 68, 75, 81–2, 97–100, 168
Pantheon, 218
paradise, 19, 24, 28, 33, 36, 67–8, 79,
  81, 94, 116, 133, 141, 172, 186–7,
  241, 244ff., 250, 256–7, 261, 263ff.,
  268, 272, 278, 282, 284, 288, 296, 309,
  316, 327, 331, 337, 349
Paradise Lost, 116, 260
paradox, 17, 52, 62, 64, 67, 69, 73, 90,
  97, 103
Parnassus, 85–6, 216

Parthenon, 56ff., 72, 94, 103
Pascal, Blaise, 298
Pasqual, Father, 34
passion, 19ff., 32, 48, 87, 97, 103, 116ff.,
  143, 150, 162, 168, 176, 184, 189, 201,
  227, 242, 248, 268, 277, 291, 308, 311,
  322, 331, 335
Patmore, Coventry, 78
Patras, 91
Patroclus, 169
Paul, St., 71, 145, 261, 334, 348
Pedrillo, 303
Peleus, 259
Pendeli, 104
Pericles, 59
Peter, St., 280ff., 306
Peter Bell, 198
philosophy, *see* metaphysics
Phyle, 91
Pigot family, 8, 40, 183
pilgrimage, 223, 290
pillar, *see* column
Pindar, 224
Pisa, 213, 228
place, 56, 82, 86, 90, 104, 106, 120, 159–
  161, 216ff.
Plato, 91, 182, 268, 324
Po, 176–8
poetics and poetry, *see* rhetoric
politics, 81, 328ff., 331
Poliorcetes, 258
'Pomposus', 34
Pope, Alexander, 43, 50, 53, 55, 58, 70,
  72, 123, 159, 270, 272, 275, 298
'Portrait of a Lady', 160
Portugal, 81ff., 96
Potemkin, Prince, 316
power, 12ff., 60, 69, 87, 92, 97, 102, 116,
  130ff., 200ff., 203, 216, 219ff., 258ff.,
  301ff., 308, 309–10, 317, 329ff., 335,
  337
Powys, T. F., 65, 341
predestination, 132
Prelude, The, 191, 192, 197ff., 228
primitivism, 263ff.
Prior, Matthew, 29
'Probus', 34
progress, 51, 251
Prometheus, 223, 231, 236, 246, 250,
  274, 285
Proteus, 202
prophets and prophecy, 26, 36, 58, 60,
  98, 129, 136, 138, 140, 165, 175, 245,
  251, 284
Puerta Santa Maria, 83

Pulci, Luigi, 278
pyramids, 241
Pyrrho, 66, 220

race, 15, 16ff., 20, 26, 35, 63, 140, 168, 235, 248, 257ff., 340
Radcliffe, Anne, *see* tale of terror
Rabelais, Francois, 287, 340
rainbow, *see* iris
Rape of the Lock, The, 61
Rasselas, 340
Raucocanti, 310
Ravenna, 47, 173, 176, 213, 232, 311
Read, Herbert, 164, 167
Reade, Charles, 316
recollection, *see* memory
revenge, 174–5, 240, 297
religion, 3, 27, 81, 86, 103, 112, 130, 132ff., 141, 174, 178, 219, 325, 328
Richard III, 61, 114, 127
rhetoric, 51, 54, 73, 75, 82, 88–9, 92, 106, 116–17, 154, 158–61, 166–9, 173, 176, 194, 217, 219, 223, 279, 283, 287, 291, 342
Rhine, 187
Rhone, 184
rhyme, 158, 160, 169ff., 174, 184, 185, 204
Richards, I. A., 124, 335
Rilke, Rainer Maria, 73, 96
river, 37, 84, 134, 147, 176, 178, 184, 217, 226, 232–3, 254, 256, 259, 266, 338, 343
Robbe Grillet, Alain, 217
rock, 17ff., 20, 68, 81, 104, 172, 174, 184, 210, 217, 255, 307, 338
Rochester, Earl of, 4, 29, 44
Rogers, Samuel, 112
Romaic, 73–4, 95
romanticism, 46, 148, 161, 168
Rome, 27, 96, 107, 163, 203, 206, 208, 213, 216ff., 224, 228, 235, 26off., 311
Romilly, Sir Samuel, 329
Romulus, 96
Rousseau, Jean Jacques, 3, 189, 200ff., 264
rose, 16, 21ff., 134–5, 153, 196, 348
Rothschild, 329
Rowlandson, Thomas, 271
ruins, 27, 62, 71, 80, 82, 96, 152, 219, 340
Rumi, 162, 229
Rushton, Robert, 79
Ruskin, John, 196, 266–7
Rutherford, Andrew, 77

Rycaut, Paul, 106

sacrilege, *see* desecration
St Peter's 203, 207, 214, 218ff., 222ff., 258, 261
St Petersburg, 294
St Sophia, 222
Salvatore, 337
Salsette frigate, 149
Samson Agonistes, 238, 241
Samuel, 136, 138
Saragoza, Maid of, 16, 83, 211
Satan, 53, 279ff., 289
'Satanic school', 279
satire, 33, 43–60, 258, 270–85, 328
Sappho, 304, 324
satori, 218, 234
Saturn, 333
Saul, 131, 134, 136
scapegoat, 116, 133, 245
Schliemann, H., 70
scorpion, 117, 186, 233, 236, 238, 241–2, 256
Scotland, 17, 54
Scott, Sir Walter, 40, 45, 51, 55, 118, 150, 185
sculpture, *see* art
sea, 21, 80, 93, 96, 101, 106, 117–18, 121, 123, 125, 137, 157, 184, 192, 209, 224, 226, 229, 239, 241, 248, 259, 264ff., 293, 297, 300ff., 319ff., 337,
Sedley, Sir Charles, 4, 29, 44
self-knowledge and self-transcendence, 22, 90–1, 101, 130, 135, 142, 170, 184–5, 216, 218, 265, 293, 301, 329
Selim, 121
senses, 32, 148, 215, 318ff., 325
Seraglio, 301, 312ff., 318–19
serventismo, 183, 264, 296, 328
Sestos, *see* Abydos
Seville, 87, 294, 300–1
sex, 11, 15, 20, 29ff., 59, 87, 233, 240, 247–8, 265, 266, 271ff., 283, 289ff., 297–8, 313, 318ff., 328–9, 347
Shakespeare, William, 83, 92, 94, 111, 155, 166, 173, 194, 213, 240, 275, 294, 330
'She was a phantom of delight', 155
Shelley, Mary, 40, 188, 257, 348
Shelley, Percy Bysshe, 3, 48–9, 72, 126, 135, 139, 164, 182, 188, 195, 202, 220, 227, 244, 246, 262, 267, 275, 316, 348
Sheridan, R. B., 48, 52, 243
shipwreck, 36, 68, 164–5, 169ff., 240, 263, 300ff., 313

shock, aesthetic, 45, 90, 155
Shooter's Hill, 326
Sickels, Eleanor M., 162
silence, 76, 86, 123, 131, 148, 154, 193,
    196, 217, 250, 256
sin, *see* guilt
skull, 62ff., 93, 102–3, 140, 145, 209,
    221–2, 338, 340
slave, slavery, 15, 20, 33, 102–4, 306,
    310ff., 313
sleep, 115, 139–40, 151, 309, 341
Sligo, marquis of, 115
Smith, Mrs Spencer, 68, 71, 130
Smyrna, 106
snowflake, 17ff., 196, 274, 338
Society for the Suppression of Vice,
    52
Socrates, 21, 46, 200, 258, 265, 293
society, 3, 48, 306, 326, 330ff., 332, 335
solitude, 19, 47–8, 80–1, 95, 104, 148,
    157, 165, 171–2, 202, 213, 215, 245–6,
    301, 306, 312, 319, 349
soul, *see* clay and spark
Southey, Robert, 15, 51, 53–4, 135, 150,
    275–85, 279ff., 292, 346
Southwell, 5, 9, 15,
Sourvaroff, 312, 316ff.
space, *see* time and space
Spain, 81ff., 96, 122
speech, *see* language
Spenser, Edmund, 55, 89, 91, 98, 100
spider, 119, 126, 256, 312
Spider frigate, 68
star, 4, 18, 25, 130, 137, 141–2, 147,
    150, 152–5, 188, 193, 196, 198, 203,
    219, 221, 227, 234, 250, 266, 320,
    342–3
Steno, 278
Sternhold and Hopkins, 129
storm, 17, 31, 38, 68ff., 117, 197, 199–
    200, 210, 226, 228
style, *see* rhetoric
Stylite, 223
Sufism, 49, 75, 78, 142, 154, 174, 196,
    206, 348
suicide, 21, 172, 233, 260
Suli and Suliotes, 99, 103, 211, 329
Sulla, 201
sun, 30, 32, 57, 80, 83, 94, 122, 150,
    234ff., 237, 254, 258, 265, 285, 300,
    309, 322
sunflower, 302
superman, 93, 274, 288
swimming, 37, 57, 225, 239–40, 266,
    303, 309

Swinburne, Algernon Charles, 16, 78,
    227, 251, 302
Switzerland, 170, 228
symbol, *see* ideogram, imagery
Symons, Arthur, 92, 278
systole and diastole, 186–7, 199, 213,
    268

tale of terror, 3–4, 51, 63, 233
Tasse, 169, 174, 206, 214, 216, 220
Tattersal, John Cecil, 37
Taylor, Henry, 118
Tempest, The, 303
temple, 11, 14, 35, 58ff., 65, 72, 82, 88–
    93, 96, 103, 138, 214, 218, 221ff.
Tennyson, Alfred Lord, 78, 121
Tepelene, 91, 97
Terence, 271
Terni, 216
The Waste Land, 159
theatre, 92, 98, 163, 205
Thermopylae, 91
Theseus, 96
Thetis, 322
Thomson, James, 135, 189, 220
thought, 6, 12, 35, 70, 87, 103, 247, 292,
    319, 323
Thrasimene, 216, 227
Thyrza, 74ff.
time and space, 32, 38, 40, 56–7, 69, 82,
    87, 92–4, 96, 103, 106, 120, 123–4,
    141, 143ff., 147, 150, 155, 161, 176,
    183, 195, 206ff., 215, 217ff., 225,
    231, 234–5, 241, 251, 256, 261ff., 275,
    319, 336, 344, 349
Tintern Abbey, 33, 51
Titian, 337
tomb, 5, 27, 31, 35, 37, 62ff., 69, 82, 86,
    88, 90, 92, 103, 119, 134, 147, 153,
    162, 166, 217–18, 273, 312, 320
Tonga Islands, 264
Toobonai, 265, 343
Torquil, 264ff.
torture, 238ff., 243, 261
To the Lighthouse, 202, 334
tower, 75, 78, 82, 92, 103, 218, 340, 225,
    232, 235, 256ff., 268, 340
Townshend packet, 80
Traherne, Thomas, 28
Trajan, Emperor, 214
tradition, 20, 26, 35ff., 39, 44, 77, 93,
    99, 129, 132, 174, 195, 264, 275
travel, 66–7, 82, 79, 148, 184
tree, 10, 11, 14, 17, 58, 111, 147, 151,
    162–3, 172–3, 201, 210, 338

Trinidada, 300
Trinity College, 46, 63, 75, 91, 97–8, 131, 134
Troy, 56, 70, 264, 310, 311, 322
Turkey, *see* Greece and the Levant
Tuve, Rosamond, 277

Ulysses, 307
Ulysses, 243
United States, 262, 268
unities, 56, 266, 281
Urizen, 257
Utraikey, *see* Loutraki

Valenciennes, 9
vampire, 300, 303–4, 339
Vatican, 223
Vaughan, Henry, 226
Vedanta, 226, 246
Venice, 9, 41, 56, 94, 96, 144, 153, 158–161, 206ff., 214, 216, 218, 220, 226, 232, 238, 278, 290, 341
Venus, 5, 87, 259
Venus de Medici, 214
Vernet, 337
Verona, 206
via negativa, 139, 142, 145
Vicenza, 206
Victorians, 47, 93, 270, 304
Virgil, 23, 91, 173, 220
Virgin Mary, 28, 264, 267, 304, 314, 336
vision, and visionaries, 19, 58–9, 90, 114, 138–9, 174, 208, 213, 263, 281, 333
Vivaldi, 160
volcano, *see* earthquake
Voltaire, 200ff., 228
vortex, 25–6, 117, 153, 159–60, 169–70, 183, 213, 232, 246, 256, 262, 312, 319
vulva, 301, 313, 320ff., 325

Walpole, Horace, 63
Walton, Izaak, 161
wanderer, 36–7, 49, 54, 65ff., 76, 87, 94, 104
Wandering Jew, 116, 233
war, 5, 12, 14, 23ff., 32, 82–4, 89–90, 98–100, 106, 125, 127, 130ff., 166ff., 186ff., 200, 225, 250, 258ff., 271, 273, 308, 314ff., 321, 325
warship, 264, 336
water, 18, 94, 106, 213, 338
waterfall, 266
Waterloo, 186, 314
weather, *see* climate

Webster, Lady Frances Wedderburn, 295
Webster, John, 171
Wellington, Duke of, 211, 317
Werther, 328, 330
West, Paul, 182, 183
Westminster Abbey, 327–8
Weston, Stephen, 23, 36
Whigs, 112
Whitehead, Alfred North, 207
whirlpool, whirlwind, *see* vortex
wilderness, 19, 222, 233, 245, 324
Wilkes, John, 60, 282–4
Wilmot, Mrs, 98, 155
wind, 25, 65, 86, 123, 137, 157, 162, 184, 199, 202, 214, 254, 256, 259, 310
wine, 11, 43, 47, 63–6, 82, 100, 254, 309, 331, 340, 347
Wingfield, John, 37, 42, 88
wisdom, 12ff., 28, 33, 34–5, 46, 59, 87, 89, 91–2, 97–8, 103, 137, 139, 145, 154, 200ff., 208, 217, 219, 221, 259, 265, 268, 299, 301ff., 304, 308, 314, 329, 337, 343
Wisdom of Solomon, 346
wit, 4, 6, 44, 49–50, 64, 103, 202, 236, 270, 275, 278, 308, 331, 332
Witch of Endor, 136
Wither, George, 11
wolf, 83, 211, 315
woman, 30, 32, 39, 47–8, 80, 82–5, 121, 130, 146, 160–1, 232, 242, 254, 277, 290, 294, 298, 300, 302, 318ff., 323, 326, 333, 344
womb, 22, 32, 226, 248, 264ff., 266, 269, 301, 320ff., 338, 339
Woodhouse, A. S. P., 135
Woolf, Virginia, 13, 28, 341
Wordsworth, Dorothy, 41, 146
Wordsworth, William, 3, 14, 18, 24, 44, 48, 49–51, 72, 92–3, 130, 135, 146–9, 156, 159, 164, 173, 177, 182, 188ff., 197, 227–8, 256, 262, 316–7, 329
Wright, John, 270
Wyatt, Sir Thomas, 31
Wycherley, William, 271

Yeats, William Butler, 120, 228, 265
'Yew-trees', 135
yuga, 162

Zaehner, R. C., 345
Zen, 142, 148, 196
Zitza, 75, 97–8, 105
Zoroaster, 345
Zuleika, 93, 115, 121, 268